CHRISTIANITY IN
THE TWENTIETH CENTURY

CHRISTIANITY
IN THE
TWENTIETH CENTURY

JOHN A. HARDON

DOUBLEDAY & COMPANY, INC.

GARDEN CITY, NEW YORK

1971

TABLE OF CONTENTS

INTRODUCTION

The purpose of this volume is to offer a concise history of Christian thought and practice in the twentieth century, built around the theme of the "Age of Communication."

It is not a mere chronology of major events, nor a summary of religious movements. Episodes and trends are the raw data out of which the narrative is woven. The story is not simple. No religious history can be described in a single volume, much less what has happened in the Catholic, Protestant, and Orthodox traditions since 1900. I believe the past seven decades are among the most significant since apostolic times. They promise to become the watershed that divides two eras of Christian history, the centuries of dismemberment and the age of re-union. Ironically they also reflect a new division in Christendom, a deep-down cleavage that threatens to separate the nominal followers of Christ from those who believe in him as the incarnate Son of God.

Both tendencies are valid reflections of what has happened during these crucial years. In the pages that follow assessments are made and judgments expressed on this seeming contradiction: that Christianity is discovering its union in Christ under the inspiration of his grace, and at the same time is being torn asunder by forces that, in some quarters, are threatening its existence. Anyone familiar with the story of the first seventy years of the first century is not surprised at the paradox. It is part of the genius of a faith whose very survival is a mystery.

CHRISTIANITY IN
THE TWENTIETH CENTURY

THE TWENTIETH CENTURY: DAWN OF A NEW ERA

It is quite possible to write a history of contemporary Christianity without reference to secular events and happenings of the twentieth century. There are so many movements and countermovements in today's society that any study of the Christian world based on these developments would make a useful contribution to religious scholarship.

But I consider the time factor so important that around it everything else revolves. The decades since 1900 are more than seventy years that might just as well apply to any other period of history. They mark the beginning of a new age in human civilization and, correspondingly, of the Christian religion.

It seems only right, then, to first take a hard look at this age. What is it? What makes it different? Why is it modern in a sense that could not be said of any other since the rise of Christianity?

There is some risk in taking such an approach. It may appear too secular for what is supposed to be a historical analysis of the Christian religion. What have computers and electrons to do with faith, and why the long prelude before getting on with the real business?

My plan is to define briefly, but sharply, what I consider the typical features of the century in which we live. These features were not chosen at random. They are the fruit of many hours of reading, reflection, and prayer. Only when they were clarified did I feel free to go on with the history proper. I was convinced that until these (or equivalent) aspects of the modern age are identified, it is impossible to say what desperately needs saying both to those who are crushed by what they consider tragedy and those who are blind to what is going on.

Not all the following aspects of twentieth-century culture are equally important, while admitting there is no simple way of sifting out their effect on religion. Some are more closely related to things of the spirit and therefore more influential in determining the physiognomy of the Christian Church. Others are less clearly connected with religion, but for that very reason may be overlooked in a study, like this one, which looks to a deeper understanding of *why* Christianity has entered on a new era of its history.

Moreover, some of the features of this "New Age" are clearly subordinate to others, e.g., Psychological Man is partly a creation of our Knowledge Explosion. Yet there is so much value in seeing each of these foci on its own merits that treating them separately is justified.

One more disclaimer. Even with this preview of our century on its secular side, the sacred history that follows is itself only the beginning of a new understanding of Christianity—at once more sober than some idealists prefer and more hopeful than the pessimists claim.

Knowledge Explosion

Those who write about the expansion of man's knowledge since 1900 use terms that appear exaggerated. They talk about the *Discovery of the Universe*,[1] *The Research Revolution*,[2] and *Science, the Endless Frontier*[3] to show that more information and deeper insight have been gained in our century than in all the previous generations of man's existence

There is no doubt that the sheer accumulation of facts and the discovery of laws is beyond anything conceivable as recently as the French and American revolutions. More significant has been the advance in knowledge of the fundamental nature of matter, living and inorganic, down to the smallest mass (from one viewpoint) and the most basic forms of energy (from another) that constitute the empirical universe.

Some might object to speaking of a second, and greater, scientific revolution in the twentieth century. They argue that actually there was no break in continuity of research such as occurred between classical times and the Renaissance. They further point out that there was no slackening in pace from the use of quantitative chemical methods of

Lavoisier (1743–1794) to the nuclear physics of Einstein (1879–1955) and Fermi (1901–1954).

Certainly terms like "revolution" and "continuity" are relative. But if we grant the name "revolution" to what happened before 1900, we must grant it *a fortiori* to what happened since.

Discovering such facts as the earth's revolving around its axis, the telescope, and the vacuum pump was extraordinary. It upset all previous ideas which these discoveries implied.

On the other hand, none of these inventions touched so intimately on the inner nature of the visible world, and less still on the secret of life—human and subhuman—as did, for example, establishing the processes of biochemistry and the structure of the cell, finding and exploring the powers of atomic energy, and applying all this to the limitless range of man's personal being and social communication.

Compare the strange theories about the composition of matter before the Curies, husband Pierre (1859–1906) and wife Marie (1867–1934), along with their French compatriot, Antoine Henri Becquerel (1852–1908), discovered radioactivity.

Again compare the efforts made for millennia to share one's thoughts with others by the written or printed word, with the telephone, perfected by Alexander Bell (1847–1922), the radio, started by Guglielmo Marconi (1874–1937), and television, made possible through the research of Joseph Thomson (1856–1940), Lee De Forest (1873–1961), and Edwin Armstrong (1890–1954).

Medicine had to wait almost three centuries after William Harvey before the myth of spontaneous generation was exposed by Louis Pasteur (1822–1895), who proved the transmission of disease by bacteria. The same with the discovery of vitamins, hormones, antibiotics, sulfa drugs, penicillin; of genes and chromosomes as hereditary transmitters; of the continuity of germ plasm and nonhereditability of acquired characteristics; of the laws of genetic mutation.[4]

Every one of these inventions was made by men whose lives spanned the last and present centuries, and whose contribution to human knowledge has literally produced a new language with thousands of vocables in all the cultures of mankind.

But this is only part of the picture, even if we add the fact that mathematics has been used in the exploitation of physical reality to an extent never dreamed in the age of Descartes. He opened the door to the prospect of exploring matter to its depths when he divorced body from spirit, and gave the exploration a dignity it might otherwise never have attained. It was left to our age, however, to enter the Cartesian treasury and find there such riches as children are now enjoying from their mothers' wombs before they are born.

The accumulation of new knowledge involves not only things material, from subatomic particles on earth to the constitution of rock from the surface of the moon. It also includes hitherto unknown data of past history, unexplored reaches of man's psyche, and previously untapped resources governing social phenomena.

Every phase of this expanding universe of the mind has made an impact on religion, which in the West is mainly Christianity. We shall examine the effects of the impact in a later context, but something must be said at this point about the real meaning of what some call the Knowledge Revolution while others, more accurately, describe it as the Scientific Revelation. Revelation is not too strong a word for the exposure of reality that has taken place, mainly since the turn of the century. Like other revelations, it unveils things formerly unknown. It not only promises but already confers benefits previously never thought possible. It demands of most people implicit faith in its assumed (and unprovable) principles, and has developed a circle of elite that would do credit to the most elaborate religions of history.

THE NATURE OF REALITY. Since the origins of man's reflective thinking, he has been asking himself: What is the real? Already in the first millennium before the Christian era, the Hindu *Upanishads* raised the question and answered it by saying that the real is the unseen; some went so far as to claim that everything else was *maya* or illusion.

So, too, the ancient Greeks, for whom the spirit was both real and substantial; it had, or could have, independent existence. Aristotle described God as *Nous* (Mind), without extension or parts, in a word, immaterial; and called man a rational animal, whose soul (*psyche*) was not only real but more real than the body. The latter was, after all, passive and determined by the soul; but the former was the active and dynamic principle of life, incorruptible, indivisible, and immortal.

If this kind of dualism prevailed until recent times, it is slowly changing in favor of another attitude, ushered in by the growing revelation of the world's storehouse of happiness available here and now, in the present world of space and time, and without waiting for the promise of beatitude beyond the grave.

It is not quite accurate to call this materialism, or to label the findings of science a threat to things of the spirit. Carl Jung, among others, believes that we have seen in our day a "metaphysics of the mind" supplanted by a "metaphysics of matter," and he regards this as "an unexampled revolution in man's outlook upon the world."[5] The conclusion is correct, but the base is too narrow. What actually happened is that preoccupation with empirical values, made known and available to an extent impossible even a hundred years ago, has centered man's attention on things of this world and diverted his attention from the world to come. This world is increasingly enjoyable in body and spirit, thanks to the growing accumulation of knowledge about the cosmos and its laws of operation. The joys of a world to come are ostensibly available only to the spirit since the body is left behind.

What, then, is reality by the standards of today's philosophy? It is everything that can be experienced in space and time. The unreal is whatever is claimed to exist but does not square with this norm.

Today's vocabulary is studded with words that suggest the dramatic change in outlook. Synonyms for real are tangible, actual, visible, factual, known and provably knowable, not supposed or hoped for, not imagined or expected, the existing and now experienced. The unreal is just the opposite. Words like spiritual and supernatural or mystical and metaphysical, are practically synonymous in current literature with the illusory and nonexistent.

Sigmund Freud was speaking for the age when in 1927 he wrote *The Future of an Illusion*. Religious ideas, he concluded after a lifetime of clinical practice, are born of the need to make tolerable man's helplessness in his environment and are conceived in man's memories of his own childhood and the childhood of the human race. They owe their vitality to mankind's hostility to culture and the intellectual renunciations that culture demands. Religious concepts, therefore, are all illusions. "Just as they cannot be proved, neither can they be refuted. The riddles of the universe only reveal themselves slowly to our inquiry. To many questions science can as yet give no answer." Scientific study is our only way to the knowledge of reality.[6]

On these premises, religion belongs to the realm of the unreal. It is unrelated to reality and motivated by wish fulfillment.

THE BASIS OF TRUTH. Parallel with this shift in the concept of reality has been a change in the notion of truth in answering the question: How do we know what is true?

If truth is that which conforms to reality, then the true is measured by the same yardstick as the real. If we further ask how the real is attained, we go back to the methodology of modern research, which is simplicity itself. All that a man has to do is make a hypothesis, experiment with what he conjectured and, if he persists, he is bound to discover something new—if only that his guess was wrong! But if there is any value to his hypothesis, he will sooner or later arrive at some new knowledge that perhaps no one else ever had.

A classic example was the discovery of chemotherapy by Paul Ehrlich (1854–1915). Ehrlich speculated that, since some dyes selectively stained bacteria and protozoa, substances might be found which could be selectively absorbed by the parasites and kill them without damaging the host. His faith in this hypothesis enabled him to persevere in the face of long-continued frustration, repeated failure, and attempts by his friends to dissuade him from the apparently hopeless task. After years of experimentation, he found that trypan red had some activity against protozoa. Taking this as a cue, Ehrlich finally developed salvarsan, an arsenic compound which is effective therapeutically against syphilis. It was the six hundred and sixth compound in the series, and a standing tribute to the power of faith in an idea overcoming great difficulties.

At the heart of modern research is search for the truth by way of supposition. You do not start with conviction and deduce certain conclusions; you begin with conjecture and arrive at a workable theory.

The whole process is built on an adverb. *Maybe* what I surmise has some merit; *maybe* it doesn't. Only testing will tell.

Even after experimenting and the discovery of what looks like the truth, the result is not really certitude but, at best, a more probable conjecture that can be used safely for still further experimentation.

The case of Ehrlich and his theory of chemotherapy bear this out. He searched for substances which are selectively absorbed by pathogenic organisms on the firm belief that drugs cannot act unless fixed to the organism. Today many active drugs are known to be therapeutic and yet not selectively fixed to the infective agents. Ehrlich's hypothesis was mistaken, yet he opened a new science of medicine and received the Nobel Prize for his achievements.

There is an unspoken implication in this method of going from the unknown to the known. The universe is saturated with laws of energy or, to change the figure, it is more filled with fixed ways of acting than the heavens are filled with stars. Anyone who methodically searches in the warehouse of nature is bound, almost in spite of himself, to run into some of these laws and "discover" what had been unknown before.

But then we come up against a problem. Is this the only way of arriving at new knowledge or, what comes to the same thing, of testing old knowledge to verify its validity?

The issue is critical for religion, any religion, which claims that its source of knowledge about man and his destiny is not the conjectural fruit of trial and error, but a revelation from God to be accepted on his word as incontestably true.

Three words have entered the epistemology of our times, and they raise grave questions for those who still believe in religious truth: *provisionalism, pragmatism,* and *horizontalism.*

No one doubted that the enormous changes in science and technology would have repercussions in the philosophy of knowledge. What many do not yet realize is that the central objective of philosophy, truth, is now on trial. In the course of a single lifetime, then in a decade, now in a year we are finding new basal facts and whole attitudes of viewing the universe are undergoing change. So far from slowing down, the process shows every sign of speeding up. The term *provisionalism* has been coined to express something of what is happening. It is not mere skepticism, which is negative, but a growing conviction that whatever we think now, people in a very short time will probably be thinking differently and better. From having been a secure commodity, truth has become a moving function. For the time being, we hold on to certain beliefs, while fully recognizing that it is only for the time being. As the search for more knowledge goes on, our stock of insight into reality keeps growing, but the fond hope for a stable and sure knowledge of anything must forever be abandoned. It belongs to a former age.

A logical corollary is *pragmatism.* Writing in 1907, William James conveniently defined the true as "only the expedient in our way of thinking." And anyone who has been watching the trend could see the same emphasis on the changing character of reality, on the relevance of knowledge to practical situations, on the need of testing truth by its ability to "work," and on the instrumental nature of ideas.

According to the pragmatic viewpoint, every truth has practical consequences. They are the test of its truthfulness. Pragmatists apply this principle to every contingency. If you ask them: How is the real to be recognized?—they answer: by the values developed through its being known. What justifies and explains religion? Its ability to satisfy psychological needs and generate useful values in society.

Less familiar but equally important is *horizontalism* to describe the way truth is acquired and distinguish it from the methods of pre-scientific days. No discovery of any consequence is possible without making use of what has been gained by others. A vast store of scientific wisdom is now available only because investigators have pooled their contributions. Publication of experimental results and observations to make them accessible to others and open to criticism is one of the basic principles of modern research.

This may be a statement of technique; it may also express a concept of knowledge. What the human race knows at any moment is the accumulated wisdom of the past (historical horizontalism) and the shared wisdom of the present (geographical horizontalism). No more and no less. Any claim of a vertical access to reality by way of divine communication, whether from the prophets of old or from religious authorities today, is unscientific in the basic sense of untrue.

The issue at stake is not trivial. This is more than the familiar rationalism which dismisses revelation as a valid source of knowledge. Men like Paul Tillich, who could not possibly be accused of indifference to religion, are redefining the meaning of nature to declare that the only source of knowledge is the world of space and time; that the trouble with scientists is their inability to understand the universe. So they foolishly lapse into atheism or agnosticism, because they do not see that the God whom they deny or question is not so distinct from the cosmos (physical and psychic reality) as they suppose. Tillich approvingly quotes two pantheists to exlain what this means.

> The phrase *Deus sive natura* (God or nature), used by people like Scotus Erigena and Spinoza, does not say that God is identical with nature but that he is identical with the *natura naturans,* the creative nature, the creative ground of all natural objects. In modern naturalism the religious quality of these affirmations has almost disappeared, especially among philosophizing scientists who understand nature in terms of materialism and mechanism.[7]

In more simle terms, the growth in knowledge in recent decades confirms what hoary philosophers like Erigena and Spinoza had been saying long ago: the "naturalist" view of the world—as opposed to the supernaturalist—identifies God, not of course with the *totality* of things, the universe as such, but with that part of nature which gives it meaning and direction. No doubt there is more to God than the "universe" that we know; but you do not depend on a God independent of the universe to learn what the world (including man) is all about. If only men will search in nature and share with other men, there is no limit to their acquisition of truth.

Electronic Communication

Among the findings of modern science, none gives greater promise of changing the world than the discovery of electronic communication. The first beginnings of electronics are so recent and their development so sudden that we have to shake ourselves into realizing what has taken place. Philosophers of the visual arts use strong language to get across to people what is happening: that our century is witnessing such drastic change in intercommunication as compares with the origin of the alphabet or the discovery of print. They speak of three revolutionary stages that have occurred so far, and we are now in the fourth. Each of the preceding three had traumatic implications for religion, and the fourth is already making its presence felt in our time.

FROM LITERACY TO PRINT. As far as anthropology can trace the ancestry of the human family, the earliest culture of which we have record was preliterate and oral. This is not to say, however, that preliterate people were necessarily prelogical.

There are many cultures that still qualify as nonliterate and whom some comparative religionists call "primitives." A fair estimate would place their number at one tenth to one sixth of the human family. They have remained from time immemorial out of general and influential contact with other peoples and as a consequence are said to possess religious beliefs which characterized mankind nearer the origins of human history than other, major religions like Hinduism, Judaism, and Christianity.

These people are by no means barbarian or uncivilized. Authors who speak of them as preliterate, without pejorative connotations, imply what is factually true: that their culture commonly antedates the arrival of human literacy. It is well to keep this in mind for later reference, because part of the crisis in today's world is the sudden impact of electronic communication into societies that never passed through the intermediary steps of literacy and print, common to the rest of the world.

Taking the term "preliterate" in its most extensive sense it refers to all such people, either long since dead, or those very much alive but lineal descendants of the former.

Their cultural pattern was (and is) essentially tribal, without suggesting that "tribalism" equals "barbarism" or that "tribesmen" are generally "wildmen." Belonging to a tribe implies a certain closed world; to other peoples across the seas or beyond the mountains, but also enclosed within the tribe itself. A tribe is a self-contained unit, and at the same time a very self-conscious unit. Everyone knows about everyone else. There are no secrets. What one does, others see or hear about, soon and with instant reaction.

Communication of ideas in tribal society is better described as communication of feeling. If the vocabulary is limited, by literate standards, it is more than sufficient to express what the people have to share—for two reasons: because they are not given to much speculation, which demands a sophisticated and extensive vocabulary, and because where people live together in close and constant relationship, the myriad of thought and feeling that call for extra words and phrases in writing are supplied by the context of daily life or the tone and gesture of the living voice.

Preliterate might better be rendered "nonliterate," to avoid the notion that writing, i.e., *literae*=letters, is necessary to convey thought or emotion; as though unwritten speech were closer to some prehuman state of man's evolution from primates.

Once this is admitted, it is not hard to see why so-called primitive cultures have survived over the centuries, since they were quite self-sufficient in terms of basic human satisfaction. It also explains why these cultures are able to "rise" so quickly from their tribal state to what literate people call civilized society. Actually literacy, for them, is not always progress in fundamental values. It may be the entrance into a world of fantasy, cerebration, and anxiety that is often more barbarian than the traditionally primitive culture from which they were emancipated.

Tribal cultures are oral societies living in an aural world. They communicate by word of mouth, and they receive by word of ear. One effect is the high sensitivity they develop, not only of the faculties of speech and sound, but of the sense of taste and touch, which are so necessary to complement the spoken word in order to convey all that one person wishes to say to another. This partly explains why serving a delicately cooked meal partakes of ritual language in tribal communities; and why symbolic touching of one's own or another's body is so closely tied in with primitive religion.

The advent of writing cannot be exactly dated. Five thousand years before the Christian era is a fair estimate. Nor is it important to trace the sequence of man's varied efforts to share his thoughts and feelings by means of pictorial writing, like the cuneiform, hieroglyph, or ideogram. It was the coming of phonetic script that made the difference. Specifically and especially it was the rise of the alphabet, directly from the Near East and developed by the Greeks and Romans, which created a totally new situation in Western culture. Scholars agree that the beginnings of phonetic writing should be credited to the Semites, and religious historians see in this a providential preparation for *The Scriptures,* i.e., the Writings par excellence, which contain the principal record of God's communication to man.

The alphabet was a revolutionary advance over the use of letters to represent ideas or even syllables. It meant that, for the first time, man could articulate his thoughts and feelings by means of single sounds expressed in a few easily remembered written forms. No expert in Sinology knows all the eighty thousand Chinese symbols, and even the ten thousand normally used by scholars are beyond the capacity of most people to learn. How much easier to use only twenty to thirty signs.

In a relatively short time, the alphabet passed from one language to another, from the Phoenicians and Hebrews to the farthest reaches of Eastern and Northern Europe. Due to its simplicity, writing became the common possession of ordinary people, and was not limited (as still obtains in large parts of the Orient) to the priestly or privileged classes. The experience of three and a half millennia confirms the opinion that, except for the alphabet, civilization as we now define it would not have come into existence. It was the alphabet that quite alone has detribalized men and made them civilized individuals. Cultures, it is said, can rise far above civilization in other ways, as in art forms and economy, but they remain essentially tribal without the phonetic alphabet, as do the Chinese and Japanese.

There may be value in listing some of the changes that take place whenever a people become alphabetically developed. From being oral and auricular they become literate. The eye replaces the mouth and ear. From a strong sense of community, they become more individualized. Their consciousness becomes more personal, locked up within themselves; their visual functions are intensified; intuition is replaced by rationality, and the world of linear space and time becomes normative of reality.

Much has been said in praise and blame of phonetic writing. Socrates, who was not a writer, feared that the invention of the alphabet would produce "forgetfulness in the minds of those who use it, because they will not practice their memory. Their trust in writing, produced by external characters which are no part of themselves, will discourage the use of their own memory within them." He quoted with approval the criticism once made to the god Thamus who taught men how to read and write:

> You have discovered an elixir not of memory but of reminding; and you offer your pupils the appearance of wisdom, not true wisdom. For they will read many things without instruction and will therefore seem to know many things, when they are for the most part ignorant and hard to get along with, since they are not wise, but only appear to be wise.[8]

Socrates was not against the art of phonetic writing, as Plato carefully pointed out. What concerned him, however, as he stood at the crossroads between an oral and literate civilization, was the prospect of men becoming learned without being wise, of being intellectual without having virtue, and of acquiring great erudition without really knowing what they appear to know.

Another feature of phonetic culture that deserves attention is the relative case with which an aggressive society possessing the alphabet can translate an adjacent society into its cultural mode. It is a one-way process, always in the direction of a literate society absorbing the nonliterate one; never the other way around. Again the Greeks seemed to have sensed this, as illustrated in their Cadmus myth. The Greek King Cadmus is said to have introduced the alphabet to Greece and, as a result, had sown the dragon's teeth which sprang up as armed men.

Viewed in this light, the conquest of victorious Rome by Greek culture becomes more intelligible. Also the influence of a small band of Palestinian Semites like Peter, Paul, and John with their written Gospel takes on new meaning. The implications for modern Christianity in contact with the heavily tribal cultures of the Orient are part of today's history.

All the effects of literacy were accentuated with the discovery of printing. Johann Gutenberg (1397–1468) is generally considered the first European to print from movable type. If 1456 is accepted as the date of his great invention, when he issued the Mazarin Bible, this would give an even eighty years to the publication of John Calvin's *Institutes of the Christian Religion.* During that period a new form of Christianity came on the scene, whose principles, historians agree, were strongly shaped by the rise of a print civilization.

There are two ways of looking at what happened. One approach assumes that the advent of typography accelerated the latent individualism of sixteenth-century society and, at the same time, homogenized whole masses of persons to a standard pattern, of which the printed book was both symbol and contributing cause. Uniformity gradually replaced variety among people, and conformity to the common ethos became a test of acceptance in the new, book-determined society.

A print culture tends to produce uniformity or, in Shakespeare's terms, "commodity." Printed books, the first uniform, repeatable, and mass-produced items in history, helped to produce the uniform commodity culture for the sixteenth and later centuries. "That smooth-faced gentleman, tickling Commodity," wrote Shakespeare, "Commodity, the bias of the world."[9] Accommodation to prevalent norms, we would say today.

A different analysis of the impact of print on human culture sees the invention of printing as only the last stage of a centuries-old development in the relationship between space and discourse. Historically the process began with hieroglyphs or ideograms, whereby sound, which is fleeting, was given a degree of permanence by being reduced to marks in space. The next step occurred when the alphabet was created, for then words became broken into separate elements, each having its own spatial sign.

This went on for millennia and might never have reached the climax of print except for the growing belief that all the wisdom of the ages is locked up in written form. The driving urge to tap this treasury of knowledge and make it available to everyone helped to create the Renaissance, which took its name from a revival of the classics of antiquity, and the Reformation, whose motto was *sola Scriptura* and whose basic objection to Catholicism was that Christians were deprived of access to the biblical, i.e., written Word of God.

On these premises, the negative consequences of multiplied literacy are dismissed as unimportant. The schism between thought and action, decay of dialogue and its replacement by solitary exposure of reading mind to written word, substitution of impersonal type for vital contact with human beings, specialized information about things instead of intimate knowledge of people, organized packets of scattered data without integration into the whole of life—all of this, and more, has been charged to the introduction of print. But what matter, provided the riches of past experience are made easily and widely accessible to present and future generations?

When Carlyle wrote, "All that mankind has done, thought, gained or been, it is lying as in magic preservation in the pages of books,"[10] he was voicing the judgment of post-Reformation, Euro-American man. To this day, Western society identifies civilization with education, and education with knowledge of the printed page.

A new epoch was born when one person's ideas suddenly became the common property of thousands who read and reread his published works, and felt that he had capsulized the spirit within the narrow lines of a book. The value of this myth has not changed substantially since Gutenberg, except that now it is being challenged by a new concept of communication created by the science of electronics.

THE MASS MEDIA. So much is being said nowadays about the communications age that it may be difficult to recognize the forest for the trees. Phrases like "the fall of the tyranny of print, the medium is the message, participation mystique, putting on one's environment, hot and cold personalities," are familiar. But their frequent use and exploitation have blurred the significance of what historians of the next century may well consider the greatest single development in man's culture since the Stone Age.

What changes are being introduced by the new media that are bound to have lasting influence on Christian thought and institutions? It is not too much to expect this influence to be at least as great as that exercised by the discovery of print and the dissemination of books which accompanied the Protestant Reformation.

The first immediate effect of electronic media—the telephone and telegraph, radio and television, radar and computer, photography and film and their derivatives—is to collectivize those who come under its influence. Words like "tribalization" and "mass participation" vaguely suggest something of what occurs. Simultaneously millions of persons find themselves equally involved in seeing, hearing, and feeling the influence of a single man or woman with whom they establish instant rapport. This is one side of the involvement. Instinctively they also sense that unseen multitudes of others are equally captivated by the same experience—which now takes on cosmic proportions.

What makes this collectivized experience revolutionary is that it comes on the heels of half a millennium of isolating literacy. Western man has been suddenly plunged into an intense, depth participation with others. From a coldly rational culture that had come to worship books, people are now exposed to people, with all the terrifying possibilities of such exposure. Visual contact with lifeless print is now extended to warm intimacy with living persons, where the whole man, body and spirit, thought and emotion, becomes profoundly absorbed— and the absorption is active, not merely passive; and communitarian to a degree that staggers the imagination. Two hundred million joined with Pope Paul VI when he addressed the United Nations; five hundred million witnessed the spectacle of man first setting foot on the moon.

The news media have increased the impact of sheer impressions by geometric proportion. When I read a page, I get only so much data per unit of time. When I watch the television screen, I am bombarded with countless data all at once. To call this multisensorial is to say very little; myriad-sensorial would be nearer the truth.

Never before has so much power been so easily available for divinizing or demonizing the human spirit, depending on the virtue or treachery of the one who directs the media. He determines their ideology; and their influence is inevitable, provided they are shrewdly adapted to differences of place, person, and time, and exploited with maximum awareness of human needs and wants.

This influence includes the printed word. The modern press was at first unwilling but is now becoming an enthusiastic partner (or confederate) of the electronics media.

Those who predicted, with Oswald Spengler, "the death knell of Western literate man," have been surprised. Electronics has not suppressed man's literacy, nor killed his desire to read. It joined forces with communication. It is a planned system, both as to formal organization and communication content. Everything from radio transmitters to film studios is constantly altered to fit the changing needs of society.

Always in focus is the impact which the media can make on the people for whom they are intended.

Words like exploitation and manipulation are really out of place to describe what those who control the media are doing. There is always some rational purpose behind whatever they present or portray. It may be as harmless as selling an article of clothing or advertising a new car. Or it may be the broadcast of a battle scene or the mass demonstration of thousands of students. But given the magnitude of the audience, regularly tens of millions in a single country; given the variety of people who witness the ad or the spectacle—an impact is made on a large segment of society for which those who direct the media are responsible. Their responsibility is only part of the problem and is not our direct concern. What is relevant for our purpose is that agencies so powerful in shaping the minds and wills of humanity are exercising their influence, to say the least, with small regard for the principles of Christianity.

Psychological Man

One more change characterizes modern times. We might call it the rise of Psychological Man. Like the knowledge explosion and electronic communication this too has a history that should briefly be seen to better understand what it means.

Until very recently, psychology was part of philosophy and was never separated from the study of man as man. With the coming of Descartes (1596–1650), something new entered Western speculation. Man was split into two parts: irrational animal and a soul that participated in the sublimity of God.

It was left to those who came after him to carry the dichotomy to its logical conclusion. Among others, Wilhelm Wundt (1832–1920) set up an exact parallelism within man between his physical and psychological activity. In America, William James (1842–1910) did the same, except that he went beyond Wundt in drawing conclusions on which others could build the "irrational man." According to James, the brain is the organ of human thought and what he called "holy thoughts" are only a form of cerebration. They well up from the unconscious. Freud went beyond James in asserting that the unconscious is the basis of all mental and emotional disorder; that to rule the unconscious is to master the human personality.

All of this would have been merely academic information except for the spirit of the age.

Not satisfied with discovering the unconscious in the human psyche, clinical psychologists developed a new science on the subject. Their findings, joined with the researches of analysts in allied fields, produced a volume of literature.

It is immaterial how Western man came to be so preoccupied with the realm of the unconscious (or subconscious) in human activity. It is not even important, for our purpose, to be technical in describing the various states of awareness that specialists distinguish. Psychic awareness is now recognized as operating on another level than consciousness; that human beings act and react to stimuli below the threshold of conscious motivation.

This area of subliminal awareness has developed into a science and is being put to use in a way that few historians of modern culture have yet been able to describe. But the fact is certain and the effects are consequential—especially in the story of contemporary Christianity.

How do we describe "the unconscious" in its relationship to human action? It is the unawareness of the bases (any or all) for a judgment that a person makes. He may be unable to identify the sequence of reasons for what he does, his judgment or attitude. It may be impossible for him to verify the elements, overt or implied, in a decision he makes. His motives for doing something, or abstaining from something else, for believing this or denying that, for feeling the way he does may be quite unknown. He may have only an unexplainable urge and feel the urge persisting in spite of conscious reasons to the contrary. He may experience an unaccountable interior drive without apparent cause in his conscious life; or an unclear sense of duty or fear or attraction, for which there is no assignable cause. He may unwittingly be influenced by a person he sees or a statement he hears, that shapes his own thought long before the age of reason and quite apart from rational reflection.

The psychological sciences have assumed these data and clarified them systematically. The unspoken premise is that human beings are not always the rational animals so neatly defined by Aristotle. Many of their actions are not rational, that is, not immediately traceable to reasoned discourse nor directly responsible to their free will.

That was one side of the picture. There are in man hidden forces which operate to influence his conduct as a human being, and all the while he may think he is acting with intelligent deliberation.

Experimentation with human beings and animals, singly and in crowds, has furnished another set of data. It has been found that people (and animals) respond to stimuli in unexpected ways. Repeated stimulation reveals definite patterns, and these in turn are used at will to produce effects which only those who know the laws of stimulus and response can predict.

Some call this the depth approach to influencing human behavior; others have coined other terms. The fact is that a large segment of Western society now uses the findings of psychology and psycho-analysis to persuade its people. The persuasion is most prevalent in the field of advertising. Billions of dollars' worth of American products, for example, is being affected and some would say revolutionized by this approach, which is still in its infancy. According to one estimate, two thirds of America's largest advertisers have geared campaigns in this direction, inspired by what marketers call "motivation analysis."

But the issue is more serious than such popularizers as Vance Packard would suggest. *The Hidden Persuaders* are not only professionals who probe our everyday habits for hidden meanings, to have us buy what we do not need with money we do not have.

Once the recesses of the spirit are probed, the results are open to other and more devastating uses. If products of manufacture can be sold by appealing to unsuspecting urges, so can ideas and attitudes, ideologies and states of mind.

No doubt other explanations are possible and many factors besides this one have been operative. But the mass influence on vast popula-tions in the present century must, at least partly, be traced to this cause. How otherwise explain the sudden change in thinking and believing of multitudes, or the drastic reversal in policies of whole na-tions?

This is not saying that men like Hitler or Castro made studies in depth psychology and then carefully applied their conclusions to manipulate the people. Nor does it mean that charismatic leaders consciously exploit the subconscious areas of human behavior. It does mean that too much has been learned about the human "uncon-scious" and too many policies have been shaped by the science of psychology to question the impact or doubt its influence in Western society.

Scientists who study the modern media write almost casually about the social effects of mass communications. They talk about "controversial questions" that will take years to explore, and maybe never solve. Does the show of violence and crime on television cause juvenile delinquency? Does pornography encourage sadism? Does international propaganda help to cause war, or advance peace? Widely different opinions can be found on these and similar questions involving the effects of mass media on public taste, morals, politics, adult education, and crime. Why is there so much controversy about these matters?

Two principal causes, it is said, are the shortage of conclusive scientific evidence on media effects and the tone or urgency that often surrounds the questions about effects.

Scientific research on communications effects is far too scarce to provide the information needed for an understanding of the subject. As one scholar testified recently concerning the effects of television on children, "The effect of television on children is controversial not because some people are against crime and others for it; it is controversial because so little is known that anyone can inject his prejudices or his views into the debate without being proven wrong." Even the available research findings are not always unequivocal, especially if one tries to interpret them as evidence for or against particular courses of social action.

Often there is an apparent social urgency in discussions about the effects of mass media, especially concerning such salient and insistent social problems as juvenile delinquency, crime, and public morality. This social anxiety makes people impatient with a slow, objective, and dispassionate scientific orientation toward the problems and encourages a search for immediate opinions and social remedies.[11]

The conclusion is that no one really knows how influential the media are and until some distant day no one will ever find out. All the while two parallel forces are operating on a large segment of human society. Man's inner spirit—his emotions, instincts, and passions—is being analyzed and classified and the stimuli to which it responds are systematically organized. At the same time, the means are being developed for deeply affecting this spirit and evoking its response—suddenly and simultaneously in millions, with dramatic effects to which every major country in Europe and America testifies.

The implications for Christianity are a matter of record. Or, more accurately, they have become the experience of Christians everywhere. Their faith makes heavy demands on personal and social commitment.

All the while the ideological climate, produced by the media, makes this commitment increasingly difficult, even in the depths of one's heart, and next to impossible in the marketplace. They are caught in a dilemma. If they adjust their principles to the value system produced by the media that surround them, they compromise on the faith. If they reject the system or try to adjust it to Christianity, they become strangers to the society in which they live, or the objects of hatred for opposing what everyone else accepts.

It would take an Augustine to do justice to the crisis in which Christianity finds itself today. The least we can do is to know what the issues are and, for Christians, trust in the final outcome.

I

FAITH AND UNBELIEF

Christianity is unique among the religions of the world in proclaiming the acceptance of mysteries as a condition for salvation. The same word, *faith,* does not mean the same thing in Christianity that it means, for example, in Judaism or Islam.

From the first century of its era, Christianity professed to communicate certain truths about God and his dealings with men which are beyond the human mind to comprehend: the Trinity of persons in one God, the duality of natures in one Christ, the real bodily resurrection of the dead. None of these is rationally provable, and yet all are to be simply believed on the authority of God's revelation.

As might be expected, not everyone was willing to accept these mysteries, even when they admired the personality of Jesus and were inclined to follow, as a beautiful ideal, the ethical principles he taught and so tragically exemplified in his life.

Since apostolic times, people who were otherwise well disposed to Christianity were not ready to subscribe to all of its mysterious teachings. The Gnostics about whom the evangelist John wrote in his book of Revelation, were so called because their *gnosis* (spiritual insight) considered irrational the allegedly suprarational doctrines proposed to the less-enlightened faithful.

The story of Christianity has not changed. In every age have risen men whose sincerity could not be questioned, but who became convinced that some (or all) of the Christian dogmas are unacceptable to the critical and intellectually honest mind.

In the fourth century, Arius found it impossible to subscribe to the idea that a human being was literally God walking the streets of Palestine. In the eighteenth century, David Hume said he could not accept Christ's physical resurrection from the dead. In between were the Pelagians and Nestorians, the Eutycheans and Iconoclasts, with many others, all essentially saying the same thing: that some principle or practice of historic Christianity, in their judgment, was incompatible with sound reason or human experience.

There are two ways of looking at this characteristic of the Christian religion. It is possible to see it only, or mainly, as a periodic conflict with established principles which the Church must protect as part of its divine mandate. Or it may be seen as conflicting, indeed, with the faith once and for all given to the apostles, but also as something more.

In the early fifth century, Augustine caught something of this deeper meaning when he observed that "many things lay hidden in the Scriptures" until certain persons came along and "began to trouble the Church with questions. Those things were then opened up which lay hid and the will of God was understood. Was the Trinity fully treated before the Arians opposed it? Was penance properly described before the Novatians raised their criticism? So, too, baptism was not clearly explained before the rebaptizers protested against the teaching."[1]

In this respect, Christianity in the twentieth century is no different from what it was in the age of Augustine. What makes a great deal of difference, however, is the attitude one adopts in looking back over the recent decades. He can see there mostly confrontation between faith and unbelief or he can trace the designs of providence in having issues raised which may be painful and costly while in process, but that are bound to clarify the faith and deepen the commitment of those who, perhaps, believed too lightly or whose loyalty had never been tried.

There is a problem in trying to assess the immediate past from either perspective: of defensive confrontation or of profitable challenge. Christianity is not monolithic. It is not even united on some admittedly basic issues.

How to make historical sense of what happened in the area of faith since 1900, affecting both Christianity in general and the Christian Churches in particular? The best approach seems to be to combine the two, while recognizing that, in spite of their divisions, Christians are not so divided that anything which touches one tradition leaves the others untouched; or that whatever concerns the essence of Christianity will not influence all of its forms.

Rivals and Challenges to the Christian Faith

If ever Christianity had to take stock of its own identity and recognize itself in the world of religion it has been in modern times.

This is mainly due to the rapid diffusion of opinions brought on by the electronics media. Ideas may now become ideologies overnight.

FAITH AND REASON. As the nineteenth century drew to a close, it offered anyone who wished to make the inventory a formidable list of charges against the Christian faith for being inadequate to meet the demands of the next hundred years.

Immanuel Kant led the critics by stating categorically that man should recognize no authority superior to his own mind and will, and therefore everyone creates his own laws of religion and morality.

If there is a categorical imperative—that is, a law for the will of every rational being—it can command us only to act always on the maxim of such a will in us as can at the same time look upon itself as making universal law. For only then is the practical principle and the imperative which we obey unconditioned.

We need not now wonder, when we look back upon all previous efforts that have been made to discover the principle of morality, why they have one and all been bound to fail. Their authors saw man as tied to laws by his duty, but it never occurred to them that he is subject only to *laws which are made by himself* and yet are universal, and that he is bound only to act in accordance with a will which is his own.

I will therefore call my principle the principle of the Autonomy of the will in contrast with all others, which I consequently class under Heteronomy.[2]

Just as Kantian ethics became independent of any other premise than the will, so religion (including the Christian) becomes a product of reason and not a communication from above. Revelation may be admitted as a hypothetical aid, but not something essential for man's perfection or the fullfillment of his destiny.

Karl Marx followed the lead of Kant by questioning the Christian interpretation of history as the working out of divine providence, and conceiving human development as part of God's design for the whole universe. The main difficulty with the Christian view of history, according to Marx, lay in the fact that God's will is unknowable to man's direct experience.

More reasonable was the Marxian interpretation which is economic. The production of the goods and services that support human life, and the exchange of these goods and services, are the real bases of all social processes and institutions. Other factors may also play a part. But the most important creator of history is economics. It is not, as Christians claim, any sort of mysterious deity on whom Christians rely in the naïve expectation that "for those who love God all things work together unto good."[3]

Marx had logic on his side. If the Christian faith was so powerful to influence men's lives, why had it so miserably failed to stem the tide of injustice and the exploitation introduced by industrialism?

Lesser minds than Kant and Marx, and disciples of both, added to the chorus of criticism that reached its peak in Nietzsche. His *Der Antichrist*, published in 1895, was to become the battle cry of all who had seen or tried Christianity and found it wanting. It also summarized every intelligent charge against the religion of the Nazarene, as Nietzsche called it, since the close of the apostolic age.

Even if they had wanted to, Christian thinkers could not remain impassive to the Nietzschean "eternal indictment of Christianity." Religious faith was not merely doubted or dismissed as fancy. It was denounced in the most unmeasured language.

> In Christianity neither morality nor religion has even a single point of contact with reality. Nothing but imaginary *causes* ("God," "soul," "ego," "spirit," "free will"—for that matter, "unfree will"), nothing but imaginary *effects* ("sin," "redemption," "grace," "punishment," "forgiveness of sins"). Intercourse between imaginary *beings* ("God," "spirits," "souls"); an imaginary *natural science* (anthropocentric; no trace of any concept of natural causes).
>
> This *world of pure fiction* is vastly inferior to the world of dreams insofar as the latter *mirrors* reality, whereas the former falsifies, devalues, and negates reality.[4]

In the years after Nietzsche's death in 1900, his theme found its way into the literature of all nations where Christianity was established. Names like Julian Huxley in England, John Dewey in America, Ernst Haeckel in Germany, Jean-Paul Sartre in France are typical of men who agreed with the author of *Antichrist* that the Christian faith is at best a pious fancy and at worst the enemy of all progress in the only real world that exists.

COMPROMISE AND SURRENDER. Confronted with the growing suspicion of Christian belief as illusory, a new kind of apologetics developed in some quarters, trying to bridge the gulf between faith and reason —now presented as the dichotomy of faith *or* reason. Either you followed your reason and were no longer Christian, or you still believed, but only at the sacrifice of rational thought.

One of the earliest twentieth-century efforts to escape the dilemma became known in Catholic circles as Modernism. Formally condemned by St. Pius X in 1907, it attracted to its cause a number of outstanding leaders in England and continental Europe. The Jesuit George Tyrrell (1861–1909), the Oratorian Lucien Laberthonière (1860–1932), and the biblical scholar Alfred Loisy (1857–1940) were kindred spirits who felt that unless the traditional concept of faith was revamped, the Church had no chance of survival in the climate of scientific criticism.

After their formal censure, the Modernists protested they were wrongly condemned; they never really meant what the papal documents *Lamentabili* and *Pascendi* attributed to them. When three years later, the Pope further required of all clerics a solemn oath against Modernism, the authors of the movement became permanently identified with a new brand of Catholicism. A half century later it was still very much alive and defended on a scale that was quite impossible in the early nineteen hundreds.

The original Modernists, as viewed by Rome, placed the foundation of the Christian faith in agnosticism. Human reason, they confessed, is entirely restricted to phenomena, the external, sensible properties of things. The mind has neither the right nor the power to transgress these limits. Therefore, it cannot raise itself to God nor come to know his existence.

Accordingly, God cannot be the object of true knowledge; nor can his activity in history ever be recognized.

If you asked the Modernists about the motives of credibility, i.e., the evidence from miraculous phenomena that makes the faith reasonably credible, "they dismiss this as intellectualism, an absurd system, and long since dead."[5]

How does a Christian, then, pass from agnosticism in the secular order to faith in the order of religion? Nothing from outside of man can explain it. Faith is uniquely from within. In fact, it is part of man's nature, "a kind of motion of the heart," hidden and unconscious. It is, in Modernist terms, a natural instinct belonging to the emotions; "a feeling for the divine" that cannot be expressed in words or doctrinal propositions, an attitude of spirit that all people naturally have but that some are more aware of having.

There can be no question, on these premises, of revealed truths which the Church can formulate in precise dogmas. There is only this semiconsciousness of the divine that may be variously stimulated by music or ritual or the sight of a beautiful scene.

The Protestant effort to avoid the quandary posed by modern rationalism goes back to the early nineteenth century, when Friedrich Schleiermacher redefined religion as sentiment and faith as a particularly intense kind of internal sensation. His influence has been enormous. To this day Protestants may be divided into those who follow Schleiermacher and those, like Barth and Brunner, who opposed his "religion of feeling" and insist on the acceptance of scriptural revelation as the only valid basis for the Christian belief.

Schleiermacher might have remained buried in his thirty-four volumes except that he was called upon to serve a new apologetic need. As the sacred writings of the non-Christian world began to accumulate, Christian scholars were demanded an account of their faith—now in competition with the beliefs of Hinduism, Buddhism, and Islam, and the numerous tribal cults of Africa and the Orient.

They were pressed to explain how these non-Christian religions were either like Christianity or different. If alike, what do they have in common; if different, what is the difference? Again the same pressure to validate the Christian religion on scientific grounds, and escape Nietzsche's charge of contradicting reality.

Out of a dozen writers who took up the challenge, Rudolf Otto (1869–1937) has been the most prominent. A disciple and editor of Schleiermacher, he found in the master a key to the problem. Otto's *Das Heilige*, first issued in 1917, must stand with the *Institutes* of Calvin as a classic in Protestant world literature.

Its central thesis is an insistence on the part played by the numinous in religious consciousness. Otto coined the word *numinous* to denote the essentially nonrational and nonmoral which constitutes what people call "holy." He described the numinous as composed of two kinds of feelings: awe and self-abasement at the Terrifying Unknown (*Mys-*

terium Tremendum), and enchantment (*fascinatio*) which the Unknown induces in anyone who allows himself to be charmed.

Although Otto's immediate teacher in this analysis was Schleiermacher, he was able to trace *The Idea of the Holy* (English title) directly to Martin Luther. From Luther he learned that "faith is the centre of the soul . . . most closely akin to the Greek 'enthusiasm' . . . For in opposition to the 'rationalizations' of the schools, the nonrational elements are maintained and fostered."[6]

Otto never let go of this nonrational basis of religion. It enabled him to place all religions on the same fundamental level. They are all equally devoid of intellectual principles of acceptance (credibility), content (doctrine), and of defense (theological analysis). Even when he spoke of the "rational elements" which should protect people from fanaticism, he never retouched the essence of religion—whether Christian or non-Christian, which is irrational. It is by origin and continued existence a psychological phenomenon whose objective validity is beyond the reach of intelligent appraisal.

DOUBT AND DISBELIEF. All sorts of consequences follow, once religion is defined in purely subjective terms. If Christianity, no less than Animism, at its center is a psychic phenomenon with emotional overtones; it becomes strange to still talk about objective religious truth or the assent of the mind to God's revelation.

Such terms as *certitude* and *conviction* belong to operations of the mind. They are not expressions of feeling. If the Christian faith is fundamentally a mood or a sentiment, we cannot really speak of being convinced or certain, or, for that matter, of denying or being in doubt. We affirm or deny with the mind, and we are said to doubt when our judgment is suspended between two mental alternatives.

There is something symbolic in the admission which George Tyrrell, the father of Modernism, made in a letter he wrote, in June 1900, to his friend Hausman, telling him that he never once resisted what in Catholic theology are considered doubts against the faith. Tyrrell had been a Catholic twenty-one years, and a priest for nine. "My lower rationalism, my imagination, my senses and passions," he confessed, "are all singularly sympathetic with doubt and even denial. But I do not 'fight down' my doubts, as I should in some cases advise others to do. Rather I go deliberately in search of every difficulty in that line lest I be haunted by the thought that new revelations might rob me of my faith, or that those who deny have reasons for their denial that I have not felt." He concluded by observing that his faith is "very different from the tranquil belief of those who have faith in the faith of others. This is impossible to me; for there is no man or body of men on earth whose belief would have the least influence on mine."[7]

Sixty-five years later, another English priest, Charles Davis, said the same thing when he left the Catholic Church "for conscience" sake. His own personal attitude, like Tyrrell's, was a compound of "imagination, senses and passions," and of how he "felt." When these conflicted with the Church's claim to speak in the name of Christ, the exodus, for Tyrrell as for Davis, was inevitable.

Viewed in this light, the crisis of faith for so many Christians takes on a different meaning. Scores of books have been published, with more in the offing, on *Atheism in Our Time, Belief and Unbelief, Culture of Our Post-Christian Era, Faith and Doubt, The Faith to Doubt, Varieties of Unbelief,* and kindred titles, concerned with the "loss of faith" among recent believers.[8]

The author of one of these books has already made history. John A. T. Robinson was Anglican Bishop of Woolwich, England, when in 1963 he wrote *Honest to God,* affirming that "All I can do is try to be honest, honest to God and honest about God."

A century from now, Robinson's short confession of unbelief will be read as the witness of millions who in our day still called themselves Christians but who no longer believed in the cardinal mysteries of Christianity.

"Our image of God must go," was the catchy title of the press announcement of Robinson's book.[9] In a few hours of publication, the first printing was sold out. In one year, half a million copies were printed, and ten translations in all the major languages of Europe and America were on the market. The nearest parallel in printing history was Ernest Renan's *La Vie de Jésus* (1863), in which the French ex-seminarian repudiated every element of the supernatural in the life of Christ. One difference between Renan and Robinson was that the Anglican prelate suddenly became the idol of the communications media.

Robinson admitted that his exposition amounted to a spiritual revolution, since the still prevalent Old and New Testament picture of God must disappear. "In fact, the coming of the space-age has destroyed this crude conception of God—and for that we should be grateful."[10]

He opened the revolution with the statement that outside the reality surrounding us there is no God: "The word *God* denotes the ultimate depth for all our being, the creative ground and meaning of all our existence. So conditioned for us is the word *God* by associations with a Being out there that Tillich warns us that to work the necessary transposition, 'you must forget *everything* traditional that you have learned about God, perhaps even that word itself.' "[11]

Some writers are creative thinkers, others are collective reflectors. Robinson belongs to the second class. On his own admission he was inventing nothing new; he was only saying, in more popular language, what more perceptive minds had been writing in professional journals and books. Three men especially were his guides: Rudolf Bultmann, Dietrich Bonhoeffer, and Paul Tillich. Significantly all three had studied at the same universities, Berlin and Tübingen, the strongholds of such influential scholars as Hegel, Schleiermacher, and Harnack.

Each of his masters furnished Robinson with part of his necessary tools. From Bultmann he borrowed demythologization of the Scriptures: "It is impossible to use electric light and the wireless and believe in the miraculous world of the New Testament."[12] Bonhoeffer gave him an idea of the Church of the future, whose "historicity is [no longer] deified as an object," that ultimately "produces a magical concept of the sacraments," undermines the absolute authority of the Word of God, and sets the institutional Church apart from the community which forms it.[13] Tillich taught him to substitute "ultimate concern" for God, since "the decisive thing is that even monotheism can be idolatrous, which means that the God of monotheism, the theistic God . . . can become an idol," when it makes "God a transcendent object, the creation an act at the beginning of time, the consummation a future state of things."[14]

Robinson campaigned against the heart of the New Testament, and with particular vehemence against the myth of Redemption.

> The doctrine of the Atonement is not—as in the supranaturalist way of thinking—a highly mythological, and often rather dubious transaction between two parties, "God" on the one hand and "man" on the other, who have to be brought together, and which goes on to explain, in Anselm's words, "why God became man."
>
> But even when it is Christian in content, the whole schema of a supernatural Being coming down from heaven to "save" mankind from sin . . . is frankly incredible to man "come of age," who no longer be-

lieves in such a *deus ex machina*. Yet Church people continue to explain the Atonement in such terms as this, picturing the interplay of two personified parties: "The relationship between God and man has been broken by original sin. Man could not pull himself up by his own shoestrings, and thus the only hope of restoration was from God's side. Yet it was from our side that things had to be put right. It appeared hopeless. But God found the answer. For in Christ, he himself became man, and as man reconciled us to himself."[15]

The Bishop of Woolwich was not playing with words. He was not setting up a straw man to later knock down. He consciously restated the historic dogma of the redemptive Incarnation in plain words to make sure he was not misunderstood. It was not theology that he wished to revise, for the sake of some more simple doctrine; it was the faith of Christianity. When he called this faith a "myth" that should be "thrown out," he meant it.

In spite of all the publicity that Robinson received, he would scarcely rate, on that score alone, inclusion in a survey of Christianity. Robinson is important because he symbolizes the beginning of religious tribalism that must be better known if the events taking place in nominally Christian cultures are to be correctly assessed.

One of the features of tribal society is the spontaneous acceptance by a group of people of whatever a persuasive leader proposes they should do. What matters is not so much what he says or how convincingly he argues his case, but that *he* says it—the right thing, at the right time, in the right way. History has known many such leaders. Paul of Tarsus, Savonarola, and Napoleon Bonaparte immediately come to mind.

He was saying the right thing: the Gospel teaching should be simplified and made intelligible to all the people, and not only to armchair theologians talking to each other in uncut foreign periodicals. He was talking at the right time: when Christian institutions are being asked to prove their claim to survival and the Catholic Church had begun its first ecumenical council in a hundred years. He spoke in the right way: with disarming openness, admitting that "as I watch or listen to a broadcast discussion between a Christian and a humanist, I catch myself realizing that most of my sympathies are on the humanist's side."[16]

All of this would be informative but not unusual until we see what impact Robinson made with a small paperback of less than 150 pages

—multiplied and advertized simultaneously on five continents. It was —to use a biblical term—miraculous.

People of every shade of religious persuasion hailed the author as a modern Jeremiah who had the courage of his convictions. Tillich, Bultmann, and Bonhoeffer became minor prophets. To suggest that Robinson had ceased to be a Christian was unpardonable.

It is instructive to read what reaction Robinson aroused in other professed Christians. A group of Lutheran religious in Germany felt obliged to match honesty for honesty, and take issue (among others) with "a leading Catholic newspaper [which] writes, 'The voice of Robinson's book is that of a genuine Christian attitude.' "[17] Their profession of faith is symptomatic of a little-known phase of Christian unity—where Protestants are teaching Catholics the meaning of what it means to believe.

> The English Bishop in his move to push aside the old picture of God and of traditional Christianity makes reference to his honesty and his courage. It is, then, no coincidence that the book's title is *Honest to God*. These key words appeal to most people.
>
> But does such honesty today require so much courage? After the preparatory work done by such atheistic giants as Nietzsche, the heart of man is already poisoned and thus open to any new teaching, such as this, in which God is deposed.
>
> In this respect, "being honest" is today not made very difficult. On the contrary, nowadays those in the large sphere of Christian theology who have the courage to leave the biblical message as it is are looked upon with disdain.
>
> Nowadays one needs courage to confess that God lives who made heaven and earth. To have honesty enough to testify that God, the Lord of life and history, is the Judge of mankind.[18]

This anguished concern about the inroads of unbelief into Western society found a strong echo in the ranks of Roman Catholicism. The four sessions of its Vatican Council (1962–65) singled out estrangement from the God of faith as having reached critical proportions: "Atheism must be accounted among the most serious problems of our age."[19]

Under the almost untranslatable word *atheismus* the Council included a whole spectrum of attitudes and presuppositions. Some expressly deny God and claim that we cannot affirm anything certain about him; or so scrutinize the concept of God as to make the term practically meaningless; or so extravagantly praise the greatness of man that belief in God becomes a sort of anemia, on the premise that we cannot know any absolute truth because everything in life is relative; or conjure up such a figment of the deity that he is no longer the God of revelation; or become so preoccupied with secular pursuits that any religion, including the Christian, seems like a waste of time.

Roman Catholics have been especially susceptible to the ravages of this climate. Their religion requires acceptance of formulations of faith which the Church is presumably authorized to proclaim. So it had done; but what happened? A surprisingly large number of people would give verbal adherence to the Church's teaching, until some intelligent critic came along or, as in moral matters, until acceptance of certain doctrines called for heavy sacrifice.

Nominally they might still profess to be loyal members of their Church. But many had already ceased to believe with "that obedience by which a man commits his whole self freely to God, offering the full submission of his intellect and will to the One who reveals, and freely assenting to the truth revealed by Him."[20]

Their faith became, in Tyrrell's words, a convergence of personal feelings, or, in the language of the electronics culture, a tribal impulse on a par with political affiliation and sometimes with less dedicated loyalty.

Anatomy of Conflict

Except for mass communications, the practical (or ideological) atheism of chronic unbelievers would have had no major influence on the rest of society. But all of this is now radically changed, as a single book like *Honest to God* demonstrated.

The net effect on many Christians, Catholics, Protestants, and Orthodox, has been to create confusion twice confounded: once because the psychological pressures became so incessant, and once again because the arguments against historic Christian beliefs were so persuasive.

Psychological pressures against the faith could be all but irresistible. In a major address at the Vatican Council, the General of the Society of Jesus identified them with brutal clarity:

This new godless society operates in an extremely efficient manner; at least in its higher levels of leadership. It makes use of every possible means at its disposal, be they scientific, technical, social or economic. It follows a perfectly mapped out strategy. It holds almost complete sway in international organizations, in financial circles, in the field of mass communications: press, cinema, radio and television.

It is like the City of Man of St. Augustine. And it not only carries on the struggle against the City of God from outside the walls, but even crosses the ramparts and enters the very territory of the City of God, insidiously influencing the minds of believers (including even religious and priests) with its hidden poison producing its inevitable fruits in the Church: naturalism, distrust and rebellion.[21]

The speaker of these lines paid dearly for his outspokenness. The press and networks of the world reacted to the exposure of their role in collectivizing modern society away from the Christian faith. Yet, as he later publicly stated, it was Pope Paul VI who had personally recommended that such a formal declaration be made at the Council on the unequal contest being waged between millions of believing Christians and those who control the means of production and communication in the present century.

The logic of the opposition is familiar to anyone who knows the history of the Church. What Adolf Harnack said in his 1900 lectures on *The Essence of Christianity* was no different from what the Roman Celsus had argued in the year 178, or what David Hume was saying in 1750. But a new factor entered the picture since Harnack first told his audiences that Christ was just another man, whom fanatical admirers had raised to the dignity of a god.

The new dimension was a marvelous growth in the power and size of secular agencies as teachers and guides of a man's whole life, including things of the spirit.

No part of the Christian world has been spared. Apart from numerous national organizations in most countries, world agencies have come into existence and been remarkably successful in shaping the life and thought patterns of millions. Inevitably and without even intended proselytism, the international character of some of these bodies has favored policies that are indifferent, if not inimical, to established Christian values.

When UNESCO was founded in 1946 to promote world peace by removing social, religious, and racial tensions, its first director general was Julian Huxley. In the world of scholarship, Huxley was a philosopher who defended the thesis that "religion of the highest and fullest character can coexist with a complete absence of belief in revelation in any straightforward sense of the word, and of belief in that kernel of revealed religion, a personal god."[22] One of the latest UNESCO publications begins a criticism of Eastern Christianity with the statement that "The social role of the Orthodox Church in czarist Russia was vividly and accurately described by Lenin: 'They are not just officials in cassocks, but defenders of serfdom in cassocks.'"[23]

When the new president of the World Bank addressed its board of governors in 1968, he outlined with mathematical precision how the agency would distribute its hundreds of millions of dollars to "undeveloped" nations. The heart of his plan was to tailor disbursements to the nations' willingness to learn "the extent to which rapid population growth slows down their potential development, and that, in consequence, the optimum employment of the world's scarce development funds requires attention to this problem."[24] Among the methods indicated was "national administration of population control programs," which in the context of the address would include abortion and sterilization. Not surprisingly this draconian measure drew opposition from such representatives of Christian countries as the Spanish Minister of Finance who stated that this "goes beyond economic considerations to higher levels affecting morals" and poses "serious problems for the individual conscience."[25]

When Marxism was in its infancy, Lenin promised it international success if only dedicated believers used every possible means to publicize their creed. "Every sacrifice must be made," he urged in 1920, "the greatest obstacles must be overcome, in order to carry on . . . propaganda systematically, perseveringly, persistently and patiently, precisely in those institutions, societies and associations—even the most reactionary —to which proletarian or semi-proletarian masses belong." This is the same Lenin who never tired repeating that part of this evangelism is re-education in the meaning of religion. "The explanation of our program," he had already said in 1905, "necessarily includes an explanation of the true historical and religious obscurantism. Our propaganda necessarily includes the propaganda of atheism."[26]

By mid-century, some one hundred million Christians were living under Marxist rule. This was mainly due—more than military coercion —to the successful indoctrination of nominal Christian leaders in the principles of dialectical materialism. When men of the stature of

Tillich could declare that "Marx is right in emphasizing material reproduction as the foundation of the whole historical process," or that "the Marxian analysis of society, brought up to date, is able to give a meaning to the present world situation" which Christianity cannot supply—the power of ideological propaganda becomes certain.[27]

When, in 1948, a conference on freedom of information was held in Paris, a draft text for an international convention was drawn up. But the United Nations, in spite of repeated efforts, did not succeed in sanctioning the agreement.

Consequently, all that exists of the right to freedom of information is the rhetorical statement of Article 19 of the Universal Declaration of Human Rights:

> Everyone has the right to freedom of opinion and expression; this right includes freedom to hold opinions without interference and to seek, receive and impart information and ideas through any media and regardless of frontiers.[28]

The inability of the nations to agree on this simple declaration explains many things in the history of Christianity in the present century: the driblets of information about the expulsion of religious communities from France in 1903 and the confiscation of Church property in 1906; the squelched knowledge about Benedict XV's efforts to prevent and then terminate the First World War; the labeling of Christians as rebels while the Church was persecuted in Mexico, from 1917 on, and in Spain, during the so-called Civil War (1936–39); the conspiracy of silence on the heroic sufferings of bishops, clergy, and people through two generations of agony in Russia and satellite territories; the incredible saddling of guilt on German Catholics and Protestants for the Nazi genocide of the Jews under Hitler; the indifference to the "holy war" waged against Christians in Islamic countries like Sudan and Biafra, commonly pictured as a purely political (and domestic) affair; the creation of an image for evangelical Protestants as "Bible fundamentalists" and religious fanatics; the misrepresentation of almost every major issue of Vatican II by sustaining the polarity between "conservatives" (with the Pope) and "liberals" (against the Pope) in the Roman Catholic Church; and the saturated secularity in thousands of pages of daily print and hours of news media in cities where Christians, except under protest, are given very little else ever to see or hear.

Three factors have stood in the way of implementing the "freedom of information and ideas" proposed to the United Nations and as a result adversely affected Christianity: money, monopoly, and vested ideology. News services are business enterprises. Long before radio and television became standard media in the 1930s and 1940s, the sale of news was subject to all the pressures of economic competition. In the news market, controversial events and personalities are the most salable commodities. They could either be actually controversial and perhaps newsworthy; or they could be shaped and developed into matter for controversy. The several years of confrontation in the press between Suenens and Paul VI, or Hans Küng and the Roman Curia are examples of such development.

News services and media, both global and national, are subject to the laws of economy in another way. They are either completely in the hands of the government (as in Soviet countries) or practically controlled by a relatively small number of people (as in France and America). In either case, the monopoly serves to filter and accommodate information to the preferences of those in charge. Vice President Agnew's comments on media monopoly in politics could be underscored in the area of religion: "A small group of men, numbering perhaps no more than a dozen . . . decide what forty or fifty million Americans will learn of the day's events in the nation and the world. We cannot measure this power and influence by traditional democratic standards, for these men can create national issues overnight."[29] Indeed, the real history of Christianity in this century cannot be written without taking stock of the corresponding power of the communications media over religion.

The ideology of persons and bodies would necessarily affect whatever information they relayed to the consumer. But when this is opposed, on principle, to the Christian ethos, the results are predictable. Some countries, like Mexico and France, have taken measures to protect their citizens against at least some of this influence. In 1959 the Mexican Chamber of Deputies approved recommendations of a special committee. One of its provisions was to prohibit broadcasts "contrary to social customs or showing violence or crime in a favorable light."[30] The French have had a similar precautionary ruling since 1949.

Needless to say such protective measures are aimed especially at America. Specialists in mass communication are perfectly frank:

The fact that nation after nation, knowing full well what United States practices are, should specifically write into their own laws and codes provisions to prevent such things in their own countries speaks more loudly than anything they may say directly about United States programs themselves. If real exchanges of programs with such nations are to occur, in the kind of worthwhile dialogue which television makes possible, some revision of our current television *value systems* is in order.[31]

As a historian reads the movement of events, he can scarcely believe that as late as 1930 the American Supreme Court in a famous case could still argue that "We are a Christian people."[32] The 1930s were the dividing line between a pre- and post-television world. Since then, an uneven struggle has been taking place between competing philosophies—the Christian which believes in certain truths that created Western civilization, and the non- (or anti-) Christian which, in Bertrand Russell's words, must prevail if the future welfare of mankind is to be insured. "The whole system of Christian ethics," he is being quoted, "both in the Catholic and in the Protestant form, requires to be re-examined, as far as possible without the preconceptions to which a Christian education predisposes most of us."[33] It was no coincidence that Russell's ninety-fifth birthday was celebrated by the major networks of the English-speaking world.

Two Attitudes

Anyone who looked at Christianity in the seventies with only the conflicts and confusion in view might well speak about a post-Christian era or about the Church in its last stage of existence.

If statistics mean anything, the secularization of large parts of Europe and America is ample evidence that the faith of their fathers is no longer the faith of millions of nominal Christians. As sociologists of religion define it, secularization is the progressive abandonment of explicit religious motivations on the level of belief, conduct, and institutional life of a person.

The story in a dozen Western countries is much the same: in the United States, about fifty million first and second generation former Catholics and Protestants no longer affiliated with any church; in England, less than twenty per cent of the Anglicans ever attend divine service; in Denmark, Finland, Norway, and Sweden, where (in 1968) only a fourth of the young people, under twenty-five, reported accepting without reservation the existence and significance of a personal God; in Germany "skyscrapers of delight" built for the most up-to-date practice of prostitution; in France and Italy upwards of one third of the electorate voting Communist; in Peru, Chile, Brazil, and Argentina most of the male population of baptized Catholics seldom assists at Mass.

Some argue that things had never really been different in former times. People had only become more aware and maybe more concerned than before.

Comparisons aside, multitudes of people who call themselves Christians in the 1900s are weak and wavering in every perceptible aspect of their faith. If a contrast must be made, it is the new confrontation of religious belief with the pursuit of knowledge to an extent unknown in previous history.

The present century admires the scientific achievements it has produced, with respect that borders on idolatry. Whether admitted or not, this admiration is for man and his native powers, his intellect and imagination, his courage and daring.

One effect has been to suggest that the time is ripe for the dethronement of gods from their dominant position in man's interpretation of his destiny, in favor of a naturalistic type of belief system. The supernatural must be swept out of the universe in the flood of new knowledge which is natural. It is predicted that soon intelligent and educated men and women will be no more able to believe in the Incarnation or Resurrection, the Real Presence or life of grace, than they can now believe the earth is flat, that flies can be spontaneously generated, that disease is a divine punishment, or that death is always due to witchcraft.

Those who try to have the best of both worlds, the comfort of Christian security and acceptance by the non-Christian majority, have been caught in a struggle that only the genius of a Sartre or Hemingway could describe but that countless others had come to experience personally.

But that is not the whole story and, in fact, not its most important feature. It is as though Luke, when he wrote the Acts in the first century, had spent all his time telling about the turmoil brought on by Christians trying to live the teachings of Christ in a decadent Roman Empire.

So, too, in the present century, where unbelief has been rampant, faith has also been strong. And where shambles have been made of what were once noble Christian institutions, new edifices of piety are being built—not mainly of stone, but in ways that might never have been possible except for the trials which occasioned them.

Development of Faith

According to the theory of natural selection, organisms which best adjust to their environment are known to flourish and reproduce their kind. Something like this happens in the realm of the spirit. Wherever the faith of a people is seen to be strong and reproductive this is due in large measure to the challenges which believers had been required to face. Their growth in faith is at least partly the result of coming to terms (without compromise) with the culture in which they have lived.

THE MEANING OF PRAYER. Among the areas of Christian belief that have been deepened in modern times, the concept of prayer enjoys a primacy all its own.

Along with accumulating titles on *The Christian Failure, Difficulties in Christian Belief, Objections to Roman Catholicism,* and *The Psychology of Unbelief* has grown a parallel literature that received less publicity but has been closer to reality.[34] Men like Barth and Heiler, Rahner and Daniélou, Hatzopoulos and Berdyaev—each from a different vantage point—have insisted on prayer as both the language of faith and its surest preservative. Few have improved on Heiler's description:

> Prayer is the great bond of union of Christendom; and not only of Christendom, but of all mankind. Prayer is the most tangible proof of the fact that the whole of mankind is seeking after God; or—to put it more accurately—that it is sought by God. Mankind at prayer is a proof of the universal revelation of God. For it is precisely in prayer that we have revealed to us the essential element of all religion.[35]

These sentiments found expression in every major pronouncement by the churches when their leaders addressed themselves to the great issues of the age. Roman Catholicism, speaking through its ecumenical council, urged the faithful—especially priests—"to listen to St. Paul's exhortation, 'Pray without ceasing.' For the work in which they labor will effect *nothing* and bring forth *no* fruit except by the power of

the Lord who said, 'Without me you can do nothing.'"[36] Protestants
and Orthodox urged the same thing. The World Council of Churches,
meeting at Uppsala, told its members that if "regular and disciplined
prayer and intercession . . . need to be recovered and renewed in
every age," it is a critical necessity today. On its positive side,
secularization is an affirmation of the true potentialities of man and
the world. In its negative sense, it becomes an ideology of a closed
world that can destroy man's freedom as an heir of heaven. On both
levels, to cultivate valid secularization and resist demonic secularism,
"Christians need periods of silence and prayer in communion with
the living God. In this churches should give them help, suggesting
ways of praying with relevance to their daily lives."[37]

The literature on prayer is immense and yet, in most ways, no
different from similar writing in the past. What is different, however,
is the ready correlation that authors (and church leaders) make between faith and prayer.

Prayer, they explain, is conceivable only in the atmosphere of faith,
a faith that deeply qualifies the human spirit and enables it to
penetrate beyond the veils of space and time. The man who believes
sees what those who do not believe do not see, and appropriately call
illusions and dreams; he hears what they do not hear and even feels
what they cannot feel. Those who do not believe do not pray. This
is a good functional definition of faith. Faith prays, unbelief does not.

At this juncture, Catholic and Protestant theologians have been
sharing their respective insights. Both traditions, divided on so many
fronts, were called upon to interpret, in Christian terms, the prevalence
of so much evil in the world. How explain the atrocities of two
world wars, of the genocide of the Jews under Hitler, and of millions
destroyed by the Communists in Europe, Asia, and Africa? How to
make sense of the crimes against God in whole nations forcibly
turned away from the worship of his name, and the tragedies in
countless homes caused by divorce and alcohol and drugs and resistance
to lawful authority?

Either Christianity can somehow come to grips with these events
or, in the worst Nietzschean language, it is a parasite in the body of
humanity.

Comparable, therefore, to the new understanding of personal sin by
the sinner who discovers God's forgiveness has been a new penetration
into cooperative evil, by society which looks to God's mercy to mankind

—with the confident hope that he will bring greater good than might otherwise have been possible—except for all the corporate sin.

The faith which inspires this patient confidence in God stands in contrast with another faith, also occasioned by the spectacle of corporate crime, which is the materialist faith of revolution. Few men have described these opposing creeds more sharply than the French existentialist Albert Camus (1913–1960). Confronted with massive evil, "man from the very depths of his soul cries out for justice." Two solutions are open to him:

> Historical Christianity has only replied to this protest against evil by the annunciation of the kingdom and then of eternal life, which demands faith. But suffering exhausts hope and faith and then is left alone and unexplained. The toiling masses, worn out with suffering and death, are masses without God.
>
> Historical Christianity postpones to a point beyond the span of history the cure of evil and murder, which are nevertheless experienced within the span of history.
>
> Contemporary materialism also believes that it can answer all questions. But, as a slave of history, it increases the domain of historic murder and at the same time leaves it without any justification, except for the future —which again demands faith.
>
> In both cases one must wait, and meanwhile the innocent continue to die. For twenty centuries the sum total of evil has not diminished in the world. No paradise, whether divine or revolutionary, has been realized.[38]

It is to such depths of ultimacy that Christians in this era resort when, in prayer, they tell God they trust him to bring good out of evil, and, what is harder to believe, great good out of great evil. Unlike revolutionaries who rebel against a god who gave man the freedom to oppress and destroy, and unlike those (like Camus) who despair because they see no prospect of relief after death, believers understand that "The cross is at the center of Christianity. Just as Christ carried out the work of redemption in poverty and under oppression, so the Church is called to follow the same path in communicating to men the fruits of salvation."[39] They are confident the harvest will be rich, even in this life, seeing that endurance has been so great.

One more aspect of prayer has deepened in Christian life under duress. While admitting that man does not have here a lasting city, that he is really a pilgrim on the road to a better life in the world to come, modern conditions have made the experience of suffering more acute, and the consequent urge to rebellion stronger than it once was.

Whatever the reasons, one effect on the Christian faithful has been to make them look more than ever to God for assistance in solving the cosmic problems of the age. For all its success, science has failed to minister to the needs of the soul. They lie outside its orbit and, for the most part, its range of interests.

Never has mankind enjoyed such an abundance of wealth, resources and economic power, and yet a huge proportion of the world's citizens are tormented by hunger. The annual military budget of a single country, it is estimated, would feed the five hundred million people of India. That same country is urging the Indians to reduce their population, if need be by sterilization and terminating pregnancy. America is the wealthiest nation in history; it also has the world's highest rate of emotional disturbance and millions of its people depend on medication to obtain some semblance of tranquility.

If human wisdom was all that man needed to achieve happiness, the advancements of science and technology should, by now, have produced something near Utopia. Instead, a specter of unrest, revolution, and the prospect of nuclear annihilation. The lesson has not been lost on those who believe that without divine grace even earthly peace and contentment cannot be attained.

It took the accumulation of genocide and racism, of cultivated violence on a grand scale and of widespread disorder in thousands of homes, to convince those who may have been in doubt, that the words *nature* and *grace* are not just convenient syllables.

Grace was found experientially to be all that theology had been saying about it technically. It is whatever human beings need over and above what they are born (*nati*) with and into. As we look at ourselves or at other selves, humanity seems to be so complete and has no need of anything but its own *native* powers—individually and collectively—to accomplish the goals set before it.

Quite the contrary. We are in the deepest sense incomplete, unfinished beings and require by divine dispensation something to supply what is absolutely needed to reach our destiny. This mysterious something is grace. All that we have or that the world can give will never get us where God wants us to arrive—at true happiness here and hereafter—unless we receive help from him beyond our natures and all the natures of humanity. And the bridge that spans from what we are to what we are to become is prayer. This is locked up in the casual statement "We must pray to be saved," where *saved* means that fulfillment which God intends his creatures to acquire by doing his will "on earth as it is in heaven."

In 1934, John Dewey gave a series of lectures at Yale in which he took issue with this supernaturalism and urged his audience to give up the belief in dependence on God to "make up" for what Christianity claims man still needs to attain the perfection of human society. "Men have never fully used the powers they possess," he argued, "to advance the good life, because they have waited upon some power *external to themselves and to nature* to do the work they are responsible for doing. Dependence upon an external power is the counterpart of surrender of human endeavor."[40]

Thirty years later, these sentiments were cited as partial explanation for the wave of violence and revolution that struck America. A whole generation had been reared on a philosophy of humanism that promised the secularist equivalent of heaven on earth, but minus prayerful dependence on God. When the earthly paradise did not come, anger and frustration broke out in a flood of revenge against institutions that trained people to expect the millennium and had not even prepared them to cope with disillusionment.

INHERITED SIN. The media have made people conscious of one another in a way that was not possible in pre-electronic days. This new awareness moved in various directions. It strengthened the bond of solidarity among like-minded persons who became conscious of each other's existence and outlook as only the telephone, radio, and television could bring about. It deepened the knowledge of the cleavage that still separates those who might live in the same country or city, but discover how different (and opposite) their attitudes are; or they are members of the same national or world-wide organization now reminded that about all they have in common is the same organizational name.

Christians have also learned a great deal in the process—beginning with a heightened understanding of sin. Those who lack the faith have practically lost all perception of sin, which they equate with a deluded state of mind. But those who believe in man's freedom to transgress the will of God see a new dimension to man's sinfulness —made clearer and more meaningful as they look to the future.

To appreciate what this means we may turn for a moment to the sixteenth century, when Luther and the Reformers brought a deepened realization of man as sinner and in need of God's redemptive grace. One contributing factor to this realization was the development of the art of print. Coming at the dawn of the printed page—with the prospect of thousands of copies of a sermon like one of Luther's homilies on the catechism—it took no time for a whole nation to share in his own painful sense of guilt and awful need of a Savior.

Moods and feelings are communicable, and to this day anyone who reads Luther sympathetically begins to share in his conviction that everything *we* do is selfish and laden with evil. If there is any goodness in man, it is *all* due to God's mercy and none to any good in ourselves.

Something like this happened in the present, socially conscious age. But the emphasis is different. It is not a question, as in Luther's day, of people being shaken to realize their own sinfulness through the disarming confession of guilt by an eloquent sinner. It is the discovery that sin has roots and ramifications in society which, until recently, had only dimly been seen.

Historic Christianity always held that man is a sinner twice over: once because of the fall of the parents of the human race, and again by reason of his own willful transgressions against God. The first sinfulness has been differently interpreted in Catholic and Protestant thought. Catholicism views original sin as the lack of that unique friendship with God which a person would have enjoyed from the moment of conception, had the first head of the human family not lost original justice for himself and his progeny. This friendship is restored with baptism, of water or at least of desire. Classic Reformed Protestantism, on the other hand, sees original sin as a complete loss of any capacity on man's part to do anything proceeding from himself that merits eternal reward. Any virtue he practices is exclusively the work of God.

So, too, personal sin has distinct connotations in Catholic and Protestant theology, depending on how man's nature is understood and how much freedom he is credited with when he chooses to do evil rather than submit to God.

But sin, it is now seen, has a third dimension—beyond original (as commonly believed) and personal—which is social. This new concept is based on two accepted facts: that when a person is born he brings with him the past history of the world from which he came, in-

cluding a long line of progenitors of whom he descended; and that
he is entering a society with present and future history that will
deeply influence him in the years to come. Another name for this
phenomenon might be social solidarity—either in sin (as we are con-
sidering it) or in virtue (as could also be reviewed).

De Fraine and Schoonenberg among Catholic scholars, Wheeler
Robinson and Richard Niebuhr among Protestants, and Orthodox
theologians like Meyendorff and Schmemann took notice of this idea
of human sinfulness—brought to the surface by the focus on society
in contemporary Western civilization. Yet the insights of scholarship
are only reflections of a growing realization among Christians everywhere that society—today as in no other period—plays a major role in
shaping man's moral existence.

The influence may be in either direction: toward greater holiness
and the benefit of mankind, or greater evil and the detriment of the
human family.

> In our era, for various reasons, reciprocal ties and mutual dependen-
> cies increase day by day and give rise to a variety of associations and
> organizations, both public and private.
>
> But if by this social life the human person is greatly aided in responding
> to his destiny, even in its religious dimensions, it cannot be denied that
> men are often diverted from doing good and spurred toward evil by the
> social circumstances in which they live and are immersed from their
> birth.[41]

Society can mold character in two ways: in terms of the past which
an individual has inherited, and the future he is entering and by
which he will be profoundly affected. Some writers decided to call
this "original sin," but the phrase demands careful explanation.

"Original" would here mean not an inheritance of nature, but the
acquisition by a person. He is born as this individual, in the latter
half of the twentieth instead of the first century; in a society which
is American or French or Italian, instead of Austrian, Finnish, or
Indian. And he is born of these parents, just this father and mother
who procreated just this child at their age in this city, on this street,
with these neighbors and friends—and no other of a near infinite
number of possibilities.

All the factors that make a person a person are original to him,
and they are in their way as much inherited as the nature that a
child receives from the couple who share with him their humanity.

Original in this context means original to man as a person, beyond the inheritance of nature as a human being. The distinction is not commonplace. All that Christianity has always believed about inherited guilt from Adam and Eve is not changed by this additional insight. This is not a resurgent Pelagianism which denies that "original sin is transmitted with human nature, 'not by imitation, but by propagation,' and that it is thus 'proper to everyone.' "[42] It is sober acknowledgment that socialization and collectivization of modern man have immersed him in other men's moral values and actions to an unprecedented degree.

Just as men are ministers of grace to one another by preaching the Word of God and witnessing to Him in their lives, so they may also be "graceless situations" to each other with opposite results.

This means that a child enters a family whose ancestry has developed certain predispositions in the moral order which may, in a sense, be called hereditary. Science does not, of course, hold that character is directly transmitted from parent to child. But so many elements of man's nature are hereditary that, taken together, they deeply affect the offspring.

As theologians are coming to see it, before anyone is born there have been generations of behavior that are part of the social heritage from which he came. Such influences as attitudes and outlooks, and habits of conduct, though hard to define and impossible in any single case to prove, are nevertheless real. It is not too much, therefore, to speak of the history of sin as an accumulation of estrangement from God and a corresponding tendency toward selfish preoccupation with this-worldly values, apart from God.

Parallel with coming from a hereditary background of his own "history of sin," the person enters a world that begins to affect him morally by its environment the moment he leaves the womb. To the extent to which the society that surrounds him is good, the influence will be salutary; but if the society is bad, its effect will be evil.

The first impact is through example, operating on the will in a direction that is often hard to resist. We are all influenced by the example of other people. If their conduct is morally evil, we are first of all deprived of the help of good example. Then we begin to feel the urge to what is evil. The sinful conduct of others suggests that "This is one possible way of acting. It is definitely attractive and makes sense, the more you think about it. Why not do the same?"

No one who understands human nature questions the importance of good example, and not only in children. Those with whom we associate are at once teachers and the mirrors in which the norms of our moral life find reflection. Their approval or disapproval, even when not voiced or explicitly stated, is a constant check on our conduct, either to confirm us in what we are doing or dissuade us from a course of action.

The impact of example becomes stronger when it is joined, as generally happens, with social and psychological pressures. Our instinct to "belong" to the group among whom we live becomes a powerful inner drive that urges us to be (or become) what others are. Conformity is not easy to resist, any more than example.

> The meaning which the environment has for our liberty is considerable. This becomes evident when good examples are missing and bad examples prevail on a large scale. In that case, doing the good excludes one from the group, which is hard to bear. The others, even though unconsciously, do not consider me as one of their number. The duty which I believe must be performed does not belong to the current style of life. It is agreeable to neglect that duty; that makes life easier, more glamorous, fuller. It makes you belong; it is a status symbol. Thus the attraction of evil may assume the form of a challenge: Let us see whether you are up to this.[43]

So strong is the desire to belong that, if not accepted, a person is tempted to strike back. This is especially the case when exclusion was deliberate. A man is excluded from certain positions; he cannot find a decent house to live in, people avoid or calumniate him. Whatever he says is labeled irrelevant, or fundamentalist, or (for a Catholic) preconciliar. His least action is interpreted in the negative light of those who set the cultural pattern in which he moves. He is deprived of many things which make life more pleasant and to which he tries to cling. His choices become more and more restricted because every major decision means another loss of something he considered precious.

He tries to philosophize about his position and tells himself that truth has never been popular with those in power and generally disdained by the clever. But gradually, unless he is made for heroism, his sense of truth is crippled under so many assaults, rude or subtle, even while he may continue to verbalize the opposite of what he is coming to believe. He allows himself to be intimidated by the kind of questioning which alternates pity with punitive sanction. Finally he agrees to relegate truth to a dark corner of the subconscious or a whispered conversation with friends.

Nor is this all. As the number of conformists increases and a culture becomes less responsive to Christian ideas, its whole value system becomes dimmed and the obscuration affects every member of the society to which a man belongs.

In former days conformity to societal patterns was often legislated by political *fiat*, amd even today millions are obliged to submit to agreement with the party line at the risk of imprisonment or loss of their ration cards. But the pressure is no less determined or effective in the so-called free cultures of the West, where believers are entangled from childhood in a web of circumstances that make Christianity increasingly difficult to live.

The Cosmic Christ

Christians are learning from experience that the collectivized climate into which they are born is decreasingly Christian in many parts of the world. They are also aware that the situation, though aggravated, is nothing strange. In the first centuries of the Church's existence, Christians regularly paid for their loyalty with their lives. In the intervening years, Christianity has never had it easy, wherever its adherents remained faithful to the cause.

Accordingly, what those who do not share the faith might call an impasse, the faithful see as the beginning of a Christian renaissance —with a comprehension of Christ's role in society that promises to be more universal and penetrating the more society needs his salvific grace.

The ecumenical movement is only symptomatic of the gravity of these needs: that not only individuals need Christ as Redeemer, but humanity itself needs him as Lord.

Both relationships are valid. Christ is believed to be man's personal Savior; he is also considered mankind's Source and Destiny. The writings of St. Paul have always witnessed to both, but the Pauline view of a cosmic Christ—and not only the redemptive—is finding a powerful response among people who know that unless society itself is Christianized the individual Christian cannot thrive. He can at best survive.

In the first and only general assembly held on American soil, the World Council of Churches in 1954 opened its final message on this theme:

> To all our fellow Christians, and to our fellowmen everywhere, we send greetings in the name of Jesus Christ. We affirm our faith in Jesus Christ as the *hope of the world,* and desire to share that faith with all men. May God forgive us that by our sin we have often hidden this hope from the world.[44]

Ten years later, the Vatican Council opened its statement in the most important of sixteen documents on the same Pauline note:

> Christ is the Light of nations. Because this is so, this Sacred Synod gathered together in the Holy Spirit eagerly desires, by proclaiming the Gospel to every creature to bring the light of Christ to all men, a light brightly visible in the countenance of the Church.
>
> The present-day conditions of the world add greater urgency to this work of the Church, *so that all men,* joined together more closely today by various social, technical and cultural ties, *might also attain fuller unity in Christ.*[45]

Even as the world is becoming more homogenous in earthly terms, the hope is that Christ might enter into his own to unite mankind in a global, Christian community.

Two foci are relevant here, found in St. Paul but now being elaborated with an urgency that suggests a return to apostolic times. The first has to do with Christ; the second with the world.

While St. Paul says a great deal about Christ the Savior—as the letter to the Romans testifies—he sees more in Christ than serving only the contingent function of saving sinful man.

Paul's vision of Christ sees him as the keystone of the cosmos and the Lord of all creation. By natural right as the Son of God, he is ruler of the universe, to whom all nations belong and under whom everything is subject. And by acquired right, through the Redemption, he enjoys dominion even as man over the whole earth.

The Pauline epistles to the Colossians and Ephesians bring out this master idea. The two letters are almost duplicates and were occasioned by the Gnostic speculators who conceived the cosmos as composed of a universe of hierarchical beings, among whom, as a creature, was Jesus Christ. Their theory was consistent with the popular Oriental tendency to synthesize the world under one orderly whole, which they called the *pleroma*.

Taking issue with this reductionism, Paul undertook to place Christ where revelation sees him, not inside the world as an aeon or demigod, but as Ruler of the Universe, of angels as well as men. To add solemnity to his thesis, Paul wrote in the form of a hymn whose literary structure is unsurpassed in the New Testament. It came as a diptych to set forth two kinds of primacy of Christ in the world: in the order of natural creation (Colossians 1:15–17), and then in the order of grace, which is the Redemption (Colossians 1:18–20).

The whole universe, then, with Christ as Ruler is the true *pleroma* or fullness of Christianity. As a result, all things are already permeated with a special presence of God, and correspondingly the whole world shares in the fruits of salvation.

In Pauline language, therefore, Christ is related to the world as its beginning, origin and the world's Alpha. He is also its final purpose and consummation, the world's Omega.

Writers, like Teilhard de Chardin (1881–1955) have coined the term "Cosmic Christ" to synthesize what this means. The expression is misleading and may be mistaken if understood in a pantheistic sense—as though the world of space and time was a kind of vesture of the Almighty or the whole cosmos, the orderly universe, is in the process of evolutionary incarnation of the Logos of the Father. Some have so interpreted Chardin—not without grounds in a writer who was more poet than theologian.

Shortly before he died, Chardin wrote in his journal a short outline of what he called his thesis. He was writing on Holy Thursday and next to the outline he wrote, "What I believe."

He said he believed three things: first in a passage from St. Paul, I Corinthians, verses 28 to 30 of the fifteenth chapter; second in four stages of development, identified as cosmo-genesis, bio-genesis, noo-genesis and Christo-genesis; third in two evolutionary movements of the universe, an upward trend from lifeless matter through living things to rational man, and a forward thrust ever moving nearer to the perfect man who is Christ, the incarnate Son of God.

Even those who rightly disagree with Chardin's evolutionary theory admit that he captured the imagination of millions. He symbolized the unspoken desire of a Christian world looking to the future with hope—after six decades of war and totalitarian tyranny.

As he read St. Paul, Chardin saw Christ coming into the world to undo the evil caused by Adam's fall. Through the merits of Christ, those who are saved will, on the last day, rise from the dead together with Christ into heavenly glory. God will then have achieved the goal he set for mankind. He will be acknowledged by all and, in heaven, will reign in all. When this history is finished, Christ's work of redemption will have been completed. He will turn over the community of men who have believed in him and give them to the Father.

Chardin read this Pauline passage and came to consider it the summation of the whole universe. Prior to Christ's coming, he distinguished four stages in the evolution of the cosmos: from elemental to organized matter, from organized matter to earth, from inorganic terrestrial matter to life, and from living things to the origin of man. With the origin of man, or hominization, biological development is believed to have reached its end-point. From then on, the only significant evolution on earth is spiritual and social. Man on the physical side of his nature is complete, but his spirit is still in the process of growth.

This spiritual growth is first of all geographic. Human beings with minds, hence noo-genesis (*nous*=mind+*genesis*=origin), gradually cover the globe with inhabitants (hence noo-sphere) much as the earth's surface was already covered with matter (cosmo-sphere) and living beings less than man (bio-sphere).

The same human growth is also communal. Not only are people multiplying and gradually covering the earth numerically but they are meant to develop socially. In a historical sense they find continuity with those who preceded them; in a linguistic sense they find kinship with those about whom they hear and read and with whom they communicate their thoughts; in an organizational sense they discover spiritual unity between themselves and all who belong to the same society—whether political, cultural, or religious.

Facilities for such collectivization have not been lacking since the dawn of man's entrance into the cosmos. But nothing comparable to present-day means—physical transportation and psychic transmission—all indicative, in Chardin's terms, of the trend toward greater centration of the human race, had been available in past ages.

Teilhard called this the upward movement of humanity which, he said, is matched by a forward projection toward ultimate destiny.

The forward evolution is not deterministic but deeply volitional: on the part of God who freely decided to enter the stream of humanity in order to draw mankind to himself, and on the part of men who are called to respond in freedom to God's invitational grace.

The goal invisioned from the myriad sons of men is finally to become one family of God—more and more united on earth by the bonds of loving fellowship; and after the last day of this earth (and the first day of the new world) by the indissoluble bond of a shared vision of the Trinity.

Some have called it Chardin's vision of the universe. This is unfortunate, because Chardin, for all his genius, had serious limitations in his logic and especially in the language he used. Part of the history of twentieth-century Christianity is that Teilhard de Chardin was frowned upon by the superiors of the religious order to which he belonged. He was forbidden to publish his major works and obeyed the injunction. He was also the object of two critical documents from Rome, in 1952 and 1967, which stated that his writings abound "in such ambiguities and indeed serious errors as to offend Catholic doctrine."[46] However, there was never a formal condemnation.

Both attitudes, of the Jesuit superiors and the Roman officials, were justified. Chardin was often extreme in his theory of complete, universal evolution leaving open the question of a special divine creation of each human soul. He was ambiguous about the origin of spirit from matter, which obscured the real distinction between reality that is spatial and dimensional, and reality that has no extension in space but can think, choose, and love. He was so preoccupied with evolution as progressive that he failed to give adequate attention to regression, which is the result of human willfulness and malice. His picture of a universe in process made it often difficult to retain a God who is absolutely transcendent and immutable, who changes all things while himself remaining unchanged.

Nevertheless, the essential image of a world moving through change toward an ultimate goal which is the Kingdom of God under the lordship of Christ is acceptable to Christians. Chardin caught the popular fancy for other (and lesser) reasons than this essential one. He was not the only, and not the best, exponent of what promises to become the turning point in the Christian concept of history. Scholars, in every tradition, have addressed themselves to the same question: What is the meaning of history reflected in the present times? Names have been given to variant interpretations—all true, in their way, and yet different in their stress on the interplay between Christ and human culture.

The exclusive Christian reads history as the story of a rising Church and growing Christian civilization, to replace the dying paganism of ancient Greece and Rome, or of modern secularism. For the dualist Christian it is an ebb and flow of conflict between spirit (Christianity) and nature (the world), typified in the writings of John; for the syncretist, it is a continuous adjustment of Christian absolutes to the relativisms of human laws and situations.

One interpretation seems to predominate. To call it *conversionist*, as Richard Niebuhr (1894–1962) does, may sound pejorative but is accurate.

> The conversionist, with his view of history as the present encounter with God in Christ, does not live so much in expectation of a final ending of the world of creation and culture, as in awareness of the power of the Lord to transform all things by lifting them up to himself.
>
> His imagery is spatial and not temporal; and the movement of life he finds to be issuing from Jesus Christ is an upward movement, the rising of men's souls and deeds and thoughts in a mighty surge of adoration and glorification of the One who draws them to himself.
>
> This is what human culture can be—a transformed human life in and to the glory of God. For man it is impossible, but all things are possible to God, who has created man, body and soul, for Himself, and sent His Son into the world that the world through him might be saved.[47]

The critical terms in this analysis are *culture, world,* and *all things.* They envision a Christianization of society, and not only the salvation of persons. They also recognize that, from the Christian standpoint, the crisis of our age is the tragedy of trying to save individuals where society is dechristianized. The two are inseparable. Christians live in the hope of future generations developing a culture that so respects the teachings of Christ as to give people not only the promise of heavenly glory but a foretaste, in this life, of God's kingdom.

II

THE BIBLE AND TRADITION

All major religions have their own scriptures. The Hindus have the *Vedas*, Buddhists the *Tipitaka*, Taoists their *Tao Teh Ching*, and Moslems the *Koran*. Just what constitutes a sacred writing and how the scriptures are to be understood are so varied and divergent as to defy analysis. And much of the difficulty that a Christian faces in studying other systems of faith arises from this basic difference—between the Bible of Christianity (and Judaism) and the equivalent sacred literature of other living religions.

Historic Christianity considers the Bible a special communication of God, in which the prophets in the Old Testament and Jesus of Nazareth in the New revealed to the chosen people the secrets of divine wisdom and the means of salvation for mankind. The Christian Scriptures are not just an important piece of religious writing; nor, as in Islam, only basic guidelines of moral conduct. They are believed to have been co-authored by God, who gave the inspiration, and the hagiographer whose faculties of mind, will, and execution were mystically directed by the Spirit, yet without prejudice to the native qualities of the human agent.

One result of this uniqueness has been the concern of the Church to trace the data and text of the Bible to its earliest possible sources. Hence biblical archaeology and papyrology are distinctively Christian sciences. Since the events described in the Bible and the narratives it contains pertain to certain periods of history, to know their historical context—as language and geography, culture and biography, and even economics and biology—becomes invaluable as a means to better understanding the sacred text and coming closer to its authentic and original wording.

Moreover, Christianity assumes that to have the biblical text is one thing—even when its authenticity is assured. To know its true meaning is something else. In every age since apostolic times Christians have wrestled over the interpretation of the Bible and wars have been fought over the differences. The science of biblical hermeneutics is also very Christian, and so distinctive that Oriental scholars in the Hindu tradition, for example, are baffled by what to them seems such wasted effort: whether Jesus' words, "I and the Father are one," should be taken literally or symbolically. Hinduism allows for *avatars*, or incarnations of the deity; and *advaita*, or the identity of God and the universe. It makes no claim to possessing objective religious truth and even the search seems illusory.

The story of Christianity and the Bible in the present century is, in one sense, no different than it was before 1900. Biblical science and investigation have kept pace with developments in Western culture, and, except for one important factor, there would have been nothing new to report beyond more expeditions to Palestine and more commentaries published on the Scriptures.

What makes the difference is the extraordinary advancement in secular knowledge that challenged the Christian faith in its biblical foundations. Four areas of confrontation have occurred: with the social and physical sciences, with history and psychology. Each has already left its imprint on Christianity.

Social Consciousness

One characteristic of the modern age is social consciousness. This is partly the result of the communications revolution and partly its cause, since one of the conditions for making people aware of each other and having them want to live together is the presence and prospect of contact with one another. The very notion of a community, from a small group to a national or global society, is conceivable only if —and to the extent to which—people can be in physical and psychological contact. Without this, a community is only an abstraction. Unless I can reach another person by being with him physically (and he the same toward me) and we can share thoughts and sentiments mutally, the idea of a society is only that and nothing more. It is not yet a real society.

This means that as Christians in today's world became more aware of what a society—any society—implies, they began to ask themselves questions about Christianity. By all the standards of its ecclesiastical nature, the Church is supposed to be a *society* of believers who follow the teachings and Lordship of Jesus Christ. The oral and visual media focused attention on what the Church itself ought to be, something more than a theoretical community. Christians either actually formed a society or they could not seriously talk about belonging to the body of believers whom Christ first inspired and still animates to constitute the *Corpus Christi*.

While every Christian tradition was brought to face this question, Protestantism was constrained to answer it more immediately. For four centuries it had stressed the image of a Church for which the written word of God was paramount. All the major confessions of faith said about the same thing. According to the Augsburg Confession, the first definition of the Christian Church was to call it "the assembly of all believers among whom the Gospel is preached."[1] The Westminster Confession (1648) synthesized this primacy of the written word of God and set the pattern for the Anglo-Saxon Protestant world:

> Although the light of nature, and the works of creation and providence, do so manifest the goodness, wisdom and power of God, as to leave men inexcusable; yet are they not sufficient to give that knowledge of God, and of his will, which is necessary unto salvation.
>
> Therefore it pleased the Lord at sundry times, and in divers manners, to reveal himself, and to declare that his will unto his Church; and afterwards . . . to commit the same *wholly* unto writing.
>
> The *whole* counsel of God, covering *all* things necessary for his own glory, man's salvation, faith and life, is either expressly set down in Scripture, or by good and necessary consequence may be deduced from Scripture.[2]

These and similar affirmations made the written word of God basic and comprehensive of the Church's faith, ritual, and moral demands. It was a book which united the followers of Christ, and allegiance to this sacred writing was normative of Christianity.

But if the Church today was so obviously social in nature, and not only biblical, what should be said of the Church in apostolic times when the Bible itself came to be written? Or from another angle, what must be taught about the Bible—especially the New Testament, as the product of divine inspiration, indeed, but also of the early Christian community?

This changed attitude was behind the development of what is better known as Form Criticism, from the German *Formgeschichte,* which literally means "History of Form." As a broad discipline, Form Criticism studies the literary structure of historical documents that preserve an earlier tradition. Its basic assumption is that the earlier, oral use of the tradition shaped the material and resulted in a variety of literary forms found in the final written record. A critical study of these forms sheds light on the life and thinking of the people who preserved the tradition.

Five writers, all German, are credited with having done most to establish Form Criticism as a type of New Testament exegesis: Martin Dibelius, Karl Schmidt, Rudolf Bultmann, Martin Albertz, and George Bertram. Their essential contributions on the subject cover a period of less than half a dozen years, from 1919 to 1924, beginning with Dibelius' *Die Formgeschichte des Evangeliums;* but their impact on biblical criticism has been monumental. Catholic, Protestant, and Orthodox scholars have taken stock of Form Criticism, and contemporary Scripture interpretation is everywhere colored by contact or conflict with the ideas of this school of thought.

ORIGIN AND PRINCIPLES. While the norms of Form Criticism have been applied to the whole New Testament and, in fact, to the whole Bible, their main application has been to the synoptic Gospels of Matthew, Mark, and Luke. John's Gospel was too evidently the production of one author writing in the more "developed" stage of Christianity to fit into the scheme of form-critical principles.

Chronologically the form critics built on the work of many forerunners: Olrik's studies of the folk tales of common people in all nations; Gunkel's identification of oral traditions imbedded in the Old Testament; Wellhausen's attention to the gradual development of Hebrew religion from a nomadic stage through that of the prophets to the religion of the Law. But more radically, Form Criticism rested on the premise that identification of written sources does not fully bridge the gap between Jesus and the written Gospels. A period of oral tradition had intervened and called for serious investigation. The prevailing sociological interest encouraged investigators to ask what part the total group of early Christians had in handing down—if not in creating—the Gospel.

Protestant writers saw in Form Criticism a reaction to the biblicism inherited from the Reformation, whose bias against tradition cut off a large segment of knowledge about the origins of Christianity. "Our problem," they admitted, "results from the overly bookish, much too literary point of view which characterized our religious inheritance as Protestants." The balance was being redressed.

> We need to correct and supplement with a more "social," more organic conception of religion; and right here Form Criticism may come to our aid practically, by helping us to see that Christianity, i.e., the Christian faith and way of life, is something more than, and prior to, the documents in which it is reflected, recorded and handed on. It was so in the first century—for the spiritual movement that eventuated in the Christian Church existed before any documents were produced; existed before any of the early communities or their teachers thought of compiling the traditions into orderly presentations; and the same order is important today.[3]

Form Criticism rests heavily on this sociological factor to the point of minimizing the evangelists' role in personally writing down the extant tradition. It views the synoptic Gospels as a collection of many separate units whose present order is the result of late editorial grouping and so does not necessarily reflect the acutal sequence or even historical content of the teachings and actions of Christ.

It holds that these units can be classified according to their form, and that the *Sitz im Leben,* or life situation, in the early Church determined the form each unit finally took. While form critics differ among themselves on how far the tradition gives a true picture of the historical Jesus, they generally agree that the Gospels are primarily witnesses to the life and teaching of the early Church. They are viewed as preserving this developed tradition in the form in which it had been selected and shaped by use in worship, instruction, counseling, and controversy. The best parallels to the Christian Gospels, therefore, are not the cultured literature of the classic writers in the golden age of Greece and Rome, but the popular compositions of ancient times, the sagas that preserve the traditions of the common people.

CRITICAL EVALUATION. A proper estimate of Form Criticism should begin with its fundamental thesis: that the native force behind Christian tradition in the early Church was not historical but utilitarian; that the dynamism which produced the Gospels was not a desire to preserve the memory of what Jesus had preached and done, but a need to serve the interests of a nascent community that was mysteriously inspired to worship and follow a great but entirely human religious leader.

In the nature of things, such necessity would not lead to writing a life of Christ with scrupulous fidelity. It would rather obscure and embellish, if not distort, the facts to meet the demands of an idealistic faith. If this looks like playing fast with the truth, Dibelius explained, people should not be scandalized.

> In the opinion of the [early] Christians, it involved no falsification.
> These things [Jesus' instructions] were the expression of the will of God, and if a man understood the will of God better than others had before him, so that he was able to adapt this expression to the requirements of a work-a-day life, then with God's help by the Holy Spirit it was permitted him to do anything which might make the saying useful for a better understanding of God's will.[4]

Among the crucial areas of the Gospel that form critics explored in greatest depth were the miracle narratives, which were compared with the healing tales of Greek and Roman mythology. "Within a certain compass," the argument ran, "we have an analogy here to the building of the Gospel tradition."[5] The analogy, said the critics, is mainly in the form in which the wonder stories of pagan mythology are cast: first a statement about the nature and circumstances of an illness, then the cure effected and the means used, and finally the result of the cure on bystanders. It was an easy and logical step from similarity of structure to similarity of meaning.

Moreover, form critics were slow to give much credit to the role of eye and ear witnesses in preserving the oral tradition. They objected that nobody could remember all the details of Christ's discourses as found in the evangelists.

Such criticism was possible only among those who had come to equate intelligence with literacy, and were so wedded to the printed word that an accurate memory without a written record was unthinkable.

Meanwhile, rabbinical studies showed there was nothing remarkable about the early Christians' ability to remember the essentials of Christ's life. Oral communication was the ordinary mode of instruction among the Jews, who concentrated on the Torah as the focus of Hebrew thought. Jewish scribes considered it a cardinal principle of pedagogy to have the disciple listen to the master and repeat his maxims with fidelity. The good disciple, they used to say, was like a cistern built of lime which loses not a drop. The highest praise of a rabbi was to have said about him that "he has not uttered a word which he had not heard from his teacher."

Form Criticism received its most serious setback with the discovery of the Qumran documents, between 1947 and 1956. These Hebrew and Aramaic manuscripts from the first centuries B.C. and A.D. showed conclusively that a Jewish community of high-minded zealots lived in Palestine during the time of Christ. Their ascetical practices and almost mystical interpretation of the Law made it quite unnecessary to postulate (as many form critics had done) Greek or Hellenistic infiltration into the "simple message of the Gospel."

POSITIVE CONTRIBUTION. In evaluating the influence of the first-century community on the canonical Gospels, we should distinguish two elements: the matter or content and the form. There are no valid grounds for supposing a community creation or distortion of the four Gospels, including John. But in shaping this material to suit the particular needs of the young Church, in selecting and abbreviating, in the emphasis and application, the community certainly played an important part.

The very existence of four accounts of just one shows how different writers answered to different communal needs. If to this we add that the Gospels were primarily catechetical and instructive, and their writers were addressing believers in the Word who wanted a concise statement of their faith in Christ the Lord, we see the impress which the Christian society in apostolic times had on the format of the Gospel message without affecting its substantial matter.

In this light, Form Criticism has made valuable contributions to scriptural thought and, in spite of its vagaries, may be considered a major benefactor in the contemporary biblical renaissance.

Among Protestants generally, there came increased attention to the early tradition that preceded the written Gospels and out of which they arose. There had been nothing like it since the Reformation. In marked contrast with the former concentration on the plain word of the Bible, exegetes now began to look more and more to the apostolic community for an explanation of the early Church; and to the same source for an adequate understanding of the person of Jesus Christ.

It seems almost like a reversal of history for a leading Reformed scholar, Oscar Cullmann, to say that first-century Christianity forces us to the conclusion that Peter was the apostle on whom Christ bestowed some kind of primacy.

> All Protestant interpretations that seek in one way or another to explain away the reference to Peter seem to me unsatisfactory. No, the fact remains that when Jesus says that he will build his *ekklesia* upon this rock, he really means the person of Simon. Upon his disciple, who in the lifetime of Jesus possessed the specific advantages and the specific weaknesses of which the Gospels speak, upon him who was their spokesman, their representative in good as well as in bad, and in this sense was the rock of the group of disciples—upon him is to be founded the Church, which after the death of Jesus will continue his work upon earth.[6]

Cullmann was not saying that Peter had successors in this leadership of the Christian community; nor even that in his own day he exercised primatial and juridical authority. But enough was granted about Peter's unique role in the apostolic Church to make Cullmann's work a milestone in the ongoing dialogue between Roman Catholicism and other Christian churches which also consider themselves catholic.

Moreover, once the gospels are admitted to reflect the mind of the Church within a generation of Christ's death and resurrection, his divinity no longer remains a matter of dispute as an expression of the faith in apostolic times. This shift of emphasis from the biblical text to the believing community is not trivial. Those who would deny Christ's divinity must now cope with the fact that the earliest Christians believed their Master was God; and it is no longer sufficient to argue the question on purely textual grounds. Again Cullmann is warrant for the conclusion that the whole of ancient tradition already saw Jesus as a divine being who became incarnate.

By their claim that the Gospels are "community creations," the form critics drew attention to an aspect of the New Testament that had not been emphasized, and that offers valuable insights into the meaning of its message. Communication of knowledge implies two things, both creative in their way: the speaker or writer and his audience or readers. When the Gospels are approached from both angles at once, the resulting image is startling.

Take the Gospel of Luke. Christian antiquity from Irenaeus to Jerome testified that the spirit which animated the writer of the Third Gospel was Paul's. We know that Luke was Paul's companion on the latter's journeys to the gentile world and his biographer in the Acts of the Apostles.

Converts from paganism needed to see the universality of Christ's message. Though himself a Jew, he intended his Gospel of salvation for all nations. From genealogy to resurrection Luke stressed the cosmopolitan character of the Messiah and his mission. Where Matthew, writing for Jews, carried the ancestry of Jesus only to Abraham, the father of the chosen people, Luke went back to Adam, the father of the human race. His birth is the promise of "peace to all men of good will," and not only to the Hebrews. At the presentation in the temple, the aged Simeon foretells that the child in his arms will be a "light of revelation to the gentiles." As a prelude to the public life, Luke in common with the other Synoptics gives the prophecy of Isaiah, "A voice of one crying in the wilderness," but he carefully added the note of universality, ". . . and all flesh shall see the salvation of God." Three times in two verses comes the same accent, "every valley . . . every mountain . . . and all flesh."[7]

Correlative with a need for assurance that Christianity is ecumenical, ethnic converts had to be shown the loving kindness of the Savior and the deep concern for human frailty in the Church he had founded. Hence the preoccupation that has made Luke's "the Gospel of mercy." He alone records those gems of compassion: the Good Samaritan, the parable of the lost sheep, the lost coin, the Pharisee annd Publican, the tears of the sinful woman at the feet of Jesus, the conversion of Zacchaeus, Christ's pardon of his enemies and the repentance of the good thief who is promised Paradise on the day he was executed. In contrast with the Mediterranean religions of fatalism and facing the wrath of angry *numina*, Luke's presentation was a natural way for Christianity to enter a world that was looking for tenderness in God.

Luke's interest in giving honor to women in the time of Christ had the same and perhaps wider motivation. Among the Greeks and Romans the status of women had reached the lowest ebb in history. Even in the highest classes of Roman society, they had become the instruments of masculine pleasure. Cicero and Seneca each married twice; Ovid, Octavian, and Pliny the Younger had three wives; Caesar had four; Pompey and Sulla had five. Concubinage was the rule among those who could afford the luxury.

Luke wanted to teach the converts what their new faith held about the dignity of women. He literally filled his Gospel with passages and events which exalted the role of women and emphasized what an important place they had in the life of Christ. He told of Elizabeth the mother of John, Anna the prophetess, the widow of Naim, the great sinner whom Jesus forgave, the daughter of Abraham whom Christ delivered from the bondage of Satan, the woman who proclaimed the mother of Jesus blessed, the widow in the parable asking mercy from the unjust judge, Martha who labors and Mary who prays, the daughters of Jerusalem who wept for Jesus on the way to Calvary.

Above all, Luke is the evangelist of Mary, whose role in the nascent Church becomes so striking that here, too, biblical Mariology is finding a place in Protestant exegesis comparable to its honored role in Eastern Orthodoxy and Roman Catholicism.

All of this may be traced, in great measure, to the rediscovery of the Gospels which Form Criticism has substantially assisted. If some critics made a fetish of literary forms, others profited by examination of these forms to see in the New Testament not only two but three converging factors: the guidance of the Spirit, the individuality of the writer, and the whole complex of human elements that made up the original Christian communities. They, too, were authors of the inspired text, as instruments of the Spirit through whom he directed its composition, and for whom he produced the Scriptures, in a way that Christians are only beginning to recognize.

The New Testament was written in an age of illiteracy. It was also written for the Christian community, and not only of the first but of the twentieth century. Its written form is a guarantee of preservation and delimitation of God's inspired word. Its purpose—to teach the nations—is seen as relevant more than ever today, in a world not unlike that of ancient Palestine, where society (and not only the individual) is the intended beneficiary of Christianity.

Supernatural and Demythology

There has never been a period in the Church's history when the supernatural elements of Christianity were not called into question. In the first century it was the supernatural character of Christ, whom the Gnostics wished to reduce to a created aeon. In the fourth century it was the supernatural grace necessary for salvation which Pelagius reasoned out of existence. In the Middle Ages it was the supernatural presence of Christ in the Eucharist which the Albigenses excluded as too carnal for the spiritual needs of man.

With the rise of Deism in England and France, the whole spectrum of Christian supernaturality was either denied (as with Blount and Tindal) or doubted (as with David Hume), or brushed aside as incredible (in Voltaire and Rousseau).

By the nineteenth century, enough nominal Christians were embarrassed with Christ's divinity and the need for redemptive grace to produce a rash of exponents of what has been called rationalism. Men like Ernest Renan and Ferdinand C. Baur, David Strauss and Albrecht Ritschl, each in his own way redefined the supernatural as somehow subordinate to human reason. Schleiermacher, we have seen, cut the ground from under both sides of the dilemma. He denied the premises of reason and the historic faith by claiming that religion (including Christianity) was essentially a nonrational feeling.

With this kind of momentum behind it, the present century would have brought nothing novel to the scene. But things had changed.

What happened was another aspect of the phenomenon which produced Form Criticism. The mounting sense of solidarity among peoples in Europe and America gave credence to two myths that have entered the stream of Western culture: that a completely new era had dawned for the human race, and that Christianity can survive only if it radically adjusted itself to the changed ethos.

The man who did most to recommend this reassessment in the world of scholarship was Adolf Harnack (1851–1930), German Church historian and theologian. Through more than twenty volumes of books and several hundred monographs, he argued to an *Essence of Christianity* which could remain true to the spirit of Jesus of Nazareth but shed its dependence on an outdated dogmatic ideology.

He rested his case on the sharp contrast between two different worlds of thought: the mythological time of the apostles and the scientific era of today. The first was the age of miraculous fiction; the present of established fact.

> We know that the Gospels came from a time in which the marvellous may be said to have been something of almost daily occurrence. People felt and saw that they were surrounded by wonders, and not by any means only in the religious sphere.
>
> Miracles, then, could not possess the significance for that age which, if they existed, they would possess for ours. For that age all wonders

were also extraordinary events, and, even if they formed a world by themselves, it was certain that there were countless points in which that other world mysteriously encroached upon our own.[8]

So much for apostolic times, when "the strict conception which we now attach to the word 'miracle' was as yet unknown." Then we turn to our own day: "We are firmly convinced that what happens in space and time is subject to the general laws of motion, and that in this sense, as an interruption of the order of Nature, there can be no such things as 'miracles.'"[9]

Lesser minds than Harnack further developed the same thesis: that if Christianity is to have any meaning for modern man it must come to terms with his thinking. It cannot hide behind the signs and wonders of the Gospel or the angels and demons of the Apocalypse to keep his allegiance in faith.

The stage was set for the drama of demythologization that began shortly after 1900 and is still going on.

Fundamental to demythology is a dogmatic assumption that the whole language and spirit of the New Testament are mythical in character. The world is viewed as a three-storied structure with the earth in the center, the heavens above and the underworld below. Heaven is the abode of God and of celestial beings, the angels. The underworld is hell. Rudolf Bultmann's description of the earth is representative:

It is the scene of the supernatural activity of God and his angels on the one hand, and of Satan and his demons on the other. These supernatural forces intervene in the course of nature and in all that men think and will and do. Miracles are by no means rare. Man is not in control of his own life. Evil spirits may take possession of him. Satan may inspire him with evil thoughts. Alternatively, God may inspire his thoughts and guide his purposes. He may grant him heavenly visions. He may allow him to bear his word of succour or demand. He may give him the supernatural power of his Spirit. History does not follow a smooth unbroken course; it is set in motion and controlled by these supernatural powers.[10]

Into this world of supernature, the New Testament implanted the event of the redemption as the subject of its preaching. It proclaims "in the language of mythology" that God sent forth his Son, a preexistent divine being, who appeared on earth as man. He died the death of a sinner on the cross and thus made atonement for men's sins. His resurrection marked the beginning of a cosmic catastrophe.

Death as the consequence of sin is abolished and the demoniac forces are deprived of their power. The risen Christ is exalted to the right hand of God in heaven and made Lord and King of the universe. He will come again in the clouds of heaven to complete the work of redemption.

What is modern man to make of these demands on his credulity? "All this," as Bultmann says, "is the language of mythology, and the origins of the various themes can be easily traced in the contemporary mythology of Jewish Apocalyptic and in the redemption myths of Gnosticism. To this extent the *Kerygma* is incredible to modern man, for he is convinced that the mythical view of the world is obsolete."[11]

Can anything be done? Yes, provided we distinguish between the true Gospel message and obsolete mythology. In other words, theology must perform the radical surgery of "stripping the Kerygma" or preaching message of Jesus "from its original mythical framework." In plain language, demythologizing it.

All of this is familiar in hundreds of writers who preceded Bultmann, back to Hierocles in the patristic age, for whom the resurrection of Christ was just another piece of fiction. The innovation was the claim that a whole culture had grown up in modern times, where *everyone* who could think for himself no longer accepted first-century myth for twentieth-century truth.

There was no variation in the two notes constantly played by demythologists. First-century man was unlettered; he was simple, credulous, and prone to accept the marvelous as miraculous. Twentieth-century man is educated; he is intelligent and therefore skeptical, empirical and demands scientific proof for anything he even provisionally accepts as true.

"It is impossible," and not merely difficult, "to . . . avail ourselves of modern medical and surgical discoveries, and at the same time to believe in the New Testament world of demons and spirits." Then the universal refrain, "We may think we can manage it in our own lives" by stultifying our intelligence. "But to expect others to do so is to make the Christian faith unintelligible and unacceptable to the modern world."[12]

There was no letting up on the basic theme. If the uncultured man in the time of Jesus of Nazareth was a creature of his age, if *his* uncritical disposition to believe everything in sight made *him* fall into the pattern of *his* society, the same must be said of the man of today.

He, too, is more than most people suppose the creature of his age. Comparable to the closed tribal culture of ancient Palestine is the increasingly tribal society of a cosmic Palestine, shaped and molded by the media that envelop Western man like the atmosphere.

However, demythologists did not analyze their own premises: Whether "modern man," taken as a symbol of today's culture, is really as unable to believe in the supernatural as they make him out to be. Less still did they ask why he is that way, when and where his caste of mind is antisupernatural. Is it because the supernatural in the Gospel is objectively untenable, and should not have been accepted in the first place? Or is it objectively valid but contemporary man is not subjectively disposed to believe what seems to clash with the scientific mentality? Or is the supernatural really valid, and reconcilable with authentic science, but those who think otherwise have read into (and helped create) a *Zeitgeist* which denies on *a priori* grounds the possibility of intelligent faith? The basic question is the last one. Can modern man be as learned and critical as the latest scientific research makes him, and at the same time loyal and committed to the supernatural as the Gospels demand that a follower of Christ should be?

Transmitting this failure of demythologists to question their own mythology, what if—in spite of the layers of the incredible that cover the Gospel message—a Christian today nevertheless still wants to believe? Two avenues are open to him. He can either blind himself to the world of present reality—the computer and atomic fission—and believe in spite of the psychic pressure to disbelief. Or he can reinterpret the supernatural of the Bible to satisfy the modern mind. There have been advocates for both ways.

The first approach has a noble ancestry. Among others, Søren Kierkegaard (1813–1855) held that Christian belief is essentially unreasoning. He placed truth in the individual person, to be discovered fully by accepting faith through a blind trust; despite the paradoxes and even absurdities of Christianity. His often-repeated statement that "truth is subjectivity" linked up truth with the existing subject, instead of with its object. As a result, he dispensed the believer from the need of satisfying his mind about the objective validity of Christian revelation. A Moslem could as well, and truthfully, believe in the supernatural claims of Mohammed or a Buddhist in the Four Noble Truths of Buddha.

Demythologists who accepted the Kierkegaardian notion of faith were also ready to take Martin Heidegger's theory of knowledge. Man, they decided, is a being in time. He is *Dasein in Zeitlichkeit*, which they translated "being in temporality," i.e., one who is constantly changing with the passage of time. What the Gospels narrate took place or was said in time which is past history. But a historical moment does not, so to speak, prolong itself from the past and through the present and future, except insofar as it has the power to evoke an "existential" confrontation. Such confrontation or decision-making, where I choose the Christian religion and dedicate myself to the same, is not possible with a merely "historical" inquiry into the words and deeds of Jesus. The Christian story is "sacred history," which means factual data that have been sacralized, overladen with nonfactual and mythological lore that belongs to a former, credulous age.

What a believer must do, to save his rationality, is liberate the historic (or timeless) elements of the Gospel from the merely historical (and transitory) details which overlay them.

This brought demythology to its second approach, of reinterpreting the supernatural in the Bible. In order to do this, the world of apostolic times had to be shown as permeated with a Gnostic propensity, seeing aeons and demiurges everywhere, and interlarding the simple teachings of Jesus with a caricature of Christianity.

The centuries of struggle between Gnosticism and the historic Christian faith, which fought to free itself from such mythology, were passed over in silence. Instead the canonical Gospels were charged with being still myth-ridden and in drastic need—finally today—of being cleansed of the incrustation.

But even this was not enough. No matter how much of the alleged Gnostic debris is removed, the Gospels are yet too mythical to be accepted at face value.

At this point, as many types of demythology appeared as there are concepts of a secularized Christianity. Some went all out in favor of a creedless, riteless, and churchless religion that is only a shadow of what the great minds of Christian history had believed. Others, at the opposite extreme, wanted to retain whatever could be salvaged of the supernatural, but not at the price of alienating "modern man." He must be the norm of what is tenable, not the reported experiences of the evangelists.

Demythology affected Christian churches in various ways. Those with a strong biblical orientation, mainly Protestant, were "shaken to their foundations," in Tillich's terms, by having to rethink their whole concept of the Bible as the foremost (if not the only) repository of God's revealed word. Remove the supernatural from the New Testament and what is left, if a Christian has no recourse outside the sacred text and no criterion for his faith besides what he believes is an inspired message from on high?

Those who were less dependent on the Bible for all that Christianity is supposed to teach were also not exempt from the general tendency to demythologize. Anglicans, Roman Catholics, and the Eastern Orthodox were (and are) brought to a similar impasse. What if the doctrines of the Councils could be treated as ruthlessly as the text of Matthew or Mark? What if the same distinction were operative here as in the case of the New Testament—that the formulas of Nicaea or Chalcedon should be re-examined on the basis of what they *really* mean, by sloughing off what is historical (because mythical) from what is historic (and still true)? And what if the institutional Church is reluctant to perform this radical demythologizing on tradition—as the experts had already done on the Bible—where would the believers stand? Among others, James Pike and Hans Küng exposed the issue for Anglicans and Roman Catholics, much as Rudolf Bultmann helped to bring the matter to a head in contemporary Protestantism.

The Bible as History

There was no evading the situation created by demythology; two antithetical positions had risen in Christian circles. One was willing to accept the words of the Bible in much the same sense as they had been understood since the canon of the New Testament was settled in the second century. Others insisted this was impossible in view of the completely changed attitude toward the supernatural brought to a climax by modern scholarship and investigation.

Some would still hesitate to draw the lines so sharply, and no doubt many were torn somewhere between. But objectively the one position is not the other. And the experience of millions of confused believers by mid-century confirms the opinion that a real polarization had taken place: between those whose faith in Christ and his Gospel was still vital and others who may have given all the appearance (sincerely professed) of being Christian, but whose firm belief in supernatural mysteries—Christ is God, he rose from the dead, he is bodily present in the Eucharist—had become weak and vacillating and, in some cases, had died.

Called upon to give an account of their faith, those who believed in the mysteries of the New Testament approached the problem on different fronts: how are the Scriptures true history, and in what sense is the Bible divine revelation?

DEVELOPMENT OF A CONCEPT. It is difficult to recapture what used to be the prevalent notion of history until fairly recent times. Under the influence of a mathematical view of the universe, this theory was mainly that of a closed system. Other factors also played a part. Preoccupation with empirical data; stress on space and time relationships in the record of past events; the sudden impact of acquired knowledge of the material world, with its features of dimension, number, and quantity. If we couple these factors with the already dominant print culture of the West—with lineal and carefully boxed pages of information in precisely designed books—we get closer to understanding why history came to be regarded as a science, with all the consequences which this term implied.

There were exceptions, of course, but the historian who went against the stream ran the risk of being dismissed as "writing for edification" or "promoting a cause." Part of this attitude came from the idea that history was functional. Past events could be classified with sufficient accuracy to become the basis for assured generalization, from which it was possible to forecast the future development of mankind. The historian's task was conceived as the demonstration that "the movements of nations are perfectly regular, and that, *like all other movements*, they are solely determined by their antecedents." The resulting definition of history was evident, as voiced by one of its eloquent spokesmen in the nineteenth century: Henry T. Buckle (1821–1862), best known for his projection of a panoramic history of civilization.

> If he cannot do this [predict the future on the basis of the past], he is no historian. He may be an annalist, or a chronicler; but higher than this he cannot rise, unless he is imbued with that spirit of science which teaches us as an article of faith the doctrine of uniform sequence.
>
> To seize this idea with firmness and to apply it on all occasions without listing to any exceptions, is extremely difficult; but it must be done by whoever wishes to elevate the study of history from its present crude and informal state, and do what he may towards replacing it in its proper rank as the head and chief of all the sciences.[13]

Involved in this notion of history as a science was a philosophy of determinism. This meant that human actions, "being determined solely by their antecedents," must have the character of uniformity. Given the same circumstances, people always behave in the same way.

This conception of history as a deterministic science by no means disappeared. It is still the heart of Marxist doctrine and had much to do with shaping the philosophy of Fascism in Italy and Nazism in Germany.

The reaction, however, was unquestionable, and is closely associated with the realization that faith and fate are more than alliteratives. As a man's faith recedes, fatalism takes over. Those who believed came to realize that there is more to human events—and therefore to history—than brute data unfolding themselves through inner necessity. There are wills, and their free exercise, in the universe: of God who freely guides mankind and of men who freely reject or respond to his will.

Accordingly, the New Testament came back to its own—among those who saw Christianity as a historical religion and not only a religious ideology. They were no longer—or not so much—defensive of the Gospels as history just because they contain more than statistical facts or place names and dates. The teachings of Christ did not have to be traceable to antecedent philosophies, and his miracles to known laws of nature.

There was another gain, too, from an unexpected side. All the stress on history as a science demanded that the New Testament also qualify, somehow, as scientific. The process of development of this concept gave biblical studies an invaluable foothold in the field of scholarship.

Centering on the Gospels, they came to qualify as history which is sacred and are no less historical for not being secular in the style of Tacitus or Pliny.

Unlike profane history, the subject of the Gospels is mainly a human being who professed to be divine. Those who heard his words exclaimed, "This is intolerable language; how could anyone accept it?"[14] And of his actions, "Whatever kind of man is this. Even the winds and the sea obey him."[15] Yet the Gospels are no less credible, as history, because they record the sayings and deeds of a remarkable man. In one sense, everything human of historic consequence is unique and unrepeatable.

Likewise the purpose of the Gospels was much higher than to tell a story or describe the accomplishments of a religious leader. They were written to share the "good news" of salvation with those who already had the faith and with multitudes who would come after them in search of the person and teachings of Christ. Critics could question the evangelists' objectivity because they had an "ulterior motive" (Bultmann's phrase) for writing, to persuade their readers that Jesus was the fulfillment of the Messianic prophecies (Matthew), that he professed to prove his eternal Sonship from the Father (Mark), that he came to save men as the hope of all nations (Luke), and that he is the Word of God who became flesh to enlighten mankind (John).

But almost a century of investigation of contemporary sources had shown that if the Gospels are unhistorical because their authors wrote to convince, then all ancient history is a contradiction in terms. No historian worthy of the name writes without a purpose beyond the bare collection of facts. Among the ancients, Thucydides (460–399 B.C.) is properly rated a scientific historian, of whom David Hume wrote that, "The first page of Thucydides is the commencement of real history."[16] Yet Thucydides was no mere chronicler, as the opening paragraph of his classic *Peloponnesian War* clearly shows. He wrote with a definite, preconceived motive: to immortalize the memory of a war that he considered of cosmic significance.

Correlative with purpose and sympathy are the elements of interpretation which secular historiographers discovered cannot be separated from true history. They came to distinguish between what may be called the outside and the inside of an event. By the outside they meant everything belonging to it which can be described in terms of bodies and their movement, e.g., Caesar crossing the Rubicon. By the inside of the event they meant that aspect of it which can only be described in terms of thought, e.g., Caesar's defiance of Republican law. "The historian" they concluded, any historian, "is never concerned with either of these to the exclusion of the other." His work may start with factual data, "but it can never end there. He must always remember that the event was an action; and that his *main task* is to think himself into this action, to discern the thought of its agent."[17]

The application of this judgment to the Gospels is more than the coincidence of time: the philosophers of secular history should be saying precisely what those who considered the New Testament historical believed to be true. The one attitude helped to shape the other. In the heyday of deterministic scientism, the Christian Scrip-

tures were put on the defensive to explain how they could be genuine
history when they were so obviously filled with miracles and unprecedented human volition. As the climate changed to a more
balanced concept of history, the Gospels became more acceptably
historical, another example of how deeply the mood of an age affects
the peoples' willingness to accept an idea—here the critical one that
the biblical foundations of Christianity are at least as scientifically
grounded as the exploits of Caesar or the story of Hannibal crossing
the Alps.

As long as the more narrow notion of what constitutes history prevailed, writings abounded on the *Quest of the Historical Jesus*. Albert
Schweitzer's book with that title appeared in 1910. At that date, he
still argued that Jesus could not have been all that the Gospels picture
him to be, since the evangelists hid the true portrait of the master
behind their own mystical dreams. The "historical Jesus," in Schweitzer's language, was a zealous preacher who mistakenly proclaimed the
immediately imminent breaking-in of the Reign of God in the sense
of the late Jewish apocalyptic. Anticipating the Last Judgment, Jesus
preached repentance, that is, a life lived in fervid expectation of the
New Eon. He was convinced that he was destined by God to be
the future Messiah. Out of this messianic consciousness, he went to
his death in the false hope of bringing the New Eon into early
realization. Only that and nothing more.

Fifty years later, even those who were sympathetic with Schweitzer's
merely human Jesus were critical of his approach to history, which
they called "a sort of pseudoscientific remythologization."[18] In his effort
to rescue the Jews of history from the mythological haze of his admirers,
Schweitzer had enveloped Jesus in a new haze of his own making.

Once the notion of history had opened to a broader vision, the
Gospels came to be recognized as authentic historical narrative written
with religious purpose. This concept was incorporated in the *Constitution on Divine Revelation* which the Vatican Council issued in
1965. If the statement could have been made in 1865, it would not
have reflected the struggles and controversies of a whole generation,
now seen as resolved for those who believe.

> Holy Mother the Church has firmly and with absolute constancy
> held, and continues to hold that the four Gospels . . . whose historical
> character the Church unhesitatingly asserts, faithfully hand on what

Jesus Christ, while living among men, really did and taught for their eternal salvation until the day He was taken up into heaven.

The sacred authors wrote the four Gospels, selecting some things from the many which had been handed on by word of mouth or in writing, reducing some of them to a synthesis, explaining some things in view of the situation of their churches, and preserving the form of proclamation but always in such fashion that they told us the honest truth about Jesus.[19]

Terms like "historical character," "faithfully hand on," "really did and taught," "the honest truth about Jesus" had been clarified in a long process of refining.

EXCAVATIONS AND DISCOVERIES. The historicity of the New Testament is more than a matter of theory. The ultimate validity of the statements and events it describes is, indeed, a matter of faith. But from the standpoint of history, they need support and confirmation from contemporary sources, literary and archaeological, to substantiate what Christians believe is founded on facts and is not mythology.

Confirmatory evidence for the historical foundations of Christianity, outside the Bible, had been accumulating for centuries. A single collection, the Migne edition of the Fathers of the Church, was published (between 1844 and 1866) in 379 volumes of Greek and Latin texts. They are a monument of data from the earliest Christian times testifying to the authenticity of the apostolic record.

But biblical and Christian archaeology as a formal science is a recent development. Much as the notion of history went through a process of growth, so the principles and methods of archaeology did not mature until the late nineteenth and early twentieth century. Among other factors, the use of the stratigraphic method was chiefly responsible for the change. Initiated on an amateurish level by Schliemann at Troy, around 1870, it was professionalized by Flinders Petrie at Tell el-Hesi in Palestine (1890), and brought to a high state of accuracy by two Americans, Reisner and Fisher, in the early 1900s. Today, careful study of the successive strata of human occupation in an ancient site is considered the first duty of an archaeologist.

Along with stratigraphy goes typology, the study of types of objects made by hand, which may be divided into classes, types, and varieties roughly parallel to biological families, genera and species. While the methods of stratigraphers correspond to those of geologists, the methods of typologists are similar to those of biologists.

At the same time that biblical archaeology had been transformed by these new methods, the study of written remains was also revolutionized. The progress achieved by philologians in interpreting ancient writing was accelerated in recent decades by the use of more scientific methods of decipherment, constructing grammars and dictionaries, and developing philological research that was unknown to scholars even a century ago.

Just as a point of reference, the first scientific excavations in Bible lands were not undertaken until after 1890. English, Austrian, and German excavators were later joined by Americans, French, and others; but only in the late 1920s was enough verified material available to say that biblical archaeology had established itself in the field of science.

No sharp line of demarcation can be made between Old and New Testament archaeology. Almost every find relative to the Old Testament has direct bearing on the New—and vice versa.

Nor is it possible here to do more than briefly survey the numerous archaeological discoveries in Palestine and elsewhere in the Mediterranean world that served to validate the historicity of the New Testament narrative.

From early 1900 on, a mass of private documents in the vernacular Greek (*Koiné*) of the Hellenistic-Roman period began to accumulate. This discovery made it certain that the authors of the Greek translations and original Greek books which now form the New Testament were writing the actual spoken language of their time, influenced only slightly by literary Attic Greek. Many details of life and speech have been clarified by these extraordinary papyri.

Since 1930 there have also been remarkable finds of New Testament papyri from the second century A.D., far earlier than anything previously known, and a whole history of lost Gnostic literature from the third and fourth centuries has come to light from discoveries in Upper Egypt.

The value of these Gnostic manuscripts can be appreciated from the competitive role they played in the early Church. At one time there were twenty-one Gospels rivaling the canonical four, all claiming authenticity and apostolic origin. The Church's sifting of the apocrypha from their genuine counterparts had been known since the second century. But not until the twentieth were complete manuscripts available to illustrate and substantiate what formerly had been done.

Since the Gnostic writings were discovered, it also became clearer that the theories they propounded were actually more bizarre than had been supposed. Any suggestion, formerly made by critics of the Gospels, that the evangelists borrowed from Gnosticism, could now be made only by those who ignored the new findings.

Clearance of tombs of the New Testament period in and around Jerusalem brought to light scores of inscriptions in Aramaic, Hebrew, and Greek. The Aramaic inscriptions yielded the first living evidence of the precise language used by Jesus, since all Aramaic literature until then had been lost.

Moreover, on the ossuaries (bone caskets) of the persons buried in the first century A.D. were found many names, commonly used by the Jews in the time of Christ, along with rarer ones. Names like Miriam (Mary), Martha, Elizabeth, Salome, Sapphira were inscribed, together with Joseph and Jeshua (Jesus), Simon and John, Matthew and Ananias. The title "master" or "teacher" was also found (*didaskalos*), as Christ calls himself in the Gospel of John; although the designation previously had been cited as evidence of a second-century date.

What looks like an unexpected gap in the archaeological information is the failure to locate any synagogues in Palestine from the first century. With one possible exception, all the synagogues appear to be either pre-Christian or from the second century A.D. or later. All of this indicates a wholesale destruction of synagogues at the time of the First Revolt (A.D. 66–70). It also corroborates other archaeological evidence for an almost complete break in the continuity of Jewish and early Christian life in Palestine.

Until modern times, the oldest extant codices of the New Testament were from the fourth and fifth centuries. Fragmentary papyri were no older. But in 1931 the Chester Beatty papyri, named after their owner, were identified as containing thirty leaves from the Gospels and Acts dating from the first or second half of the third century, together with twenty more leaves from St. Paul and the Apocalypse. Old Testament manuscripts in the same collection amounted to a hundred and eighty leaves from nine books, dating back to the second century A.D.

The Beatty papyri substantiate the essential soundness of the existing biblical texts. No striking or fundamental variation is shown either in the Old or the New Testament. There are no important omissions or additions of passages, and no variations which affect vital facts or doctrines. Such deviations as exist, touch only on minor matters like the order of words or the precise words used.

Equally significant is the Bodmer papyrus of St. John's Gospel, published in 1956 and named after its owner, M. Bodmer of Geneva, Switzerland. Written in Egypt before the year 200, this Greek codex consisted originally of 154 pages. It is still almost perfectly preserved for the first fourteen chapters of John, with the other chapters in a fragmentary state. Together with the Beatty papyri, this manuscript is of epoch-making value in confirming the extant texts of the New Testament beyond anything comparable in any other subject or field of similar antiquity.

The Bodmer manuscript is so much like the Vatican Codex of the Bible (fourth century) that this most ancient text of the whole Scriptures may now be safely equated with what Christians used within less than a century of the apostolic age. Even certain dramatic omissions are the same in the Bodmer and Vaticanus, e.g., the twelve verses from John 7:53 to 8:11, describing Christ's mercy toward the woman taken in adultery. Though accepted in the biblical canon, this passage was more likely from St. Luke or one of the synoptics.

We get some idea of the significance of these modern discoveries when we recall that the oldest substantial manuscripts of the ancient Greek and Roman classics are five to twelve centuries removed from the reported composition of Herodotus and Homer, Caesar and Pliny. The Greek historian Herodotus, e.g., lived about 484–425 B.C. Yet the earliest documentation of his *Histories* is not available until more than a millennium after his death, in two manuscripts, the *Mediceus* and *Florentinus*, both from the tenth century of the Christian era.

Equally important discoveries relating to Christian archaeology were the Dead Sea Scrolls, first unearthed in 1947. Over sixty manuscripts and innumerable fragments were excavated at the site of the ancient Qumran community, located close to the Dead Sea in Palestine.

The principal texts include a set of rules for the monastic community, namely *The Manual of Discipline, A Zadokite Document* (discovered earlier at Cairo), and a *Formulary of Blessings;* two collections of hymns, for the initiants and a psalm of thanksgiving; several commentaries, on the Books of Michaeas, Nahum, and Habakkuk; a long oration of Moses which was a paraphrase of the Law; an epic on *The War of the Sons of Light and the Sons of Darkness;* and a manual for the future congregation of Israel, the so-called Messianic Banquet.

Conservative scholarship holds that the scrolls were composed at various dates between 170 B.C. and A.D. 68.

The burning question is the relation of these documents to Christian beginnings. Some extremists claimed that we have here the rude clay of which the Christian Church was later molded, with the implication that the latter is not really unique but merely continuous with its Judaic predecessor among the ascetics at Qumran. Nothing could be further from the facts. There is in the Dead Sea Scrolls no trace of any of the cardinal theological concepts of Christianity—the incarnation of the Son of God, original sin, redemption through the cross and the life of divine grace, the sacramental system, or the universality of the Gospel *kerygma*.

On the other hand, there are numerous affinities on which balanced scholarship has agreed and which cast abundant light on the meaning of the Christian faith. The scrolls furnish a picture of the religious and cultural climate in which John the Baptist conducted his mission and in which Jesus of Nazareth was initially reared.

Among the affinities between the thought and language of the scrolls and that of the New Testament, the most prominent touches on the communal nature of the Qumran sect and the Christian community. The Qumran group had a variety of inspectors who were overseers and whose duty it was to admit new members, pass judgment on those in probation, direct the interests of the community, and, when necessary, dismiss those who failed to live up to prescribed regulations. This spiritual leader was called "teacher" or "right-teacher." In the fourth Gospel, Jesus is hailed as the teacher sent by God, appointed by the Father to bring the light of truth to all nations.

In the *Manual of Discipline*, the community is promised to become a veritable "temple of God, a true holy of holies," provided it abides by the community regulations. This is more than superficially like the words of St. Paul to the Corinthians, "Holy is the temple of God, and this temple you are."[20]

Members of the Qumran body styled themselves "the elect" or "the elect of God," with an accent that is familiar in the writings of St. Paul, who spoke of himself as an apostle of Jesus Christ, "according to the faith of God's elect," and in St. Peter who said he was an apostle of Jesus Christ "to the elect who are sojourners of the dispersion."[21] In both sources, the Qumran and Christian, the faithful declared that they stand in the eternal congregation of God, hold direct converse with him, and "share in the lot of the holy beings." They enjoyed a community of goods, practiced obedience to superiors, and were told to abstain from divorce with the right to remarry. Thus in the *Zadokite Document* we read, "one of the traps is fornication, by marrying two women at the same time, even though the principle of creation is, male and female He created them." And in Mark we read, "Because of the hardness of your heart he [Moses] wrote you that precept [allowing a bill of divorce to put away one's wife]. But from the beginning of creation God made them male and female."[22] Some commentators have been so struck by the similarity they rushed to conclude that the *Zadokite Document* is Judaeo-Christian.

Comparable to the Christian emphasis on the struggle between light and darkness is the theme of the Qumran manuscripts that speak at length of two spirits, the Prince of Light and the Angel of Darkness, with constant opposition between them. While the idea is a commonplace of ancient Iranian and later Jewish thought, it suggests a development that became part of the structure of Christianity. It should be noted, however, that the New Testament subjected this doctrine to an essential change by contraposing the Angel of Darkness not with an Angel of Light but with Christ or the Holy Spirit, with never a suspicion that the two were equally matched.

Even more striking is the parallel between the meal of the Palestinian monastery and the Lord's Supper. There was no transformation of the elements in the Dead Sea documents, but otherwise the two ceremonies were quite similar. Speaking of communal duties, the Qumran members were told that "when they prepare the table to eat and wine to drink, the priest must be the first to extend his hand to bless the first portions of the bread. And if wine is being drunk, the priest must be the first to extend his hand to bless the first portion of the bread and wine." So, too, in describing the Messianic Banquet, "When they gather around the table to eat or to drink wine, and the common board has been spread and the wine mixed, no one is to stretch out his hand for the first portion of bread and wine before the priest. For it is he who is to bless the first portion of bread and wine, and the first to stretch out his hand to the bread. After that the Messiah of Israel will place his hands on the bread."[23]

In the spite of these analogies, the early Church was very different from the Jewish community which some have identified with the Essenes and others, with more caution, describe as the Dead Sea

Covenanters. The Jewish ascetics were legalistic in the extreme and attached to externals. Their observance of the Sabbath was more demanding than the burdens laid down by the Pharisees. They were a closed sect, socially, psychologically, and even physically, and were forbidden association with others at the risk of being excommunicated for consorting with outsiders.

Future research may reveal new correlations between Qumran and the Church of the Apostles, especially in heightening the spiritual idealism of the Jewish people at the time of Christ. It will also show that, while Christianity appealed to the best in human nature and made demands on generosity beyond anything hitherto suspected in Judaism, its inspiration did not come from the Prophets alone but from a new dispensation which the followers of Christ believe was a communal fulfillment of the Old Law.

The Bible as Revelation

Interest in the Bible has never been higher than today—if statistics on the number of copies of the Scriptures sold, translations available, and publications on biblical subjects are a good index of the times. This may seem strange if all the talk about the dawn of an audiovisual age is true.

It is not strange, however, if we reflect that the Bible was originally a people who banded together in common allegiance to a great leader; and if the same media of sight, sound, and touch that first gave rise to Christianity are becoming dominant in modern culture. It was the person of Christ, his spoken words, and the actions he performed that created the Christian community. It is the same person, his words, and the events of his life that are now capturing the imagination to a degree that was only partially possible in the era of print, when the Bible (as the name describes) was mainly a *Biblion*, i.e., a paper or scroll, that people read, and not a personality around whom those who believed had gathered to serve and venerate.

The same evidence of a biblical renewal in Christianity suggests that every tradition has found new meaning in the Bible, and that what had been a sword of division in the sixteenth century is becoming a source of unification in the twentieth.

Roman Catholics, it is said, are rediscovering the riches of the Bible as distinct from the Church's tradition; and Protestants are finding that tradition must complement the Bible. Also within Catholicism and Protestantism, as in Eastern Orthodoxy, the Bible is becoming a touchstone of something so deep and imponderable, it cannot be expressed in words, and yet is fundamental. It divides those who really believe in a supernatural Christianity from those who have adjusted their lives to the humanism of Western society.

All these aspects of the Bible are somehow comprehended by the term *revelation,* which is the divine counterpart to the human element that makes the Bible true history. On both levels, the Scriptures have undergone sharp development in recent decades. In both cases, the growing collectivization of modern culture was the main reason, or at least the principal catalyst, responsible.

REVELATION AS COMMUNAL EXPERIENCE. People judge things by their own lights, and they describe religious concepts according to the way they think. Their thinking, in turn, is affected by the cultural patterns and predispositions of the age. We would expect Aristotle, the logician, to call man a rational animal; and Adam Smith, the prophet of industrialism, to say "man is an animal that makes bargains."

So, too, with revelation. We are not surprised that John Calvin, writing in the sixteenth century, placed biblical revelation ahead of the Church and insisted that "the writings of the prophets and the preaching of the apostles . . . must certainly have preceded the Church," and not the other way around. Without the Bible "the Church itself would never have existed."[24] And until very lately, most Protestant confessions of faith included some equivalent of Calvin's teaching: that the Bible is a special divine creation out of whose acceptance grew the Church, variously conceived according to different interpretations of the biblical message from God.

Equally understandable is a current expression of judgment by a recognized Protestant authority on the Bible.

> It remains true that the proper place for the Bible is in the Church. The Church existed before the creation of scripture; it is the environment of scripture. Both Church and scripture witness to Christ; but the Church came first, and the scripture was produced within the Church for the use of the members of the body. Those who stand outside the believing community cannot do so fully, for they must to a certain degree cut against the grain rather than with it.[25]

Both judgments, Calvin's and today's, reflect the times in which they were written. They also reflect the change in attitude—notably in

Protestantism—toward the Bible as God's revelation to the original Christian community in the first century; and his continued revelation in and through the faithful to the end of time.

It is informative to trace some of the factors that contributed to the changed outlook. In the first place, the same process was at work in the development of the Bible as history. Every archaeological find and the accumulating knowledge of Christian origins added new evidence to the same conclusion: that Christianity came on the scene as a communal religion, with the concept of society built into its very essence. Part of this social dimension was the Bible, but only a part. Except for the Church there would have been no Bible; and, to this day, the Bible is honored and followed in the spirit of Christ only where the community of believers is vital.

More influential, however, than the study of Church history was the unfolding of modern events. It is not coincidental that the earliest clear statements in official Protestant circles, favoring a reassessment of revelation as extra-biblical, came only after the nations had been plunged into world conflict.

In one country after another, the same refrain began to be heard. God's revelation is in the Bible, indeed, but only because it was entrusted by Christ to the Church. It is the Church he founded to which he disclosed the mysteries of faith; and the disclosure is biblical only because the Bible belongs to the Church.

In 1934 the Free Reformed Synod in Germany declared: "The Word spoken by God once and for all is heard by the Church, through the free grace of the Holy Spirit, in the twofold but united and mutually complementary witness of the Old and New Testaments, i.e., in the witness of Moses and the prophets to the coming of Jesus Christ, and in the witness of the Evangelists and Apostles to the Jesus Christ who has come." A few months later, at Barmen, representatives of all the major Protestant bodies in Germany repeated, more briefly, that Jesus Christ, present and working in "the Christian Church [which] is the community of believers," constitutes the true object of man's allegiance.[26]

The German Calvinist editor of these historic statements added his own commentary to what this shift of focus implied:

Here it is stated plainly that the Bible is not a book filled with religious truths or moral laws, nor a collection of pious writings, but a witness to Jesus Christ, to God's Word, who exists outside of us but who comes to us.

The Protestant "Scripture principle" was thus cleansed of all obscurities and distortions. In the Church of God it is not a question of an infallible book, a "paper-pope," but of Christ clothed in the words of His witnesses, the apostles and prophets, of the Christ who by His Spirit proves Himself a living Lord who still uses the words of His messengers to announce His presence today, where and when He wills. At Barmen the false positions of Protestant orthodoxy and liberalism were broken through, and the true approach to the Bible found.[27]

If these words sound revolutionary, they were, and the passage of time has only confirmed their significance. Born of the crisis precipitated by the Nazi persecution of the churches in Central Europe, they later became the foundation for the ecumenical movement. Seeing themselves pushed to the wall to give witness to their faith, Evangelical Protestants defined it in terms of Christ, speaking to the Church, and, as such, no less audible today than he was when he spoke on Mt. Thabor to the first disciples.

Even the strange criticism of "an infallible book" and "the false positions of Protestant orthodoxy and liberalism" were part of the drastic change in concept of what Christian revelation really means, and where the Bible fits into this revised approach to faith.

Some had become disenchanted with any claims to infallibility, whether of the Pope (who did not speak for Protestants) or of the Bible, which years of radical criticism had practically dissolved. They would fall under the ban of liberalism. Others were disillusioned with an infallible Bible that seemed irrelevant for the times. What possible meaning could a Christian make of the gas chambers or the stockpiles of human hair from the heads of three million victims at Auschwitz? Unless he had faith in a divine person and believed that person was speaking today in the community of believers, faith would be impossible. Conservative biblicism was no refuge from the horror of the concentration camps.

Ten years later, America's entrance into the Second World War had the same effect on Protestantism in the New World. Before the war were over, the United States would deploy twelve million men in service and register over a million casualties.

As in Germany, so in America, Protestant Christians who looked for strength in their faith to sustain them under trial found it in Christ who reveals himself far beyond a book (the Bible) or a place (Palestine) or a time (the apostolic age).

During the years of its history (1908 to 1950), the Federal Council of Churches reached a peak in 1943, when its thirty denominations published a joint document on "The Relation of the Church to the War in the Light of the Christian Faith." The ten-thousand-word manifesto began with a statement on "Revelation."

With the Barmen Declaration in Germany, it divides world Protestantism into two eras: one in which the Bible and the second in which the Church is the main repository of God's message to mankind.

> In speaking of the revelation of God in Jesus Christ to us, we speak of a situation in which two stages of disclosure are involved.
>
> There is first the need that the man Jesus of Nazareth be disclosed to us, men of the twentieth century. This disclosure comes mainly in two ways. On the one hand there is the written record in the New Testament of his words and deeds . . . On the other hand, there is the Christian Church, a living community in which his spirit is still present and active. The written record and the living community cannot be separated. Each involves the other and neither can be reduced to simple dependence on, nor to simple parallelism with the other. Through both at once, the person Jesus of Nazareth makes his impress and finds his interpreters in our day, not perfectly but in the manner of all vital communication in history.
>
> There is hidden within this historical disclosure another that gives it an added dimension of meaning and efficacy. In Jesus of Nazareth, known to us through written word and living church, was present, we believe, the redemptive Word and Will of God . . . What is meant by saying that God was in Christ is, in essential part, that Jesus Christ has been able through the centuries and is able now to awaken in men the profound personal response we call faith. Herein is made concrete and contemporary the revealing of God in Jesus Christ to us.[28]

The implications for the future of Protestantism are considerable. Revelation is sharply distinguished between God's communication of himself in the person of Christ, and man's response to the disclosure. In other words, it is possible for God to reveal and man not to respond. Moreover, God's self-manifestation is to be found both in the Scriptures and in the Church. It is in this living community that Christ's "spirit is still present and active," and "the New Testament . . . must be interpreted by the Christian community."

The lesson behind these sentiments has not been lost on Catholics, who for so long had been charged with subordinating Scripture to the Church's teaching. When the Vatican Council came to treat of this delicate question it no longer had to remain on the defensive. The ground was ready for all Christians to see that neither the Bible alone nor tradition alone is sufficient guide for the faith.

> There exists a close connection and communication between sacred tradition and Sacred Scripture. For both of them, flowing from the same divine wellspring, in a certain way merge into a unity and tend toward the same end.
>
> Sacred Scripture is the word of God inasmuch as it is consigned to writing under the inspiration of the divine Spirit. Sacred tradition takes the word of God entrusted by Christ the Lord and the Holy Spirit to the Apostles, and hands it on to their successors in its full purity. Thus, led by the Spirit these successors can in their preaching preserve this word of God faithfully, explain it, and make it more widely known. Consequently it is not from Sacred Scripture alone that the Church draws her certainty about everything which has been revealed. Therefore both sacred tradition and Sacred Scripture are to be accepted and venerated with the same sense of loyalty and reverence.[29]

The Roman Catholic position shows a profound respect for the Bible and gives it coequal status with tradition as revelatory of God's word. It also avoids bickering over trifles, in the face of the momentous fact that Jesus Christ is revealed in the New Testament *and* in the New Community he founded.

Naturally, the Council went on to identify tradition in a way that Protestants do not profess: that the task of authentically interpreting the word of God, whether written (Bible) or handed on (tradition) "has been entrusted exclusively to the living teaching office of the Church."[30] To further explain that this teaching office (the *magisterium*) is the episcopate in union with the Bishop of Rome was only to take the logical step of describing Roman Catholic Christianity. But the essence of Christianity was agreed upon. It is the acceptance of Christ, revealed as much in the Bible (to remind Catholics and Orthodox) as in tradition (to remind Protestants); and that neither source has a monopoly on Christian revelation.

SCRIPTURE AS CONTINUED REVELATION. If the Protestant Churches discovered tradition as God's revelation to the believing community, Catholicism rediscovered the Bible as the same revelation, completed at the end of the first century and yet continued—indeed enriched and deepened—into the twentieth.

So much has happened in the Catholic biblical renaissance, all in less than a hundred years, that the best way to see what some have called the "Saga of the Bible" is to place it in chronological sequence.

It began rather unpromisingly with the publication of a few books in the nineteenth century by Catholic writers who were eager to get into the stream of biblical scholarship—and went beyond the limits of established orthodoxy. The First Vatican Council curbed their tendency to question the validity of Christian doctrine because some exegete had discovered a new meaning for a Greek vocable.

The matter became more serious when scholars like Lenormant and d'Hulst urged a novel idea of inspiration, which allowed that the Bible actually contains errors in matters of history, touching on Christian belief.

To meet this budding threat to the faith, Leo XIII in 1893 published the letter *Providentissimus Deus,* which set the pace for Catholic biblical studies. Leo's purpose was forthright: to clarify the Church's teaching on the absolute truth of the inspired Scriptures. There may be scribal errors in manuscripts, the meaning of a passage may be doubtful, a translator may be at fault. But in the original Scripture, as it left the hand of the hagiographer, there was no lapse from the truth.

By the same token, the Church simply disallows any restriction of divine inspiration to certain points of the Bible, such as those pertaining to doctrine alone, and forbids the concession that in some points —no matter how minor—the sacred writer may have erred. The formula expressed by Leo is that every Scripture is as necessarily inerrant as it is necessarily impossible for God to be the author of error.

One other principle of Leo has been fundamental to biblical studies in the twentieth century. It practically defines Catholic hermeneutics or the science of interpreting revelation. Close adherence to Catholic tradition should be combined with up-to-date scholarship in the history, linguistics, and archaeology of the ancient Mediterranean world. Events have since proved the wisdom of this twofold principle, and the difficulty of maintaining a sound balance between the two—loyalty to the Church and fidelity to scientific progress.

Leo's historic document was not academic. He anticipated the practical need of establishing a professional center for biblical studies in Palestine. Seeing the sad state of contemporary Catholic exegesis, he

encouraged the Jerusalem foundation in 1890 of the *École Biblique,*
with the Dominican Semitics scholar, Père Lagrange, as its first head. In
order to keep the Catholic world posted on the progress of Scripture
studies during those turbulent years of strife for orthodoxy, Lagrange
founded in 1892 the quarterly *Revue Biblique,* which has attained
international recognition.

In 1902, Leo XIII founded the Pontifical Biblical Commission to
promote biblical studies among Catholics and to safeguard the same
from the inroads of rationalism. Two years later, it was empowered
to confer the academic degrees of the Licentiate and Doctorate in
Sacred Scripture. And in 1907 a papal decree of Pius X stated that
decisions of the Commission oblige as much in conscience as those of
other Roman Congregations. The present name of this organization is
the Commission for Biblical Studies, which is not officially a part of
the Roman Curia.

The number of decrees issued by the Commission has been remarkably few—with increasing attention to give scholars guidelines for
study rather than to impose restrictions on their research.

From its establishment in 1902, to the accession of John XXIII, the
Biblical Commission published fifteen decrees. Their variety and scope
are an index of the Commission's work to the eve of the Second
Vatican Council. They also reflect the progressive development of an
authentic biblical theology in the Catholic Church.

Eleven of the decisions occurred in the pontificate of St. Pius X, each
dealing with a controversial issue connected with Modernism: the
admission of error in "implicit citations" in the Bible from profane
sources (1905); historicity of statements not intended to be taken
literally (1905); Mosaic authorship of the Pentateuch (1906); Joan-
nine authorship and historical validity of the fourth Gospel (1907);
authenticity of the prophecies in Isaiah (1908); affirmation that the
first three chapters of Genesis correspond to "objective reality and historical truth" (1909); authorship and time of composition of the
Psalms (1910); priority, authorship, and original composition of Matthew before the fall of Jerusalem in A.D. 70 (1911); Marcan and Lucan
authorship of the second and third Gospels, and canonicity of the infancy narratives (first two chapters) and Christ's bloody sweat in the
garden in Luke (1912); authorship by Luke, a disciple of Paul, and
historicity along with the miracle narratives of Acts; also the Pauline
authorship of the pastoral epistles (1913); Pauline responsibility for

the Letter to the Hebrews, "pending later judgment of the Church" (1914).

During the next forty-four years, only two decrees were published by the Commission, indicating the end of a period of crisis. Moreover, the issues handled were rather internal and minor, compared to those in the previous decade: the Apostles were not in error even though they spoke of an early second coming of Christ (1915); the writer referred to Christ's resurrection in Psalm 15, and Christ's words about, "What does it profit," in Matthew 16:26 and Luke 9:25, refer to the eternal salvation of the soul and not only man's temporal life on earth (1933).

In the same four decades, two other statements were issued by the Commission, but not as decrees. In 1940 an Italian author (Dolindo Ruotolo) published a severe criticism of the Church's attitude toward scientific exegesis, in favor of a spiritual interpretation independent of the literal sense of the Bible. The following year, the Commission defended the current practice in a letter to the bishops of Italy and insisted on the priority of the literal meaning of Scripture. It also defended the freedom of scholars to go beyond the Vulgate (though approved by Trent) to such manuscript texts of the Bible as were becoming available in the original Hebrew and Greek.

In the other direction (1948), the Archbishop of Paris (Suhard) received a similar letter from the secretary of the Commission on the literary genre of the first eleven chapters of Genesis which deal with man's origin and fall, the blood and Babel—up to the call of Abraham. The main thrust of the letter was to admit the exegetical problems raised but also to reject the position of "anyone who *a priori* contends that these narratives contain no 'history,' in the modern sense of the term."[31]

The foregoing survey of a much misunderstood phrase of Catholicism also shows the development in the Church's attitude toward the Bible. From being regarded as a watchdog, the Commission became more and more the guide and animator of scholarship. Its original "decrees" were really answers (*responsa*), and later on were called directives (*instructiones*).

A chart for the future, the most elaborate and encouraging directive set forth by the Commission since its beginning, was published under Paul VI in 1964. Typical of the treatment of theological issues by certain media, the New York *Times* changed the whole focus of the document by giving it a negative slant: "Vatican Cautions Students of

Bible: Rejects as Dangerous and Invalid Any Conclusions Not Arising from Faith: Inquiry Limits Defined: Modern Historical Methods Accepted If Scholars Are Wary of 'Prejudices.'" A more objective caption was "Vatican Green Light to Bible Scholars," in another newspaper.[32]

Through several thousand words of careful direction, this *Instruction on Historical Truth of the Gospels* offered for years to come the broad lines characteristic of Gospel Truth. There were no surprises in the directive, whose main purpose was to help the Catholic exegete in his labors. He is urged to rely not only on his own resources, but also on God's help and the light of the Church.

Scholars are encouraged in their pursuits and their growing number is hailed with pleasure. They and their critics are counseled to charity, which is needed in this area so prone to emotional discussions. A chance remark gives a clue to the tone of the instruction, that not even Jerome was always successful in handling the biblical problems of his day.

Throughout the decades of the Commission's existence, two other factors were continuously operative to sustain the Church's devotion to the Scriptures. The Biblical Institute was founded in Rome in 1909, and a series of papal letters encouraged the faithful to study and use the inspired text in their daily lives.

In keeping with the intention of its founder, Pius X, the Pontifical Biblical Institute endeavors to be "a center of higher Scripture studies and related sciences in the spirit of the Church." Under the direction of the Society of Jesus, its purpose is twofold: to prepare teachers of Scripture for seminaries and universities, and train experts in the biblical sciences. Authorized to confer the Licentiate and Doctorate degrees, the *Istituto* has gained international recognition through the quality of its graduates and learned publications. Not commonly known is that Augustin Bea, rector of the Institute for nineteen years, was the confessor and close friend of Pius XII. Created cardinal by John XXIII in 1959, he became the first head of the newly formed Secretariat for Christian Unity and exercised immense influence in shaping the Catholic Church's policy toward Protestants and Orthodox. The Bible, he hoped, would become the bridge to reunite a dismembered Christian world.

If Leo XIII initiated the Catholic biblical renewal at the turn of the century, Benedict XV preserved it in the aftermath of the First

World War (1920), and Pius XII gave it definitive form.³³ The latter's encyclical *Divino Afflante Spiritu* in 1943 was more than a vote of confidence in scientific research or a protest against the growing fad of an intuitive explanation of the Bible. It marked the first stage in a new period of challenge and crisis in Roman Catholicism.

Growth in Biblical Realism

Fifty years had passed since Leo XIII had encouraged Catholics to study the Bible without fear of the burgeoning sciences, and with confidence that the faith would not lose but profit from its encounter with the world of investigation. During the half century, progress had been made, but there were also casualties. Men like Lagrange had suffered at the hands of co-religionists who were more zealous than learned, and whose zeal sometimes lashed against the tentative efforts of scholars to decipher the mysterious text of the Scriptures.

They needed protection from the well-intentioned but ill-advised, and support from the Church's highest authority. One sentence in *Divino Afflante* has become classic. After admitting progress and urging scholars to utilize all the resources of history, archaeology, philology, and allied sciences, the Pope concluded on a note of freedom that some consider unique in the annals of Roman documentation:

> There remain many things, and of the greatest importance, in the discussion and exposition of which the skill and genius of Catholic commentators may and ought to be freely exercised, so that each may contribute his part to the advantage of all, to the continued progress of sacred doctrine and to the defense and honor of the Church.³⁴

That was in 1943, and the statement was hailed as a major breakthrough in delivering Catholics from the "fundamentalist literalness" of certain segments of Protestantism.

As far as most exegetes were concerned, Rome had not misjudged the situation and its trust in their loyalty proved to be well founded. This is so true that even to mention the opposite minority risks giving the wrong impression. Scholars of the stature of Fonck and Lagrange, Dyson and Bea, Merk and Benoit, Vosté and Barton—to name only a few—witness to the ability of highly trained specialists to accept the Church's historic interpretation of the biblical word.

By the early sixties, things had begun to change. Most Catholic writers, especially professional exegetes, caused no problem. When they raised difficult questions or struggled with the demands of their science, they wrote mainly in learned journals and their conclusions were modestly presented as tentative or subject to revision. Like their fellow scientists in other fields, they avoided the glare of publicity and the penchant for making generalizations.

RADICAL REVISION. But there were exceptions. And except for the fact that this is the communications age, there would have been nothing more to record. Not a single one of the ideas of nominally Catholic writers who use the Bible at variance with Catholic tradition is new. What is new and revolutionary is the projection of these ideas on a national and global scale, multiplied, visualized, and synchronized with similar ideas elsewhere—until the impact on Western culture is so powerful that the Catholic Church seems to be rocked to its foundations.

Every major country, notably in the Anglo-Saxon world, has these representatives of a new approach to the Bible, minus a wholehearted reliance on the Church's historic tradition.

From Germany, Catholics are told St. Paul should be re-explained when he writes in Ephesians about the apostolic foundations of the Church. In answer: Who are the successors of the Apostles?—the people are told, "the whole Church, not just a few individuals." Consequently, "apostolicity can never mean power through which the Church might rule. It is not a question of others submitting to the Church. The Church must itself submit by accepting the authority of the apostles." Where is the authority to be found? In the New Testament, "Apostolic succession," instead of somehow uniquely residing in the historic episcopate, "entails a continuing and living confrontation of the Church with the original, fundamental testimony of Scripture."[35] The Bible, therefore, stands in judgment on the Church; not the Church on the meaning of the Bible.

Canadians are told to re-examine the Bible in the light of modern scholarship and discover that all the references to divine justice in the Scriptures are anthropomorphic. "God is not a judge who punished." Both testaments demand re-evaluation.

> According to the Old Testament authors, the justice of God is not the quality whereby God rewards the good and punishes the wicked. God is just when he intervenes in the lives of the underprivileged, especially the orphans and widows, to save them from the injustices of men . . . God is just when he defends the cause of the innocent. God is just when he

establishes those who have been exploited by wicked men. God is just when he saves the poor.[36]

There is no change in the New Testament. St. Paul "tells us in the epistle to the Romans that in the Gospel of Christ, 'the justice of God is revealed.' This justice is the power of God unto salvation to everyone who believes. God is just when he justifies sinners."[37] The *only* concept of justice in God is where he redeems. He never willingly inflicts punitive pain.

English readers are recommended to get over their childish ways. "There is a parlor-game in which a whispered message is passed down a line from player to player and comes out unrecognizably distorted at the end." Sometimes the result is whimsical. Invariably it is ridiculous. The tragedy is that many Christians are playing the same game, only with disastrous results, when they still take the Bible literally on such primitive notions as angels and devils. They need to be enlightened.

> *Angel* is a lazy translation for "messenger." It is the God who rules and directs the world by his word that is thus appearing to man. The criterion of what the Bible teaches is not what its human author believes, it is rather how he uses his beliefs to enlighten us about God. The human author of Genesis believed in a flat earth and solid sky, but the Bible does not teach this; it teaches that God made both earth and sky, whatever their nature. Similarly, there can be little doubt that the human authors of the Bible believed in the existence of angels, but this alone does not justify us in regarding the Bible as teaching their existence.[38]

The devils in Scripture are no less symbolic. They are merely dramatic ways of depicting wicked people who resist the will of God (Old Testament), or of describing those on earth who refuse to believe in the Son of God (New Testament). In neither case are they real creatures distinct from the creator. They are biblical symbols of man's attempted independence of God.

American Catholics are instructed on the postconciliar approach to such doctrines as the Real Presence, Mary's virginity, papal primacy, and a sacrificing priesthood. Cardinal Bea is first quoted and then corrected on what divides Catholics from other Christians. According to Bea, "First and foremost, the fundamental teaching of the Catholic Church will not be changed. Compromise on points of faith that have already been defined is impossible. It would be quite unfair to our

non-Catholic Brethren to stir up false hopes of this nature." So far
Bea. Now the corrective.

These remarks of Cardinal Bea are predicated on a concept of dogma
that has been for some time, and is today, widely accepted in Catholic
theology. In current Catholic usage, the term *dogma* means a divinely
revealed truth, proclaimed as such by the infallible teaching authority
of the Church, and hence binding on all the faithful now and forever.[39]

Given this unilateral approach to the Bible, ecumenism becomes an
impossible pursuit. "Having taken irreversible steps on its own, Catholicism must demand that others take the same steps. If Christian reunion is conceived in this light, it seems to be a one-sided affair. The
other Churches would have to come to where the Catholic Church
now is." Clearly this would be intolerable. The solution to the impasse
is to rethink the meaning of defined doctrines, to see they are not so
irreversible as men like Bea thought they were.

This rethinking depends on an existentialist approach to knowledge,
and specifically on Heidegger's analysis of truth. "Dogma has the value
of revelation if, and only if, it is grasped by a mind presently influenced by God's active self-bestowal."[40] Or more plainly, revelation
is dogma only insofar as a person assimilates what was revealed. The
whole shift, therefore, is away from God's communication of objective
truth to man's subjective understanding of what he believes.

Dogmas are revelation experienced. They are different for different
people at different times. Accordingly instead of speaking of *orthodoxy*
(right doctrine), the Church should use terms like *orthology* (right
speech) or *orthophony* (right words). "While right speech has its
value, the rightness of speech depends on a great variety of circumstances, some of which are not within the control of the Church. Thus
the Church may be forced to change the canons of right speaking."[41]
But all of this is premised on the assumption that faith is primarily
man's way of grasping revelation, rather than God's demand for the
acceptance of revealed truth. No one, therefore, should be held responsible either for the degree to which God communicates himself
to man, nor the manner in which man understands God.

Once this is admitted, then a major obstacle is removed from the
path of Christian unity. "Many Catholic dogmas, such as original sin,
transubstantiation, and perhaps the virginal conception of Jesus . . .
that have traditionally divided the Churches 'are capable of radical
reinterpretation.'"[42] Those who believe that original sin is inherited

from Adam should reformulate their ideas in terms which include the Unitarian belief that this sin is only the bad example of society. And those who profess the real bodily presence of Christ in the Eucharist should reword their "dogmas" to cover the Baptist position which holds that this presence is purely symbolic.

Irish Catholics are given almost the same recommendation, to stop thinking that because somewhere in the past the Church has defined certain doctrines, they are objects of special veneration. It must sadly be admitted that too many people still labor under this illusion.

> It would be nothing short of self-defeating to deny that we are still, all of us, subject to some extent to the kind of attitude to tradition and change which was the product of the ages of controversy. In our normal unreflective attitudes we do still think of tradition as the authoritative imposition on successive generations by the teaching hierarchy of the Church of dogmatic propositions which we have to believe to be saved.
>
> There is no excuse for our overlooking these things any longer. We do now have both the peace and the knowledge which enables us to construct a reasonably adequate theory of tradition and change.[43]

No doubt, some would still prefer "the sinister peace of those whom much of the world has begun to ignore." But those who are alert to the times will recognize that "the second Vatican Council was itself . . . too much subject to the hangover from the ages of controversy to succeed in producing a fully developed theology of tradition."[44] As they read the present age, when controversies have been laid to rest, they discover that "tradition is the whole life of the community as it advances through history. As it advances, it undergoes the changes proper to all historical existence."[45]

Applications of this theory to Christology or Mariology are frankly minor compared to its implications in the moral order. Arguing that "there is nothing in the New Testament even vaguely approaching a ruling on contraception,"[46] today's Catholics are free to revise the Church's formal teaching on the subject in the light of the "historical existence" in European and American society.

Holland has had more than its share of revisionists, arguing from the Bible to a new form of Catholic Christianity. A particular target of their attention is the priesthood, which, they say, can no longer be understood as a sacrificing ministry, demanding special sacramental ordination.

The ground on which the new priesthood should be built is the vision of an "apostolic secularity." This means that the primary role of the Church of the future must "not consist in ecclesiastical ministerial functions," i.e., the Mass and administration of the sacraments, "but in the labor of all Christians within the community of human beings." Instead of a "special ministry," the new ecclesiology will take as its starting point "the common priesthood of all believers."[47] If this seems strange to Catholics, it is only because they have not properly read the Scriptures.

> In the New Testament, ecclesiastical ministers were called bishops or presbyters, and there is not a single indication of the fact that they functioned as officers of cultic sacrifices. However, from about the days of Eusebius—that is, since the end of the third century—ecclesiastical ministers are also named *hiereis-saerdotes* (priests).
>
> How could this development come to pass? . . . It seems pretty certain that it is connected with the then evolving theory of the Eucharist as sacrifice.[48]

The mandate given by Christ to the apostles at the Last Supper to "do this in remembrance of me" is ignored. And the whole tradition of the sub-apostolic Church is bypassed, e.g., Ignatius of Antioch (A.D. 107) declaring, "Let that celebration of the Eucharist be considered valid which is held under the bishops."[49]

If a sacrificing priesthood was a third-century development, Christ did not institute the sacrament of orders and anyone—layman or lay woman—can "celebrate Mass" and perform all the traditional priestly functions. In order to leave no doubt, the issue is restated in the clearest terms. It is untrue to claim, as the Catholic Church now teaches, "that the possibility of an authentic Eucharistic celebration is totally dependent on the more or less accidental presence of officially empowered ministers." How so? Because "the power to celebrate the Eucharist is bestowed in principle on the common priesthood," and without benefit of another sacrament, which some receive "for reasons mainly of discipline."[50]

Finally the French and Swiss are reassured that all the confusion of ideas in the Church is necessary and, in fact, part of the price of an authentic faith which may coexist with positive doubt. Catholics have been misled into thinking that true faith does not include suspension of judgment. If they reread the Old and New Testaments they will be "struck by the breadth of the concept of faith" there presented, that "goes far beyond our usual understanding of the term."[51] This broader concept allows for doubt in matters of faith, and without scruple that one is doing wrong.

Doubt is a spiritual exercise, for it presupposes vigilant watch over one's actions and permanent openness to truth. Denial is easy, and the conformist who adopts other people's beliefs for the sake of peace is taking the easy way out. The kind of doubt we are speaking of is a noble exercise of faith. Without it (for those who cannot do otherwise than doubt) there would be no faith.[52]

There is no mincing of words here. This means real doubt as the "suspension of judgment," which causes a person "to remain uncertain as long as one is not personally convinced."[53] If, as a result, "the spirit is torn in pieces" or "inner desolation" follows, it is better to be honest with oneself than be a conformist to the Church's ready-made dogmas.

CONTRIBUTING FACTORS. The number of authors who wrote in this vein has not been large and, by the late sixties, the publishers who favored their writings were almost predictable. Yet the receptivity given their ideas bears some explanation. For months on end, week after week, Pope Paul would deplore the harm being done to the faithful. He spoke of "the revolutionary mentality," where a man "substitutes his own spiritual experience, his own feeling of subjective faith, his own personal interpretation of the Word of God." Such a one "is certainly producing something new, but it is ruinous." He recalled in dismay that people who call themselves Catholics want to "re-establish unity at the expense of doctrinal truth." He reminded those who should know better that "We cannot demolish the Church of yesterday in order to construct a new one today. We cannot solve difficult questions and weaken demanding laws with historicist adaptations to subjective interpretations."[54]

By 1970, anyone familiar with papal statements could assemble a critical vocabulary about "irresponsible initiatives . . . laicist mentality . . . distortion . . . deformation of freedom . . . arbitrary change . . . conformity to the mentality and manner of our time." Always the Pope's concern was that God's unchangeable truth was being twisted to fit the changing circumstances of the age.

What happened? Admittedly those who were guilty of distortion were not many, but their effect was enormous because the media exploited every shred of conflict which this aroused. It made no difference to *Time* or *Le Monde* or *De Tijd* that not one of the writers previously quoted was a professional exegete. What mattered was that the historic faith of Catholicism should be called into question by its own professed members; that "those who claim to speak and define

God's word should have their right not on an abstract and untenable theological doctrine but on fidelity to Scripture."[55] It was assumed that Scripture was first understood in the subjective sense of the Church's critics, and then it became normative for passing judgment on the Church's teaching.

This exploitation of writers who often had no higher title to fame than their iconoclasm must be taken into account in any analysis of "what happened?" Some of them (known to the author) had personal crises with the faith and yet opted to remain members of the Church in good standing. Publishing houses for years associated with Catholic books or periodicals decided to promote theological revolutionaries and foster "their independence in the face of a quasi-tyrannic authority." Interestingly, by 1970 the same publishers had decided that the "era is pretty clearly at an end."[56] The demolition was fairly complete.

Less familiar but a potent factor was that authors who caused the Pope most anguish received open or covert support from certain members of the hierarchy. When Bishop Shannon of St. Paul was about to leave the episcopate in 1969, he argued his case against the Church mainly on the premises of Hans Küng.[57] Later in the same year, when the bishop-delegates to the Synod at Rome spoke on collegiality, the prelates from Belgium, Canada, and Holland were conspicuous for their criticism of how modern popes have been exercising the primacy. The bishops' "interventions," reported by the Vatican press,[58] practically formed a mosaic of ideas from writers who were known to be irritated with the Church's perennial tradition—and not only on the primacy.

Twenty years in the life of the Catholic Church were long enough to witness the Church's growth in biblical realism. In 1943, Pius XII recommended, without qualification, that "the skill and genius of Catholic commentators may and ought to be freely exercised."[59] By 1966, under Paul VI, the scope of this freedom—otherwise repeated verbatim—was strongly qualified. It was to be exercised, as before, "to the continued progress of sacred doctrine and to the defense and honor of the Church." But, as a generation of experience had proved critically urgent, also "to the preparation and further support of the judgment to be exercised by the ecclesiastical magisterium."[60] What began as a renewal had become a revolution.

III

WORSHIP AND MINISTRY

Ritual is a good index of religion. As a people believes, so it worships. The human sacrifices to Re and the libations of wine to Jupiter tell us more about the faith of pre-Christian Egypt and Rome than all the learned monuments of antiquity. When we read that the humanist scholar Erasmus was not known to have once celebrated Mass in the twenty-eight years of his priesthood, we get some idea of the state of Catholicism in the sixteenth century. Our age is no exception.

Distinctive Features

In order to arrive at a balanced perspective, we shall first look at the main features of Christian ritual as reflected in all the churches—Catholic, Protestant, and Orthodox—and then take each of them separately in its own historical context. Some elements are common to the whole of Christendom; others are seen only in one tradition.

If religion is an expression of the deepest aspirations of a people, the times in which they live will naturally affect their religious profession, including worship. Sometimes there was a negative reaction against the age, at other times almost slavish conformity; but always the cultural patterns of the "secular world" have been active in the realm of the sacred.

In saying this, one distinction should be kept in mind. It is inaccurate to talk about the "age" as though it were all uniform throughout the world or, for that matter, mainly in the Christian West. The United States is not Canada, and certainly not Mexico or Brazil; it is even less Germany, or Spain, or Montenegro. The obverse is equally true. England is not Ireland, and the Scandinavian countries are not Latin America.

One feature, however, which typifies the secular culture almost everywhere and is one of the main theses of this book is the increasing sense of nearness produced by the media and rapid transportation. The effect on religion has been to make it more communitarian in worship. All ritual is already communication; but the experience we are describing goes deeper. It is almost as though people thought there was no value to prayer unless done in a group, or unless there is a "sense of togetherness" while people are praying. Passages from the Gospels like the words of Christ "where two or three are gathered together in my name, there I am in the midst of them" are being interpreted by some to mean that Christ is quite absent from those who invoke him unless at least two or three are doing the invocation in company.

Slogans like "the family that prays together stays together" are part of this attitude. But they also indicate another reason for the stress placed on joint or group worship in modern Christianity. With all the development in the physical means of contact between people, Western society—at least in the large urban (and suburban) areas—has become a lonely society.

More than one writer has pointed out that modern man's last resort to share his spirit with others is the liturgy. Almost every other avenue has been closed to him in the computerized civilization of the West.

Also by way of reaction, the infinitely complex structure of contemporary secular living has made demands for greater simplicity in the one place where, hopefully, complication is not desirable—in man's relationship with God. We shall see that this observation will have to be modified as we compare the liturgical renewal in Catholicism and Protestantism. But, in the main, ritual practices in every Christian tradition have become more simple, which is not the same as becoming artless, or secularized—although that, too, is a quality in some forms of Christian ceremony when authentic religious values and the sense of God's transcendence begin to wane.

With increased literacy and rising sophistication it is almost natural that people would look for more intelligibility in their worship. They want to not only participate but understand what the words and gestures mean and better assimilate the symbolic meaning of the rites in which they are expected to share. Not a small amount of the tension in contemporary Catholic ritual arose from the fact that people had matured in every field of secular culture—perhaps too much, too soon; and all the while they had not grown in a better understanding of the sacred signs they were supposed to use.

It is unthinkable that the audiovisual arts which are so much a part of present-day society would not have their impact on the sacramental forms of Christianity. But the influence is not necessarily strongest where it seems most prominent. Many of the extremes of liturgical jazz and ritual fantasia that have entered the Churches are neither so common nor, certainly, so commonly accepted as to indicate a decisive trend. For the most part, our audiovisual customs are passive and imply a maximum receptivity on the part of the one hearing (audience) or seeing (vision) others in action. They include, of course, a certain degree of activity but no more than is needed to benefit from another person's performance. Fifty thousand people may attend a sports event, but only nine or eleven men are active; the rest are looking on.

In Reformation times, John Calvin criticized the Catholic Mass because, in his words, the congregation was only a crowd of spectators watching the priest at the altar. The issue he raised is a perennial problem in Christianity, which believes that the liturgy is not only a form of collective religious experience. It is also, and mainly, a means of giving corporate honor to God. On both levels, the Churches have been struggling with the use of sight and sound in the ritual—as an active experience for all the participants and active adoration for all the worshipers, and not only for the priest or minister who leads the community in prayer.

Depending on the country and its culture—or on a smaller scale, the city or even parish—the activism that characterizes a people has also affected their religious cult. Worship in some instances has become a symbol of social preoccupation and the very extremes to which this has gone in some sectors only emphasizes the tendency. The situation is similar to what happened in the days of John Wesley. He was so disturbed with what he considered the ritualism of the established Church that he decided to form a new denomination, stressing the apostolate to the poor and the care of widows and orphans and those in moral distress. His point was that worship should not be divorced from service, and that it is possible for sacramentalism to obscure the demands of Christian love.

As the ecumenical movement spread throughout the Christian world, the call for a more ecumenical liturgy grew apace and, among Protestants, has been the single most influential factor in their drive for reunification. America is an exception in this regard, but estimates show that fifty per cent of American Protestants change their denomination every time they change residence. In terms of the liturgy this has been active as both cause and effect. Mobility from one denomination to another naturally tended to homogenize the churches' ritual customs. As a result of the more uniform cultic tradition, churches have come to question the need for their denominational separateness, and mergers in American Protestantism are almost a description of its history since 1900.

Corresponding pressures have developed between Catholicism and Protestantism, and the urge on Rome to permit intercommunion is part of the crisis in twentieth-century ecumenism.

One more element of Christian ritual which has grown out of cultural change is also a barometer of the faith. The term *ritual* is analogous, and may be compared to the word *creed*. Both are symbolic manifestations of internal attitudes: one in the order of belief and the other of worship.

We have seen something of the demythology, of the Bible and tradition, that swept over sections of Christianity. Where this occurred, and where the faith was more symbolic than real, nominal Christians influenced the churches' ceremonial and their corresponding liturgies have been desacralized. The consequences are a matter of record. The faithful are caught between the option of remaining affiliated with a church whose ritual is only minimally religious, or being cut off entirely from any semblance of communal religion. In the United States, over half the Episcopal clergy are "converts" or transfers from less creedal and liturgical denominations—which shows the magnitude of the problem in Protestantism. But the situation in the Catholic Church is also critical, as the number of clergy leaving the active priesthood suggests.

On the other hand, and occasioned by the desacralization, has been a deepening of religious fervor in the liturgy and a heightened desire to make it more valid. Recognizing that worship without faith is meaningless and that the essence of ritual is to glorify God, the spiritual side of the liturgy is being stressed—and rediscovered—to an extent that only the next decade will more fully reveal. Phenomena like Pentecostalism have other roots besides this one; but a partial explanation is the hunger among believing Christians to worship God and not merely feel togetherness when they are supposed to pray.

As we shift from this broader analysis to the major forms of Christianity in historical survey, a word on procedure may be useful. The main reason for taking Catholicism, Protestantism, and Orthodoxy separately is that the ritual history of each is so different. Where they have been mutually influential, this will be pointed out.

Roman Catholic Church

The "Liturgical Movement" has become a byword in the Catholic vocabulary and, for those familiar with the Church's modern history, almost synonymous with the developments in Roman Catholicism in the present century.

Three stages of this movement are discernible, with the latest still in process and having no prospect of finalization for years to come. Stage number one began building up in the sixteenth century and reached its crest with the liturgical reforms under Pius X (1903–1914); stage number two continued to the second Vatican Council (1962–1965); and the third stage since the council closed. It is best to call them "stages" without implying steady growth or continous progress. The movement has had peaks and troughs and, some would add, progress and setback, as the largest body in Christendom undertook to adjust its whole ritual posture to the needs of the age.

THE HISTORICAL SETTING. Among the less-known contributions of the Council of Trent (1545–1563) was its restoration of a strong liturgical life among the faithful. Aware of the fact that neglect of the sacraments and loss of fervor in prayer were greatly responsible for the terrible conditions of the Church in the sixteenth century, the decrees of Trent dealing with worship started the Counter Reformation where the Church most needed reform, in the moral and spiritual lives of the people.

In its laudable effort to safeguard the validity of the sacraments and insure doctrinal orthodoxy in ritual forms, Trent stressed the objective side of the liturgy and gave special prominence to what had to be done in order to protect the essentials of Catholic piety. Yet it also opened the way for exploring the subjective needs of worshipers—but without much encouragement from Rome. The Protestant departure was too near and too painful to risk another schism in Catholic unity.

All the while voices were raised urging ways of celebrating divine service to bring out more clearly its original, uncomplicated lines, and to produce a living liturgy in which the participants had a rightful share. Gradually there developed a historical science of liturgy, with Mabillon (1632–1707), Martène (1654–1739) and Lebrun (1661–1729) taking the lead. This gave the movement a sound footing, though colored by a strong emphasis on restoration of the past.

Unfortunately the movement became compromised by political and religious troubles, and ended by drifting into the backwash of a narrow Jansenism. Led by Antoine Arnauld (1612–1694), the Jansenists succeeded in quashing the practice of early and frequent reception of the sacraments. According to Arnauld, sinners should perform a long and solitary penance before absolution, and communion should be forbidden to everyone "in whom there is not yet the purest love of God, unmixed with any lesser affection."[1] Rome waited fifty years before condemning Arnauld, mainly because so many bishops in France and Holland had sided with the Jansenist leader.

Jansenism had penetrated every country in Europe and Anglo-Saxon America and should be seen as the backdrop against which the modern liturgical movement came into existence. Late in the nineteenth century, Catholics were still generally prohibited from receiving the Eucharist until adolescence and a series of documents from Rome (1885 to 1890) witness to the need for special permission to receive daily. In 1890 religious superiors were forbidden "to prescribe by their own authority the days on which their subjects have either to abstain or to receive Holy Communion."[2]

Essential to the Jansenist spirit, which derived from Calvinism, was a rigid concept of morality stemming from the idea of a depraved human nature. Joined to this was a strong antipathy to Roman authority in the area of morals and the liturgy.

PIUS X TO JOHN XXIII. Several factors conspired to make Pius X the pioneer in the Catholic liturgical revival. The Pope's own antecedents, his years as a parish priest, and above all his personal devotion to the Eucharist made him conscious of the harm done to souls who only seldom received the sacraments and whose ritual practices were divorced from the needs and difficulties of daily life.

Furthermore he realized that the root of the problem lay not among the faithful but among those who were to guide the people in the way of salvation. Theologians were undecided, e.g., on what precise conditions were required for frequent reception. In principle they agreed on the value of the Eucharist as a means of sanctification; but in practice they were divided on the proper dispositions that were needed. The majority held for stringent conditions, not excluding the conquest of inordinate affections. If a man was too ardent in loving his wife, he should abstain from communion!

Every important phase of Catholic worship and sacramental practice was radically improved during the short pontificate of the former Giuseppe Sarto. In 1905 he issued the decree on frequent communion whose basic provision was to interpret the word *frequent* as "daily" and to reduce the necessary dispositions to a minimum.

> Frequent and daily Communion, as a thing most earnestly desired by Christ our Lord and the Catholic Church, should be open to all the faithful, of whatever rank or condition in life: so that no one who is in the state of grace, and who approaches the holy table with a right and devout intention, can lawfully be hindered from receiving.[3]

To appreciate how lenient this was, it may be recalled that moralists, utterly free from doctrinal Jansenism, were nevertheless very strict in the conditions demanded for licit reception. The standard manual in *Moral Theology* through the 1800s was authored by St. Alphonsus Liguori (1696–1787). The founder of the Redemptorists instructed confessors that the Eucharist could be given daily only to people who "live free from affection to any venial sin . . . much given to mental prayer and strive towards perfection, no longer falling into sin, even fully deliberate venial sin."[4] Needless to say, few persons qualified.

Five years later, still opposing Jansenism, the Pope declared "the abuses we are condemning arise from the fact that those who distinguished one age of discretion for Penance and another for the Eucharist were in error." He decided there must be no such distinction. "The age of discretion for Confession is the time when one can distinguish between right and wrong, that is, when one arrives at a certain use of reason, and in like manner, for Holy Communion, is required the age when one can distinguish between ordinary bread and the Bread of the Holy Eucharist, which is also the age when a child attains the use of reason."[5] The formal decree is very explicit, and has never been rescinded:

> The age of discretion for both Confession and Holy Communion is that in which a child begins to use his reason. This is around the age of

seven, more or less. From that time on a person begins to be bound by the precept of both Confession and Communion.[6]

For confession, it was assumed that slight faults could be committed, and the child needed strength to overcome them; for communion it was likewise assumed that the child needed sacramental grace to grow in the love of God and of neighbor. In each case, the focus was on a human nature far more noble than the one conceived by Jansenist theology. Pius X also adverted to the changing times, when the social climate in which children were being reared was increasingly seductive for the young. They needed divine assistance from the dawn of reason.

Thematic in all of St. Pius' legislation on the liturgy was a concern to catholicize the ritual expression of the faith, in contrast with the Jansenist approach to Christianity. In the documents, he spoke of the "Jansenist poison"[7] which limited God's salvific work to the predestined—capable of rigorist asceticism; which denied man's free cooperation with grace and opted for an individualistic approach to God, apart from the historic Church founded by Christ as the sacrament of salvation. The Pope also wanted to make sure that Catholic worship was thoroughly biblical yet not burdensome, and he urged the faithful to become more conscious of the Christian calendar.

A series of reforms was instituted along these lines. In 1903 was promulgated what a Protestant commentator called "the great musical directive in Roman Catholic Church history." After emphasizing that sacred music must possess holiness, goodness of form, and universality, the Pope praised Gregorian chant in words that good Gregorianists have memorized:

> These qualities are found most perfectly in Gregorian Chant, which is therefore the proper chant of the Roman Church, the only chant which she has inherited from the ancient Fathers, which she has jealously guarded for so many centuries in her liturgical books, which she directly proposes to the faithful as her own music, which she prescribes exclusively for some parts of her liturgy, and which recent studies have so happily restored to its original integrity.[8]

Few elements of contemporary history illustrate more clearly the sweeping changes in Christian piety than a comparison of this praise of Gregorian chant and the *de facto* liturgical practices in many parts of the Catholic world.

In 1911 the Roman Breviary was revised. The Sunday office was restored to its dignity. On week days the ferial office regained prominence. Many accessories were no longer obligatory: the offices of the Blessed Virgin and the Dead, along with other prayers like the gradual and penitential psalms. Invocations were shortened and the Litany of the Saints was relegated to the Rogation Days, connected with Ascension and St. Mark's.

Encouraged by these reforms, liturgists in Germany organized in Holy Week of 1914 the first Liturgical Week for laymen at Maria Laach, the Benedictine abbey near Koblenz. Many consider this the beginning of the most prominent phase of the liturgical movement—active participation of the laity. At Maria Laach, the dialogue Mass was introduced with participating laymen. Scholarly publications followed: the *Liturgiegeschichtliche Quellen und Forschungen* (1918); the *Ecclesia Orans* series from 1920; the *Jahrbuch für Liturgiewissenschaft* (1921), which became the *Archiv für Liturgiewissenschaft* (1950). Similar Liturgical Weeks were sponsored elsewhere, until in 1930 the First International Liturgical Congress was held at Antwerp in Belgium.

Periodicals on the liturgy began to appear in all the major languages of Europe and America. *Orate Fratres* (later *Worship*) started publication in 1926 under the Benedictines at St. John's Abbey in Minnesota; *La Maison-Dieu* began at Paris in 1945. One evidence that this revival was late taking root in Anglo-Saxon countries is the fact that Rome had a regular journal on matters liturgical, the *Ephemerides Liturgicae,* since 1881.

One writer whose publications caused some stir on the score of orthodoxy was Dom Odo Casel, of Maria Laach. His "mystery-theology," developed in the twenties and thirties, aroused great interest among Catholics and Protestants alike.

Casel was challenged by Jesuit scholars (Umberg, Hanssens, and Prümm) on his main thesis: that the Mass is a liturgical re-presentation of all the mysteries of Christ's life and not only the sacrificial death on the cross. He appealed to the newly discovered practices among tribal peoples, quoting in support the authority of Alfred Loisy:

> Liturgical symbolism, Loisy rightly declares, presents itself in the primitive cults as a naïve imitation and in the course of religious development it strives toward a more and more idealized symbolism. However, if this symbolism would remain religious it must always in-

corporate within itself a considerable amount of mystical realism; without this it would only be a spiritual entertainment and an aesthetic pleasure, a theatrical presentation, but not a holy action, an offering or a sacrament.[9]

It was unfortunate, at the time, that Casel identified his theories with known Modernists like Loisy. It gave his critics ready ammunition without coming to grips with his thesis. It also strengthened the suspicion that in his effort to account for the whole span of Christ's action in the Mass and, indeed, in all the sacraments, Casel was obscuring the distinctive bodily presence of Christ in the Eucharist. His critics urged that he seemed to reduce the difference between Christ's presence in the Eucharist and the other sacraments almost to one of degree rather than of kind. Some of his followers took this interpretation, although Casel himself unquestionably believed in a real corporeal Christ under the Eucharistic species.

Apart from the controversy, Casel touched on a crucial aspect of the liturgical renewal in the Catholic Church. He brought to light a concept of mystery which, many feel, had been overshadowed by the aftermath of the Reformation. As he saw it, the ancient understanding of Christian Mystery was of an altogether concrete visible, tangible, and audible reality. When the liturgy was enacted, its actuality consisted not only in concrete circumstances but in an *action* which transpired before the eyes of the spectators, in which they themselves took an active part. "*Do* this in remembrance of me," Christ was recalled as saying.

In pre-Reformation times, Casel argued, the Catholic liturgy embraced as part of its very nature this "plastic objectivity." With the Renaissance stress on literalness we meet the "one-sidedness of a silent, passive devotion" *to* Christ. Even the Mass came to be conceived in these terms. The Reformation denied the objective dispensation of grace through the sacramental mysteries. Trent protected their objective character by clear definitions, but in the process something of their subjective value lay undeveloped. The great need is to restore that rich idea of the early Church, when the Mass (and all the sacraments) were seen as man's active cooperation *with* Christ in reliving now what the Savior had done in times past.

Casel's insights have been justly censured for theological imprecision and sometimes for ambiguity that verges on illuminism. He conceded as much by reworking his language and deepening his knowledge of the Old Testament. The latent Hellenism he thought he saw in the Christian mysteries later turned out to be Hebrew revelation which he had previously missed.

But Casel also represents a turning point in the Church's contemporary understanding of sacramental worship. Man's collective consciousness, his cultivated pragmatism and awareness of power as a human being to do things and produce effects that truly emanate from inside his own mind and will, are reflected in the active communal participation which Dom Odo spent a lifetime advocating as essential to the liturgy in the modern world. People see themselves as coproducers, and not merely onlookers, in every enterprise, including that which pertains to the spirit.

By 1922 Rome gave formal approval for Dialogue Masses, and six years later Pius XI published a special *Constitution on Sacred Music* in which strong recognition was given of the need for active involvement by the laity. "It is absolutely necessary," the Pope said, "that the faithful should attend the sacred actions, not as outsiders or silent spectators, but thoroughly imbued with the beauty of the liturgy . . . so that they may join their voices to those of priest and choir in accordance with antiphonal rules."[10]

While specialists and scholars were discussing the needs for more open liturgical forms, zealots were busy—notably in Germany—urging practices and advocating such principles that the bishops and finally Rome intervened. One of the issues was the right of the Holy See to direct ritual reform. A meeting of the German hierarchy at Fulda in 1940 organized a liturgial referendum to deal with the crisis which involved such figures as Romano Guardini and Josef Jungmann favoring, and Max Kassiepe and August Dörner opposing the liturgical innovations.

To meet the double challenge, sparked by the German situation but soon penetrating elsewhere, Pius XII issued three encyclical letters on the Church, the Bible, and the Liturgy—to encourage authentic progress and check the swelling tide of aberration.

In *Mystici Corporis* (1943), the Pope clarified the fundamental premise of Catholic worship: that when Christ offers the Eucharistic sacrifice, it is the whole Church which joins with Christ as priest and victim in the oblation. In *Divino Afflante Spiritu* (1943), he opened the door to retranslating the Scriptures for liturgical use by going beyond the Latin Vulgate (fifth century) to the earlier Hebrew and

Greek manuscripts. And in *Mediator Dei* (1947), he explained the priesthood of all believers, the importance of personal piety to make the liturgy effective, and the necessity of a historic priesthood to consecrate the sacred elements at Mass. Frequent confession, benediction, thanksgiving after communion, and the recitation of the Breviary were highly recommended.

The single most influential factor that spurred on the movement for greater lay involvement was the war experience—actually from 1941 to 1945—when several million Catholics in service and civilian life found in the liturgy the solace and strength they needed during those terrible years. Emergency adjustments of ritual and administration of the sacraments, but especially the discovery of how much the Mass and communion, confession and anointing meant in times of crisis and peril of death awakened a deep sense of appreciation even among nominal Catholics. When seven hundred American army and navy chaplains were asked in 1944 whether "the public recitation of certain permissible parts of the Mass in the vernacular would result in a more fruitful lay participation," eighty per cent answered with an unqualified affirmative.[11]

During the next decade, special concessions were made by Rome for different countries. In 1947 Belgium could have an evening Mass on Sundays and holy days; in the same year a bilingual *Rituale* was approved for France; in 1948 Japanese bishops were permitted evening Masses under certain conditions; in the same year a few Polish priests were allowed to celebrate evening Mass daily; a year later the Holy Office authorized the translation into Mandarin Chinese of the Roman Missal, except for the Canon; also in 1949 India began to have regular evening Masses and the Eucharistic fast was reduced for a number of dioceses. At the same time Indian bishops were practically ordered to expedite new ritual books in the most important native dialects. In 1950 a German *Rituale* was formally approved by Rome, and in the next year the Easter Vigil was restored, at first experimentally for one year. In 1952 an official German translation of the Canon of the Mass was made. Next year the universal Church had evening Masses approved and the Eucharistic fast drastically modified.

The fast before communion shows the rapid pace in Catholic liturgical practice. Complete fast from food and drink, from midnight was widespread in the fourth century, and by the Middle Ages was mandatory everywhere. Within ten years all this was changed. In 1953 the obligation was reduced to complete abstinence from solid food but permission for water at any time and for liquids (except alcoholic) up to one hour before communion was granted. Four years later, the permission was extended to solid food and alcoholic beverages up to three hours before receiving. And in 1964, at the close of the third session of the Vatican Council, Paul VI reduced the precept to complete abstinence from everything except water and medicine for only the last hour.

Pius XII's constitution in 1953, *Christus Dominus,* was more than a legislative document. It typified the Church's ability to adapt to changing circumstances, provided the alteration of a divine law is not involved. Reasons for the radical modification were historical ("new conditions of time"), psychological ("grave difficulties apt to deter people"), humanitarian ("travel . . . health . . . labors . . . missionaries . . . late hour"), sociological ("workmen in factories, transportation, shipping . . . mothers . . . children"), and especially sacramental ("to promote the reawakened devotion toward the Eucharist").[12] An unpredecented growth in reception of the sacrament among Catholics was the immediate result of this adjustment to the times.

Further changes, approved by Rome, up to the eve of the Vatican Council included simplification of the Mass rubrics (1955), setting conditions for concelebration (1957), vernacular hymns at the Eucharistic sacrifice (1958), and omission of prayers after Mass (1960).

In his message at the opening of the Second Vatican Council in 1962, Pope John XXIII told the Fathers why he had convoked the solemn assembly: "The greatest concern of the ecumenical council is this: that the sacred deposit of Christian doctrine should be guarded and taught more efficaciously." On his recommendation, the council first undertook the *aggiornamento* of the sacred liturgy, whose essence must be preserved at all costs, but whose expression should be accommodated to "the new forms of life introduced into the modern world."[13]

SECOND VATICAN COUNCIL. A cursory estimate of the Vatican Council's reform of the liturgy would say it was revolutionary. Certainly many of its provisions called for a complete overhauling of ritual forms. The impression in some Catholic circles is that something like a nuclear bomb hit the uniform pattern of the Church's worship since the Constitution *Sacrosanctum Concilium* was promulgated by Paul VI on December 4, 1963.

In spite of appearances to the contrary, the Council's reforms were only that and nothing more. Years of study by the Church's finest experts, building on the experience of a half a century of widespread adaptation to present-day needs produced a body of norms which are in many ways less radical than the changes made during the Counter Reformation. There was nothing, for example, comparable to the exuberant number of saints' feasts suppressed by the Council of Trent. One major difference between Trent and Vatican II is that the critical need in the sixteenth century was to produce some semblance of liturgical unity in a forest of competing multiplicity. In the twentieth century, the need was to expand and diversify what the Church recognized is an essential unity.

The main contribution of the twenty-first ecumenical Council to liturgical reform was its precise, yet existential definition of the liturgy. Without a clear notion of what to improve it would have been naïve to talk seriously about improvement. According to the Council, the Christian liturgy is the public worship of God, in which the whole Mystical Body, Christ the head and the faithful as members, is engaged. Its purpose is to honor and thank the Divine Majesty, to ask God's mercy and the help of his grace, and to direct the faithful in the way of salvation.

The focus of the liturgy, therefore, and the aim of all its expression is God. It is theo-centric, because God is the center of all genuine ritual; and, it is theo-final because the glory of God is the decisive reason why there are any rites in Christianity at all. Man's satisfaction and the benefits that a worshiper acquires are useful and highly desirable. But they are not the ultimate goal of the liturgy—no more than the real purpose of religion is to profit the believer. Religion is either directed to God or it is spurious.

Nowhere in the sixteen documents of Vatican II is the reader more conscious of being in the atmosphere of faith, that deeply qualifies the human spirit and penetrates beyond the veils of space and time; that sees and feels what those who do not believe do not see and cannot feel. Those who believe, worship. Those who do not believe, do not worship, which is not the same thing as going through a prescribed ritual.

Four relationships of man to God are identified in the *Constitution on the Liturgy*, and repeated in other documents of the Council. They are so fundamental that without them anything else said about the liturgy would be meaningless. Those who worship do so because they acknowledge the divine transcendence, they recognize God's goodness, they understand his mercy, and they appeal to his infinite generosity.

The Council uses different words to express each relationship. They are familiar words, but the conciliar documentation gave them an uncommon depth of meaning. Christian worship is intended (1) "to praise God" and by it "God is perfectly glorified," (2) to be a "eucharist" instituted for "giving thanks to God," (3) like Christ "to heal the contrite of heart" as a means for the "achievement of our reconciliation," and (4) to effect "the sanctification of man" through the channels of "grace poured forth upon us."[14]

God is first of all to be worshiped because he is God. He is the Being who cannot not exist, whose existence is from eternity to eternity, and who therefore wants as the first law of the Christian religion that those who profess the faith "become true adorers whom the Father seeks."[15]

He is also to be worshiped because of his great goodness to mankind and to each person in particular. Everything we possess is from the divine bounty, and among the special reasons for being grateful is "the unspeakable gift" we have received "in Christ Jesus."[16]

God deserves to receive worship because man has sinned and deserves to be punished. So true is this that an accurate, though incomplete, definition of the liturgy would say it was that "through which the work of our redemption is accomplished."[17] To exclude man's sinfulness from the ambit of Christian ritual is to dechristianize it. If the greatest sacrificial act of the perfect Man was his voluntary death on the cross to redeem the world, the continuation of that act through the sacraments and the Mass must have the same bearing on deliverance from sin and its consequences.

Finally, Christians worship God in order to obtain through the sacramental rites the infusion and increase, the healing and restoration of the divine life of grace which is necessary for salvation. In two paragraphs are summarized all that distinguishes Catholic Christianity as a cultic religion from every other form of ritual approach to God.

Incorporated in the Church through Baptism, the faithful are destined by the baptismal character for the worship of the Christian religion. . . . They are more perfectly bound to the Church by the sacrament of Confirmation, and the Holy Spirit endows them with special strength so that they are more strictly obliged to spread and defend the faith.

. . . Taking part in the Eucharistic sacrifice, which is the fount and apex of the whole Christian life, they offer the Divine Victim to God, and offer themselves along with It. . . . Strengthened in Holy Communion by the Body of Christ, they then manifest in a concrete way that unity of the people of God which is suitably signified and wondrously brought about by this most august sacrament.

Those who approach the sacrament of Penance obtain pardon from the mercy of God for the offence committed against Him and are at the same time reconciled with the Church. . . . By the sacred Anointing of the sick and the prayer of her priests, the whole Church commends the sick to the suffering and glorified Lord, asking that He may lighten their suffering and save them. . . . Those of the faithful who are consecrated by Holy Orders are appointed to feed the Church in Christ's name with the word and the grace of God. Finally, Christian spouses, in virtue of the sacrament of Matrimony, whereby they signify and partake of the mystery of that unity and fruitful love which exists between Christ and His Church, help each other to attain to holiness in their married life and in the rearing and education of their children.[18]

So much for the definition of the liturgy, in which the Council drew on the Church's past wisdom and applied it to the present age. But definition is not yet reformation, and the council's objective was to lay down norms for reforming, in the sense of reshaping, the spectrum of Catholic worship to meet the needs of today.

Like the definition of the liturgy, so its reformation is summarized under four principles—out of which the practice is expected to grow.

Heading these principles is a set of norms that quite alone would identify the liturgical reformation as distinctively Catholic. It is assumed that public worship is regulated, and "the regulation of the sacred liturgy depends solely on the authority of the Church, that is, on the Apostolic See and, as laws may determine, on the bishop."[19] No single provision of the Council promises to be more severly tested than this one: that ritual changes are valid only if authorized, and authorization belongs to the teaching Church, which is the bishops under the Apostolic See.

Regulation, however, assumes that something needs to be regulated, and for this the Council indicates the sources on which the revised liturgical forms are to draw. They are "theological, historical and pastoral investigation," which means being scientific; "experience derived from recent liturgical reforms and from the indults conceded to various places," which concerns the practical; and assurance that "no innovations [be made] unless the good of the Church genuinely and certainly requires them," which is essentially the exercise of prudential judgment.[20]

Overarching the use of these means is the main focus of the liturgy of the future. It is to be biblical, "for it is from the Scriptures that lessons are read . . . that actions and signs derive their meaning" and most of the ritual prayers and sayings have come.[21]

Following this broad perspective are three normative premises without which there might be a liturgical renewal but not a thorough reform. They imply that certain aspects of the Church's cultic life had got out of hand, and that a new spirit needs to be infused. By its nature, the liturgy should be communal and hierarchic, instructive and pastoral, and fully adjusted to the culture and traditions of the people by whom it is used.

The Church's rites are, in a sense, public and social by nature. But this fact should be actually manifest. Consequently, whenever the rite in question makes "provision for communal celebration, involving the presence and active participation of the faithful, this way of celebrating them is to be preferred, so far as possible, to a celebration that is individual and quasi-private."[22] Both factors are necessary to make the rite communal: physical presence of an assembly, and the audiovisual involvement of a group.

Unlike casual group prayer, even though organized, the liturgy should include persons who are exercising different functions on diversified levels—something like the combined melody in a musical symphony, where each member has a share in the production of a masterful whole. Everyone does his part, but no more. So, too, "in liturgical celebrations each person, minister or layman, who has an office to perform, should do all of, *but only,* those parts which pertain to his office by the nature of the rite and the principles of liturgy."[23] As experience shows, this puts a maximum restraint on the natural tendency to self-display; it also helps to create an inspiring ensemble, in which everyone somehow shares and without whose contribution the corporate worship of God would be impossible or only as perfect as it is truly cooperative.

Although its primary purpose is cultic, the liturgy is also meant to be didactic and directional. The faithful are supposed to learn from participating in the Church's ritual, "for in the liturgy God speaks to His people and Christ is still proclaiming His Gospel."[24] A score of corollaries follow. Ritual prayers and symbols should be marked by a "noble simplicity," and "normally should not require much explanation." Since the Bible is the best source of instruction, "there is to be more reading from Holy Scripture," and that more varied and suitable for circumstances and times. The sermon must become an essential "part of the liturgical service," and its content should draw "mainly from scriptural and liturgical sources."

While the stress will be on the vernacular, "the use of Latin is to be preserved in the Latin rites." But the mother tongue is to be increasingly used in the offering of Mass and the administration of the sacraments.[25] This, too, can be instructive: in teaching the mysteries of faith and revealing the Church's essential unity.

Of far-reaching consequence was the Council's decision to adapt the liturgy to the culture and traditions of different people. First a general attitude: "the Church has no wish to impose a rigid uniformity in matters which do not implicate the faith or the good of the whole community." This has a venerable ancestry, testified by the variety of liturgical rites in communion with Rome—like the Alexandrian used in Egypt and Ethiopia or the Byzantine among the Greeks, Russians, and Ukranians.

But here the council was looking to the future. It wished to provide for new peoples yet to enter the Church. Their "genius and talents" (culture) and "way of life" (tradition) are, if possible, to remain intact and even admitted into the liturgy itself, provided they are "not indissolubly bound up with superstition and error" and "harmonize with the true and authentic spirit" of Catholic Christianity.[26] The scope envisioned by this provision was the creation, if necessary, of new rites.

Parallel with such complete innovation was the foresight of needed adaptations in the Roman rite "to different groups, regions and peoples, especially in mission lands," as long as "the substantial unity of the Roman rite is preserved."[27] A single detail like the Chinese respect for deceased ancestors or the American tradition for efficiency has deep implications in adjusting the liturgy.

NEW LITURGY. Faithful to the spirit of the Council, Pope Paul VI authorized the most complete revision of the *Roman Missal* since the Council of Trent, and a corresponding revision of the rites for all the sacraments.

For centuries the Mass used to begin with a psalm said at the foot of the altar in preparation for the confession followed by a number of penitential prayers. It was almost universally a dialogue between the priest and his server. In the revised ritual, the act of penitence which begins the Mass will always be performed by all present, priest and faithful, as a single family. "Each will acknowledge before God and his brethren that he has sinned."[28]

The offertory is another example. According to Justin's *Apology*, about A.D. 150, the offertory was a very simple rite. After the Gospel and homily, "we all rise to our feet and raise up prayers, and the bread and wine and water are brought. The one presiding raises up prayers and thanksgiving as best he may. And the people reply, 'Amen.'"[29] In the reformed ritual, the offering is symbolic, when the elements for sacrifice are carried to the altar. But the actual prayers are reduced to a minimum, and taken almost verbatim from the first-century liturgical document, the *Didache*, discovered at Constantinople in 1873 and fully authenticated only in the twentieth century. The passage from the *Didache* was prescribed "regarding the Eucharist." A synoptic comparison is revealing:

Didache	*New Missal*
Thou, Lord Almighty, hast created all things for the sake of thy name, and hast given food and drink for men to enjoy, that they may give thanks to thee. But to us thou hast vouchsafed spiritual food and drink and eternal life through Jesus, your Son.[30]	Blessed be thou, Lord God of all things, because we have received bread (wine) from thy bounty. We offer this fruit of the (vine) earth and of men's labor, that it may become for us the Bread of Life (a spiritual drink).

In keeping with the desire for greater simplicity, the rubrics no longer require that the chalice be plated with gold; the altar need be covered with only one cloth, instead of three; and, while statues in church are commended, they are not to be "excessively multiplied."

To better symbolize active participation in the Eucharist, at least some of the faithful should receive portions of the consecrated host which the celebrant himself receives. Women are permitted, within limits, to assist the priest at the altar. In funeral Masses, a wide option of prayers is given to meet a variety of family situations. Always to be kept in view is the common priesthood of the faithful, which they are to exercise according to their state of life.

What complicates the picture is that the reform of the liturgy coincided with a positive revolution in theology, and the two movements were either confused or overlapped—with results that only time will fully reveal.

In two countries the coincidence had more serious effects than elsewhere, mainly because of the publicity received. In 1966 the Dutch hierarchy approved a controversial catechism that was disapproved by Rome; and supported some very extreme decisions of the Netherlands Pastoral Council (1970). Both events had direct bearing on the liturgy. In 1969 the American bishops ordered a nation-wide survey of diocesan and regular priests—along lines similar to the Dutch program.

Thematic to the whole issue is the nature of the priesthood, whether it is cultic or essentially functional and the correlative meaning of the Eucharist, as presence, sacrament, and sacrifice.

Sample references from Dutch and American statements, backed by some of their bishops, indicate the gravity of the problem.

According to the Dutch Catechism, the general priesthood of the faithful is "truly the central and important thing," whereas "the priestly office whereby bishops govern the Church is [only] a *service* through which the people of God are priestly." Hence "it is *not surprising* that the Reformation took another view of this office [and] shrank from admitting that Christ's salvation was so earth-bound that it could be found in men with holy orders."[31] Not surprisingly, the Dutch Pastoral Council decided that the priestly ministry is conferred not by episcopal ordination but by the Christian community.

The parallel document, which "the American bishops have commissioned," is nominally "a comprehensive study of the Catholic priesthood in the United States and of American priests living abroad."[32] Its function, however, is substantially the same as the vote of the Dutch council of priests and laity. Thousands of priests were asked to give their "opinion" on the most fundamental mysteries of faith: whether "ordination confers on the priest a new status or a permanent character which makes him essentially different from the laity within the church," whether "the priesthood as we know it is a transitory institutional role," whether "being a priest really means being the liturgical leader of the Christian community," whether "there is no ontological difference between the priest and the laity, since all share in the common priesthood of Christ given at baptism; the difference is mainly one of assigned duties in the church."[33]

During the Council sessions, two conflicting concepts of the priesthood came into view. The English *peritus* to the Council, Charles Davis, publicly admitted this of himself, shortly after he broke with Rome. But the actual confrontation took several years to develop, and, where fully mature, faced the Catholic Church with its most serious ritual crisis in four hundred years.

What added fuel to the controversy was the calculated pastoral nature of the revised liturgy, and the absence of theological terms in official Roman commentaries. This aroused the suspicion of some who felt that Rome was soft on the unorthodox or at least unaware of what was going on. Among other "concessions," had not Paul VI practically eliminated (1966) the centuries-old Friday abstinence and Lenten fast?

In 1969 a group of European theologians published their criticism of the forthcoming *Novus Ordo Missae*, the New Form of the Mass, and the former Assessor of the Holy Office, Cardinal Ottaviani, wrote a personal letter to Paul VI. According to the critics, "the *Novus Ordo* represents, both as a whole and in its details, a striking departure from the Catholic theology of the Mass as it was formulated in . . . the Council of Trent."[34] Ottaviani later publicly declared his complete adherence to the New Liturgy.

What the cardinal and those who drafted the ten-thousand-word critique objected to was the great stress on the Mass as a communal experience, of priest and people, and the corresponding underplay, as they saw it, of the Eucharist as sacrifice and sacrament. The Mass, they felt, was being, "Protestantized."

The indictment of the new missal provoked counterdefense. Paul VI defended the reformed liturgy and pleaded for patience and objectivity, while admitting that some of the changes made were extraordinary, but with no compromise on the faith.

Several times in public addresses, the Pope returned to the same defense, aware of the dangers of schism, compounded by the fact that some who still called themselves Catholic no longer believed in the "traditional essence" of the Mass. Thus delegates to the "European Assembly of Priests," which met in Rome during the synod of bishops (1969), drafted a formal statement to that effect. Complaining that "the ministry of the priest is today still considered essentially under its cultic aspect," offering Mass and distributing the sacraments, they declared that such "distinction between the sacred and profane is completely alien to the Gospels. It is taken from the pagan and pre-

Christian religions."[35] No priest is empowered to say Mass, any more or less than any layman.

The most dramatic change, occasioned by the strong reaction, was a complete redrafting of the definition of the Mass. Compare Article 7 of the *New Order of the Mass* (April 3, 1969) with the same Article 7 of the *New Roman Missal* (March 26, 1970). Only the latter text is definitive.

New Order	*New Missal*
The Lord's Supper of the Mass is the sacred *synaxis* or assembly of the people of God united under the presidency of the priest to celebrate the memorial of the Lord. Therefore in the local congregation of the Holy Church the promise of Christ is fulfilled: "Where two or three are gathered in my name, I am there in the midst of them" (Matthew 18:30).	At the Mass, or the Lord's Supper, the people of God are called together to celebrate the Memorial of the Lord or the Eucharistic Sacrifice. The priest presides and represents the person of Christ. For this reason, the promise of Christ, "Where two or three are gathered in my name, I am there in the midst of them" (Matthew 18:30), is particularly applicable to such a local assembly of the Holy Church. At the celebration of Mass, in which the Sacrifice of the Cross is perpetuated, Christ is really present in the community itself which is gathered together in His name, in the person of the minister, in His word, and especially in a substantial and continuous manner under the Eucharistic species.

Another aspect of Catholic piety that touches on the liturgy but has deeper implications for the Church in Northern Europe and America is the sudden decline in popular devotions. Novenas and benediction, rosary services and the Way of the Cross, days of recollection and parish missions in some parts of the United States are practically extinct, and elsewhere have become increasingly rare.

Although a drop in devotional practices could be seen before the Second Vatican Council, it became pronounced only after the midsixties. No single reason fully explains what happened. The Council itself encouraged such practices, adding only the obvious precautions:

Popular devotions of the Christian people are to be highly commended, provided they accord with the laws and norms of the Church, above all when they are ordered by the Apostolic See.

Devotions proper to individual churches also have a special dignity if they are undertaken by mandate of the bishops according to customs or books lawfully approved.

But these devotions should be so drawn up that they harmonize with the liturgical seasons, accord with the sacred liturgy, are in some fashion derived from it, and lead the people to it, since in fact, the liturgy by its very nature far surpasses any of them.[36]

There is no evidence that the decline in extra-liturgical piety was due to zeal for liturgical purity, or that excessive devotion suddenly brought on a reaction. A host of other factors, some vague and others more clear, contributed to what has been described as the rise of Puritanism in Roman Catholic worship.

Cultural pressure was a factor. Writing in 1954, the Oratorian convert from Calvinism, Louis Bouyer, charged that the Baroque and Romantic mentality induced a false notion of worship. "The chief focus of liturgical life," he charged, "was no more the Mass, which included too many elements out of harmony with the mentality of the times. Instead, Solemn Exposition of the Blessed Sacrament, a ceremony created and developed just in time to satisfy the new tastes of the age." Moreover, "all this was pervaded with that type of sentimental piety, those pantings after divine love, capable of competing successfully with the ecstatic expressions of human love fashionable in the poetry of the time."[37]

The ecumenical movement also played a role. Since many devotions involved the saints, some Catholics thought this would injure the cause of Christian unity. Priests removed statues from churches and on rare occasion rosaries were publicly torn in the pulpit to symbolize the changing times.

Closer to the real reason was the gradual accultration of Catholicism to the environment. Not unremarkably, decrease in popular devotions followed the practice dominant in a country, or a region, or even in sectors of the same city. As expressions of religious faith waned among the people in general, Catholics soon fitted into the same pattern. Not only public devotions, but the gamut of external marks of religious identity, e.g., among priests and religious, began to decline. Those who reflected on the process defended what was happening on the score of making themselves more acceptable to the world and less ostentatious in their piety.

Public and private invocation of the Virgin Mary exemplifies this accommodating tendency. The most famous Marian shrine in the Catholic world, after Lourdes, is Fatima in Portugal, where the Virgin is said to have appeared several times between May 13 and October 13 of 1917 to three children at Cova da Iria, north of Lisbon. They reported her message recommending the frequent recitation of the rosary, mortification for the conversion of sinners, and invocation of her Immaculate Heart. The apparitions were declared worthy of belief in 1930 and devotion to Our Lady of Fatima was authorized under the title of Our Lady of the Rosary. Millions of pilgrims have visited the Portuguese shrine, which has none of the dramatic appeal of Lourdes, and in 1967 Pope Paul VI personally went to Fatima where he pleaded for greater reliance on Mary's intercessory power with Christ and for the daily recitation of the rosary. His visit and message were practically ignored by the news media of certain countries and were a source of embarrassment in Catholic circles where the cultural climate was unfavorable to "religious emotionalism."

CLERGY IN CRISIS. The sweeping changes in the Catholic liturgy authorized by the Council contributed to an identity crisis among the clergy, the official custodians of the Church's ritual and sacramental life. But equally critical was the dilemma which the Council itself raised for some people by simultaneously stressing two quite different roles of the priesthood in the Catholic Church.

In the Constitution on the Liturgy, the accent was on the priest's function as dispenser of the sacraments, his "cultic" role as this came to be known. In the later decree on the Ministry and Life of Priests, another emphasis appeared. In the most unequivocal terms, it was stated that "priests, as co-workers with their bishops, have the primary duty (*primum habent officium*) of proclaiming the Gospel of God to all."[38] The words *prophetic* and *ministerial* have been used to describe this second dimension of the Catholic clergy.

Objectively the two roles are compatible, as historic Catholicism understands the priesthood; but subjectively they touch on a most critical issue: how are priests to view their place in the modern Church?

Underlying the problem were questions of faith: whether any form of ministry as mediation between God and man is still valid, on the assumption that for many neither God nor the need of his grace is viable any more; whether the particular kind of ministry, professed by the Catholic Church, should not be reformed in the twentieth century as it had been in the sixteenth, where the essential function is no longer mediatorial but only ministerial.

But even assuming the fullness of Roman Catholic belief, there were still the practical questions posed by stressing the duty of a priest as prophetic leader and the instrument of God's message to the faithful. Two questions especially came to the surface with lightning speed and with devastating consequences. Accurate figures are not available; but the loss of several thousand priests to the active ministry in less than five years after the Second Vatican Council was symptomatic. Celibacy and the priests' autonomy became the subject of hundreds of articles, scores of books, and as recently as 1969 threatened to sever the relationship of at least one country's hierarchy and the Holy See.

Defenders of optional celibacy and of greater freedom for the priest uniformly urged both privileges as necessary means for implementing the new-found responsibility in the priestly ministry, beyond ritual and the liturgy that, some said, for too long had dominated Catholic thinking.

Before 1950, there was no serious opposition to clerical celibacy in the Catholic Church. Among the exceptions was the formation of a Polish National Church in the United States, one of whose provisions (in 1921) was for a married priesthood. The argument was that no church, outside the Roman Catholic, requires celibacy of its ministers. But the privilege was for a long time opposed by the laity "who thought it might soften unduly the lives of the priests,"[39] so that at first few of the clergy dared face the opposition.

A year before, Benedict XV excommunicated a minority of priests in Bohemia who, among other things, urged the abolition of celibacy and formed a schismatical church to implement their program.

With the cessation of hostilities after the Second World War the problem arose of what to do about the priests—chiefly among those conscripted into the armed forces—who had contracted civil marriages during military service. Some had families already and were canonically excluded from the sacraments. After due processing, many of them were laicized. Their marriages were blessed by the Church, but they were not to exercise their priestly ministry. Although fully sanctioned by ecclesiastical authorities, these concessions were not generally known; and no policy was established.

In 1954, the same Pius XII who approved these laicizations published a major encyclical on "Holy Virginity," in which he upheld the traditional Catholic practice and corrected some popular misconceptions on celibacy.

The next year, the Pope issued a confidential document to all bishops in the world in which they were told to know whom they raised to the priesthood. They were, above all, to make sure beforehand that the men ordained knew exactly what a life of celibacy involved. The trouble Rome had was with priests who, after ordination, raised doubts about their real fitness or true motivation or right intention in receiving the sacrament of orders. Most of these *post factum* representations had to do with celibacy. This part of the document reads like a synopsis of what the media would later publicize on a world scale. It is also the best commentary on this publicity because it reveals the root cause of the problem: the massive ordination of some thousands of men who, if they had been more carefully screened, might not have assumed a burden which they were not naturally equipped to carry.

In the Roman directive, the hierarchy was told that "the chastity problem should ordinarily be resolved at least during the year preceding theology." This meant up to four years before actual ordination. One year's freedom from grave lapses was the absolute minimum before major Orders. "If after repeated testing doubt still remains regarding the student's vocation, he must be refused the priesthood."[40] No matter what other qualities he may have, they cannot compensate for certain necessary dispositions in the celibate priest.

When the Vatican Council opened, there was some talk about loosening the celibacy requirement for diocesan clergy. A number of prelates wanted the matter aired at the Council and were circulating petitions to that effect. Finally in October 1965, during the last session of the Council, Pope Paul VI personally informed the assembled Fathers that he intended to preserve the ancient law of celibacy of the clergy for the Latin rite.

The papal announcement was met with prolonged applause. The only parallel for the move since the Council began was the Pope's decision a year before to remove the subject of birth control from the agenda and turn it over to a special commission appointed by himself.

Pope Paul's action on both counts was in line with the attitude of his predecessor. John XXIII did not want birth control publicly debated before the Council. He was also adamant on celibacy. As recorded by his private secretary, Loris Capovilla, the Pope's dying wish was that priestly celibacy remain intact. This fact was brought to light seven years later, when some were appealing to his memory in favor of an optional married clergy. "Pope John was a fearless champion and enthusiastic defender of the law of celibacy. He praised it his whole life through, most significantly when he was on the point of death."[41]

From 1965 to 1970, a series of statements emanated from Rome, confirming and re-emphasizing the commitment to celibacy required of all priests in the Latin rite. Five conciliar documents treated of celibacy and one, *The Decree on the Ministry and Life of Priests*, explicitly declared, "Celibacy was at first recommended to priests. Then, in the Latin Church, it was imposed by law on all who were to be promoted to sacred orders. This legislation, to the extent to which it concerns those who are destined for the priesthood, this most holy Synod again approves and confirms."[42]

Parallel with the agitation in favor of birth control came a rising crescendo in the public press against mandatory celibacy. Paul VI's encyclical on *Priestly Celibacy* only fanned the flames of opposition in quarters that insisted priests should be free to choose whether to marry or not.

Then in 1970 the Dutch hierarchy bent under pressure of its "Pastoral Council" and approved its vote to abolish clerical celibacy. This sparked a reaction throughout the world.

Most of the Catholic hierarchy took strong exception to the Dutch prelates. Among the severest critics was Cardinal Bengsch, Bishop of Berlin. In a lengthy statement, he reminded the Dutch episcopate that collegiality meant agreement with the rest of the hierarchy, in agreement with the Pope. In the name of collegiality, they were "secularizing the message of Christ." The crux of the problem, he charged, was not whether the Church wants married priests. There are and always have been such in Roman Catholicism. The real issue is whether the Dutch still believe in the Catholic concept of the priesthood. Once the priesthood is defined "according to criteria proper to the social sciences of the day, and if the Church's mission is taken almost exclusively as an aid to the autonomous and secular development of man, then, of course, priestly celibacy will seem to be nonsense."[43]

The bishops of Yugoslavia, behind the Iron Curtain, listed sixteen reasons for not abrogating the law of celibacy. Reason seven read: "Celibacy as a witness is particularly necessary today when a wave of pan-sexualism is sweeping over the world, and sex is becoming the idol to which youth, real love, the joy of a pure conscience and life itself are sacrificed."[44]

The episcopate of Thailand took a different approach. They described the situation in Asia, where Buddhism is faithfully practiced.

Thailand is a predominantly Buddhist country, and in the whole country there are no fewer than two hundred thousand bonzes who strictly observe celibacy either for life or temporarily. In the teachings of Buddha and in the practice of twenty-five centuries, Buddhist monasticism has shown the world the value of celibacy for the honor of religion, in order that the bonze may be an example to believing people and as a means of purification.

It is for lack of a spiritual life, not nourished by prayer, mortification, and meditation, because of conformity to the world, that we now sadly witness a defection that is so harmful and unworthy of God's love.[45]

A new level of confrontation was reached in 1970 when Cardinal Suenens gave an interview to the Paris newspaper *Le Monde*, in which he publicly berated the Pope for refusing to listen to the pleas of so many distraught priests and seminarians who want to marry. Suenens accused the Pope of blocking two popular movements in the Church—optional celibacy and contraception, which "the world press reflects."[46] The answer would be to let each country decide for itself, whether to have optional or obligatory celibacy. His views were shared, among others, by those American bishops who encouraged the poll of several thousand priests about their desire to get married.

Along with optional celibacy, Catholic priests in some countries felt they needed more freedom in their ministry, always assuming that administration of the sacraments was only part (for some the lesser part) of their role in the priesthood. They chafed under a discipline which seemed to treat them like children, in which they were not given full opportunity to develop their talents for working with the laity, and were caught up in an "authoritarian structure" which they found repressive.

No set pattern is traceable among priests in this category. There were young, middle-aged, and old among them; men in religious communities and those "incardinated" in dioceses; the newly ordained and others who had years of "successful ministry" to their credit. Priest authors who tried to describe the situation found it hard to put into words, and yet all recognized what was happening—those who felt stifled and their confreres who did not consider themselves threatened.

Some of this ambiguity became world-wide knowledge when the English liturgist and *peritus* at the Vatican Council, Charles Davis, left the priestly ministry in 1966. Some months before his resignation, he analyzed the problem. He emphasized the lack of correspondence between the close personal relationships that many priests have with lay people and the institutional structures under which both still live in the Church.

> The slowness of existing structures to change is in fact having a noteworthy effect. Increasingly the Christian activity of reflective and earnest lay people is being carried on outside those structures or with only a nominal connexion with them. Catholics are meeting, discussing and acting together in informal groups, while having little outside the liturgy to do with the formal organization of the church. They look to sympathetic priests for support.[47]

Davis' own status was unique. He was professor at a school of theology, and not tied down to "liturgical duties" as were others for whom he ostensibly spoke. In fact, most clerical writers who took issue with the "institutional Church" and thought it hindered "the proper fulfillment of their role as priests" were not personally inhibited in pursuing the "prophetic" and "noncultic" side of the ministry, as "community formers" and "leaders of informal Christian gatherings."

Without minimizing the problem for many in the priesthood, the American bishops in 1968 suggested that its solution lay with the men themselves, and not with an upheaval in the Church's organization. The cost of adjusting the ancient Church to modern times was admittedly high, and the price was prohibitive if anyone tried to do it alone. Hence the urgent need for priests to work together as teams, to meet and discuss things in common, and be ready to support one another in a way that makes their celibacy meaningful.

> Priests must never become so involved in their personal pursuits, even in serving their people and others, that they no longer notice their brother priests whose needs may be deeper than their ability to express them. Priests often require special support because they bear in their hearts not only the cares of their own lives but the sufferings of their people and no small part of the solicitude of the Church herself.[48]

Brotherly charity among priests, they counseled, was a necessary condition for celibacy; and celibate charity which united like-minded men in the ministry could live with the problems of the age. Their corporate wisdom would resolve the paradox which to many seemed a contradiction; that the Catholic priest is not only a leader of men or teacher of God's word, but also a mediator with God and the channel of God's grace through the sacraments.

The Protestant Churches

It would be strange for the Catholic Church to go through a liturgical renaissance without a similar renewal taking place in world Protestantism. The churches of Reformation origin are also revising their traditional stance on ritual and, if anything, more drastically than their counterpart in Roman Catholicism.

The Protestant liturgical revival on a global scale started in 1910, at the World Missionary Conference in Edinburgh, Scotland. It was the first time the conference had met on the basis of national representation, and its most pressing problem was to reduce some fraction of the disunity which hindered the progress of the missions. The Anglo-Saxon element dominated the conference, primarily because of the large number of missionaries from English-speaking countries. Among these, the presence of Anglican societies in the High Church tradition proved decisive for the future of Christian unity and of Protestant liturgy.

Before Edinburgh the "High Church" groups had kept aloof from missionary conferences, suspecting the "Protestant" mind of their organizers and feeling they would have to keep silent about their Catholic interpretation of Anglicanism. "Low Church" segments had previously represented the Anglican Communion. Once the liturgical-minded High Churchmen joined, the mood began to change. Worship became one of the mainstays of Protestant evangelism and the liturgical movement entered the stream of world Protestantism.

Forty years later, the newly constituted World Council of Churches held a meeting at Lund in Sweden (1952) to assess the progress and to lay plans for the future on "Ways of Worship and Intercommunion." The decisions reached at Lund have been, in their way, as important as the Constitution on the Liturgy of the Vatican Council. Specific recommendations were made, to become the lode star for every important phase of Protestant ritualism in modern Christianity. The Churches were asked to concentrate on seven norms:

1. The cultivation of a sympathetic and reverent attitude by all Christian people towards all forms of worship, both "liturgical" and "nonliturgical," in which God confronts man.

2. Detailed scrutiny of the grounds upon which the worship of each communion is based, and in this light the re-examination of its attitude to that of others.

3. Reflection on the question: How far does the fact that there are varieties in forms of worship within the same communions make it possible to conceive of a similar rich diversity within a united Church?

4. Study of the liturgical movements going on in various parts of the world, coupled with study of the roots of modern antagonism to Christian worship in all its forms.

5. Thorough examination of the relationship between the unique sacrifice of Jesus Christ and man's response in worship and life.

6. An examination of the existing situation in which some Churches regard the preaching of the Gospel as well as the eucharistic act as essential for worship, whereas others regard the Eucharist as by itself containing the essential elements of worship.

7. A more detailed exploration, theological, metaphysical, and psychological, of mystery in relation to worship.[49]

This called for a complete reassessment of Protestant Christianity and a readjustment to what seemed imperative in the cause of Christian unity. Each step was filled with implications respecting the main families in Protestantism—the Lutheran, Reformed, Anglican, and Free Churches; and the main forms of Christianity that are not Protestant—Roman Catholicism and Eastern Orthodoxy. It was impossible to take the Lund recommendations seriously without touching on the foundations of Reformation ecclesiology.

Since then much has been written by specialists on every phase of the Lund report. What is more significant, each phase has been implemented in the interests of a more Christian way of life. Moreover, the liturgical development has been somewhat different in each of the four major traditions of twentieth-century Protestantism.

LUTHERANISM. Evangelical Churches have been strongly confessional in their teaching of the Gospel, with insistence on loyalty to the great confessions of faith—the Apostles' and Nicene creeds, the Confession of Augsburg and the two Catechisms of Luther. Even when they are less doctrinal and more biblical, they retain a firm hold on what they consider essential dogmas, to a degree not present in other inheritors of the Reformation. Articles of belief are a matter of principle with Lutherans.

As they entered the modern liturgical movement, their attitude was not so much to explore new types of ritual as to make sure that, in becoming more liturgical, they did not become less doctrinal. Worship forms and hymnology are traditional with the Lutheran bodies. No great need for progress there. More difficult to keep in balance was the increasing pressure for ritual unionism among the churches without losing in dogmatic stability.

Lutheran delegates to the World Council were explicit in what this meant to them. Where other, less doctrinally firm, denominations had no scruple melting their cultic differences, Lutherans were not so complacent. Among the official reports of the world ecumenical assembly was the explosive observation that, "The *best* preparation for the fuller unity to which we look forward would be the extension of the practice of intercommunion between different Churches."[50] The Lutherans were less sure. If some of their American co-religionists were ready to compromise, the United Evangelical Lutheran Church of Germany stated its case with quiet frankness. It could not, on principle, practice intercommunion.

> The plea to approach church unity by establishing intercommunion is based upon a definite conception of the Lord's Supper. If we agreed to this plea we should have to acknowledge that our own conception of the Lord's Supper is the same as, or only insignificantly different from, this underlying conception. We cannot admit that. In our opinion the whole question is not concerned with slightly diverse theological opinions or a certain mode of ordering the Lord's Table, but with the particular gift of the Lord's Supper as we understand it, i.e., the real presence of the Body and Blood of Jesus Christ in the elements of bread and wine.[51]

Their fellow Protestants listened to the objection respectfully, but went on, in spite of it, to state that "the extension of the practice of inercommunion, with all its difficulties, appears to be the best way forward."[52] This contrast in ritual posture gives some idea of the tensions which the liturgical renewal has uncovered—and not only between Protestants.

The same year this confrontation occurred in Europe, American Lutherans with clear doctrinal positions were re-examining the whole sacramental system, to discover *What the Symbolical Books of the*

Lutheran Church Have to Say About Worship and the Sacraments.
It is a revealing document. Arguing that the number of sacraments
varied with different theologians down to the Middle Ages, the Americans found that the symbolical books—Luther's Catechisms, Augsburg
Confession, Formula of Concord, and the Smalcald Articles—commit
themselves to no specific number. Two new sets of terms are accordingly introduced, *major—minor,* and *essential—secondary,* to describe
the difference between the traditional Catholic number of seven and
the ordinary Protestant idea of only two sacraments.

As a result, seven sacraments are somehow replaced within the ambit
of Lutheran theology. Two sacraments are essential, holy baptism and
the sacrament of the altar, to which is added "the sacrament of
Repentance" as a third "major" sacrament. Moreover, the symbolical
books are said to "expressly concede the designation of sacrament to
Holy Ordination." But then a qualifying admission that "the minister
of the Sacrament of Order may, but need not be, except for the sake
of love and peace in the Church, in bishop's orders. Episcopacy is not
a universal, apostolic tradition."[53]

The stand on Holy Orders reflects a growing divergence in the
Lutheran Churches between the Romanizing and Evangelical elements.
The former argue to the need for a full-blown episcopacy, with power
to ordain coming directly from the institution by Christ; the latter
would have remain what Protestant tradition has made them, delegates
of the people who have no sacerdotal power beyond the common
possession of all baptized Christians.

Matrimony is likewise admitted "with qualifications" to belong among
the sacraments: "Wherefore, if anyone wants to call it a sacrament, he
ought to differentiate it from the preceding ones." While confirmation
and holy unction require a special explanation, they also "could be
called sacraments . . . in an improper sense of the term," as "rites
received from the Fathers, which even the Church does not require
as necessary for salvation."[54]

True to Reformation principles, the sacraments are said not to confer grace in virtue of the rite performed. Yet in further explaining
what this means, Lutheran theologians defend the baptism of infants
before the age of reason—and of personal profession of faith, on the
score that "if God did not accept the Baptism of infants, He would
not give the Holy Ghost nor any of His gifts to them."[55] Since he

does, baptism must take effect even without a positive contribution on the part of the child baptized.

If there is one distinctive feature of the Lutheran liturgical movement, beyond its deep concern for integrity of faith, it is the rediscovery of the place of confirmation in the total life of a dedicated Christian.

Why confirmation? Because from the standpoint of Lutheranism, this sacrament belongs in the total religious education which the Church considers necessary to produce something more than nominal believers. For six years, 1957 to 1963, the Commission on Education of the Lutheran World Federation studied every significant aspect of confirmation and then published its findings on the one sacrament which "affects every person directly and plays a crucial role in establishing lasting concepts of the church and of the individual's relationship to it."[56] Since members of the commission were drawn from many countries, its report may be taken as representative of the best Lutheran thought on the subject. Twenty-six different Lutheran rituals were first examined, then evaluated, and a final set of conclusions was made.

Topping the list of these conclusions was the urgent need for redetermining "the special place of Confirmation in the total catechumenate of the Church." On a practical level, it seemed unwise to confirm adults right after baptism. The same applies to young people who are baptized, say, in their teens. Ideally "Confirmation is meaningful only in view of the practice of Infant Baptism. Confirmation refers to the elementary instruction given during the children's catechumenate."[57] This makes confirmation the closing worship service to several years of previous instruction, similar to the Bar Mitzvah among the Jews.

If confirmation is so closely identified with baptism, "in the service which concludes this part of the catechumenate the uniqueness and soteriological importance of Baptism must be clearly expressed in the liturgical forms which are being used."[58] Otherwise the faithful will either consider confirmation a kind of second (and more important) baptism, or they will miss the relationship of both sacraments to salvation.

Similarly, confirmation should be the capstone to serious and prolonged study of one's religion. "Basic instruction in the faith . . . must have a special place in the order of Confirmation."[59] It is not a mere adjunct of the ritual, and still less a dispensable commodity.

Most pertinent from a pastoral viewpoint, "the liturgical order must clearly indicate that this is a *confirmatio* [strengthening] in the full sense of the word and that this *confirmatio* takes place daily in the life of the Christian through the faithful use of the Means of Grace, through living membership in the congregation and through practicing the imitation of Christ."[60] Words could not be plainer on the contemporary Lutheran realization that the sacraments are channels of grace, and that they require human cooperation to derive their fullest efficacy.

As Lutheran liturgists see the direction all this is taking, they sense that more is happening than most people suppose. They feel that Lutheranism is stressing where the notion was present, and restoring where it may have been obscured, the "churchly function of the priesthood for the communication of these [sacramental] signs." Indeed, they are willing to agree that, while Luther suffered from the abuses of his day, he never intended to remove the *sacerdotium* (priesthood) from the Christian community. "His basic intention remained directed toward her renewal not toward her dissolution and destruction."[61] The present liturgical development is therefore also a renovation of the sacred ministry.

REFORMED TRADITION. Protestants in the Reformed family derive from John Calvin on the continent and John Knox in Scotland. Less homogeneous than Lutherans, the inheritors of this tradition are generally called Presbyterians in England and America; and they belong to a variety of Reformed churches throughout the world.

Like the Lutherans, Reformed Protestants have taken the liturgy seriously and, in fact, more seriously than had ever been true since the sixteenth century. During Reformation times, the Calvinist doctrine of predestination placed extraordinary emphasis on Christ's sacrifice on Calvary as uniquely salvific. Any compromise with this uniqueness, it was felt, would derogate from the all-inclusive value of Calvary.

Calvin had used the Epistle to the Hebrews as mainstay for his position, and cited two classic passages as proof against the sacrifice of the Mass: "Christ by a single offering, has perfected for all time those who are sanctified [so that] there no longer remains a sacrifice for sins." Our only duty is to "continually offer up a sacrifice of praise to God, that is, the fruit of lips that acknowledge his name."[62] Since the Passion, no more is either possible or necessary for mankind.

But this is not the sixteenth century. Reformed scholars are now asking whether the Eucharist has been given its due sacrificial meaning. The report to the Faith and Order Commission of the World Council suggested an evaluation:

> Doubt is cast upon the interpretation of the Epistle to the Hebrews traditional in Calvinist Churches, according to which the sacrifice at the heavenly altar is held to imply the abolition of sacrificial praise on earth. The Epistle is interpreted as justifying the idea, traditional in Orthodox liturgical worship, that in the Eucharist the crucified, risen and ascended Lord unites His worshippers with Himself in His eternal self-offering to the Father.[63]

The reference to Orthodox liturgical theology is basic to a correct understanding of the new trend in Reformed thought. The two theologies have a parallel history. In 1621 the new Patriarch of Constantinople, Cyril Lukaris, changed what had been "traditional in Orthodox liturgical worship" to conform to Calvinist stands. Fifty years later, his successor, Patriarch Dositheus, authorized a lengthy *Confession* which some have likened to the definitions of Trent. This *Confession* is now an accepted norm of faith in Byzantine Orthodoxy, and unqualified on the subject of the Eucharist.

> We believe that the Body Itself of the Lord and the Blood That are in the Mystery of the Eucharist ought to be honored in the highest manner, and adored with *latria*. For one is the adoration of the Holy Trinity, and of the Body and Blood of the Lord.
>
> Further, that it is a true and propitiatory Sacrifice offered for all Orthodox, living and dead; and for the benefit of all, as is set forth expressly in the prayers of the Mystery delivered to the Church by the Apostles, in accordance with the command they received of the Lord.[64]

It was this Orthodox belief which had, since 1948, become part of the shared ideology of the World Council of Churches and since 1922 of its parent Faith and Order Commission. Leading the Orthodox membership in 1922 was the "Oecumenical Patriarchate of Constantinople." In the same year, there were twenty-three Reformed bodies on the same Commission, including the two large Presbyterian Churches in America, the Church of Scotland, the Reformed Church of Hungary, and the Presbyterian Church of India.

If the Orthodox influence on Reformed sacramentology was admitted, it was also resisted. Christian Reformed scholars in the United States and their Dutch counterparts have been outspoken. They maintain that the only sense in which the word *sacrifice* may be used of Eucharistic worship is to describe an offering of praise and thanksgiving in gratitude for the blessings received from the one sacrifice on the cross. In no sense, according to them, should people think of Christ still offering himself to the Father, and nothing in the words or actions of liturgical practice should even suggest the idea.

Although the objectors are numerous and their arguments have weight to support the traditional view, they are being answered from within their own ranks by dedicated Calvinists who call for a revision. The protest of the Reformation, they explain, was directed against the abuses of the Church of that time, above all against the concept of merit, "which was actually even promised for the sacrifice of the Mass," against traffic in religious commodities, and the low moral conduct of the clergy. "So it came to the abolition of the office of priest, however long the expression itself remained current. The offertory was cut out of the Mass and altars were broken down," but with the result that "the idea of the Altar proved to be ineradicable."

Priesthood and altar, then, were set aside. "But has attention really been given to what the Scripture has to say about both? The sacrifice of our Lord once for all on Calvary was emphasized. As at one time against the Gnostics, the historicity of this sacrifice has rightly been underlined. Yet a solitary historical fact can be so tied to its place in history that it sinks into the past with just that place and hour." This should be revised.

> When the Church of old conceived the idea of the Mass as representing the sacrifice of Calvary, she intended to express something true. . . . The Church does not merely remember the death of the Lord; she "represents" the sacrifice itself, letting herself into the suffering and death of Christ, into His obedience. In that way she proclaims His death "until He comes."
>
> The same is true of the priesthood. What is the biblical priest? Neither teacher nor preacher, but he who offers the sacrifice, i.e., of God's love. He is there *for* others, their servant for Christ's sake. He is intercessor, too, and God's instrument in the work of forgiveness and redeeming love.[65]

If the language of this new approach to sacrifice and the priesthood is still Calvinist, the spirit behind it is clearly pre-reformational. Nor was it limited to theological exposition, but has found expression in revised rituals. The new liturgies of Lausanne and Geneva give a liturgical form to the collection of gifts for the Church. For the first time since Calvin, an offertory was introduced and concluded by appropriate words pronounced by the officiating minister, and the Lausanne rite specified that the alms be placed on the Holy Table with a sacrificial prayer.

One of the new Genevan formularies for the Lord's Supper brings back the pre-Reformation scheme of the Eucharistic canon, and supplements the words of institution with a statement that was unknown in Reformed liturgy until the present century.

> We remember, then, O our God, the sufferings and the death of Thy Son; His Resurrection and His Ascension, and while awaiting His return, we praise Thee for having regarded the sacrifice which He offered on the Cross once for all, and accepted His perpetual intercession on our behalf in the heavens. Receive also the homage of our hearts which offer themselves to Thee and consecrate themselves to Thy service in a living and holy sacrifice.[66]

Reformed liturgists point out that this is the first time in their history that the "great theological idea" so familiar to the Orthodox finds entry, namely, the concept of a mystical relation between the liturgical act of the Lord's Supper and the eternal oblation which Christ the High Priest continually makes of his death to the heavenly Father.

ANGLICAN COMMUNION. The typical features of Anglican worship are to be found in *The Book of Common Prayer*, originally written by Thomas Cranmer in 1549. The revised version of 1662 remained practically unchanged until the present century. Characteristic of Anglicanism is the name "Common Prayer," which grew out of successive Acts of Uniformity, requiring all people in England to follow the ritual standard imposed by the Crown. After two offenses on this score, "such person shall suffer imprisonment during his life."[67]

As Anglicanism grew out of its state-dominated church forms, the liturgy also became more varied, but *The Book of Common Prayer* remained essentially constant.

In the face of persistent ritual controversies, stimulated by the Oxford Movement under Newman, Pusey, and Keble, a Royal Commission on Ecclesiastical Discipline was appointed in April 1904. It held 118 meetings and reported in June 1906, recommending the issue of "Letters of Business" to the Convocations (governing body of Anglican clergy) with a view to a complete Prayer Book revision. The Crown issued Letters in November of the same year, and the subject was put before the bishops and lower clergy for nearly twenty years.

After long and heated debate, it was decided that the 1662 Book should be retained, but that a new parallel Book should be made, the use of which would be optional. Finally in 1927 the bishops were ready with what promised to be the most complete break with traditional Anglican ritual since the Elizabethan era.

Actually the new Book represented a compromise. Its alternative Eucharistic rite came very close to the medieval Mass service, with a new canon, the use of *Kyrie Eleison*. The rites of baptism and matrimony also approximated pre-Reformation forms and the reservation of the blessed sacrament (under both species) was permitted under narrowly guarded conditions. The Requiem Mass which High Churchmen had denounced in the 1870s was made legal. Reacting against the Low Church tradition, prayers for the dead were formally sanctioned. In the same way, the sacrament of anointing was restored, at least partially, "as a sacrament of healing."

In the Convocations and in the English Church Assembly, the proposed Book passed with large majorities (517 to 133 in the Assembly, where the bishops voted 34 to 4). But hopes for getting final approval were short-lived. Protestant opposition within and outside of Anglicanism, combined with the sense that it failed to satisfy the more advanced wing of the High Church party, led to its rejection by Parliament. It passed the Lords (where prelates were strong) by 241 votes to 88, but was rejected by the House of Commons in a historic vote (238 to 205) on December 15, 1927.

Aware that Parliament had to be placated, the liturgical experts amended the Book more in accordance with Protestant demands. The amended version was accepted by the Anglican Assembly (396 to 153), but failed to satisfy Commons. By a vote only slightly different than before, Commons refused to approve (266 to 220) what the Church requested on June 14, 1928.

Historians of Anglicanism consider the two parliamentary rejections of the new *Book of Common Prayer* a turning point in the Church of England. In almost four centuries of existence, its dependence on civil authority—in matters as deeply religious as the liturgy—was seen to be deeper than many had supposed.

In spite of its lack of formal approval, the revised manual was issued in 1928 and continues to be sold in a variety of editions designed for liturgical use. Although legally distinct, Anglican churches in countries outside of England are, in effect, branches of the mother body. Their own Books of Common Prayer differ verbally, but not substantially, from the unauthorized English prototype.

Since 1928 the liturgical situation in world Anglicanism has further polarized. The pro-Catholic and pro-Evangelical elements in the Church have worked out a *modus vivendi,* mainly by having certain parishes (or dioceses) favor one or the other side of liturgical faith and piety. There is no easy way of distinguishing one type of ritual preference from another, except the actual experience of belonging to, say, a High Church congregation where Masses are said, and publicly advertised; or to a Low Church community where only a Communion Service, and never the Mass, is available.

A careful distinction should be made, however, between High Church ritualism and High Church Anglo-Catholicism. It is quite possible for Episcopalians to be very "High Church" liturgically, yet doctrinally favor a position which is essentially no different from Protestant bodies that have no priesthood and no claim to a historic episcopate.

Accordingly, not all visible signs of "high" liturgical practice—vestments, incense, and altar vessels—are necessarily evidence of what some would call "Catholic worship." The converse is, of course, commonly true: that the absence of external forms of "sacerdotalism" generally indicates an evangelical and not Catholic creedal understanding of Christianity.

The clearest index of where a particular church or pastor stands on the spectrum of both ritual and doctrinal liturgy is the kind of order of worship that is used. There is no question, on the one hand, that *The People's Anglican Missal* is High Church and Anglo-Catholic. And, on the other hand, there is also no doubt that the *Book of Common Prayer According to the Use of the Anglican Church of Canada* is basically Low Church and Evangelical. A comparison of the two liturgical manuals could be made on almost every level of approach to the Eucharist, with evident contrast.

Thus in the *Anglican Missal,* reference is consistently made to the "altar," but in *The Book of Common Prayer* it is always the "Lord's Table" or the "holy Table," but never the altar. A similar contrast between the "Mass," and "Lord's Supper" or "Communion."

The *Missal* uses the Ordinary of the Mass, according to the Roman Rite, literally in translation; and has the full sequence of liturgical feasts, along with such post-Reformation saints as Ignatius of Loyola and Thérèse of Lisieux, Thomas More and Vincent de Paul. There are special Masses for the Chair of St. Peter in Rome and the Lateran Basilica. In the Province of South Africa is permitted the commemoration "after the Prayers of the Mass of the day," of about twenty "Anglican Servants of God," including William Laud (January 10), John Keble (March 29), and William Wilberforce (July 29).

Conversely in the *Book*, all the Saints' Days are of biblical figures only: angels, apostles, disciples, and evangelists. Not even pre-Reformation saints like Bede the Venerable or Francis of Assisi are included.

When the two manuals reflect on their respective concepts of the Eucharist, the difference is unmistakable. In explaining "How to worship at the Eucharist," the *Missal* stresses the importance of knowing what the "Real Presence" means:

> The real and whole Christ is here, after a fashion which enables us to receive him. He is present everywhere as God, but not in such a way as to enable us to receive him as our spiritual Food. In his humanity, he is present only (a) in heaven where he continually makes intercession for us in the presentation of his eternal sacrifice; and (b) in the Sacrament which he has ordained to be the means whereby his heavenly presence and sacrifice is made available for us on earth.[68]

In the rubrics for the Anglican Church of Canada, the words of institution are repeated in the Lord's Supper ceremony, but ritual reference to the consecrated elements is distinctive. As the celebrant "delivers the Bread," to the communicant, "he shall say, The Body of our Lord Jesus Christ, which was given for you, preserve thy body and soul unto everlasting life"; and "if the consecrated Bread and Wine be all spent before all have communicated, the Priest shall consecrate more according to the manner before prescribed." Also, "if any of the consecrated Bread and Wine remain, the Priest and other Communicants shall reverently eat and drink the same." Nothing is to be left over. Then to leave no room for doubt, a final rubric is added:

> Whereas it is ordained in this office for the Administration of the Lord's Supper, that the Communicants should receive the same kneeling —which order is well meant, for a signification of our humble and grateful acknowledgment of the benefits of Christ therein given to all worthy

receivers, and for the avoiding of such profanation and disorder in the Holy Communion as might otherwise ensue.

It is here declared, that thereby no Adoration is intended, or ought to be done, either unto the Sacramental Bread or Wine there bodily received, or unto any Corporal Presence of Christ's natural flesh and blood. The Body of Christ is given, taken, and eaten in the Supper, only after an heavenly and spiritual manner. And the mean whereby the Body of Christ is received and eaten in the Supper is faith.[69]

It is not surprising, in the light of the foregoing, that the Anglican Church of Canada has a broad policy of intercommunion with other, less liturgical and also less creedal bodies. It finds no great disagreement, in practice, between its own Eucharistic theology and that of the dominant Protestant denomination in the country, the United Church of Canada, for whom "the Lord's Supper is the sacrament of communion with Christ and with His People, in which bread and wine are given and received in thankful remembrance of Him and His sacrifice on the Cross."[70]

Taking Anglicanism as a whole, this is far more common than the strong countermovement toward the Catholic belief in seven sacraments, the Real Presence, and the Mass as a propitiatory sacrifice. Nevertheless, the Catholic liturgical movement in Anglicanism is very active. There are bishops and clergy in every country where the Church is established who struggle for identity as Anglicans, yet also wish to be Catholic. They sometimes find it next to impossible to decide between loyalty to their own Communion and the security which, at least historically, has been associated with Rome.

Among the most flourishing centers of Catholic ritualism are Anglican religious communities of men and women, of whom there are more than a hundred throughout the world. Together with their associates or oblates, among the clergy and laity, these communities have literally kept the liturgy alive in the Church of England and its national derivatives. Religious foundations began with the Tractarian movement and waited almost a century before recognition. The first religious community in Anglicanism to have regular Mass, the reserved Sacrament, Eucharistic adoration and Benediction was the Society of St. Margaret, Sussex, founded in 1855. Yet it was not until 1930 that the Lambeth Conference hierarchy gave formal approval to those "who have given their lives in complete sacrifice as a supreme act of worship of God and for His immediate service."[71]

At the Lambeth Conference in 1968, or less than forty years after officially approving religious communities in their midst, the hierarchy sanctioned principles and policies which some Anglicans consider the very opposite of historical Catholicism.

At great length and with complete awareness of its implications, the Conference of 452 bishops accepted the most unqualified intercommunion: "Christians duly baptized in the name of the Holy Trinity and qualified to receive Holy Communion in their own Churches may be welcomed at the Lord's table in the Anglican Communion."[72] Apparent modifications on this broad permission elsewhere in the document were mainly *pro forma,* since so many Episcopal dioceses had already been doing what Lambeth belatedly approved.

Likewise, "full communion with the Church of South India" was said to be "now open for Churches of the Anglican Communion."[73] This came less than twenty-five years after a million Anglicans, Congregationalists, Methodists, and Presbyterians had united to form what was then the boldest merger in modern times. Episcopal bodies (Anglicans and Methodists) joined with non-episcopal churches, whose confessions of faith excluded, on principle, the Catholic concept of sacraments, the priesthood, and the Eucharistic sacrifice.

The most revolutionary change, however, touched on the essence of the liturgy. For over four hundred years, the Anglican Communion had believed itself to have an episcopate traceable to the apostles. In its famous Quadrilateral passed by Lambeth in 1888 as minimum conditions for Christian unity, the English Church declared its possession and profession of "the Historic Episcopate." When the question of the validity of Orders came up in 1896, the Archbishops of Canterbury and York replied to Leo XIII that their orders were valid, since the alleged break in apostolic succession (1552–1662) was not real. Seventy years later, Lambeth was satisfied with the "common acknowledgment of a ministry through which the grace of God is given to his people."[74] In other words, the Church of England and its national affiliates were now willing to join with any Church which had a ministry claiming somehow to give divine grace to the faithful. Since no denomination in Christendom claims less, every denomination becomes a prospective partner with Anglicanism.

The liturgical consequences for Episcopalians are staggering. Yet, they are not surprising. On the eve of the 1968 Lambeth, the Anglican Executive Officer of Ireland, Bishop Dean, publicly stated that, "The episcopal office was unknown in New Testament times, and therefore unity cannot depend on the acceptance of the episcopate which must not be regarded as necessary to the 'being' of the Church."[75] It is only a useful, and dispensable, form of ecclesiastical structure.

THE FREE CHURCHES. Protestants in the Free Church tradition trace their ancestry to a reaction to the Reformers on the continent and in England. Part of the reaction was against what they considered the halfhearted Reformation which severed relations with Rome but kept many of the ritual practices of the Catholic Church.

In the intervening years, until recently, denominations like the Baptists and United Church of Christ, the Christians and Disciples of Christ were reputed to be the least liturgical bodies in Protestantism. The logic of their position was understandable. If, as they felt, Christianity is essentially a relationship between the believer and Christ, and if justification comes only by faith, liturgical practices are at best peripheral. They are hardly consistent with a religion which is first of all concerned with the individual and his own redemption through confidence in a personal Savior.

Moreover, if man is sinful to the depths of his being and incapable of doing anything meritorious on the road to heaven, what room is there for cultic practices or symbolic ritual? If some of these are permitted, it is mainly a concession to his desire for seeing and feeling religious, and beyond the essential worship of the heart.

There are still occasional tracts published in this vein, and bodies like the Quakers have retained much of their austere simplicity. But nowhere in contemporary Protestant life has the liturgical renewal been more pronounced or widespread than among churches whose original names stood for religion with a minimum of ritual. They were Separatists and Non-Conformists, Puritans and Congregationalists because they refused, in greater or less measure, to be identified with a Christianity which seemed to compromise with the severe doctrines of "faith alone" and "the Spirit alone," as beacons of salvation.

The ways this renewal has taken place are as varied as the churches themselves which, in the Free Church lineage, are almost as different as individuals. In the absence of juridical authority outside the local congregation and the stress on covenant discipleship, it is impossible to describe what is actually happening, except in general terms. A Baptist church in Mississippi may have ritual forms which no other Baptist congregation in the world uses; and, even the most detailed manuals for ministers are careful to explain that the different "orders of worship are listed here merely as illustrations of types of worship services."[76] There are also no prescribed rubrics or liturgical directives that everyone is expected to follow.

More valuable for our purpose are the reasons which their own theological writers give for this reversal of a distinctive tradition. Each reason, on analysis, is also a reflection of the crisis which nonritual Churches faced in adjusting to an age that thrived on symbolism and demanded group consciousness as the price of cultural survival.

As they read the Church's past history, Baptist writers especially are now saying that Christian worship is the human response to the revelation of God in Christ. But this necessary dialogue has been periodically distorted. The abandonment of preaching before the Reformation led to an overreaction in the opposite direction. In some segments of Protestantism, all the accent was placed on preaching, and little provision was made for an adequate response of the congregation in common praise and prayer, in offering and sacrament. Our age is witnessing a reaction against this, and the reaction is most prominent where the neglect of ritual had been most extreme.

Since Reformation times, some Churches had so interpreted the phrase "to God alone the glory" that they practically denied any role of man as free and responsible agent in living the Christian life, including his life of prayer. English commentators confess that "in Great Britain today the average worshiper goes to church to receive rather than to give, to 'get a blessing' rather than to 'make an offering.' This is to destroy the reciprocal nature of the divine-human encounter, and to pauperize the recipient of grace. We need to recover the biblical conviction that service is offering, that worship is sacrifice. Such an awareness would go far to rescue our services from subjectivity and self-centredness."[77] While speaking immediately from the English scene, this observation can also be made for Free Churches elsewhere.

Liturgists have arisen among Congregational church bodies who are telling the people that Christian worship, to be genuine, should be incarnational and sacramental. Both as revelation and response, it should involve man's whole personality, the body and senses—imagination and sense organs—thoughts and articulate words, movement and action as well as listening and understanding. Once a Christian admits that God is revealed and communicated through the material and social environment of man, who is himself flesh, the nature of man's worship is inevitable. Christian worship is embodied. Embodiment means all the senses, and not only the ears confined to hearing the preacher's voice. "The Evangelicals, like the Puritans, exalted the ear-gate at the expense of the eye-gate of the soul."[78] Their descendants today tell the people to honor God with their whole body; open eyes as well as open ears should be engaged in worship.

Unlike anything previously associated with churches in the Anabaptist and Puritan tradition, the customs now permitted and encouraged are, in plainest terms, liturgical. The free use of symbols gives some indication of the general trend. Baptists and Disciples of Christ are urged to use pictures and symbolic representations as aids to devotion. "The cross," especially, "has become to all the world a symbol of the Christian faith." Consequently, "while recognizing that the use of symbols may become too dominant a feature of worship, we nevertheless emphasize the values to be derived from the use of them."[79] Among the symbols commonly used are IHS, interpreted to stand for the Latin, *Iesus Hominum Salvator;* the triangle, signifying the Trinity; a seven-pointed star to represent the seven gifts of the Holy Spirit; a six-pointed star "to remind us of God, the Creator"; a single circle depicting eternity; and a triple circle representing the Trinity. Six liturgical colors are advertised for vestments in divine service: white for joy, red for suffering, black for sorrow, purple for repentance, green for hope, and blue for loyalty and eternity. Object symbolism is extensive, with six items most often featured in church art and architecture: the cross representing Christ, the Bible standing for the word of God, an anchor for hope, a banner for victory, a globe for authority, and a gate for protection and freedom. Religious pictures are used and, on a more limited scale, also statues, but only to heighten "the spirit of worshipful devotion," during actual service.

One aspect of ritual revival in the Free Church movement has deeply affected other Protestant bodies and also made inroads among Roman Catholics. Pentecostalism is a direct outgrowth on the cultic side of the centuries-old restraint in Churches of various doctrinal ancestry, but with Congregational structure and polity. Once the restraints were broken, the burst of ritualistic fervor knew no bounds, and the history of Pentecostal enthusiasm is only beginning—although its organized form dates from the early twentieth century.

Eastern Orthodoxy

No other part of the Christian world was more gravely affected by the course of modern events than the Orthodox Churches of the East. The effect on their liturgy has also been crucial, since, more than Catholicism or Protestantism, Orthodoxy places ritual at the center of the Christian life. The very name, Orthodox, designates both "correct doctrine" and "correct worship." In Slavonic, Orthodoxy is rendered by the word *Pravoslavie,* which means "true glory," so that when a Russian, Serb, or Bulgarian calls himself Orthodox, he proclaims his belonging to a community which praises and glorifies God in the right way.

Eastern Christianity has also been more closely identified with the State than its sister communities in the West. This fact is an important link to understanding what happened to the Church when the political powers dominating Orthodoxy fell in the course of less than half a century. The impact on everything in the Orthodox religion, notably its liturgy, was profound.

UP TO THE COLLAPSE OF THE EMPIRE. The ideological roots of modern Orthodox faith and worship were anticipated in the writings of Feodor Dostoevsky (1821–1881). His four years' imprisonment for political conspiracy led him to rediscover Christ and inspired him to write such classics of Russian literature as *Crime and Punishment* (1866) and *The Legend of the Grand Inquisitor* (1880). Essential to Dostoevsky's vision was the belief that only in Christ can sinful and divided men recover harmony and integrity. He was admired as a gifted novelist but the religious intentions he tried to communicate were lost on his contemporaries.

His personal friend, Vladimir Solovyev (1853–1900), fared little better during his own lifetime, but now he is hailed as one of Russia's greatest thinkers, and events also proved him to be a veritable prophet. What he wrote at the close of the nineteenth century pertains directly to Orthodox worship.

Solovyev's fundamental premise was that Orthodox (true) doctrine about Christ is the only sound basis for truly Christian society. What a person believes about Christ determines his concept of the human community. He told his people to beware of heterodoxy.

As true Orthodox, you have the royal road to follow between two opposite heresies, the false liberalism of Nestorius and the false pietism of the Monophysites. The former would make a final separation between the sacred and profane, as Nestorius separated the humanity from the divinity of Christ. The latter would absorb the human soul in the contemplation of the Divine and would abandon the mundane world to [its] fate; this is the application to society of monophysitism which merges the human nature of Christ into His divinity.[80]

This is the basis for the sacramental system in Christianity, and the only security for the future of its people. Deviate to either side, and all is lost. No option is left to an Orthodox believer, and much less the priest, on how he should view the twofold nature of Christ: truly human and truly divine, yet also united in one person and not two (as Nestorius urged), and this divine person not absorbing Christ's human nature (as the Monophysites held).

Now the master stroke. In one eloquent paragraph he synthesized more than a statement of Orthodox liturgical theology. He capsulized the inner workings of Providence in the world today, and showed the intimate connection that should exist between genuine sacramental piety and a truly Christian society. He divided the synthesis into two parts: one dealing with sacramental grace and the other with society's response.

Pontiffs and priests, you are the ministers of the sacraments of Christ. In revealed dogma, Christ is the principle of all truths or of the whole truth. . . . So in the holy sacraments Christ is the principle of life, of the whole life, not only spiritual but also bodily, not only individual but also social. You, sacrificing priests, were created to plant within humanity the mystical yet real seed of divine-human life; you sow within our nature the seed of matter made divine, of a heavenly corporeity. The beginning of this work, the first source of supernatural life within the body of earthly humanity, must be an absolute fact surpassing human reason, a mystery.[81]

Thus for the sacramental contribution from priests, who give people the person and teachings of Christ, at once divine and human, and forming one indivisible whole.

But there is nothing hid which shall not be revealed; the mystical elements implanted in human nature by the grace of the sacraments through your ministry must germinate, grow and display themselves in visible existence, in the social life of mankind which they progressively transform into the true body of Christ. This work of sanctification does not therefore belong only to the priesthood; it demands also the cooperation of the Christian State and Christian society. What the priest initiates in his mysterious rite, the secular prince must continue by his legislation and the faithful people must consummate in its life.[82]

If Solovyev had been heard, his fears would not have been realized. He saw the riches of divine grace, coming from the sacramental mysteries, lost in a culture where the Church lacked the freedom even to teach what Christians were supposed to do with the graces they received.

Even a great preacher like John of Cronstadt (1829–1908), who was considered a living saint and had a reputation for working miracles, failed to arouse the people to action.

As a priest, John Sergieff had a fruitful experience of liturgical prayer and his influence in bringing the Eucharist to popular attention was his chief legacy to the Russian Church. Whenever he celebrated Mass, he was overwhelmed by the transcendent drama of the mystery. He could not keep the prescribed measure of liturgical intonation; he called out to God; he shouted; he wept in the presence of visions of Calvary and the Resurrection. When he stood at the altar, he was transfigured and wanted nothing more than to have everyone in the church share in his own intense experience. Contrary to the prevalent custom of yearly communion, he demanded that all who came to his church should communicate with him.

Where the Russian custom prescribed sacramental confession before each communion, Cronstadt could obviously not hear the private confessions of the thousands at every Mass. So he daringly started the practice of general vocal confession. Witnesses reported it was an impressive, even terrifying spectacle: thousands of people shouting aloud their most secret sins and sobbing for forgiveness. All the barriers of ecclesiastical order and propriety were transgressed. Only a friend of the Tsar could have been allowed this liberty. No priest in Russia ventured to follow Father John's example with public vocal confession; but the practice of frequent communion was now initiated. His published sermons, given ex-tempore, are filled with panegyrics of the blessed sacrament.

As in Jesus Christ, "dwelleth all the fulness of the Godhead corporeally," so likewise in the life-giving Sacrament of His Body and Blood. In the small human body dwells all the fulness of the infinite, incomprehensible Godhead, and in the small "lamb" or bread, in each smallest particle, dwells all Divine fulness. Glory to Thy Omnipotence and Goodness, O Lord![83]

Cronstadt had a passionate devotion to the Church and respect for its liturgy. Such freedom as he took in the matter of confession was exceptional. He extolled the praises of liturgical laws and paid highest tribute to the benefits which those who obey these laws can expect from God. "I thank my all holy, all merciful and most wise Mother the Church," he proclaimed, "for all her offices of prayers, for the Divine services, for the sacraments and the rites; I thank her for the fasts so beneficial to me both in bodily and spiritual respects." Then by way of exhortation: "May Christians attach themselves wholly and with all their hearts to the Church of Christ. . . . May they all be zealous of the fulfillment of all her commandments and ordinances, and may they obtain in her eternal salvation through Jesus Christ our Lord."[84]

The concluding reference to eternal salvation typified Cronstadt's preoccupation. His unique concern was with things of the spirit, how people might more surely reach their heavenly home.

If John of Cronstadt was reactionary, other dedicated Orthodox urged immediate reform, arguing that, unless something were done soon, the Church might be left without a liturgy. The forces of revolution were mounting. Four converts from Marxism, Piotr Struve (1870–1944), Sergei Bulgakov (1871–1944), Nicholas Berdyaev (1874–1948), and Simeon Frank (1877–1950) led the intelligentsia in a campaign for social reform on Christian principles, which they said was impossible as long as the Church was shackled to the autocratic whims of the State.

SINCE THE REVOLUTION. Without subscribing to Solovyev's precise analysis, Orthodox commentators admit that the Revolution of 1917 marked a dividing line between two periods of their Church's liturgy. If the first could be called *monastic,* the second should be considered *mysteriological.* For centuries the dominant liturgical forms were set by the great monastic families of Byzantium. Among other reasons for this was the fact that, with rare exception, Orthodox bishops were trained as monks, and their ritual perspectives were determined accordingly.

Whatever else the Revolution did, it shifted the culture of millions from the seclusion and formality implied by monasticism to their opposites. This alone would have deeply affected the people's religious customs, including their ritual. But more profoundly, the Revolution gave the Church almost no option except to re-examine the whole range of its ritual traditions and reassess them for the modern world. Various names have been given to the new approach. *Mysteriological* carries the connotation of concern for the spiritual reality symbolized by the visible rites, and stresses the active participation of the worshiper. It also implies a theological understanding of the liturgy, as the Church's reflection on the cultus of the Christian religion.

Among the practical changes which this occasioned, the most dramatic affected the Iconostasis, which is the chief characteristic of the interior of an Orthodox church edifice. It is the screen which divides its eastern end from the part occupied by the laity. It consists of sacred pictures which may be arranged in several rows. Varying in height and in the subjects represented on them, the pictures always have three doors. Behind the central one, the Royal Door, stands a table called the Throne, on which the offering of the Eucharist is made, while the whole space behind the screen is referred to as the altar, and is reserved for the clergy and their assistants.

Unlike the custom in Western churches, in which the priest or minister is directly seen by the congregation, Orthodox Christians see in front of them not a celebrant or preacher but sacred pictures. The priest remains hidden behind the screen during the major part of the service.

This is still the dominant practice in Orthodoxy. But changes are being made. A number of churches are reverting to what is said to have been the original form of the Iconostasis. Instead of a solid screen, the chancel is separated merely by a low screen a few feet high, which allows the people to witness what is going on during the Eucharistic celebration.

Similar changes are being introduced in the Holy or Royal Door. Outside service time, except during Easter Week, the gates of the Door were kept closed and the curtain behind them was drawn. During services, at particular moments the gates were sometimes open, sometimes closed, while occasionally (when the gates were closed) the curtain was drawn as well. Many parishes, however, now no longer close the gates or draw the curtain at any point in the Liturgy; and in some churches the gates have been removed altogether, while still others keep the gates closed but have removed the curtain.

Father John of Cronstadt is credited with having started the more open type of Iconostasis, with followers in other branches of Orthodoxy and not only in Russia.

More frequent Communion is another innovation in the Orthodox liturgy. While most of the faithful still receive only five or six times a year, a growing number of churches in Europe and America have restored the primitive practice of weekly reception, always under both species. Reports from behind the Iron Curtain also indicate that believers are receiving the sacrament much more often.

Congregational singing is another development in certain parts of the Orthodox world. Like the open Iconostasis, this is rather a revival than complete innovation. It is especially popular in countries like America where the prevailing practice in other Christian churches, Catholic and Protestant, regarding hymnal participation by the laity is well established.

Parallel with the new stress on worshiper involvement is a tempering of the length of Orthodox services. Russians as a rule have longer rituals than the Greeks. Two hours for the Vigil Service on Saturday nights is not exceptional. In 1943 the Patriarch of Constantinople laid down that in parishes under his jurisdiction the Sunday liturgy should not last over an hour and a half.

Along the same lines, a number of churches in America especially have introduced the organ to accompany congregational singing. This is still comparatively rare. Even where Orthodox tradition provided for hymns by the faithful, they were to be unaccompanied by instrumental music.

When the Russian monarchy fell, three other empires collapsed at the same time: the German, Austrian, and Ottoman. Their disappearance, along with the fall of the Romanovs, changed the liturgical life of all Orthodox Christians. At Constantinople the Turks took over the patriarchate; Alexandria came under the Egyptians; Antioch went to Syria and Lebanon, and the patriarchate of Jerusalem was caught in the strife between the Arabs and Israelis.

Mass migrations became common, and adjustments to cultural interests, ethnic pressures, and the demands for national autonomy among Orthodox Churches became the order of the day.

The fall of Russia alone created six autonomous *Cirkviy* in Georgia, Poland, Finland, Lithuania, Latvia, and Estonia. Japan and North America acquired an ambiguous independence; and a vast influx of faithful into Greece, Serbia, and Romania altered the physiognomy of the Church in those countries.

A fair example of the ritual adjustments which all of this provoked is the story of the Orthodox Church in America. Its own spokesmen feel that the liturgical picture of American Orthodoxy can be formulated as a double question: *how much* of their liturgical tradition could be preserved, and *how well?*

The first question is admittedly a quantitative one. With so many Orthodox born and educated in America, they scarcely realize that only a small fraction of the liturgical treasure of the Church is really used on the parish level.

> The fact must be stated bluntly: from the liturgical point of view we are rapidly becoming a Sunday Church, and even our Sunday worship is drastically curtailed. To a great, if not overwhelming, majority of our people the liturgical life of the Church is limited to Sunday morning and two or three additional "must" days: Christmas, Epiphany, Holy Trinity.
>
> All that which was vital, so central, so essential in the liturgical piety of the past: the feasts and their eves, the "bright sadness" of the Lenten services, the unique celestial beauty of the Mariological cycle, the warm, almost personal, commemoration of the Saints, the long and solemn *crescendo* of the Holy Week—all this, although it is still dutifully listed in ecclesiastical calendars—is virtually absent from the real liturgical life.[85]

The second question is qualitative. Unlike the influence of the liturgy of former days, for many people "today, this power of worship has all but vanished." They still participate, but from the viewpoint of what Orthodoxy historically stands for, the modern believer is different. "There exists today a wall between *worship*—its spirit, its 'message' and its 'call,' and the *community* which in theory exists in order to worship God." The whole panorama of "secular" life of the people is separated from their life of worship, "as if the two hours spent in Church together, the participation in the *leitourgia* . . . had nothing to do with these problems, were not even meant to have any application to the 'practical' needs and responsibilities of life."[86]

Conscious of the need for wedding the two elements of the liturgy —the ritual and social—Orthodox leaders everywhere, but especially in the *diaspora*, have done wonders in maintaining spiritual depth while acquiring relevance to the human condition.

In many countries, the liturgical texts have been translated into the vernacular. Rubrical customs have been changed to correspond more closely to the practices of the dominant culture and a host of adaptations has been made which some churchmen heartily endorse and others patiently tolerate.

The real issue, however, lies deeper. How correct is it to speak of Orthodox liturgy as Eastern or Oriental, and thus label other, also historic liturgies Western? At stake is the welfare of Orthodox Christianity, depending on how severely the religion is identified with a certain ritual tradition. Some theologians believe the time has come for crossing the Rubicon, and deciding in favor of an Orthodoxy independent of particular liturgical forms—always assuming that the faith remains substantially the same. In general, those in America seem to favor this concept of the liturgy. Others are not so sure. They claim that in Orthodoxy the historic liturgy is the Church. Its language and ritual action, hymnology and even the Julian calendar are basically untouched since patristic times. Does the present century, no matter how revolutionary, demand that all this be changed? And if changed, how far, without risking the loss of the essence of Orthodoxy?

Symptomatic of the hard questions which the issue raises is what happened in 1923 when a conference at Constantinople devised an annual reckoning which, for all practical purposes, was the same as the Gregorian calendar used in the West. The revision was adopted for fixed feasts, while the date of Easter and its dependent holy days were still reckoned by the Julian method. Orthodox churches in Constantinople, Greece (1923), Cyprus, Finland, and Romania (1924), Georgia (1927), Alexandria (1928), and Antioch (1941) complied with this decision. But the rest of the Orthodox world, a majority, still use the Julian calendar entirely. They fear that compromise on the Western calculation of time would do injury to the purity of the Orthodox faith.

IV

AUTHORITY AND FREEDOM

Christianity has been deeply influenced by contemporary culture in the exercise of authority. This is understandable once we recognize that the Christian religion is not only a theology but a way of life. It makes claims on the human person of obedience to Christ and his teachings. Anything in society, therefore, which aids or inhibits the practice of Christian virtue will affect the believer's attitude toward Church authority telling him to hold or do what is not according to his natural inclinations.

Ecclesiastical authority is a very analogous term when applied to Christianity in general. Any attempt to trace its history in our century is possible only if we first distinguish between Roman Catholicism and other Christian traditions.

There is authority in Protestantism and Eastern Orthodoxy, and its exercise has often met the same problems and challenges that obtain in the Catholic Church. But the dialectic between freedom and authority has been most pronounced in the Church of Rome. This is partly because of its interpretation of Christ's words, "He that hears you, hears me," but chiefly because of the cultural pressures on a religious society which demands allegiance to values that may contradict the spirit of the time.

Ecclesiastical authority, however, is not the only kind present in Christianity, and one of the major changes in modern Protestantism has been just here: a shift from leadership which administers church policy to leadership which shapes and directs religious ideology. The same may be said, within limits, of Catholicism and Orthodoxy, but with such marked differences that the two should be treated separately.

CATHOLICISM

It is customary to suppose that the conflict between freedom and authority in the Catholic Church first became serious after the Second Vatican Council. Certainly the publicity which the controversy received after Pope Paul's encyclical on birth control in 1968, or his stand on celibacy in 1970, indicates that by the seventies the issue had reached a culmination point. Secular commentators spoke, almost with pity, of "the Master of the Vatican [who] pulled out the ultimate stops of hierarchy," and "decided in his solitude" to teach an ethic that "has been almost universally rejected" by those who called themselves Catholic.[1]

In reality, the whole history of Catholicism is the story of conflict, and the highly publicized confrontation between papacy and people under Paul VI has its roots in apostolic times. It was in A.D. 96 that Pope Clement I rebuked a group of Corinthian insubordinates and warned "any who should disobey what has been said by him [Jesus Christ] through us."[2] The encounter in the twentieth century was only a more dramatic version of what happened in the first.

Rise of Modernism

The immediate prelude to the modern conflict in the Catholic Church came in the closing years of the pontificate of Leo XIII. In January 1899 he wrote an apostolic letter to Cardinal Gibbons of Baltimore, in which he deplored a movement that has since come to be known as Americanism.

The actual details of what some defendants have nicknamed "The Phantom Heresy" are immaterial. It is also irrelevant whether a man like the Paulist founder and convert from Methodism, Isaac Hecker, was in any way guilty. Most likely he was not.

It was almost prophetic, however, that the Pope focused on the one issue that six decades later was to send reverberations around the Catholic world. He deplored the misguided zeal of those who felt that basic Christian virtues should be trimmed to fit the new cultural ideas. Stress was being wrongly placed on the active virtues, e.g., humanitar-

ianism, eugenic reform and democracy, while the passive attitudes of
humility and subjection to authority were depreciated. It was also
recommended that the Church should relax as far as possible the rigor
of her requirements for converts, emphasize only what Catholics held
in common with other Christians and minimize points of difference.

But the greatest threat to authentic Catholicism lay deeper. It was
the arrogance of those who disputed the Church's right to teach,
through the bishops and the Pope, what the people were to believe and
do on the way to salvation. "The followers of these novelties," he
warned, "judge that a certain liberty should be introduced into the
Church, so that, limiting the exercise and vigilance of its powers,
each one of the faithful may act more freely in pursuing his own
natural desires and potential. They claim that this is called for in order
to imitate that liberty which, though quite recently introduced, is now
the law and foundation of almost every civil community."[3] Then followed a passage that could have been written seventy years later:

> Those who argue in this way set aside the wisdom and providence
> of God. By a solemn decision, he affirmed the authority and teaching
> office of the apostolic see; to guard the minds of Catholics from pre-
> cisely such dangers as those of the present time.
> The license which is commonly confused with liberty; the passion
> for saying and reviling everything; the habit of thinking and expressing
> everything in print—have cast deep shadows on people's minds. If
> there was ever need for this teaching office (*magisterium*), it was never
> more useful than today, to preserve men from being seduced from fol-
> lowing their conscientious duty.[4]

Every principal issue of the forthcoming clash with authority was
voiced in this much-maligned document of 1899. The basis of authority
would be man's accumulated knowledge instead of the revealed "wisdom and providence of God." Moral freedom to do what is right would
be substituted by "the license" to do what is liked. In the name of freedom, the most sacred power of the human spirit, to keep thoughts to
oneself or share them only with trusted friends, would become a "passion for saying and reviling everything." Instead of an honest effort to
communicate what is true, "the habit of thinking and expressing everything in print" changed the purpose of communication. It became persuasion and the desire to arouse.

Correspondingly the concept of authority in the Church would be
forced into a mold prepared by the secular culture in which Catholics

were expected to live. This culture was increasingly democratic and its government not only for the people, but "of the people and by the people." So, too, the Church's exercise of leadership should depend more on group consensus from below and less on "commands from above." Modern science was offering men greater development of their "natural potential" and more opportunity to satisfy their "natural desires." Both called for more liberty of enterprise and less need for a Church to tell people what to do, and less still what to think.

In the first decade after Americanism was "duly laid to rest," the confrontation that Leo anticipated in Western society began to take shape. The pattern that started to emerge has remained fairly constant ever since. The human mind and appetite have discovered new means of satisfaction that were unknown before. It is up to the same collective human genius which found the sources of satisfaction to determine the conditions of its use. Since most people are not able to decide what these conditions are, it devolves on their leading thinkers to arrive at this decision and on their elected representatives to administer what has been finally decided to be good.

We have already seen the rise of Modernism at the turn of the century and its influence on faith. Its leading spokesmen also set the stage for a new approach to the Church's claims to authority, and their revision of the meaning of obedience has yet to be improved upon.

After Pius X condemned the Modernists in 1907, various bishops in Europe and America took up the same issue and began to alert the people to what was going on. The best known supporting pastoral came from Cardinal Mercier of Belgium, at the beginning of the following Lent. But its reputation comes not so much from what Mercier said as from the book-long refutation published by the founder of Modernism.

The ex-Jesuit George Tyrrell had frequent difficulties reconciling his own convictions with the teachings of the Church to which he had converted thirty years before. Now he saw himself the champion of a new age, and felt obliged to refute the cardinal and through him the Pope. He was flattered to be singled out as "the most penetrating observer of contemporary Modernism," and frankly pleased to defend its claims to being, indeed modern, but also validly Catholic.

Tyrrell rested the defense on a concept of the Church which, he said, begets a different notion of authority than the familiar one of papacy and hierarchy. Mercier had charged him with fostering a crude religious subjectivism, where every man's own conscience was his only guide. Tyrrell called this "blank nonsense" and suggested that the Primate of Belgium had never read what the Englishman wrote.

Tyrrell protested that he was the very opposite of nonconformist. "My consistent aim," he argued, "from first to last has been to defend the Catholic principle, *securus judicat orbis terrarum* (confidently judges the whole world), against every sort of individualism— whether that which makes each man's private judgment its own rule, or that which imposes the private judgment of one upon all the rest."[5] The first he would call egotism, of which he was unjustly accused; the second was tyranny, of which he accused the Church of Rome.

There was a middle ground, and the only true form of Christianity in which Tyrrell believed.

> The alternative, Your Eminence, is Catholicism, the subjection of the private and individual to the public and collective mind of the Church.
>
> That the religious life of the Church is the source and criterion of doctrinal truth; that experiment is the criterion of theory as the fruit is of the tree, is a point that I will not even discuss. It is a truth that theological pride hates and picks against, but which it dares not deny in the teeth of the Gospel or merely in the name of a discredited knowledge-theory.[6]

In less complicated language, Tyrrell's idea of Catholic authority was based on an accepted theory of the Church as a Christian society. If everyone in the Church had equal access to understanding God's revelation, and if no one had special competence in religious matters —then the *only* norm for determining truth from error is the collective judgment of the Christian people. Stress is placed on the word *collective*, whether taken as a historical accumulation of knowledge or geographically as the here-and-now agreement by a sufficiently large number of persons.

Tyrrell was offended at being lumped together with "the uneducated and half-educated multitudes" who thought there was no choice between one or other of these two individualisms. As though a Catholic had no alternative to "absolute self-sufficiency" except "the new-fangled dictatorial conception of the papacy"—defined lately by the Vatican Council, "of a privileged private judgment to which all must submit."[7]

There was an option: reliance on the combined judgment of a multitude of Christians; and the more numerous their expressed opinions, the more secure their judgment.

This analysis was made in 1908. It could not have offered a more timely formula for Catholics who were getting impatient with one man in Rome directing their lives. Tyrrell also symbolized the beginning of a new polarization of attitudes toward ecclesiastical authority. In the 1800s it was still the Gallicans who said a council was above the Pope and Ultramontanists who said the opposite. The rift would become deeper and revolve around something more fundamental. The question in the 1900s would be whether anyone except the community of believers had any authority or only what the community gave him.

Fifty Years of Grace

After the sudden outburst of revolt in the first decade, the prospect for the Church looked foreboding. One of the if's of history is what might have happened under other circumstances; for example, had someone other than Giuseppe Sarto become Pope when the Modernist crisis struck.

Pius X was a holy man. He was also a shrewd judge of his times and absolutely fearless when he felt the interests of God were at stake. Anyone who knew the shy Giuseppe, and recalled that as a young curate he would not even make a short detour on a journey without his pastor's permission, was astounded to read the incisive language of Sarto as pope when defending the sacred rights of his office. Modernism was "venomous," "pernicious," and "pestilential," and he spent most of his pontificate preparing the Church for what he foresaw would happen if ever the theories of Tyrrell, Loisy, and their disciples took hold.

Their ideas never died; they only remained latent, as later events were to prove. But for over half a century the Church enjoyed a remarkable "tranquillity of order" between the two segments of Christian society which critics of Roman Catholicism had tried to pit against each other. The relation of Pope to bishops, bishops to priests and religious, and those officially in the Church's service to the laity was extraordinarily peaceful.

This is all the more surprising when the same period is seen from the viewpoint of political history: two world wars, involving over fifty nations; almost continual armed conflict somewhere and the spread of Communism over one third of the globe. Yet the Church seemed to thrive under external difficulties; and its internal life, so closely related to authority, flourished.

Every aspect of faith, ritual, and moral conduct was dealt with, judgment passed on, and regulations made—with scarcely a tremor of negative reaction, compared to the explosion that was later to meet the Church's teaching after the Vatican Council.

In the pontificate of Benedict XV, the Holy Office decreed a series of propositions on the knowledge of Christ's human soul which some Christologists were impugning: that the soul of Christ while living among men had the knowledge which the blessed enjoy in heaven; that Christ's soul from the beginning knew all things in the Word of God, past, present, and future.[8]

Two years later, the same Pontiff refuted the speculation of those who held that "the historical parts of the Scripture depend not on the absolute truths of facts, but only on what they call the relative and harmonious opinion of the multitude."[9] According to this theory, Christ might never have actually walked on the waters, or changed water into wine, or multiplied the loaves and fishes. He only seemed to do so by those who later on "harmoniously" reported what they thought he had done.

Pius XI, the former head of the Ambrosian Library in Milan, issued no less than 136 official documents during his seventeen years as Bishop of Rome, the first within a month of accession—extending the start of papal elections to fifteen days after the Pope's death; and the last published three weeks before he died—urging the Catholics in the Philippines to the restoration of family life and the social apostolate.

Seeing the shambles made of the family and marriage in reputedly Christian nations, Pius XI published *Casti Connubii*, in which he denounced the abuse of the whole range of communications media—theatrical productions, books and periodicals, radio and movies, "in short all the inventions of modern science." They are being exploited "to trample and deride the sanctity of marriage and to extol or so depict divorce, adultery and all the basest vices as to make them appear free of all reproach and infamy."[10] He then specified the historic position of Catholic Christianity on all the major aspects of marriage being challenged by Western society.

To begin with, "there can be no true marriage between baptized persons without it being by that very fact a sacrament."[11] This applies to all Christians and not only to Catholics. Every valid marriage contract between two baptized people is always a sacrament. Since Christ raised marriage to the sacramental state and, in so doing, made it monogamous, no earthly power can legitimately separate the consummated union of husband and wife. "Christian marriage may not be destroyed by any human authority." The marriage of Christians symbolizes the permanent union that exists between Christ and his Church, "which union, as long as Christ shall live and the Church through him, can never be dissolved by any separation." So Christian marriage enjoys "indissolubility," and any one who leaves his or her spouse, for any reason, to marry another, "is guilty of adultery."[12]

With equal clarity, the Pope recalled the Church's position on marital morality. Almost forty years before *Humanae Vitae*, he recalled this doctrine in the most explicit terms:

> No reason, however grave, may be put forward, by which anything intrinsically against nature may become conformable to nature and morally good. Since, therefore, the conjugal act is destined primarily by nature for the begetting of children, those who in exercising it deliberately frustrate its natural power and purpose sin against nature and commit a deed which is shameful and intrinsically evil.[13]

Resting this doctrine on the Church's uninterrupted teaching, the Bishop of Rome further identified direct abortion as "murder of the innocent." Sterilization he called "a pernicious practice." Extramarital relations are "adultery," and those who indulge in premarital intercourse "will reap what they have sown . . . sadness, estrangements, weariness of common life."[14]

There was nothing astounding about this forthright presentation of traditional Catholic belief and, except for subsequent developments, would not have merited such lengthy inclusion in these pages. What should be noted, however, is the Pope's awareness of coming events: head-on conflict between centuries-old Catholic principles of marital morality and "the errors and impending dangers" from an ideology at variance with the spirit of Christ.

Equally commonplace was the general acceptance of these "hard sayings" by the Catholic community. A rundown of hundreds of monographs and articles in Catholic journals, popular and scholarly, indicated that few, if any, bishops, priests, or the laity reacted adversely to what they quietly recognized as the plain, if difficult heritage of their faith.

If Pius XI set something of a record in the number of formal documents published, his successor and former secretary of state made papal history in the frequency of his addresses and allocutions over a span of almost twenty years. Over four hundred are on record, each with its own formal title, taken from the opening words, and treating of the widest possible subjects, given before the most diverse kind of audience. In a single month, October of 1953, Pius XII addressed seven different congresses that came to the Vatican to hear a special message from the reigning Pontiff: the congress of Italian nurses, on neuropsychiatry; of International Penal Law, on the nature of crime and punishment; of the International Foundry, on human factors in business; of Italian urologists, on the licitness of anatomical amputation; of the International Federation of National Associations of Technicians, on the need for evaluating scientific progress; of the International Office of Military Medical Documentation, on the right acquisition and use of medical knowledge; of the American Society of Travel Agents, on the code of fair practice for international travel. There were also, in the same month, prepared addresses to a delegation of scientists from Denmark and to the faculty and students of the Gregorian University in Rome.

These speeches were prepared under the Pope's direction by a staff of experts in every conceivable specialty: medicine and law, political science and chemistry, journalism and electronics. When he spoke to an audience of gynecologists in 1956 on the psychological method of natural painless childbirth, the address made world headlines and sparked a whole literature of commentary in the international press. When he told a group of obstetricians in 1951 that "every attempt on the part of the married couple . . . to hinder the procreation of new life is immoral," he was taking issue with those who recommended the new contraceptive hormones.[15] According to expectation, the Planned Parenthood advocates attacked the Pope; Catholics supported him.

So accustomed had Catholics become to having the Pope speak authoritatively on a broad variety of issues, that even the solemn definition of Mary's bodily assumption into heaven was taken as a matter of course. He defined "a dogma revealed by God that the Immaculate Mother of God, the ever Virgin Mary, after completing her span of life upon earth was assumed to the glory of heaven in body and soul."[16] A thousand bishops, the entire diplomatic corps representing fifty nations, and almost a million people from every country witnessed the proclamation in St. Peter's Square on November 1, 1950. Even the non-Catholic world was impressed. Remarks like Julian Huxley's that Mary's assumption was impossible on scientific grounds, that her body would have disintegrated once it rose beyond the atmosphere, were quoted by the press as curiosities.

Yet, in the same month the Pope announced he was going to define Mary's assumption, he issued *Humani Generis* which, by any estimate, was one of the hardest-hitting documents emanating from Rome. It practically took over where Pius X left off in 1907, and warned that a storm was brewing in the Church; that what the Sarto pontiff had said was a serious threat to Catholic Christianity, was closer than ever now.

Fifty-six distinct errors against the faith or its conclusions were recited in what some unwary commentators thought was sclerotic fear in the aging Pius XII. He was seventy-five at the time. Literally every important phase of belief and conduct was being called into question: Christ's bodily presence in the Eucharist, the inerrancy of Scripture, the existence of angels and demons, the Church's necessity for salvation, original sin, and the relevance of tradition for determining the validity of moral standards.

More critical, however, than the recitation of these errors was the renewed insistence by those who propounded them that the Church's hierarchy was not the final arbiter in faith and morals. The Pope was still hopeful. Not too many writers were thinking this way. "It is a matter of regret," he worried, "that not a few of them severely spurn the teaching authority of the Church." They "tend to withdraw from the guidance of the sacred teaching authority, and are in danger of gradually losing revealed truth and of drawing others along with them into error." These "lovers of novelty pass from disdain of scholastic theology to neglecting and even despising the magisterium of the Church which bestows high authoritative approval on that branch of theology."[17]

Fortunately, for the time being, "some caution is as a rule observed in published works; there is more of it in writings intended for private circulation as well as in conferences and lectures."[18] That was in 1950, when special visitations of certain seminaries in France and elsewhere tried to ferret out those "lovers of novelty" who were privately circulating monographs and lecture notes along the lines indicated by Pius XII.

Not everyone was comfortable with the "inquisitorial" methods used by Rome, and, among others, the general of the Society of Jesus had to remind his own men that "we should accept this warning of the vicar of our Lord Jesus Christ in the spirit of faith."[19]

When Angelo Roncalli became Pope in 1958, he inherited both streams of thought in the Church: the ready loyalty of most of the faithful, and the questioning skepticism of a growing minority among the clergy. John XXIII was orthodox to the finger tips, and we got a fair idea of how traditional was his faith and piety from that masterpiece of spiritual self-disclosure, *The Journal of a Soul.* In the third year of his pontificate, while making his annual retreat, he wrote about himself and the high office to which he had been raised:

> Peter's successor knows that in his person and in all he does there is the grace and the law of love, which sustains, inspires and adorns everything; and in the eyes of the whole world it is this mutual love between Jesus and himself, Simon or Peter, the son of John, that is the foundation of the Holy Church; a foundation which is at the same time visible and invisible, Jesus being invisible to the eyes of our flesh, and the Pope, the Vicar of Christ, being visible to the whole world.[20]

Nothing he ever did or said in the five years he was Pope cast a shadow of doubt. He had the same concept of Church authority as his predecessor, whom he was always quoting; or as Leo the Great, on whose fifteenth centennial he published a special encyclical. "It is indispensable," he affirmed, "to the unity of the faith that there be union among the teachers of the divine truths, that is, the harmony of bishops among themselves in communion and submission to the Roman Pontiff." Though dedicated to ecumenism as no other Pope in recent history, he yet declared that "the center and fulcrum of all visible unity of the Catholic Church is the Bishop of Rome as successor of St. Peter and Vicar of Jesus Christ." In fact, Pope John was so utterly conservative, he believed that "the supreme and infallible magisterium was reserved by the Lord to Peter personally and to his successors," and that this is "the essential bond of visible unity of the Church."[21]

All of this would be prosaic, proclaimed by every Pope in the last millennium and professed by everyone who called himself Catholic, except that Pope John's reign marked the end of an era in the history of the papacy, and of ecclesiastical authority. Even his special provision, in 1962, that those who teach the sacred sciences in seminaries "should speak Latin and use Latin textbooks," otherwise "they should be replaced by professors more suited to this task," is like the echo of a former age.[22]

The Vatican Council: Its Teaching and Implications

Six hundred million Catholics have asked themselves, what happened? And the rest of Christendom would also like to know. In one of his talks to the preparatory commissions making arrangements for the Second Vatican Council, Pope John commented on the fact that the Apostle Peter was "the object of persecution," but that twenty centuries of prayer seem now to have given the papacy such liberty as few of Peter's successors ever had.

> By the disposition of God's good Providence, the Bishop of Rome, greeted over the centuries as His Vicar on earth, at present enjoys a personal freedom which permits him to exercise his sacred spiritual ministry, as happened to the first Pope, Peter, after he had been freed from Herod's prison.[23]

John XXIII was a saint, and his words may be taken as prophetic. Certainly, in the context in which they were spoken, they are cryptic. He said "how much strength and spiritual certainty and peace comes to the Pope from feeling himself sustained by his venerable brethren (the bishops) and beloved children over the whole world."[24] Yet, eight years later, John's successor, Paul VI, opened his heart to an audience in one of the rarest expressions of anguish ever spoken by a *pontifex maximus*. A few days before, some high-ranking prelate told the Pope that, in the widespread confusion and uncertainty besetting Catholics everywhere, the Bishop of Rome, too, seemed to be wavering, "that the Church's center, also the Pope himself, had been overcome by a certain loss of confidence about the general way things had gone in the post-conciliar period, and that they had shown themselves to be timid and uncertain, rather than frank and resolute." Then Pope Paul's reaction:

> This remark made Us think. Were We ourself overcome by loss of confidence? "I am a man," and there would be nothing strange about

such an event. Peter, or rather Simon was weak and inconstant, with alternating moods of enthusiasm and fear. In that case, We, too, should need to throw ourselves at Christ's feet and with deep humility repeat Peter's words, "I am a sinful man," but also say with immense love, "You know that I love You"; and then have to make a humble apology for Ourself to Our Brothers and Our Children, with no other purpose than to cancel in them any impression they may have had of the kind mentioned before and to assure them of all the interior certainty with which the Lord designs to strengthen Our ministry.[25]

These were not idle words. They were spoken many times before, if with less poignancy, since he became Pope in 1963; but, not with less reason for grave concern over what was transpiring in the Catholic Church.

HISTORICAL ANTECEDENTS. The roots of the present crisis are the Church's belief that Christ founded a society to teach men until the end of time what he had originally taught the Apostles. Apostolicity is the key to understanding the Catholic claims to authority. It is one of the four traditional marks of the Church set forth in the Nicene Creed, which says, "I believe in one, holy, catholic and apostolic Church." The scriptural basis is St. Paul who stressed the necessity of a divinely authorized mission. "How can men preach," he asked, "unless they are sent (apostalosin)?"[26]

As the need arose for validating the Church's teachings, first the norm of apostolicity was applied to doctrine, and then to the Church itself.

Applied to doctrine, it meant that a given teaching was orthodox if it had been held since apostolic times. Applied to the Church, it meant that the Catholic Church was the true Church of Christ because it had an unbroken apostolic succession which made it one with the Church of the Apostles in origin, teaching, and divinely authorized mission.

The apostolic origin was said to be verified in the historic episcopate and Roman primacy: both trace their lineage, respectively, in un-interrupted sequence to the Apostles and to Peter as their appointed head. This lineage is not only individual but corporate, so that the bishops under the Pope are not only inheritors of apostolic powers in virtue of their consecration, but the episcopate is apostolic as an organic unity.

Christ is believed to have conferred on the Apostles the threefold office he had received from the Father: to teach, to rule, and to sanctify. Thus he told them to "make disciples of all the nations." He gave them such authority that "whatever you bind on earth shall be considered bound in heaven; whatever you loose on earth shall be considered loosed in heaven." He communicated to them, among other gifts, the ability to re-enact what he had done at the Last Supper: "Do this as a memorial of me" and the power of remitting sins: "As the Father sent me, so I am sending you. . . . For those whose sins you forgive, they are forgiven: for those whose sins you retain, they are retained."[27]

These apostolic prerogatives were not merely functional but inherent in the sacramental powers they received from Christ. The Apostles, therefore, were not only commissioned to carry on his work, but consecrated to do so. Their authorization to teach, govern, and sanctify was intrinsic to their office and included the reception of all the graces necessary to exercise their apostolate effectively for the people of God.

They were also empowered by Christ to transmit the essentials of this threefold office to their successors in the ministry by laying on of hands. This is the basis for the historical episcopate and presbyterate and the fundamental reason why the Church is called apostolic.

However, the Apostles were not only individually called by Christ and sent into the world in his name. They were also a collegial community, bound together by their common loyalty to him and intended by him to work together, under Peter, as the nucleus of his Church.

COLLEGIALITY AND PRIMACY. Until recent centuries, the term *collegiality* was rarely used. It was generally subsumed under the concept of "hierarchy" to describe a variety of episcopal activities whenever the bishops worked together as a community.

With the rise of the modern State the concept of collegiality took on a new dimension that was only implicit in former times. There has always been a built-in tension between the rights of bishops and the rights of Rome. Stephen and Cyprian, Celestine and Nestorius, Nicholas and Photius are examples of how difficult it has been to reconcile the two authorities in the Church, episcopal on the local level and papal for all the people of God.

As the nations of Europe and Afro-Asia became divided and nationalism took root in political life, the normal tension was aggravated. It is, in fact, the one facet of history most responsible for the divisions in Christianity that have since become crystallized into churches that rival and challenge the authority of Rome. It is no coincidence that Eastern Orthodoxy has been identified for nine hundred years with Eastern political power; nor that Lutheranism has been the State religion of Norway, Sweden, Denmark, and, until recently, large sections of Germany; nor that England should have developed its own form of Protestantism which is still called Anglican.

When the question of collegiality was discussed at the Council of Trent, the issue was shelved because of this spirit of nationalism which threatened the solidarity of a united, supra-national Catholicism.

The First Vatican Council took a glance at collegiality and made a statement on the subject but did not dwell on it. Speaking of the primatial authority of the Pope, the Council explained that Christ "placed St. Peter at the head of the other apostles that the episcopate might be one and undivided." Anticipating trouble, the Council scored the "perverse opinions of those who wrongly explain the form of government established by Christ in his Church," either by denying the primacy of Peter's successors or "by claiming that this same primacy was not given immediately and directly to St. Peter, but to the Church and through the Church to Peter as an agent of the Church (*ministro Ecclesiae*)."[28]

While bishops were mentioned, and their collegial unity under the Pope was referred to, the stress was not on their relationship to each other or the Pope, but of his toward them.

By the time of the Second Vatican Council, a new ethos had entered political and religious thought. The stress now was on internationalism and, consequently, the dangers inherent in an uninhibited collegiality were considered minimal. It was felt there was not the same risk of national churches sprouting into existence wherever the national pride was unwilling to take orders from an alien Rome. Collegiality became part of the Council's *Constitution of the Church*.

Yet just because of the great potential which collegiality implied, it had to be seen in relation to the primacy, without which it could not be conceived. The bishops who worked on drafting the document recalled that no one question was more on their mind than this: how to express their faith in the episcopal community without infringing on the rights of papal authority.[29] By actual count the Roman primacy is explicitly mentioned thirty-three times in the single chapter on the episcopate, and ten times in one paragraph where collegiality is described.

Not satisfied with this precaution the *Constitution* is unique in having an appendix officially added "under higher authority" to clarify the delicate relationship of the episcopal college to the Holy See.

What is this relationship? It is said to have been created by Christ himself and therefore independent of the whims of man.

When the bishop is consecrated he receives, in virtue of the consecration, the fullness of the sacrament of orders. He receives that fullness of power which is called the high priesthood. But consecration alone does not make him a member of that community which succeeds the apostles. He must also be received as confrere by the other members of the Catholic episcopate. While his consecration makes him bishop, it must be supplemented with acceptance by the episcopate under its head to incorporate him into the episcopal college. Of course, he must also intend to accept his fellow bishops under the Pope.

A careful distinction was made among the three powers inherent in the Catholic episcopate. The first is the power of administering the sacraments, including the consecration of other men as bishops. The second is the office of teaching authoritatively and sharing in the Church's divine guidance of communicating revealed truth. The third is the right to govern and direct the people of God according to norms of conduct that are binding on the consciences of the faithful.

The first of these three prerogatives comes to a bishop in virtue of his consecration. It is intrinsic to him as a man who has received the fullness of Christ's priesthood. He should not exercise these powers except with the approval of the Bishop of Rome. But if he does, he acts validly and the sacraments he confers (including episcopal consecration) take their effect automatically.

It is quite otherwise as regards teaching authority and pastoral government. Certainly they are rooted in the sacramental consecration of a bishop. But this consecration confers only the virtual capacity, not its actual realization.

At this point, an explanatory note added to the *Constitution on the Church* is most enlightening:

> In consecration is given an ontological participation in sacred functions, as is clear beyond doubt from tradition, even liturgical. The word *functions* is deliberately employed, rather than *powers*, since this latter word could be understood as *ready to go into action*. But for such ready power to be had, it needs *canonical* or *juridical determination* by hierarchical authority.[30]

The passage in the *Constitution* which this note clarifies says that episcopal consecration does indeed confer the fullness of priestly orders which includes "the office of teaching and of governing." But this office "of its very nature, can be exercised only in hierarchical communion with the head and the members of the college."[31]

The Latin text speaks of *munera* for "functions" and *potestates* for "powers." This is equivalent to saying that episcopal consecration gives a man the objective (ontological) ability to teach and govern with divine authority in the Catholic Church. However, unless this *munus* is actuated by hierarchical authority under the Pope, it lacks the subjective (existential) determination for being put into effect.

It is immediately seen that episcopal collegiality becomes operative only if a bishop (or a group of bishops) is in actual communion (or agreement) with Rome and the rest of the hierarchy united with the Pope. In terms of what had been said above, this is centripetal collegiality. Without such communion or conformity, no episcopal mandate has assurance of divine approval, no matter how many prelates may agree among themselves on a course of action in opposition to Rome. Nor, as a consequence, are the faithful obliged in conscience to give such mandates their obedience.

There is an obverse side to this relationship between collegiality and the primacy. Bishops depend on Rome for the actualization of their authority, whether acting as individuals with respect to the people under their immediate care or as a college with responsibility to the whole Church of God. Not so with the Pope. Nothing which the Second Vatican Council says about collegiality undermines what the First Vatican Council said about the primacy.

On the other hand, "the college or body of bishops has no authority unless it is understood together with the Roman pontiff, the successor of Peter as its head." In other words, the Vicar of Christ determines whether and how much authority the bishops actually exercise. But the Pope is not determined by a corresponding approval from the bishops.

> The Pope's power of primacy over all, both pastors and faithful, remains whole and intact. In virtue of his office, that is, as Vicar of Christ and pastor of the whole Church, the Roman Pontiff has full, supreme and universal power over the Church. And he is always free to exercise this power.[32]

The Church had not changed its mind on the primacy since collegiality came to the fore. There was development but no break with Catholic tradition. No doubt the contemporary emphasis on the episcopal community brought out facets of the Church's nature that were more latent before; but, the idea of primacy already presupposed a college or body within which and over which the primate rules. When the First Vatican Council defined papal primacy it by no means excluded episcopal collegiality.

> This power of the Supreme Pontiff is far from standing in the way of the power of ordinary and immediate episcopal jurisdiction by which the bishops who, under appointment of the Holy Spirit, succeeded in the place of the apostles, feed and rule individually, as true shepherds, the particular flock assigned to them.[33]

Much had happened in the past century to call for an explication of the bishops' role as shepherds of the flock committed to their care. The development of easy communication between people and nations reduced the need for detailed directives from Rome to the bishops in the Church. Correspondingly the growth of Catholic population, from one hundred million in 1900 to almost six hundred million in 1960 made it impossible to consult Rome or depend on its guidance except in the more serious and pressing issues affecting the people of God.

In terms of principle, therefore, the issue was clear enough. Taking stock of the changed situation since 1870, the prelates at Vatican II added a welcome complement to papal primacy. Without depriving the Pope of one shred of final authority, the Council heightened the role of bishops in the Catholic Church: that they were not mere papal lackeys but men with divinely guaranteed rights in their own dioceses. Yet all the while, they were reminded that union with their fellow bishops, and with Rome, was an equally divine condition for the exercise of these rights.

THEOLOGICAL REFLECTION AND CONTROVERSY. All of this, however, was in the objective order only. Psychologically the seeds had been sown long before to read into the new term *collegiality* a form of church polity that was foreign to historic Catholicism. Instead of conceiving authority in the Church as primatial, and still less monarchical, it was reduced to a form of democracy common in present-day political societies.

The basic idea behind this reassessment of the Church as a visible, hierarchical institution is not new. It was prevalent among the Gnostics in the first century, and was part of the ideology of the Protestant Reformers. Essentially it says that when Christ founded the Church, he did not endow it with true juridical authority, vested in Pope or bishops or, for that matter, even a general council of ordained prelates. Whatever authority the Church had or has is, under God, vested only in the people of God. Contrary to the affirmation of Vatican I, the Pope, and bishops, are merely agents of the Church, i.e., of all the faithful.

The social sciences were brought to bear on the subject, and volumes were published long before Vatican II, tracing this reversal of Catholic Christianity back to the New Testament.

Unlike almost anything still left in today's society, the argument ran, the Church is holding on to antiquated notions of authority. Take the very terms, *superior* and *subject*, or *head* and *members*. They connote a form of authoritarianism that would be intolerable in the secular world. At the apex of the power pyramid are the administrative elite, who deliberate, discuss, and decide issues among themselves; then in the name of authority, they dictate decisions to subordinates who are told to submit their wills and judgments and humbly obey. St. Ignatius' *Norms of Catholic Orthodoxy,* penned in the sixteenth century, no longer hold today. He was writing for a past generation when he said, "We must put aside all judgment of our own, and keep the mind ever ready and prompt to obey in all things the true Spouse of Christ our Lord, and Holy Mother, the hierarchical Church."[34]

As some commentators read the New Testament, the authority structure of the first Christian communities had no split levels, of those ruling and those ruled. If there was a hierarchical principle at work, it was inside the community, not over and above it. There was no distinction between "I" and "We," no superior-subject relationships.

> The New Testament is anti-authoritarian in a proper sense. . . . It is anti-authoritarian in the sense that it permits no member of the Church to occupy a position of dignity and eminence. . . . Authority in the New Testament is conceived in a way which must be called democratic. . . . The New Testament is strangely silent both on commissions to command and on exhortations to obedience and submissiveness to Church authority. . . . Since the mission of the Church is the responsibility of all the members of the Church, all members have a concern in the exercise of authority.

Like all functions of the Church, the exercise of authority is a function of love. This means that love is directed to persons, not to ideas, or institutions or things. . . . Love is the only power which the New Testament knows.[35]

Others, reading the same New Testament, found Christ explicitly telling the apostles to bind and loose in his name; and St. Paul warning the Corinthians, "Once you have given your complete obedience, we are prepared to punish disobedience."[36] If this sounds like the conferral and exercise of authority, those who decided against it were willing to claim that the biblical text had been tampered with or theologically amplified.

A good instance is what Luke appears to have done in the Acts of the Apostles. He mentions that Paul and Barnabas appointed ruling elders over each new cluster of converted Christians.[37] This is contrary to fact.

Luke is making an unhistorical addition—either theologically conditioned, or based on a tradition which had developed in the meantime— when he maintains that Paul and Barnabas "appointed elders . . . in every Church." For this is borne out by the letters of Paul himself. In the first generations there were no presbyters in Hellenistic territories, at any rate in the Pauline communities of Greece and Macedonia, nor was there originally any kind of ordination in these areas. . . . Ordination in the Christian communities is the giving of authority.[38]

On these premises, the conclusion is clear: original Christianity did not ordain men for performing the liturgy or the exercise of authority. This was a later innovation, borrowed from the "Jewish tradition." As such it is an intrusion into the Catholic Church.

It naturally follows that a complete revolution of structure should take place in Catholicism. Centuries in the making, the change is still not complete.

Luther, followed by other reformers, denied the right of any human authority whatsoever to dictate a man's relationship to God. They insisted that God's authority was *not* delegated to a few men but could be found only in the words of Scripture. Thus, not only the form but even the principle of Church authority was challenged.

The reaction of the Fathers at the Council of Trent was to tighten the threatened authority. The mystique of "divine right" of authority completely identified God's will with the institutionalized form of authority, and ignored the community form.[39]

What is the community form of authority, toward which the Catholic Church will hopefully develop? It is a form modeled on the local churches in the first generation of Christians, when "the bishop was the man in their midst with a special charismatic gift for group leadership; [and] authority was in all men and all women, in the *plebs sancta.*" In present-day language, "any decision that affects the whole must be made by the whole."[40] It may not be commanded from the top down.

In less than a decade, writings were published in all Northern European languages, repeating the same theme with only minor variations. A high point was reached when a Dutch bishop in India, Francis Simons, came out with a whole volume denying papal infallibility. "A scrutiny of the traditional arguments," he argued, "seems to prove that the very structure of infallibility has to be abandoned."[41] Nor is there any hint in the Bible, Simons claimed, that the apostles' successors would inherit more than ordinary providential assistance in interpreting what the apostles themselves witnessed. Bishops have no authority in the Catholic Church beyond what inspired leaders enjoy in Protestantism.

When Simons wrote his slender polemic, he was an unknown entity. His American publisher was an obscure, box-number press whose titles were not listed in the standard directory. But *Time* favored the book with two columns of a lead article giving its author international fame.

All this studied challenge of ecclesiastical authority, especially of the Pope, was bound to have results. No significant aspect of Catholicism was left untouched.

The best known is the Dutch situation. When the Netherland bishops produced *De Nieuwe Katechismus* in 1966, they criticized "earlier catechisms that looked for brief formulations which could easily be memorized." Their presentation was "to preach Christ's message through ordinary language . . . and to throw light on present-day questions by means of the gospel."[42] Rome took a dim view of the Dutch effort and pleaded with the bishops to revise the catechism and not publish in other languages until certain changes had been made. The book became a best seller in half a dozen countries. In the meantime, Rome was having the contents examined by the cardinals of five nations and a commission of world-renowned theological advisors generally regarded as open and progressive.

The bishops of Holland were unhappy. They defended their theology in a long closely reasoned reply; it was promptly released to the major news agencies of the world. One sentence typified the prelates' approach, which they candidly felt was shared by millions who, in their words, had become "adult Catholics."

It is precisely the new discovery of our age that, even though our time presupposes as self-evident the substantial unchangeability of faith, it is a question of an unchangeability within a real historicity.

We have become especially receptive to this. Through this new discovery, the faithful who can no longer go along with old formulations, can find again their old, unchangeable faith precisely in these new formulations. To try to put the brakes on this would be a catastrophe for our faithful, and a source of new alienation from the Church.[43]

Among the new formulations of the "old faith" the bishops had sanctioned a concept of the priesthood that was not traceable to the Last Supper, and of the Eucharist that left the bodily presence of Christ in doubt. But their grievance went deeper than particular expressions of belief. They challenged Rome's right to instruct Holland on how religion should be taught to the people.

By the fall of 1968, the papal commission finished its appraisal and Rome published in the *Acta Apostolicae Sedis* the full documentary report. Ten areas of the "New Catechism" called for revision, covering such doctrines as: each human soul's immediate creation by God, original sin as not merely birth into a sinful world. Mary's perpetual virginity, the Mass as a true sacrifice, Christ's presence in the Eucharist in the fullness of his divinity and humanity, the Church's infallibility in the teaching of revealed truth, miraculous transcendence over the powers of nature, the existence of angels, and Christian marriage as indissoluble.

Underlying all the others was the careful ambiguity with which the catechism treated ecclesiastical authority.

The Cardinals asked that the new Catechism clearly recognize that the teaching authority and the power of ruling in the Church is given directly to the Holy Father and to the Bishops joined with him in hierarchial communion, and that it is not given first of all to the people of God to be communicated to others. The office of Bishops, therefore, is not a mandate given them by the people of God, but is a mandate received from God Himself for the good of the whole Christian community.[44]

Exactly a year later, the Dutch became embroiled in another confrontation with the Holy See, this time on celibacy. By a vote of ninety to six the Dutch Church's national council (of priests and laity)—with the eight bishops abstaining—passed a motion that celibacy should no longer be required of priests. By eighty-three to three—and nine abstentions—the council voted that priests who want to marry or are already married can continue to function fully as priests. Then by a ninety-three to two count (with three blanks), they voted on the main statement that celibacy should be completely rescinded.

Christmas Eve, 1969, Pope Paul wrote a letter to the bishops of Holland. He asked them, "What do you think We can do to help you, to strengthen your authority, to enable you to overcome better the present difficulties of the Church in Holland?" On the subject of celibacy, he reminded them that they are Catholics, and that "the duty of the Catholic Hierarchy" is plain enough, "in harmony with the decisions of the Second Vatican Council . . . to teach clearly and firmly that the generous practice of perfect chastity is not only possible but that it is a source of joy and sanctity; to make known and promote everywhere the indispensable conditions for its exercise."[45]

In less than three months, the hierarchies of a dozen nations rallied behind the Pope, defending his stand on celibacy and, in some instances, strongly criticizing the Dutch prelates for their weakness under organized pressure. Cardinal Bengsch of German put his finger on the extraordinary need for authentic collegiality in today's world. "Given the present ease of communications in the world," he warned, "pressure exerted by a local church to go its own way affects *all* local churches, and frequently leads, among extremist groups, to an arrogance which has no respect for others. This causes harm, not only to the universal Church, but also to innumerable faithful in their personal Christian lives."[46]

Thanks to mass media, tens of thousands of religious women in America were aroused to indignation through publicity given a situation similar to the one in Holland. When a community of nuns in California decided to update, they dropped practices and customs that the local bishop thought were essential. He appealed to Rome, which studied the case through an American representative, and then informed the women that they were to "adopt a uniform habit . . . meet daily for some religious exercise in common . . . keep in mind their commitment to education as specified in their Constitutions and

. . . observe the prescriptions of the [Vatican] conciliar decree . . . in regard to collaboration with the local ordinaries in the works of the apostolate."[47]

Led by their mother general, they gained the sympathy of the press and networks, and were finally told to either obey or disband. The majority, over three hundred, chose to disband. They decided to form a new enterprise, with married couples as well as single men and women admitted to membership. After the break with Rome, the former head of the community isolated the dilemma that she and others faced: "While I saw the break as inevitable, I didn't really want it. But I wondered how much energy you could spend fighting authority, when you could spend that same energy doing what you should be doing."[48] *Time* magazine gave her a cover picture, next to ex-bishop Shannon of Milwaukee, as symbols of "the deepening disaffection" with authority that has gripped Roman Catholics everywhere.

The exodus of priests and religious from active service in the Church during the single decade, 1960 to 1970, has no parallel since the sixteenth century. It is part of the revolution that men like Bishop Shannon symptomize, in which the fundamental issue is the perennial one of Catholic authority.

Shannon wrote a monograph shortly before he left the episcopate to marry. At the time of his departure, he insisted that "I do not intend to leave the Catholic Church." Two months earlier, in a national publication for priests, he gave what could later be read as a clue to what he meant by this statement. It is also a key to understanding what might otherwise be unintelligible: how so many trained and often well-intentioned Catholics could leave the Church and still call themselves Catholic.

Shannon redefined the Church in terms that exclude, on principle, the existence of an institution whose visible authority is vested with divine grace to teach and direct, and also to command, in the name of Christ. He rested his case, he said, on Hans Küng's thesis, that "essentially the Church is a community of believers. Its members are joined together in their common belief in the teachings of Jesus Christ. *They declare themselves* to be a fellowship of believers." No one else, certainly no Pope, council, or bishop, decides what this belief must be or what the conditions of fellowship are. On this basis, an honest man could do nothing but "leave" a caricature of the Christian community, once he realized, as this bishop did, with how much they had to reproach the Catholic Church—mainly "authoritarian dogmatism mummified in its correctness [and] casuistic morality divorced from life."[49]

The fact that these statements were borrowed from a Swiss-German theologian only emphasizes the cosmopolitan character of ideas and their influence on human action.

It is secondary whether Küng and Shannon had ever met before the bishop took his leave. They had met in the realm of ideas, and discovered a kinship of spirit that, more than anything else, symptomizes the authority crisis. A growing number have psychologically left the Church described in both Vatican councils. They prefer a Church without papal or episcopal authority, although many (unlike Shannon) still reluctantly subscribe to the external forms of Catholicism.

Year of Decision

Among the decrees of the Vatican Council, the one on the Bishops' Pastoral Office promises to be critical in the ongoing development of authority in the Catholic Church.

THE PRELUDE. Dates here are important. The decree was published in the last session of the Council, on October 28, 1965. The focal paragraph is rather prosaic:

> Bishops chosen from various parts of the world, in ways and procedures established or to be established by the Roman Pontiff, render more effective assistance to the supreme pastor of the Church in a consultative body which will be called by the proper name of Synod of Bishops. Since it will be acting in the name of the entire Catholic episcopate, it will at the same time show that all bishops in hierarchical communion share in the solicitude for the universal Church.[50]

A month before the conciliar decree, Paul VI had issued a *motu proprio* in which he specified that the synod of bishops should be so constituted as to be (1) a central ecclesiastical institution, (2) representing the complete Catholic episcopate, (3) by its nature permanent, (4) yet structurally performing its duties for a time and when called upon, (5) normally operating as a consultative body, to inform the Pope and give him counsel, but (6) it may also have deliberative (decision-making) power, when this is conferred by the sovereign Pontiff, (7) who must in all cases confirm the synodal deliberations to give them validity.[51]

The first synod of bishops was held in Rome in 1967 passing almost without notice in the Catholic world. Pope Paul's observation to the assembled prelates, "while the function of this gathering of bishops is essentially advisory, it is nevertheless of great value," scarcely received attention.[52]

Between 1967 and the next synod the Pope issued *Humanae Vitae* (July 25, 1968) on contraception, and the whole climate changed. Mounting pressure was felt in different countries which gave plausibility to the feeling that Pope Paul had acted precipitously and that he should at least have waited for the next meeting with the bishops. The fourteen months until the second synod opened in October 1969 were among the most tense in modern Catholic history since papal infallibility was defined exactly a hundred years before.

Before long the leader of those who questioned the Pope's way of exercising primacy made world headlines. Leo Josef Suenens became Cardinal Archbishop of Malines Brussels (Belgium) in 1962. For years before, and at the Council, Suenens urged a modification of the Church's historic stand on contraception, suggesting that perhaps "we have excessively stressed the first end [of marriage], procreation, at the expense of another, equally important end, that is, growth in conjugal love."[53] Under his metropolitan jurisdiction, the first scholarly defense of contraception was published in 1963 by Canon Louis Janssens of Louvain.

Suenens himself published upwards of a hundred thousand words in the one year between *Humanae Vitae* and the synod of 1969—never directly touching on contraception but constantly stressing the grave need for re-examining the method and procedure by which the Bishop of Rome exercises his primatial authority in the Church. His most explicit position was voiced in a series of interviews, up to the eve of the synod, where he elaborated what he meant by the theme of his book *La Coresponsabilité dans l'Église d'Aujourd'hui*,[54] which came out in 1968 and was quickly translated into English.

Suenens' main thrust on Church authority was for updating the primacy in such a way that the Pope would not—ever again—issue a major document affecting the whole Church without prior *dependence* on the bishops, representing the mind of the faithful. His criticism of the existing Roman machinery was incisive:

> Of its nature, that is an essentialist, bureaucratic, static, juridical, centralizing tendency; it is characteristic of men more aware of the established order and of the past than of the demands of the future,

closer to the spirit of Vatican I than to the year 2000, more anxious to repress abuses than to understand and foster the new values and aspirations which are coming to the fore in the Church as in the rest of the world.[55]

Concretely he argued for a widespread democratization in the Church's structure. Ecclesiastical law, he urged, "can only respond to the needs of the Church and the world if it also receives the *continual, living agreement* of the whole people of God for whom it is intended." Moreover, "a higher authority should *never* at *any level,* take over what a lower authority could normally decide for itself." In a word, "it is high time for us to realize that the old regime is no more."[56]

The media sustained this image of a historic confrontation up to the eve of the synod. Addressing the bishops at the opening session, Pope Paul pleaded for unity. Using Suenens' favorite term, he admitted that "Collegiality is co-responsibility." But he went on to insist on two other elements: the Pope's duty to respect the rights of the bishops and theirs to recognize the supremacy of the Pope.

Having stated his side of the case and promised his cooperation, he then reminded the bishops of their responsibility to the Bishop of Rome.

In explicit terms, the Pope's responsibility, based on "tradition and the councils," is that of "Vicar of Christ, Head of the Apostolic College, Universal Pastor and Servant of the servants of God." His rights "cannot be conditioned on the authority, exalted though it be, of the Episcopal College, which we are the first to wish to honor, defend and promote, but which would not be such, were it to lack our support."[57]

Almost as soon as it started, it became evident that the crisis was passed. The suspense that had built up for months expecting a showdown between the papalists and anti-papalists did not materialize.

Saying this, however, is only to be stating how the issues worked out on principle. In practice the synod was anything but unruffled, and the problems facing Catholic authority during the rest of the twentieth century are extremely grave.

During the synod, each prelate was invited to respond to a confidential document (*schema*) which had been circulated among the bishops long in advance. The agenda, for the synod, (also confidential) was surreptitiously released in French a month before the meeting by the *IDOC International,* headquartered in Rome.

A definite pattern emerged from the bishops' "interventions" when they spoke in commentary on the *schema* and voiced what could be interpreted as the dominant attitude of their respective countries. In general, the representatives from Belgium, Germany, Holland, Canada, Panama, and Switzerland favored greater autonomy for the bishops, singly and as national bodies. Those from the Mediterranean area (Spain, France, and Italy), the Slavic countries (Poland and Czechoslovakia), Africa, Asia, Australia, the United States, and Latin America stressed the need for greater solidarity with Rome and expressed misgivings over the tendency in some quarters away from historic loyalty to the Holy See.

TOWARD A NEW COLLEGIALITY. The complete *acta* of the synod would run into several volumes. But even a sampling of what transpired in October 1969 may give some idea of the present and foreseeable status of authority in the Catholic Church—at its critical point: the relationship of the bishop to the Bishop of Rome.

Cardinal Suenens gave the most detailed "intervention" in favor of more freedom to the bishops. The three points raised by Suenens dominated the thinking of those who, like him, felt that Rome was too wedded to the past: (1) world culture has radically changed since the First Vatican Council; (2) as a result the Roman primacy, though admitted, needs to be thoroughly restudied; (3) this study can best be done by theological experts of many different persuasions.

Cardinal Doepfner (Germany) agreed that "all the theological questions regarding collegiality should be entrusted to the International Commission of Theologians."[58] Things are too much in flux to take an unqualified position until theologians have done their work. Cardinal Willebrands (Holland), head of the Unity Secretariat, earlier proposed the same solution, except that he "demanded that the International Commission of Theologians study the doctrinal aspects of this matter."[59]

Bishop Alexander Carter, speaking, as he said, in the name of the Canadian Bishops' Conference, stated that unfortunately the Vatican today still conserves the images of a Church in "static equilibrium," whereas "the Church is very much with a dynamic force." An evolution is going on, from a hierarchical concept to the idea of a Church which must be reformed continuously. It is the evolution from a centralized static Church towards a decentralized and flexible College of Bishops. This evolution should be better explored on the doctrinal level and for that reason we ask the International Commission of Theologians to undertake this study."[60]

The Panamanian prelate, Marc McGrath, said the same thing. He took issue with the Vatican documents on the relation of bishops to Pope: "This is not in accordance with the evolution we are living to-day." It is "too unilateral, too static and too much concerned with the binonimy of the primacy and the episcopate." Again an appeal to the theologians "to give a more solid basis for the doctrine of collegiality."[61]

Joannes Vonderach, Bishop of Chur in Switzerland where earlier that summer an informal preliminary gathering of bishops was held, spoke of the Vatican presentation on collegiality as "too vague." He also strongly recommended that theologians unravel the complexity of the authority problem in the spirit of "our times," with "a growing diversity and pluriformity, also in the Church." Then on a climactic note: "Decisions should be taken collegially and therefore the Synod should have deliberative and not only consultative powers."[62] This was a direct challenge to the Second Vatican Council, which ex-plicitly declared that the episcopal synod should give assistance to the Pope "in consultation=*in Consilio*," allowing only for such decision-making powers as the Pope might concede to it.

PRIMACY AND COLLEGIALITY TOGETHER. The contrast from what used to be called the ultramontane bishops could not have been more striking, except that now the prelates were more accurately ultramarine —not only beyond the Alps but beyond the seas.

Among the Spanish delegates, Archbishop González of Madrid be-gan by drawing an analogy between the "divine life of the Father, the Son, and the Holy Spirit" in the Trinity, and the close communion that should obtain among the faithful in the Church. "This commun-ion should manifest itself in the hierarchical government of the Church, which means above all that union under the Roman Pontiff should be visibly expressed." Specifically, "the Roman Pontiff is free to exercise his supreme power over the entire Church, but for a variety of social and psychological reasons he can ask for the cooperation of the Bishops in teaching and governing the Church."[63] He both takes the initiative and determines the conditions.

Cardinal Daniélou of France opened his "intervention" with the statement that four years can be a long time. "The Church today is different from the Church of Vatican II." No doubt the Council clarified many points of faith, but since then "a serious crisis has struck the Western world: the number of priests had decreased tragically; faith, especially of the young generation, is weakened; the spiritual life and morals have worsened." This is no time for idle speculation. "The Christian world expects this Synod to produce results for meeting these conditions. To confront the crisis, a firm and united authority is needed." A clear and forthright stand to that effect will "erase many doubts not only about the authority of the Holy Father but also of bishops and priests."[64] Their claim to respect from the laity depends on their own obedience to the Vicar of Christ.

The Pope's own theologian, Bishop Colombo of Italy, made a brief synthesis of the meaning and interrelationship of primacy and collegiality. He also chided some of the Fathers for stressing one to the oversight of the other. The two cannot be separated. He then added an important clarification on the meaning of subsidiarity:

> Regarding the principle of subsidiarity, a distinction must be made between the way pastoral activity and discipline are exercised, and the way doctrine is proclaimed. Revealed truth and divine law are one and indivisible in the universal Church, namely what is taught by the magisterium, whereas other matters admit diversity and pluriformity.[65]

Colombo's distinction is essential for understanding a document like *Humanae Vitae*. If the morality of direct interference with the life process belongs to "divine law," then the matter should be considered doctrinally closed. One cannot appeal to administrative technique (like subsidiarity) when dealing with issues which pertain to mandates of God (like contraception).

Cardinal Stefan Wyszynski of Poland was permitted by the Communist government to attend the synod. He took strong exception to those prelates who seemed to be passing judgment on the ecumenical Council with their insistence that "collegiality is not clear," that "it needs expert analysis by scholars." His point was that "we should accept the conciliar doctrine on collegiality and not go further." Then he added a dramatic plea. "The world today," he observed, "is sick of too much discussion and dialogue. It wants teachers who have something to give and do not talk much." Referring to his own country, he said that "everyone including those who profess atheism, expect the Church to profess unity and loyalty, firm allegiance to the Holy See and love for the Pope. Today the enemies of the Church direct their attacks against the Pope. It is therefore more than ever necessary for priests and the faithful to show signs of unity. With the Pope, we are called upon to be confessors of the faith. Every discord among us, and every discussion which puts us at the mercy of public opinion brings harm to the people of God."[66]

Another prelate from behind the Iron Curtain, Bishop Trochta of Czechoslovakia, reminded his confreres that the Pope enjoys "the primacy"; he is "the head of the Church." It is the Pope's right to direct "the activity of the bishops to the benefit of the Church, and the bishops should participate in the concern of the Pope." The Church's hope, in confrontation with its enemies, lies in "fostering truth and charity" among its members.[67]

The solidarity of the native bishops of Africa and Asia, in supporting the primacy, was unqualified. It marked an event in the Church's history that presages the future direction of Roman Catholicism. Those who declared, with Cardinal Darmajuwono of Samarang, Indonesia, that "the Roman Pontiff possesses supreme power in the universal Church, which he can always use freely, according to the Church's needs" came from a score of countries. Spokesmen from Algeria, Ghana, Guinea, the Ivory Coast, the Malagasy Republic, Ruanda-Burundi, Senegal, South Africa, Upper Volta, and Zambia, from Ceylon, India, Indonesia, Japan, and Vietnam, and from Australia and the Fiji Islands were some of the strong defenders of papal prerogatives who stated their own and their people's adherence to the Holy See.

Raimond Tchidimbo, Archbishop of Conakry, Guinea, voiced the sentiments of the Afro-Asian hierarchy:

The spirit of peace which should animate us opposes the superficiality and impulsiveness with which some, even prelates, have made statements on very serious matters concerning the entire Church. They have disturbed also those of the faithful who are not very familiar with the internal life of the Church. In our times, the Church certainly does not lack freedom or liberty. What it lacks is humility and charity.

We bishops exercise our power, given to us by God, together with the Holy Father. At least as we Africans see it, in today's world we should insist more than ever on unity, and on obedience to the Holy Father. The Roman Pontiff is the physical sign of that unity, and we feel that we should not minimize the truth that the Pope is Peter. The Pope should continue to exercise his universal power by issuing encyclicals and other major documents without the direct participation of particular and national churches.[68]

This acknowledgment of the Pope's jurisdiction over "particular and national churches" is all the more surprising in view of the fact that twenty-nine African nations came into independent existence since 1960. Yet, though politically so conscious of their nationalism, spiritually they wanted nothing less than nationalistic Catholicism.

The American cardinals Terence Cooke of New York and John Wright, formerly of Pittsburgh and then with the Vatican, spoke in the same vein. Cooke urged the bishops to "give a witness to authentic catholicity and unity to a world which is tired of discords and divisions."[69] Wright touched on a sensitive area that Americans at least recognize as a whirlpool of difficulties wherever national (or local) interests take precedence over the universal good of the Church. He offered three principles to forestall the threatened fragmentation of Catholic unity:

1. The Conferences of Bishops should be not only national ones. Nationalism is a danger today, as it has been in the course of history to produce many schisms. Today's climate is also infected with Gallicanism, Anglicanism, Americanism, and the like. In our age of spatial discoveries, we should enlarge our vision.

2. The concept of the local and particular church should be clearly defined. Bishops are direct successors of the apostles. There are in history many examples of bishops, e.g., Ignatius of Antioch and John Fisher of England, who defended the faith and the solidarity of their union with the Roman Pontiff.

3. A bishop is not a bishop because he is a member of a conference of bishops, but because, in intimate union with the Supreme Pontiff, he exercises his own pastoral activity.[70]

Among the Latin Americans, there was no dissenting voice in upholding the undiluted primacy, without recourse to theological investigation to discover its certainty. The most elaborate defense of the papacy was given by Cardinal Vega of Ecuador, which he issued in a special communiqué to the press. He centered attention on the erroneous impression that some people were creating of a polarity between the Pope and the bishops. Collegiality, he said, is a truth of divine revelation. So, too, is the primacy. Consequently, "an authentic theological perspective will reveal their intimate unity and not tend to dissociate them. Such a false perspective would lead to the fatal extreme of placing one truth against another."[71]

In tracing the attitude of the bishops from Northern Europe, the primates of England and Ireland were transmitted—to be mentioned last. They stood by the Pope and forcefully spoke out on the very things which the critics were exploiting to embarrass the papacy. Heenan of Westminster decried "the opinion, diffused world-wide, that the Episcopal College is aiming to contest the power of the Supreme Pontiff, or at least the power of the Roman Curia. We have to avoid such an impression." In press and television let the bishops tell the world how strongly they are behind the Pope. "We have, as successors of the apostles, the duty to be concerned with the prestige of the church and of the Roman Curia." For failure in doing this, "the time after *Humanae Vitae* has not shown much unity but rather discord."[72]

In the same way, Conway of Armagh took issue with the proposal to have theological experts re-examine collegiality. There was no problem in having the International Commission of Theologians study the role of bishops in the Church and their relationship to the Bishop of Rome. Let them "prepare all the material in this regard from Holy Scripture, tradition and theologians." This will be useful, but have them do this in such a way "that not the Commission but the competent authority can make its decision."[73] As the aftermath of the papal commission on birth control had earlier proved, this was no empty recommendation.

PROTESTANTISM

In the Protestant tradition, ecclesiastical authority vested in the Pope or bishops was replaced by the inspired word of God as found in the Bible, and by the indwelling spirit which enlightens every man who comes into the world.

On its theoretical side, the groundwork was laid by the sixteenth-century Reformers who appealed against the Catholic position by arguing that once baptism was received, there is no further need for ordination or consecration, or their correlative claims to a specially conferred juridical power from God. "Whoever has undergone baptism," wrote Luther, "may boast that he has been consecrated priest, bishop and pope, although it does not beseem everyone to exercise these offices. For since we are all priests alike, no man may put himself forward, or take upon himself without our consent and election, to do that which we all alike have the power to do. If a thing is common to all, no man may take it upon himself without the wish and command of the community."[74]

Protestantism begins with the premise that Jesus Christ was a historical figure, and therefore the paramount question is posed by the historical gap between God's special advent in Christ two thousand years ago, and the sources of religious authority today. Catholic bodies, it is explained, fill the gap between Jesus Christ and the modern Christian by the *magisterium,* namely the official teaching of the bishops in communion with the Pope. This position is said to be based on the supposition that Christ delegated his authority to the Apostles and their ecclesiastically certified successors in the hierarchy and in union with Rome.

For its part, Protestantism admits that Christ conferred some authority upon the Apostles, but it believes that the Apostles were unique. Their authority cannot be handed down to others.

What, then, is the basis for the continuity of Christians today with the authoritative Jesus Christ? After more than four centuries, most Protestants would say: the written words of the Bible are authoritative, preserving concretely the message of the Savior, and assuring constant illumination from the same Savior's Spirit indwelling in the hearts of the faithful. Both facets are important for an understanding of the changes that have taken place in the Protestant concept of authority. The biblical record is viewed in a very different light than in 1804, when the British and Foreign Bible Society was founded in London "for the printing and distribution of the Bible at home and abroad." And the invisible working of grace has different implications than it had in the mid-eighteen-hundreds when Horace Bushnell (1802–1876) summarized his faith in the words, "My heart wants the Holy Ghost."

Authority of Scripture

We have already examined some of the influence of an audiovisual culture on the print-centered type of religion implied in devotion to the Bible. We also saw that a rediscovery of the believing community as creator of the Scriptures and their living form raised challenges for a faith whose focus for half a millennium had been on the scriptural, i.e., written, word of God.

What have these and other factors done to the Bible as "the Protestant conscience" and the believer's last court of appeal? They drove a wedge between two divergent approaches to Christianity, one more than ever devoted to Scripture, and the other decreasingly concerned about the inspired word of God.

The so-called liberal approach is more easily described. Nineteenth-century *biblical criticism* did not originally imply what the term suggests, "tearing the Bible to pieces." Most biblical critics were scholars who studied the Bible to better understand its meaning. They were critical in the sense that they tried to find rational or scientific reasons for their conclusions rather than to accept the dogmatic pronouncements of the preachers.

Albert Schweitzer pointed out that some of the first critics to contribute to a better knowledge of the New Testament were enemies of Christ, men who looked at the Bible critically because they hoped to destroy the religion based upon it. But Protestant divines quickly took biblical criticism into their teaching and preaching, and soon the seminaries became centers of biblical research. There were battles, of course, and the story of the first quarter of the 1900s is filled with charges and countercharges of "modernism" in which contending parties were professors in divinity schools or churchmen reacting to the "scientific study" of the Bible.

Slowly the critics won their case, although many a scholar lost his position in the process. Preachers who sympathized with biblical criticism were removed from their posts. When Harry Emerson Fosdick (1878–1969), a Baptist holding a Presbyterian pulpit, preached a sermon on the attempt of the "literalists" to force subscription to a simple biblical creed, he was attacked. Compelled to leave his Presbyterian church in New York City (1925), he became pastor of the Park Avenue Baptist Church. Under his leadership this congregation became the interdenominational Riverside Church, and Fosdick himself rose to fame on the nation-wide radio ministry, the "National Vespers."

Hailed as "America's most popular preacher," Fosdick never wavered in his dedication to the Bible, which he quoted frequently and used in a most persuasive way. But his thirty volumes of sermons, reflections, and essays are built around the concept of an ethical religion whose founder, Jesus Christ, was just *The Man From Nazareth*—the title of Fosdick's best-known book. Jesus had no such divine sonship as "Hellenistic Christianity later put into the Nicene Creed."[75]

But exegetes and preachers in America were only echoes of the

European intellectuals who were struggling with the confluence of two elements in modern Protestantism: the obvious values of biblical criticism and the literal acceptance of the biblical words (*literae*) as the word of God.

Those who favored criticism and were willing to sacrifice (if need be) something of the "old-fashioned religion" were among the leading lights in biblical scholarship. Hermann Gunkel (1862–1932) set out to show that the biblical narrative of the beginning and end of time is based on extra-biblical legends of Oriental peoples. Regarding the origin of Christianity, he asserted that it is a syncretistic religion, and that the essentials of the Church's christological doctrine are not derived from the historical Jesus.

Gunkel's theory was developed by Hugo Gressmann (1877–1927), for whom the guiding axiom was that history is the key to all religion. According to Gressmann, there is in the world no material that does not have its history, no conception of thought without its connections to previous conceptions. This maxim holds true not only in small and trivial things of life, but also concerning the prophetic religion of Israel and the origin of Christianity. Moreover, the study of history is conditioned by the law of development. "Anyone who rejects evolution can make no claim to scientific knowledge." Evolution in the field or biblical studies is an established fact and has supplanted a biblical history based on supernatural forces. Gressmann concluded that such ideas as the Messiah or heaven and hell were conditioned by similar extra-biblical concepts, not by supernatural revelation and inspiration. A Christian who believes in these concepts is actually subscribing to notions that are not uniquely Christian but that grew out of the religious history of pre-Christian peoples.

Other writers with the same outlook applied these principles to the whole sweep of biblical faith. William Wrede (1859–1906) said it was Paul and not Jesus who founded the Christian religion. Baptism is an accretion from the mystery cults; and the Lord's Supper was simply a farewell meal that Paul elevated to the dignity of a sacrament. Wilhelm Bousset (1865–1920) decided that whatever makes the Bible authoritative is not found in the Scriptures themselves, and certainly not in any revelation they convey. It is man's native instinct to believe, which attaches itself in different people to different writings. They become "sacred" by reason of this unreasoning urge to identify and simplify one's object of belief. Hindus have thus sacralized the Vedas, Jews the Torah, and Christians the New Testament narratives.

Along with this approach to the Bible as history, there developed another and more comprehensive Protestant effort to ground the authority of the Scriptures. The historico-religious school was transformed into a philosophy of religion, out of which came present-day systematic theology. Its modern creator was Ernst Troeltsch (1865–1923), who rebuilt the Christian faith on the foundations of Hegel.

Troeltsch analyzed Christianity from a historical standpoint, and found it no better (or worse) than other religions of mankind. His dictum was universal: To be historical and relative is identical. On this side of its being, therefore, Christianity has no more claim to absoluteness than Buddhism; maybe less, because it is not so ancient.

But why should that be troublesome? For the European-American mind, the last thing Christianity wants is absolutes. Christians are quite willing to settle for a religion that gives personal satisfaction, that is "good enough for me." Christianity is extraordinarily potent as "a personalistic religion."

Admittedly, said Troeltsch, there is no objective criterion by which this personal contentment can be verified. Yet that is unimportant. What matters is that "Christianity is true for me": as a Parsi could say of Zoroastrianism or a Moslem of Islam. Few men have improved on Troeltsch's definition: "Christianity becomes the gospel of the attainment and preservation of the God-filled soul. We do not ask, 'How can I obtain a gracious God,' but rather, 'How can I find my soul again, how can I learn to love again?'"[76]

Troeltsch was indifferent to being accused of making the Bible an instrument for the development of human personality, instead of God's revelation to a sinful human race. In a famous address given in Switzerland during 1918, he declared that, while Jesus is not strictly speaking necessary for the Christian religion, he is desirable for sociological and psychological reasons "as the focal point of worship and the unifying factor in the community."[77]

Even those who never read a page of Troeltsch's ponderous *Gesammelte Schriften* (1912–1925) have been affected by his logic. His influence is pervasive and some would say that, except for this Augsburg theologian, there would be no systematic theology in contemporary Protestant thought. Neo-Protestantism, as it is sometimes called, was born with him. It was "neo" because, for Troeltsch, the Reformers had retained too many features of Catholic Christianity. In his eyes, eighteenth-century rationalism was the beginning of the modern age, for it asserted the autonomy of man in religion. This freedom was to him the very core of a new Protestant Christianity, as distinct from the older form of Luther, Calvin, and Zwingli.

Is the Bible still authoritative? Yes, insofar as it gives the man who uses it the spiritual comfort and satiety he expects from religion.

At the other extreme to Gunkel, Gressmann, and Troeltsch, Protestant churchmen in Europe and America were confronted with the painful option of either giving up the Bible as normative or holding on to it with uncritical fervor—which the opposition would label as fanaticism. They took a middle course.

On the European continent were figures like Theodor Zahn (1838–1933), Ludwig Ihmels (1858–1933), Reinhold Seeberg (1859–1935), Theodor Kaftan (1847–1932), and Erich Schaeder (1861–1936). They were all dedicated to preserving the primacy of the Scriptures and succeeded to a degree that might not have been possible had the "crisis in biblical authority" not faced the Protestant world.

Zahn and associates were expert in higher and lower criticism. They, too, were interested in the meaning of words in the Bible; to find out when each passage was written, who wrote it, and to whom and why it was written. As higher critics, they recognized the need for this kind of background in order to understand the Scriptures. As lower critics, they studied manuscript texts, weighed their relative age and value, and came up with some startling discoveries. But all the while they maintained that the essentials of the faith were not impugned; rather that scholarship enhances the meaning of God's revelation—provided a man does not exclude, *a priori,* the very possibility of a supernatural communication through the medium of human language.

Lutheran Protestants, or at least those of Evangelical background, were at a distinct advantage in this contest with the intellectuals who seemed to be reducing the Scriptures to the level of the Vedas or the Zend Avesta. From the outset they distinguished between the biblical text—its literary form and material content, and the biblical faith—which the text somehow contained but was also present in the hearts of believing Christians.

Unlike the other families in Protestantism, they inherited a strong confessional tradition in a series of documents that were finished before the end of the sixteenth century and ever since had remained standards of Christian belief. Thus the *Augsburg Confession* and its *Apology*, the two *Catechisms of Luther* and the *Smalcald Articles*, while stressing the privileged status of the Bible, also insisted on the corresponding need for confessional creeds.

These were authentic creeds of Protestantism and, as over half a century of struggle is showing, the Protestant religion survives only where such creeds continue to be honored by the people.

What happened in practice was that the great confessions of historic Protestantism became, in reality, expressions of Christian tradition: to select and explain the major articles of Christian belief out of a broader and deeper context than the plain words of the Bible. They drew on the riches of Christian history and could further draw on the continuing insight of the whole of Christendom.

Underlying the Evangelical defense of the Scriptures, therefore, was the implicit assumption that *sola Scriptura* in the early Reformers need not be taken so woodenly as to exclude other sources of Christian knowledge. The Bible could remain, as the *Formula of Concord* (1577) declared, "the only rule and norm, according to which all dogmas and all doctors ought to be esteemed and judged."[78] At the same time, the accumulated wisdom of the ages, from Ambrose and Augustine to the present day, could be consulted and invoked to substantiate what the basic confessions of faith proposed as of the essence of Christianity.

Other Protestant traditions were less fortunate, except where (as among the Reformed) they approximated the Lutheran position: that the Bible is, indeed, "the only rule and norm," but it allows and needs interpretation; and that among the means of interpretation, the most useful were the confessional formularies which concentrated on essentials and correlated Protestantism with the rest of Christianity.

The best-known Reformed defender of the Bible was Karl Barth (1886–1968), who began as a pastor in Geneva, taught at Göttingen, Münster, Bönn, and Basle where he died with the reputation of having saved Protestantism in modern times. Barth's name, it is confidently said, "will go down in history as the great conqueror of liberal theology, as a prophet of a new Christianity, because he interpreted the crisis of Western civilization in the light of the Word of God, proclaiming relentlessly the divine yes against our human no, and the divine no against our human yes."[79] Without Barth, contemporary Protestantism anywhere in the world is unintelligible.

He began his literary career as an historical relativist, with great hope in the future of man's progress through the new discoveries in science and political socialism. Then came the First World War, during which he was disillusioned with human progress and had a genuine conversion. Two documents of Barth, out of a library of more than twenty volumes, synthesize his thought, especially on the one question that preoccupied his mind: What is the authority of the biblical word of God? In 1919 he published a *Commentary on Romans* (*Der Römerbrief*), which he revised two years later. And in 1934 he was the main author of the *Barmen Declaration* against the Nazi oppressors of the Church.

Typical of his openness to ideas from others as "reflectors on revelation," he completely re-edited the first draft of *Der Römerbrief*, because he felt the need of enlightenment from those who shared his own biblical faith. In the original edition, he argued to the fundamental postulate of Christianity: that there is a God, the wholly Other, whose reality is always present and active in our lives. In the second and definitive edition, he took on the "sophisticated pygmies" who would not "let God be God," but insisted on reading the divine Word through their own distorted vision of what, on their terms, the world and mankind ought to be.

He undercut the position of his own former colleagues by dismissing as extraneous all their arguments against the historicity of the Bible and the quest of a "historical Jesus." Until Barth came along, the Evangelicals, in their apologetic efforts, had often arrived at some sort of compromise between the results of biblical criticism and the religious finality of the Bible.

Trained as a critic, Barth would not accept the position of "fundamentalists," notably in the Lutheran confessional tradition. He bypassed all the historicism and psychologism of the critics by holding to a theory that revelation and redemption are phenomena which lie beyond the realm of history and psychology. He borrowed from Kierkegaard what has since become the name of the Barthian view of Christianity, "dialectic theology." The Danish Lutheran had taught him that "Paul and Plato can go quite a ways together," to the point that Barth finally settled for a cosmic dualism in the universe. God and man, eternity and time, are seen as metaphysical opposites. God is in heaven; man is on earth. God is known, but only as the unknown God.

Barth's main object was to lead Christianity away from what he thought was the cardinal error of modern religious thinkers, with their kindly attitude toward science, culture, and art; their sympathetic outlook on mysticism and their willingness to "buy" a religion of feeling. He would bring the faith back to the principles of the Reformation. It was to be a return to the prophetic teaching of the Bible, of which he believed the Reformers were the most authentic interpreters. Among those who specially influenced him was the Russian Dostoyevsky.

The Christian message, according to Barth, affirmed the Supremacy and Transcendence of God, whose infinite superiority to all human aspirations meant the worthlessness of human reason: "See what man's genius has produced—chaos!" Since the Fall, which brought man wholly under the dominion of sin, his natural capacities, including his reason, had been perverted. All "natural theology," therefore, as expounded by the Scholastics (Aquinas and Scotus) and the modern Catholic Church, and all religion grounded on experience, as found in Schleiermacher and the Hegelians, have now become impossible. God's sole revelation is in Jesus Christ and the Word of God is his one and only means of communication with man. Since man is utterly dependent on divine grace, all his boasted cultural achievements are rooted in sin.

These doctrines were proclaimed by Barth with passionate fervor, in a style at once graphic and forceful. He was most eloquent when he dealt with the role of the Gospel in the Christian life or, more accurately, in the Christian community:

> What we might call the characteristic work of the community [is] its commission to preach the Gospel to the world. . . .
>
> It cannot approve nor tolerate the way and ways of the world. It has to indicate a very different path. On the other hand, its decisive task is not to confront men with this objection, criticism and negation, nor with a program, plan or law in the performance of which men must abandon that great attempt to live without God, counterbalancing it by the opposite attempt to return to God and with His help to make everything different and better. This is what the Synagogue does. This is what Freemasonry does. This is what Moral Rearmament does. But this is not what the Church of Jesus Christ does. It has no right to make proposals to men as though they could now help, justify, sanctify and and glorify themselves more thoroughly and successfully than hitherto.
>
> No, its great and simple but very different mission is that of declaring

to them the kingdom of God, and not therefore a means to help them to do something, but the one truth that God has already begun to do something for them and that He will also complete it in spite of their opposition, overlooking and bypassing all their perversity and futility. . . . It must be only the community of the Gospel, content to be no more.[80]

In page after page of his *Dogmatik* (twelve volumes), Barth has sustained passages that go on for a thousand and more words to a single paragraph. Some have found him impossibly repetitious and caustic critics suggested that all his writings could be reduced to one jotting on a scrap of paper: "God is not man, revelation and redemption are not history, eternity is not time." Perhaps, but this very remark shows how forcefully he got his message across on the central fact of Christianity, that what the Bible proclaims is ultimately a proclamation, to be listened to because it is God speaking to man— today as the day it was written. Its authority is simply, and terrifyingly, itself. God confronts man with his Word, telling man that God is master of the universe and that man is completely under God.

Barth spoke with such conviction because he never separated the Bible (as written word) from the Word of God, the *Logos*, dwelling in the hearts of Christian believers. Moreover, he always associated the Scriptures with the Christian community, in which the words of revelation are a living and corporate presence, in a way that printed syllables in the Book could never be conceived.

He also illustrated the fact that those Protestants were most successful in warding off the solvent of rationalism who had the strongest confessional tradition on which to rely, in this case the *Institutes* of Calvin. Barth regarded Calvin second only to Augustine in his understanding of the Gospel, and accepted his concept of predestination with unswerving loyalty. He recognized in Calvin's interpretation of St. Paul the essence of Protestantism or, more accurately, of the Protestant—as distinct from the Catholic or Orthodox—form of Christianity.

While Karl Barth and his followers in Europe were developing a neo-orthodoxy along scholarly lines, practical church leaders in every country were organizing the Protestant faithful to protect the Bible "against the inroads of unbelief." The United States, with its competing denominations, saw the most extensive effort among Evangelicals (as they preferred to be called) to consolidate their forces in spite of sectarian differences.

By mid-century, Americans had successfully mobilized similar movements elsewhere. In 1966 delegates from more than thirty nations of Europe, America, and Afro-Asia met in Berlin for a historic congress on Evangelism. Their purpose was to agree on the basic principles that must underlie any effective preaching of the Gospel by the heirs of the Reformation. The summary of these principles is a reflection of decades of struggle by men who sought to find their Protestant identity in a confusion of ideologies.

"Evangelism must be trinitarian," the manifesto began, "if it is to be biblical. The Great Commission defines the program of the Church for this age by the authority of the Triune God." Thus, when Christ commissioned his followers to teach all nations, he exercised his divine authority to command. Although he is no longer on earth in visible form, he promised to be with his people in spirit, to the end of the world. Meanwhile he left his followers a visible (and readable) body of revelation in the form of a book.

> The Bible is our authority. A Bible that is an infallible rule of faith and practice is the reason for the existence of Protestantism. The Reformation rediscovered three major truths that established Protestantism as a return to New Testament Christianity.
>
> The first truth, called the formal cause of the Reformation, is that the Bible is the final and infallible authority in matters of faith and practice. This is the principle of *sola scriptura*. The second truth is justification by faith, called the material cause of the Reformation. This is called the principle of *sola fide*. The third truth is the priesthood of the believer. It is a corollary of the other two.

So much for positive affirmation. Then a strong condemnation of those who wish to be considered Protestant and enjoy the fruits of the Reformation but have lost its original spirit.

> The principle of *sola scriptura* has been rejected by liberal Protestantism. For the liberal the Bible is not authoritative, not dependable, and not authentic. This dismissal of the Bible has resulted from the acceptance of evolutionary naturalism and higher criticism.

The Protestant world during the last decades of this century seems to be faced with only one option: rationalism or Rome.

The necessity for a return to biblical authority is the reason for our gathering. We are under the Word. Let us therefore give proper place to the Word of God in all our deliberations. Otherwise only two alternatives exist. The first is to go to left-wing rationalism, in which the human mind is the supreme authority in religious matters; the second is to return to Rome, where the church is the final authority in doctrine and ethics.[81]

Protestant churches that have retained (or regained) this concept of final authority, vested in the infallible Scriptures, are also the most flourishing. Comparative figures for one denomination, the American Southern Baptists, illustrate the contrast:

Year	Members	Churches
1845 (estab'd.)	351,951	4,126
1910	2,332,464	23,248
1930	3,850,278	23,731
1950	7,079,889	27,788
1970	10,947,389	33,926

There was no similar growth in any other denomination of world Protestantism. Appropriately, the Southern Baptists have the nearest to a formal creed in the Free Church tradition, and they place the authority of the Bible first among the twenty articles in their *Abstract of Principles:* "The Scriptures of the Old and New Testaments were given by inspiration of God, and are the only sufficient, certain and authoritative rule of all saving knowledge, faith and obedience."[82] The Southern Baptist Convention is not a constituent member of either the National or the World Council of Churches.

The contrast in the mission field is equally symptomatic. As reported by its own researchers, the National Council of Churches in America showed an increase of only 4.5 per cent during a ten-year period in the number of foreign missionaries from all agencies related to the Council. In the same decade, the churches not belonging to the Council and strongly based on biblical authority, recorded an increase of 149.5 per cent in foreign missionary personnel. A similar survey of the American Protestant clergy showed an increment ratio of three to one in the number of ministers belonging to biblical as distinct from social-oriented churches in the United States.

Witness of the Spirit

The second focus of classic Protestantism, along with biblical authority, was a stress on the Spirit as abiding Master in the life and activity of every believing Christian.

The Scriptures became normative during the Reformation, in place of councils and popes. So, too, the indwelling Spirit became directive, in place of the professedly divine guidance by the Spirit residing in the Catholic hierarchy.

This dependence on the Spirit, available to every Christian, is still distinctive of Protestant Christianity. It specifies the idea of internal authority within the believer, to complement the external authority of the Bible.

It was left to modern times, however, to bring out clearly the correlation between these two elements, the Bible and the Spirit. They are related so closely that the one depends on the other, and, as the one recedes, the other enters; or, as the one decreases, the other becomes more prominent.

With the growing challenge to biblical authority, rose a corresponding trust in the working of the Spirit. Churches and people that had formerly used the Bible with complete certainty, or accepted its teaching with equanimity, came more than ever to look to the Spirit for guidance in religious matters.

Any attempt to review the main features of this movement in twentieth-century Protestantism is handicapped by so much detail as to defy classification. Perhaps the best thing is to give it a name, Pentecostalism, and trace its three principal forms of expression, illuminism, evangelism, and charismatic phenomena.

As a species of Protestant Christianity, Pentecostalism may be traced to the ministry of Edward Irving (1792–1834), pastor of a Presbyterian church in London. Irving had witnessed an outburst of speaking with tongues and some cases of healing in Glasgow, Scotland. He reported back to his congregation that what he had seen could be repeated in London if only the people prayed earnestly enough that they, too, might be filled with the gifts of the Spirit. Soon after, some of his parishioners began to speak in strange tongues and prophesy. He refused to curb these manifestations when advised to do so. By 1832 he had started a new congregation which professed to receive unusual blessings in answer to prayer.

The Irvingites were soon joined by Quakers, Shakers, Mormons, and others who preached that external manifestations are an essential part of Christian belief. More significant was the fact that Methodism in the United States began to divide along sharp lines. John Wesley, the Methodist founder, had never been much concerned with creedal orthodoxy. Experience of conversion and an awareness of the Spirit had always been more prominent in Wesleyan thought. With the advent of biblical criticism and the solvent of rationalism, many of the followers of Wesley fell back almost exclusively on personal experience as a criterion of God's saving presence. Some of these Holiness groups affiliated with the disciples of Irving, and modern Pentecostalism was born. It had the theoretical principles of Wesleyan theology and the practical experience of Irvingite phenomena. By 1970, scholars estimated a world membership in formal Pentecostal bodies of almost twenty million. If the name is extended to include traditional churches which have Pentecostal leanings, the number may safely be doubled.

The most dramatic event in Pentecostal history occurred on New Year's Eve, 1900. Before Charles Fox Parham, a lay Congregational preacher, left on a mission trip, he instructed his students at Bethel Healing Home in Topeka to investigate the subject of baptism in the Holy Spirit. When he returned, they told him that the gift of tongues was conclusively this Spirit baptism. They asked him to impose hands on one of their number, a Miss Ozman. The moment he did so, she was "filled with the Holy Spirit" and began to speak in several languages, besides talking in a strange tongue that not even accomplished linguists could understand. Before long most of the students at Bethel became similarly gifted, and went out to preach the new gospel to all who would hear them.

Parham's disciple, the Negro William J. Seymour, carried the Pentecostal message to California, where it took immediate root and began to spread to all parts of America and overseas.

During the next fifty years, Pentecostalism became established in every major country of the world. Chinese Pentecostals of pre-Mao days were recruited chiefly from Presbyterians, Methodists, and Anglicans. The Chinese had adopted Buddhist and Taoist mysticism and later on were presented as models of a Marxist-Christian denomination.

Under the guidance of American, British, Canadian, and Swedish missionaries, Pentecostalism penetrated India (and Pakistan) since the early 1920s and now poses a serious challenge to the traditional Christian churches. The concentration is in southern and central India (Maharashtra, Andhra Pradesh, and Kerala). Indian Pentecostals tend to be more contemplative in their approach to prayer, and less interested in healing. A single group, converted by the Church of God (Tennessee), reported 35,000 members in 1968. Similar conversion successes were claimed for Japan, the Philippines, and Indonesia.

Africa showed an astounding fertility for Pentecostal development. Almost without exception, the Spirit-filled groups are direct descendants of Protestant evangelistic bodies. They generally have only the rudiments of biblical knowledge—often just a few memorized texts. But the Spirit supplies for the deficiency and their experiences tend to follow the pattern of whatever Scripture passages are most favored. On the ethical side, they are often legalistic and rigorist, stressing the importance of tithing, fasting, and avoiding alcohol and tobacco. Ritually they understress the Lord's Supper, often omitted, and reflect the gamut of charismata like healing, exorcism, and the gift of tongues. By 1970, African Pentecostalism had passed the million mark, and was firmly established in such disparate places as Addis Ababa (Ethiopia) and South Africa. Social scientists write of "sectarian outbursts all over Africa, and prophets everywhere, in whom a veneer of Christian truth is overgrown by non-Christian excrescences, including anti-white rebellion and animistic survival."[83]

In Latin America, Pentecostalism has made more progress than in any other continent. It concentrates on the poorest and religiously more abandoned people, and finds no problem in adapting the most varied customs of the natives to the simple message of "receiving the Spirit" and awaiting the early advent of the Lord Jesus.

Its basic appeal in Spanish America is to the unwritten Gospel of the heart, which has great attraction especially for those with the lowest literacy, who may, of course, have a high degree of intelligence. Countries like Bolivia, Brazil, El Salvador, Guatemala, Haiti, Honduras, and Peru—with illiteracy ratios of thirty to seventy per cent of the population—are also strongly Pentecostal.

The dialectic between literate (Bible) and charismatic (Spirit) Protestantism may be more complex, however, as happened in Chile.

Pentecostalism was brought into the country by an American Methodist, W. C. Hoover, who met with little response among the *hermanos* until one day he invited them to a prayer meeting at his home in Valparaiso. Together they prayed for the blessing of the Spirit and the blessing came. "The brethren danced, had spiritual visions, spoke in tongues, and prophesied." The Methodist authorities intervened and tried to put a stop to these occurrences, but the converts answered that they had to obey the Spirit and not men. In the following year (1910), they were expelled from the mother church and formed a new denomination. Internal dissension later divided the parent body, into the Iglesia Metodista Pentecostal and the Iglesia Evangelica Pentecostal. In thirty years, these two became eight national bodies, with an estimated million members and forming four fifths of the total Protestant affiliation in Chile.

The Chilean experience symbolizes Pentecostalism in Latin America. Though highly literate, the people were only slightly educated in the Catholic faith of their baptism. Protestantism had been offered them for generations, but with only a trickle of converts. Then a sudden change of approach, from the Bible (to be read) to the Spirit (to be sensed), in reaching the natives, and the results are so dramatic that one enthusiastic writer predicted that "Pentecostalism, the youngest offshoot of the third Reformation, has dealt a decisive blow to Catholicism in Latin America."[84] What is certain is the extent and fervor of the conversions.

This brings us back to the United States where modern Pentecostalism started. Over two hundred religious bodies in America would qualify as Pentecostal. Often their names give no clue to their real character, e.g., the Church of God or the Assemblies of God. Their statements of faith are much the same, with a uniform stress on the operations of the Spirit, and their indispensability for authoritative Christianity in today's world of confusion and uncertainty.

All believers are entitled to and should ardently expect and earnestly seek the promise of the Father, the baptism in the Holy Ghost and fire, according to the command of our Lord Jesus Christ. This was the normal experience of all in the early Christian Church. With it comes the endowment of power for life and service, the bestowment of the gifts and their uses in the work of the ministry.

This experience is distinct from and subsequent to the experience of the new birth. With the baptism in the Holy Ghost come such experiences as an overflowing fulness of the Spirit, a deepened sense of reverence for God, an intensified consecration to God and dedication to His work, and a more active love for Christ, for His Word and for the lost.

The baptism of believers in the Holy Ghost is witnessed by the initial physical sign of speaking with other tongues as the Spirit of God gives them utterance. The speaking in tongues in this instance is the same in essence as the gift of tongues, but different in purpose and use.[85]

Inherent in this concept of Christianity is the direct witness of the Spirit to the heart and mind of each believer. On analysis this means a composite of three experiences received as one. The logic that binds them is irrefutable—given the Pentecostal premises. First comes the divine visitation, a baptism like that of the apostles on the first Pentecost in Jerusalem. The Spirit of God pours into the souls of those he selectively visits an abundance of internal blessings: of faith and understanding, conviction and the certainty of his presence. It is divinely infused illuminism.

Along with this comes the supernatural desire to communicate the faith and conviction to others. It is pressing and irresistible. Only those who receive it know how imperious it can be. Pentecostal commentators do not hesitate to compare themselves with the early disciples whom "the charity of Christ urged" to preach the good news. Evangelism is a weak word to describe the zeal of those who, having seen for themselves, want to have others partake of the same vision.

The capstone is the extraordinary phenomena that accompany the preaching of the Word, no less than in apostolic times. Their function is to give evidence to the action of the Spirit in the person who claims to be in special contact with God. The term *charisms* technically refers to the third of this Pentecostal triad: prophetic illumination which is the baptism of the Spirit; supernatural inspiration to go out and make disciples in the light of this new-found wisdom; and miraculous intervention by God to convince oneself and others that the original inspiration was certainly divine.

Pentecostalism is a dramatic commentary on the Protestant crisis of faith in the authority of the Scriptures as the revealed word of God. It answers to a deep-felt need for assurance of being saved and of Christ's redemptive mission to mankind. What the Bible provided in a less critical age, the Spirit now confers by his own charismatic aid—

much as he did before the Bible was written or the pages of the Gospel were ever read.

But the Catholic Church also has its crisis of faith—in the authority of the Church as infallible teacher of God's revelation. Predictably a form of Pentecostalism would enter the Catholic ranks to serve much the same purpose: answer to a psychological need for reassurance that the Church is still a safe guide on the road to salvation. What the Church's magisterium provided in "pre-conciliar" days, the Spirit is now believed to supply by a supernatural effusion of grace—much as he did before the institutional Church was fully organized or statements of popes and bishops were so commonly made.

At the Uppsala meeting of the World Council of Churches in 1968 a representative of the Pentecostal churches of Germany brought the issue to a sharp focus. He frankly told the Council what the conflict in today's world is all about. On the one hand, he stated, there are certain "unrelinquishable bases of the Christian faith—God's act of salvation in Jesus Christ, his incarnation, his being born of the virgin Mary, his miracles which he performed through the power of God, his sacrificial death of atonement on the Cross at Golgotha in order to redeem us, his physical resurrection, his ascension to the right hand of the Father, and his glorious return promised at the end of time in order to establish the kingdom of God." They are inalienable truths. If ever "these essential bases of the Christian faith were to be argued away by human logic," or, what comes to the same thing, "if the gifts of the Holy Spirit poured forth at Pentecost were regarded as identical with the human intellect, which is becoming increasingly deified," then he would pronounce a malediction. Organizations like the World Council, or any other agency with "world-wide influence," in spite of its Christian name "might be in danger of preparing the way for Anti-Christ."[86]

The delegates at Uppsala allowed this judgment to stand: that just as the foundations of Christianity were first authored by God, so they do not now "depend upon the findings of scholarly research." They derive their lasting authority from "what God, in his grace, reveals 'to babes.' "[87] It is not necessary to accept the Pentecostal movement as a preternatural descent of the Holy Spirit to recognize the perennial essentials of Christianity.

ORTHODOXY

Long before that fateful third of April 1204, when Eastern Christianity severed relations with Rome, the Orthodox had developed a concept of authority which did not include papal primacy. For want of a better word, the English *conciliarity* has been coined to translate something of what the Russians mean by *sobornost* and the Greeks by *koinonia*. Their theologians explain that "conciliarity of government," or the mystical union of the faithful through love, is the true notion of the Church's authority.

The classic idea of *sobornost* and *koinonia* grew out of historical circumstances. For centuries the Church had been faced with a series of doctrinal crises, raised by those who denied the divinity of Christ, his oneness with the Father, and the necessity of supernatural grace for salvation. With notable exception the crises were resolved mainly through conciliar action, whether local, synodal, provincial, or ecumenical. If there were many instances when the popes intervened, either to support the council or pass judgment without it, the dominant impression in the East was that conciliar rule and teaching should be identified with the ordinary mode of governing the Church.

As we enter modern times, the traditional concept was essentially the same. Depending on how the Church was conceived, its authority was generally seen as halfway between Protestantism and Roman Catholicism. Unlike Protestants, the Orthodox did not believe that decisive authority derives primarily from the people, depending on their personal and collective understanding of the Bible under direct guidance of the Spirit. The Orthodox made much of their ordained hierarchy, who were literally "priestly rulers" (*hieros*=priest and *arche*=rule).

The standard *Confession of Dositheus*, drafted in 1672 to meet the Protestant challenge, laid down in plain language how Orthodoxy looked upon this hierarchical episcopate:

> The dignity of the Bishop is so necessary in the Church that, without him, neither Church nor Christian could either be or be spoken of. For he, as a successor of the Apostles, has received in continued sucession by the imposition of hands and the invocation of the All-holy Spirit the grace that is given him by the Lord of binding and loosing. He is, therefore, a living image of God upon the earth. By the fullest sharing

in the operation of the Holy Spirit, who is the chief functionary, he is a fountain of all the Mysteries [Sacraments] of the Catholic Church, through which we obtain salvation.

We further hold that he is as necessary to the Church as breath is to a man, or the sun to the world. It has been well said in recognition of the dignity of the High Priesthood that, what God is in the heavenly Church of the first-born . . . that every High Priest is in his own particular Church, as through him the flock is enlightened, and nourished, and becomes the temple of God.

Moreover, we consider it certain that this great mystery and dignity of the Episcopate has come down to us by a continued succession.[88]

The clarity of the Orthodox position was partly occasioned by the crisis in the seventeenth century. To this day, Dositheus' creed is normative in Byzantine Orthodoxy.

Then came the Russian Revolution, itself the culmination of centuries of Caesaro-papalism. The net effect of the Tsarist control of the Church in Russia and of the Church's subservience under the Ottomans was to reduce the ideals of the Orthodox episcopate to theory, and substitute a *de facto* subordination of Church to State. As a further consequence, episcopal authority, though nominally resident in the Church's high priests, became increasingly vested in civil officials or in the collective will of the people.

There are two phases to the twentieth-century story of Orthodox authority: the oppressive ideology and legislation of the Soviet State, and the changing concept of Orthodox ecclesiology, adjusting to the revolutionary circumstances of the times. Neither side can be understood without the other, and together they form an appropriate climax to this part of our study, because the Orthodox experience under Marxist political power (some would say) is a foreshadowing of what Catholicism and Protestantism may expect from the rise of totalitarian states throughout the world, and not only behind the Iron Curtain.

Soviet Ideology and Legislation

The real beginnings of Soviet ideology, which was later to challenge every iota of Orthodoxy's right to teach and direct its people, go back to 1848, when Karl Marx and Friedrich Engels published their *Communist Manifesto*. Next in sequence were the three massive volumes of Marx's *Das Kapital*, finished posthumously by Engels by 1894. The third ideologue to shape Soviet theory was Lenin (1870–1924). His twelve volumes of writings have, as their main features: an analysis of imperialism; the need for creating and maintaining a strongly organized and disciplined Communist party to prepare and guide the proletariat revolution; uncompromising atheism; and the willingness to resort to expediency in the conflict with capitalism and religious authoritarianism.

Built on the work of these intellectual giants are commentaries, interpretations and analyses, like the articles of the *Great Soviet Encyclopedia* and the speeches of Stalin and Khrushchev. The whole ensemble is so vast in size and often so technical that few people realize the essentially simple principles on which the Soviet system is founded. Each principle clashed with its counterpart in that form of Christianity which has borne the main brunt of the conflict.

In order to appreciate what has happened to Eastern Orthodoxy in terms of its divine mandate to lead the faithful, something of the adverse forces it had to face must be seen—at the risk of talking in a vacuum. These forces were (and are) ideational. They express a philosophy of being and of man's nature and purpose that directly contradicts the Christian religion—whether in the Orthodox or another tradition. For the sake of conciseness, we can reduce them to two premises, or propositions, and briefly illustrate each in historical context. Then we can turn to the Church's reaction to this deeply conceptual challenge to its authority.

DIALECTICAL MATERIALISM. The bedrock of Marxism is dialectical materialism. This has two elements: "materialism" and "dialectic."

On the side of materialism, it is the philosophy which claims that matter, meaning the observable world of space and time, is taken "without reservations" as real in its own right. It exists independent of any transcendental source (God) and is temporally and logically prior to mind (spirit). In other words, mind appears only as an outgrowth of matter and must be explained accordingly. We think with our bodies and brain cells *only*, not with some mysterious entity which can exist independently of the body.

The dialectical part of this system postulates a universal, built-in process of transformation. All things are constantly in flux. They are in perpetual change, evolving into some new thing by reason of the inner conflict of opposing forces which constitute everything. Nothing can be said *to be*; it is always *becoming*. And the process of becoming

and the offspring would be given better care ("good living conditions for the children"), contraception is not only permissible but desirable.

In the fall of 1968 the American hierarchy published a document entitled *Human Life in Our Day,* in which they explored the implications of the Church's teaching on contraception in its bearing on the Christian conscience.

They began by recalling Newman's well-known letter to the Duke of Norfolk, to whom he explained how even in ordinary matters of papal jurisdiction, quite apart from professedly infallible doctrine, a loyal Catholic assumes that the Pope is right and obeys accordingly.

But here the issue is no passing act of papal legislation. As Paul VI declared, he intended "by virtue of the mandate entrusted to Us by Christ," to restate for today's world a "teaching that had already often been set forth by the Magisterium." Consequently, there can be no question about the *fact* that contraception is contrary to the will of God. There can only be question of the *degree of guilt* in those who, out of weakness or ignorance or confusion, practice what the Church teaches is wrong.

> *Humanae Vitae* does not discuss the question of the good faith of those who make practical decisions in conscience against what the Church considers a divine law and the Will of God. The encyclical does not undertake to judge the consciences of individuals but to set forth the authentic teaching of the Church which Catholics believe interprets the divine law to which conscience should be conformed.
>
> We feel bound to remind Catholic couples when they are subjected to the pressures which prompt the Holy Father's concern, that however circumstances may reduce moral guilt, no one following the teaching of the Church can deny the objective evil of artificial contraception itself.

So much for objective principles. As for subjective problems, the Church is a loving mother, aware of the cost that fidelity to Christ's teaching may demand of her loyal children.

> With pastoral solicitude we urge those who have resorted to artificial contraception never to lose heart but to continue to take full advantage of the strength which comes from the Sacrament of Penance, and the grace, healing, and peace in the Eucharist. May we all be mindful of the invitation of Jesus. "The man who comes to me, I will never turn away" (John 6:37). Humility, awareness of our pilgrim state, a willingness and determination to grow in the likeness of the Risen Christ will help to restore direction of purpose and spiritual stability.[40]

As a general pattern, the cultural milieu in which the various hierarchies (and theologians) lived almost determined how they reacted to *Humanae Vitae*. In countries where birth control was common and the social pressure for contraception strong, the bishops and commentators reflected both the practice and the pressure. Scandinavia, with its high index of birth limitation, was a classic example. The United States would seem to be an exception, but more recent events suggest that the sentiments of the 1968 pastoral were only minimally followed up by individual bishops in their dioceses. Those who seriously tried to implement *Humanae Vitae* paid dearly at the hands of the image-makers of America.

The media played a major role in the *Humanae Vitae* controversy, centering especially on the conflict between conscience and authority. Some, in the words of the editors, made it their set policy "to defend the Church against the Pope." They assumed that Catholics, in general, wanted contraception and that the Pope, on principle, was against it. Before the encyclical, the confrontation between Rome and (in this case) America was built up to dramatic proportions. After the document was published, the opposition seemed to be fixed—only by then the issue was more than contraception; it was the locus or even the existence of visible authority in the Catholic Church.

3. CHRISTIAN LOVE IN MARRIAGE. If Church authority and the rights of conscience were clarified by the reaction to *Humanae Vitae*, the demands of Christian love also became clearer. In the light of the Church's tradition, the Pope analyzed the ways in which every marriage—as Christians see it—is an expression of true love. Conjugal love is first of all *human*, wherein two persons freely join to live together in spirit—and not only in bodily cohabitation.

How does contraception militate against the human quality of married love? Defenders of *Humanae Vitae* argued that in contraceptive marriages the wife frequently becomes a chattel (though well-clothed and well-housed) of the husband and shares only marginally in that intercourse of spirit which makes human companionship one of the great joys of marital life.

Conjugal love, when truly Christian, is also total. "Whoever truly loves his marriage partner loves not for what he receives, but for the partner's self, rejoicing that he can enrich his partner with the gift of himself."[41] This mutuality of giving is predicated on the words of Christ that it is better to give than to receive, and the witness of St.

Paul that marriage is a complete surrender of self for the benefit of the other.

Again, how does contraception inhibit total self-giving? Theologians in Europe explained it by saying that a couple practicing contraception develop the habit of using their partner for sexual gratification, instead of cultivating ways of showing their love selflessly. Of critical importance here is to know what the word *love* really means.

> The term *love* is completely misused by many Catholics. They are blind to the nature of spousal love and attempt to reduce it to "sex appeal." Even when some admit that sexual intercourse without love is something negative, love is in fact taken to mean something completely peripheral, basically a sensual desire, which lacks all the characteristics of love in general as well as those of spousal love in particular.
>
> It is of the greatest importance to stress that the question of birth control must be considered in the light of the mystery of true love and its fulfillment in bodily donation, and never in terms of sexual attraction —today so often called "love."[42]

Besides being human and total, wrote the Pope, conjugal love is "faithful and exclusive until death." This is the way bride and groom understand it on the day when they freely assume the commitment of the marriage bond. If this fidelity can sometimes be difficult, it is always possible—provided husband and wife believe on faith that their love is supported by the grace of Christ and sustained by the inflexible teaching of the Church.

Since *Humanae Vitae* appeared, studies that were lost in scientific journals or known only to specialists were brought to light and used to support the Church's position. Other, more elaborate research programs have been instituted. Those who believe that contraception is morally wrong are also sure it is socially bad, that "birth control . . . consistently leads to the defense of promiscuity," because it focuses attention on self.[43] It makes fidelity to one man or one woman more difficult, especially when infidelity no longer has the sanctions of extra-marital pregnancy.

The last quality of marital love, according to the Pope, is fundamental for any understanding of why historic Christianity rejected contraception. Love in marriage is fruitful: "It is not exhausted by the communion between husband and wife, but is destined to continue by raising up new lives." On a right concept of this love Christianity finally builds its high expectations of the married faithful.

By its very nature, the conjugal act, while most closely uniting husband and wife, makes it possible for them to generate new lives, according to laws inscribed in the very being of man and woman. By safeguarding both these essential aspects, the unitive and the procreative, the conjugal act preserves in its fulness the sense of true mutual love and its ordination to man's most noble calling to parenthood.

Taken obversely, contraception is held to be wrong just because it tries to separate these two built-in qualities of marital intercourse—fostering mutual love *between* husband *and* wife (unitive) and communicating love *from* husband-with-wife *to* their potential offspring (procreative).

A mutual act of love, which jeopardizes the possibility of transmitting life—which God the Creator of all things has, according to particular laws, implanted therein—goes against both the divine design of marriage, and the will of the first Author of human life. To use this divine gift, while destroying, even if only partially, its meaning and purpose is to contradict the nature of man and woman and of their most intimate relationship. It is also to contradict the plan of God and his will.[44]

The defendants and opponents of *Humanae Vitae* parted company in their respective approaches on this issue. Those favoring contraception charged the Pope with preoccupation with biology and indifference to the hunger of a proliferating humanity. Those opposed parried these objections and centered on the responsibilities of Christian love.

The full implications of love as Catholic Christianity sees it are due for an extensive theological development, once the dust of controversy settles and scholars investigate more deeply why marital love is meant to be fruitful.

At the present stage of understanding, stimulated by the contraception crisis, theologians start with the Gospel principle that love is always self-giving, self-sacrificing, and self-effacing. So essential are these qualities in Christian love that, without them, love itself is destroyed. Conjugal love, therefore, is authentically Christian only if it is truly selfless and self-giving. It either contains within itself the element of self-oblation or it merely simulates what Christ told his followers they must do if they wish to be his disciples. They are to love others not only as they love themselves, which is already the high ethic of Judaic law. They are to love others as he, the God-man, loved (and loves) them, which is as far above the Mosaic code as Christ's offering of himself on the cross was greater than any oblation known to ancient Israel.

Underlying this exalted concept of love is the belief in Christ's divinity. When he told his followers to love others as he loves them, he was telling them to love their fellow men as he, who is God, loves the world he created and then became man to redeem. God's love is unmeasured, absolutely generous. It is not coerced from within or without, but sovereignly free. It is not self-seeking, but looks only to benefit the creatures whom God brought out of nothing to communicate to them, not yet existing, a share in his own infinite being. The same God, with the same freedom and generosity, took on man's humanity —only to give of his goodness and to profit nothing, as God, for himself in return.

Among all the published writings on *Humanae Vitae,* those which stood firmly behind the Pope identified this Christian concept of love as the heart of the Church's attitude toward contraception. Everything else in the Catholic tradition on the subject takes meaning from the New Testament teaching on love. Resistance to *Humanae Vitae,* said the bishops of Ireland, is a reluctance to accept the Christian vision of charity.

> Modern theories of sexual freedom all take as their starting point the fact that contraceptives separate the personal relationship or unitive aspect of sex from its procreative aspect. To admit this separation is to be inescapably committed to the very principle which lies at the root of contemporary sexual permissiveness . . .
> Love in its sexual expression is a longing for unreserved selfgiving by two people who desire to belong to each other completely in life-long love and sharing of life, *and* who desire to love together into life children who will be the living image of their two-in-oneness.[45]

One of the less publicized qualities of a contraceptive culture, the bishops concluded, is the ease with which it accepts sexual activity without reference to marriage. Catholic tradition would say this is inevitable—given a theory of love that deliberately excludes the conception of a child while performing an action whose divine purpose is to share human life.

Marriage in Eastern Orthodoxy and Protestantism

Inevitably such major pronouncements by Rome as Pius XI's *Casti Connubii* and Paul VI's *Humanae Vitae* focused attention on the

Roman Catholic concept of marriage and consequent implications in family life. Yet, there have been important developments also in the Orthodox and Protestant understanding of matrimony, as these traditions examined their historic attitude toward marriage as applied to modern times.

While Orthodox as well as Protestants sought to maintain the sacredness of marriage in the welter of growing secularization, they differed in their estimate of "sacred" with respect to marriage. Among the Orthodox, marriage is one of the seven sacraments; among Protestants, its holiness is from God, indeed, but should not be considered sacramental.

IN EASTERN ORTHODOXY. True to their view of Christianity as essentially "right worship," the Orthodox centered on the rite of marriage for better explaining its value to the people.

The Orthodox marriage service is divided into two parts: the preliminary Office of Betrothal, and the Office of Crowning. Only the second really constitutes the sacrament. On the heads of the bridegroom and bride the priest places crowns, made among the Greeks of leaves and flowers, but among the Russians of silver and gold. Until recent times, the crowning ceremony simply assumed a ritual practice with centuries of hallowed usage behind it. Pastoral implications were left undeveloped. Now the faithful are bidden to continue what their forebears had instituted because it is more than ever relevant today.

Orthodox commentators dwell on the distinctive features of the crowning ritual. They isolate three aspects as specially important: that the crowning symbolizes the small domestic kingdom which husband and wife are to begin in the bosom of their own family, the martyr's crown by which they will be called upon to witness to Christ before an indifferent and sometimes hostile world, and the anticipated glory which they, with their progeny until the end of time, have in store for them in the kingdom of eternity.

Scholars like Nicholas Cabasilas, George Fedetov, John Meyendorff, Alexander Schmemann, and Nicholas Zernov have written at length, for their own people and others, about this unique contribution to a better appreciation of Christian marriage in the increasingly non-Christian cultures of the West. A typical commentary is Schmemann's on the dignity of marriage as martyrdom.

The glory and the honor is that of the martyr's crown. For the way to the Kingdom is the *martyria*—bearing witness to Christ. And this means crucifixion and suffering. A marriage which does not constantly crucify its own selfishness and self-sufficiency, which does not "die to itself" that it may point beyond itself, is not a Christian marriage.

The real sin of marriage today is not adultery or lack of "adjustment" or "mental cruelty." It is the idolization of the family itself, the refusal to understand marriage as directed toward the Kingdom of God.

It is not the lack of respect for the family, it is the idolization of the family that breaks the modern family so easily, makes divorce its almost natural shadow. It is the identification of marriage with happiness and the refusal to accept the Cross in it.

It is the cross of Christ that brings the self-sufficiency of nature to its end. But "by the cross joy (not happiness!) entered the whole world." Its presence is thus the real joy of marriage. It is the joyful certitude that the marriage vow, in the perspective of the eternal Kingdom, is not taken "until death parts," but until death unites us completely.[46]

From another viewpoint, Orthodox leaders are telling the faithful that marriage is a form of consecration which partakes of the Christian priesthood. The occasion for this approach was twofold: the painful rift between clergy and the laity that brought such havoc into Orthodox ranks in Russia and elsewhere, and the sensed need for involving all believers to preserve and advance the Kingdom of God.

> The sacrament of ordination is, in a sense, identical with the sacrament of matrimony. Both are the manifestation of love. The priest indeed married to the Church. But just as human marriage is taken into the mystery of Christ and the Church, and becomes the sacrament of the Kingdom, it is this marriage of the priest with the Church that makes him really a priest, the true minister of that Love which alone transforms the world and reveals the Church as the immaculate bride of Christ.[47]

This is not an entirely new concept. But the stress is new, emphasizing marriage as a vocation to work in the world in order to transform it according to the teachings of the Gospel. Serious students of Byzantine society were raising the question of "whether social consciousness was to be found in the Byzantine Church." Some actually believed that "the Byzantine Church was involved only in sacramental mysticism and in an eschatological outlook with no real concern for social justice and the earthly needs of the people." A theologian from the Soviet Union blamed Byzantium for the social evil in prerevolutionary Russia. "Of all Christian cultures," he charged, "Byzantium is the one which contributed most of all to the . . . sanctification of social evil." He implied that this "social evil" was transmitted to Russia and was preserved there for centuries, from the time when Russia began to regard itself as the inheritor of Byzantium.[48]

In the light of these and similar charges, Orthodox apologists of both Greek and Slavic background have defended their Church with historical studies to prove the contrary. Yet they also felt it necessary to arouse the laity to a deeper realization of their responsibility as "priests to the world" in virtue of the sacrament of matrimony they had received.

IN PROTESTANTISM. Not unlike the situation in Orthodoxy, Protestant Churches were faced with contemporary pressures which threatened the well-being, and even the survival, of Christian marriage. Two such pressures which the heirs of the Reformation have mainly countered were the movement for greater freedom for women in marriage, and the tendency to look upon marriage as a social institution with little or no bearing on religion and the faith.

Given the wide spectrum of world Protestantism, it is impossible to generalize. The Churches reacted differently to the cultural phenomenon of "woman liberation" in politics and the secular pursuits in Western society. One pattern that may be seen, however, distinguishes biblical Protestantism from its more liberal and less doctrinal type.

Churchmen in the biblical tradition saw what was happening under duress from women liberationists and they were not impressed. There was a time, they admitted, when the word *obey* was included in marriage vows. The husband vowed to love and honor his wife and she vowed to love, honor, and obey her husband. As they read the Scriptures, the vow of obedience was based on St. Paul, who taught that wives should be subject to their husbands.

But women in the twentieth century are less inclined to vow obedience. "Deluged by books and magazine articles by advice-to-women experts, modern women view marriage as a partnership in which the husband and wife stand as individuals who maintain separate identities. Some women are outraged at the thought of a bride's vowing obedience."[49] While recognizing the common attitude, Protestant writers who consider it contrary to the Bible have been telling their people not to give in to the prevalent mores.

Women need not feel threatened. God has provided safeguards for the woman in Christian marriage. Her husband is to love her as Christ loves the Church—to have her best interest always at heart. . . . He is to love her as he loves his own flesh, for, says Paul, she *is* his flesh.

Whereas the human relationship of the husband and wife is that of the leader and the led, there is no such distinction in the spiritual realm. The wife is just as much the object of God's grace . . . as her husband. The husband who selfishly indulges in the good things God gives and refuses to share with his wife stands in danger of divine displeasure.[50]

This presupposes that the husband is ready to listen to the voice of faith and will be impressed with the threat of "divine displeasure" if he tyrannizes his wife. On a pastoral level, therefore, "adequate premarital counseling can help a young woman to avoid marrying a man who is disposed to cruelty." More basically, however, the issue which the modern Christian woman faces is her identity. "Is she going to maintain a separate independent identity apart from her husband," or will she accept the biblical image of a wife in whom the grace of Christ makes her want to become one with her husband?[51]

Parallel with a strictly biblical interpretation of women's rights in marriage has been the more familiar approach typified by the larger bodies of established Protestantism. Participants at the Uppsala meeting of the World Council in 1968 were the principal spokesmen for a "creative partnership" between husband and wife which takes into account the changed position of women in "a changing world." The Church should prepare its adherents for "new styles of living," that were, perhaps, unheard of before.

In ages past, and as recently as 1900, women were cast almost exclusively in the role of mothers of families, and their place in society was determined accordingly. But a new era has dawned.

> The relationship between men and women can be one of true partnership. Increasingly, collaboration between husband and wife is taking the place of social patterns in which women were used as agents of men's creativity and lived a life of constant child-bearing. Beyond the family relationship there is the possibility for creative partnership between the sexes. There are forms of authentic communion which do not include physical intimacy. Nevertheless, in relations between men and women there is always a sexual component. It permeates our being and maintains a tension which is creative when properly used. In professional and social relationships where men and women do not regard each other as sexual objects close partnership can be achieved. Established patterns in church, family and society which deny the full human rights of women stand condemned.[52]

Other agencies of organized Protestant thought said the same thing: that the Christian woman of the future, though married, should not look upon her status only, or even principally, as child-bearer. Like other human institutions, marriage should adjust to the culture of the times. Since "family patterns change in different social settings," therefore "Christian marriage can find its expression in a variety of ways."[53] For one couple, this may mean the procreation and nurture of offspring; for another it may take other forms. Always the operative index of choice is the woman's privilege to have her "full human rights" respected and her "personal fulfillment" recognized.

Conscious of the desacralization of marriage in countries where Christianity is supposed to be dominant, Protestant analysts spared no effort to reverse the process. In the absence of authoritative structures like the papacy, they chose the best means at their disposal: popular manuals of instruction for newlyweds and those planning on marriage. A single manual like *Harmony in Marriage* has gone through over thirty printings and typifies the spirit of millions who believe that the most necessary element for building a stable home in today's unstable society is reliance on God and his grace.

> Religion at its best burns like an altar fire in the home and God is the unseen guest day and night. Such an experience may seem difficult of realization, and it is, but not so difficult as appears. It requires daily consecration, daily thoughtfulness and daily "practice of the Presence of God." Long experience has shown that the home is more stable when the husband and wife keep their ideals by God's strength; when children learn to pray at their mother's knee; when the family go to church together as a family custom and as a conscious participation in community life.
>
> Practical results of religion in family success have been indicated in a striking way in a number of studies that have been made. These have shown that divorce is rare in homes in which the husband and wife take their church duties seriously. Time taken for private and family prayer for public worship is time spent in building up the spiritual strength of the family.[54]

From this vantage point, interdenominational writings have been more insistent than others on the absolute need for family prayer and worship to safeguard the home. Young couples are told that "if creeds and forms presented to you as embodying religion do not satisfy you, look for the truth and beauty that are deeper than all forms," or "if your church is imperfect try to make it more perfect through your influence in it."[55] Under no circumstances should religion, which is the mainstay of marital security, be abandoned.

Mixed Marriages

It would be strange, if possible, for many developments to be taking place in the modern theory of marriage without affecting the practice of marriage—among Christians of different traditions and between Christians and those who are not Christian. Mixed or interfaith marriages reveal so many important features of Christianity in the present century because they cut across elements that still divide sincerely dedicated people in the Western world.

Since it is presumed that mixed marriages are a problem for Christians who practice their faith, the focus of attention will be on partnerships where the other person is a Christian in fact and not only in name. Otherwise we would be using the wrong vocabulary. The analysis will consist mainly of reviewing the prevalent positions of the major religious traditions in the West in their respective attitudes toward mixed marriages. These positions, though growing out of centuries of the past, have reached an exceptional degree of concern in recent years. One reason may be that "communications" and "community" are more easily discussed in speculative abstractions than applied in the hard school of experience—as the millions of first- and second-generation mixed marriages testify.

WORLD PROTESTANTISM. Protestant Churches in all countries have come out often and strongly against mixed marriages. It is doubtful if a single denomination of any size has not said explicitly that its members should not contract interfaith unions. Cautions to this effect have been voiced in resolutions by the Churches individually and by church federations corporately. Special manuals for the clergy on marriage include a complete section on this matter, covering all the major Protestant religious bodies.

What is remarkable about these attitudes is their focus on marriages with Roman Catholics and their reasons for urging the people not to enter such partnerships. The universal objection is that the Catholic Church makes demands on the Protestant party which are incompatible with personal freedom. What is more objectionable, Catholicism makes assumptions that lie back of these demands to which Protestantism takes positive exception. The International Convention of the Disciples of Christ spoke for world Protestantism when it said, "We urge our young people to stand on their rights as self-respecting Christians, and that in no event they enter into marriage contract which places them in a position of disadvantage in their family relationships and in the training of their children."[56]

An analysis of the formal directives to their constituents of the major denominations in Europe and America shows that their grievances against the Roman Catholic stand on mixed marriages cover seven areas of concern. Not every Church gives all the grievances, nor is each one equally stressed, but the composite affords an accurate picture of how Protestantism views the Catholic Church in its own theology of marriage, which is the real point at issue. The directives cover the mid-century period from 1950 to 1970.

1. Protestants object to submitting to a course of instruction in Roman Catholic doctrine before marrying a Catholic. They recognize the logic of the Catholic position and frankly do not like it. As they understand it, a Protestant needs enlightenment about the religious requirements of the person whom he is to marry. If that is admitted, they ask, why should not the Protestant ask the same of his Catholic partner in order to better appreciate the life and ideals of the one he is marrying? As a rule, the more creedal Churches raise this objection; those especially, like the Missouri Lutheran and Free Methodists, who have required premarital instructions for their own people.

2. Implicit in the Catholic stand, it is argued, is the principle that: "Truth has rights which error does not possess." This makes the Catholic attitude one-sided. From the outset, therefore, a home in which one has to be right while the other has to be wrong suffers a handicap to lasting mutual esteem and harmony. Although strongly confessional bodies make most of this criticism, it is also voiced by others, e.g., the United Church of Christ, on the score that Catholicism presumes to have dogmatic possession of religious truth, something to which no one should lay absolute claim.

3. Again on the level of reciprocity, when a Christian of another Church is asked to agree that he will not interfere with the free exercise of the Roman Catholic party's religion, why should he not ask for a similar agreement in return? Not too many Churches urge this grievance in practice, even when they express it in principle. Some, however, make a great deal of it. This obtains not only among groups

like the Christian Reformed, who have an extensive doctrinal structure, but also in Churches with detailed moral and social prescriptions, such as the Adventists (vegetarianism and Saturday Sabbath), Southern Baptists (gambling prohibitions), Brethren (no alcohol), and Mennonites (simple attire).

4. Every Protestant document dealing with the subject is outspoken in its reaction to the demand that all the children of a mixed marriage be brought up Roman Catholic. There is almost no variation in what the different Churches say. They agree that the Roman Catholic demand takes away the normal liberty of a loving parent of imparting to his child the truths that are deepest and dearest to him concerning God and his kingdom. They regard this as an attack upon the freedom of conscience.

No matter how undemanding a denomination may be in its own creedal requirements, the heart of the objection is that a Catholic is obliged to bring up his offspring as Catholics, whereas Protestants wish to remain free to choose not only their children's but their own affiliation. The irritant, therefore, is the insistence on the part of Catholicism that it considers itself above denominational allegiance and claims absolute loyalty from its present and prospective members.

As in other areas, so here, the Anglican Communion has been very clear in what those who are not Roman Catholics would like Rome to do. The latest Lambeth Conference welcomed a suggestion made by some Catholic laymen that the responsibility for the Christian education of the children of a mixed marriage be regarded as the responsibility of both parents. The Conference quotes, with approval, the passage in the Declaration of Religious Liberty of the Second Vatican Council, that, "Parents . . . have the right to determine, in accordance with their own religious beliefs, the kind of religious education that their children are to receive."[57] In context, the Vatican document was talking about parents' rights to educate their children, free from state control and assisted by the civil government "to make a genuinely free choice of schools." Lambeth applied the text to Anglican or Protestant rights of parents, independent of the Catholic Church.

5. Less often stated, but also objected to is the Catholic Church's requirement that for validity the marriage must be performed before a priest and specified witnesses. Where the question is examined theologically, the premise taken is that this implies an unwarranted assumption of authority over the conditions of a marital contract. The *In-*

stitutes of Calvin dealt with this at length and certain texbooks in Lutheran and Reformed systematic theology raise the same issue today. Who ultimately has jurisdiction over the marriage bond? Is it the Church? If so, which Church; the Catholic or the Protestant (or Anglican)? If either or both, how does this square with a basic Reformation principle that jurisdiction over marriage belongs to the State? If it belongs to the State, is not the Catholic Church claiming authority over a contract to which it has no right?

6. The liabilities to which Protestants are exposed if they marry Roman Catholics are regularly brought up. Among these the one most frequently mentioned is contraception. Given the general approval of the practice by their Churches, and the official disapproval by the Church for Catholics, the resulting conflict of moral interpretation seems plain.

When faced with the dilemma of choosing between unwanted children and practicing contraception, Protestants are informed that the essential morality depends on *why* conception is limited, not on *how* it is done. In its official declaration on responsible parenthood, touching on the problem of mixed marriages, the National Council of Churches in America puts the matter in sharp outline:

> Protestant churches hold contraception and periodic continence to be morally right when the motives are right. They believe that couples are free to use the gifts of science for conscientious family limitation, provided that the means are mutually acceptable, non-injurious to health, and appropriate to the degree of effectiveness required in the specific situation. Periodic continence (the rhythm method) is suitable for some couples, but is not inherently superior from a moral point of view. The general Protestant conviction is that motives, rather than methods, form the primary moral issue, provided the methods are limited to the prevention of conception.[58]

From the same perspective, Protestants contemplating marriage with Roman Catholics are warned against possible psychological conflicts between the spouses, or within either partner, if one believes that contraception is wrong and the other thinks it is right. Since agreement on the conditions of intercourse is essential to a happy marriage, it seems foolhardy to enter a relationship in which the two partners are so liable, on moral principle, to disagree on the time, frequency, and circumstances in which coitus may be had.

7. Equally grave, although less immediately pressing, is the option

that Protestants are reminded they might lose if an unwanted pregnancy comes into their mixed married lives. Practically no distinction is made between direct killing of the fetus in order to avoid undesirable consequences, and permissible indirection abortion for the sake of the mother's life. But even where, on occasion, the distinction is adverted to, the Catholic Church's intransigence in that one-in-a-million case of choosing between mother and child is unacceptable. As explained in a directive from the National Council of Churches, "Most if not all Protestant persons would abhor the sacrificing of a mother's life in such a case."[59] The prior right, it is argued, is always the mother's, not the child's.

EASTERN ORTHODOXY. Consistent with their historic position, the Eastern Orthodox have often come out against mixed marriages of any kind, and with special concern to avoid marriage with Catholics. But their approach to the question is quite different than among Protestants. The Orthodox stress is on maintaining purity of faith and orthodoxy of worship. If permission is granted to contract a union with someone outside the pale, conditions are imposed which affect the validity of the contract.

> Mixed marriages . . . are allowed in the Orthodox Church, though not looked upon favorably. The non-Orthodox party must promise to allow the Orthodox to practice his religion and to baptize and rear the children in the Orthodox Church.[60]

When the Second Vatican Council issued its decree on the Eastern Churches and made extraordinary changes in its legislation affecting the Orthodox, the Standing Conference of Canonical Orthodox Bishops in America (SCOBA) published a set of "Guidelines for the Orthodox in Ecumenical Relations." One directive directly touched on mixed marriages:

> In some instances, involving inter-confessional marriage, the Catholic Church now permits "dual" performance of the Sacrament of Matrimony: in the Catholic Church and in the church of the non-Catholic party. The Orthodox Church does not favor this practice; in every such instance, the Priest must take particular care to receive prior permission from his Bishop.[61]

The directive from Rome permitted one of two types of ceremony: where the actual reception of the sacrament takes place before a Catholic priest, and then follows an Orthodox marriage ceremony;

or where the usual Catholic form for marriage is dispensed from, and the whole ceremony takes place before an Orthodox priest. The significance of the SCOBA attitude lies in its reaction to Rome's great openness toward the Orthodox.

The Standing Conference of Canonical Orthodox Bishops in America represents over twelve hundred parishes in North America, out of a total of fifteen hundred, and therefore accounts for most of the church membership in the United States and Canada. It includes Albanian, Bulgarian, Greek, Romanian, Russian, Serbian, Syrian, and Ukrainian groups, and reflects the strong merger tendencies among the Orthodox in the New World. In future ecumenical (including matrimonial) relations between Catholics and the Orthodox, SCOBA will be the nearest to a single juridical body in American Orthodoxy. One proviso should be added: The "canonicity" of several churches belonging to SCOBA is not accepted by all the others; and even within SCOBA, not all members fully recognize one another's jurisdiction affecting such matters as matrimony.

ROMAN CATHOLICISM. If anything is beyond doubt, it is the widely divergent concept of the nature of marriage held by the Catholic Church and by other, whether Christian or non-Christian, religious bodies.

The fundamental issue, from the Catholic viewpoint, is how differently two people can conceive the nature of marriage and yet contract validly on Catholic principles. In other words, how *mixed* can a contract be and yet be a true *marriage*? Three principal areas of "mixture" and of divergence are indicated in the ecclesiastical documentation and literature in pastoral theology on mixed marriages: lifelong permanence, marital activity, and marital fecundity. Indissolubility, contraception, and offspring are synonyms.

As regards indissolubility, the most practical question concerns mixed marriages with Protestants. In case after case presented to the former Roman Rota, decisions were rendered which stated or implied that simple belief in marital dissolubility, even though it is the motive for the marriage, does not invalidate matrimonial consent. Hence Protestants, by Catholic standards, even though they hold different opinions about this essential quality of marriage, contract validly among themselves and when they enter mixed marriages with Catholics.

The usual approach in these decisions was to say that such unions were valid even though the party concerned would not have con-more Christian understanding of the sexual relationship and its creative use for the augmentation of the life of man;

Embody a healthier understanding of the body-mind-soul relationship which does not fall into the easy dualism of body and spirit;

Take full account of the deeper (subconscious) level of the human *psyche* in order to apply the redemption wrought in Jesus Christ to these levels also.[38]

Implied in these recommendations is the belief that just as the East first gave birth to the monastic ideal in the early days of the Church, so it should take the lead in guiding religious life for today. Since "Orthodox people are deeply rooted in speculative spirituality,"[39] they are uniquely able to distinguish between essentials and adaptations. Moreover, their half century of suffering under Marxism has sharpened their vision of the rights of God—especially in the Liturgy, and the rights of man—as projected by the Communist way of life.

Religious Life in the Catholic Church

The story of Catholic religious life kept pace with the ebb and flow of Catholicism and, in one sense, was not much different from all that happened in the Catholic Church since 1900. In another sense, there is no parallel.

Men and women religious, as a class, were more educated than the generality of faithful. And although the difference is less marked now, at least in Europe and America it is still sufficient to say that they had also been more widely exposed to the influence of ideas than most lay Catholics, and correspondingly more responsive to the cultural pressures of the times. This becomes more certain if we distinguish culture as ideology from culture as social custom. Their relative seclusion from the mainstream of Western society—its politics, economy, and practical details—may seem to argue against religious being more deeply affected by cultural changes. But their involvement in the academic and professional life in erudite societies like America, England, and Germany made them, as a group, more open to changes in thought and speculative attitude than other Catholics who, by supposition, were not so engaged in the world of books or the realm of ideas.

Another difference is that in some countries the rapid growth of membership in religious orders was sparked by the growing need for laborers in the apostolate. As schools and hospitals multiplied, so did the influx of novices to communities that were to staff these institutions. There was almost a one-to-one relationship between felt apostolic needs and the recruitment of members in societies that were to meet these needs. This functional approach to vocations produced, as recent events suggest, many workers in the service of the Church but not all equipped for a lifelong commitment to the evangelical counsels.

There is no simple way of seeing the complexity of religious life in Roman Catholicism at any period, and least of all today. One approach, however, that may give a balanced perspective is to look at two historic events in twentieth-century Catholicism that had direct bearing on the subject and then review the present scene in the light of these events. The promulgation of the Code of Canon Law in 1918 and the Vatican Council (1962–1965) were landmarks in this respect. Given the nature of the Catholic Church, they explain far better than anything else what must still remain a mystery: why in a short time several thousand men and women who were living apparently happy lives under vow should leave to "go back to the world" in search of "an authentic Christian life."

CONCEPT OF RELIGIOUS LIFE UNDER THE CODE. As a visible society with laws and juridical institutions, the Catholic Church has periodically systematized its legislation in a *Corpus Juris Canonici*, a body of canon law. The collection is known as the *Codex*, or Code, to designate the approved laws and procedures by which the Church is governed in all the variety of its organizational structure. In civil government this would be called the statutes.

In the early centuries, laws were enacted for various dioceses or for the whole Church and efforts were promptly made to bring them together in a juridical synthesis. Greek collections of this type existed before the Council of Chalcedon (451); and other syntheses were made before the eighth century in Italy, Spain, France, Africa, and even England and Ireland.

By the twelfth century there was a bewildering accumulation of such codices. In 1140 the Italian Camaldolese monk Gratian did the monumental task of coordinating all the disparate church legislation. But the proliferation went on, and had regularly to be brought together, coordinated, and new syntheses published. Peak dates for the publication of these codices practically trace the Church's history of development and necessary adjustment to the changing times: under Popes

It is painful to have to grant requests for dismissal, yet in examining such requests, one comes to see the causes that led up to them. If a Jesuit drops personal prayer on the pretext that his apostolate leaves no time for it, or if, during the period of formation, he refuses all spiritual direction and guidance in his studies and work, or seeks worldly contacts and diversions while leading a completely secularized life without any apostolic purpose, it is not surprising that a day comes when in all sincerity he asks himself, "Why am I in the Society? Whatever it is I am doing now, I can do better as a layman . . ." Certainly his reasoning is logical, if that is the kind of life he wants to lead.[59]

This kind of open disclosure of the facts could have been made only on the basis of wide experience.

But the question still remains: Granting personal neglect of the necessary means to maintain a high level of spirituality, is that all? What are these "difficult times" and "serious problems" through which the world, the Church and religious life are passing—and which partly account for the breakdown in the spiritual life?

Enough has been seen of the ideological revolution taking place in Western (and Christian) society to identify some of the issues which directly affect the religious life.

A strong cult of feminine liberation, directly affecting the women and indirectly the men (priests and religious) under celibate vow, has also penetrated into religious circles. The same Suenens who stirred up so much controversy over papal authority wrote a best-seller (1962) that some calculate was read by more than a million women in convents and monasteries. In two successive cameo pictures he compared the woman of yesterday (Then) and woman today (Now). In former days, "woman lived imprisoned in a sort of immutable destiny, in the framework of an idealized pattern set by men which remained invariable. She was supposed to be docile, faithful, resigned, hard-working—but all within well-defined limits and sheltered from the draughts and winds of the outside world."

But now "a new type has been born—modern woman. She does not passively accept her fate, she takes charge of it." Much of the credit for this welcome change, Suenens believed, can be given to Marxism, and specifically to Lenin.

Lenin was able to write: "The experience of all movements of liberation proves that the success of a revolution depends upon the degree of participation by women."

This is a phrase not to be forgotten. Christianity is the greatest and most radical revolution for freedom in all history. . . . And it is in this light that the apostolic role of women who are consecrated religious stands out in bold relief. Their very womanliness, with everything positive that the term implies, cannot be betrayed or stifled.

Suenens held that religious women had been betrayed and stifled; that the convent life they led and the norms given them by Rome were incompatible with the new age. "A type of society which had imposed itself on mankind for thousands of years has disappeared, never to return." Women should be in the vanguard of the society now being shaped and religious women must take part in the liberation: "Freed from her former shackles, she develops in an atmosphere that allows her to make use of her natural gifts."[60]

This heady wine was bound to have its effect on the people for whom it was intended.

What Suenens wrote could have been taken rhetorically, and nothing much would have come of it. But there was a backlog of lethargy in many communities that resisted change, and often ignored prescriptions, no matter how highly authorized, to make adjustments to the times. Once the lethargy ceased, an avalanche broke loose that seemed irresistible.

Rome had been giving directives for years, but with minimal effect. Founders or foundresses were not to hold superior-generalship for life contrary to the constitutions (1922). Repeated election of the same person as superioress general was forbidden (1920). Doctrinal instruction was to be given regularly to all religious (1929). Novice directors should be free to give all their time to the religious under their charge (1922). Sisters in mission countries should receive professional maternity training (1936). In drawing up new constitutions, anything of a transient nature should not be included, e.g., the daily order and calendar, specific exercises of piety; also to be excluded were letters of exhortation, theological and juridical questions, ascetical instructions, and mystical considerations (1937).

This list could be extended through pages of citation (and repetition), indicating the Church's awareness of changed circumstances and varying conditions of time, place, and personality. A French bishop summarized the attitude of certain institutes that he knew. He was speaking during the mid-sixties:

The Modern State and Christianity

In order to classify the variety of political structures under which Christianity has lived in the twentieth century it will be useful to see them in terms of their relative autonomy or independence of the Church, and their philosophy of civil government. Both factors are characteristic of the modern State and, depending on each (or the two together), we have the different kinds of political society that, in varying degrees, either cooperated with the Church or became an obstacle in the Church's prosecution of its religious aims.

TOTALITARIAN SECULARISM. Although the concept is ancient, the term *totalitarian* is recent. It was coined by Mussolini to embrace a new idea of total absorption by the civil power. It meant, "Nothing outside or above the State, nothing against the State, everything within the State, everything for the State."[1]

In this new type of society, which came into being since 1900, the governing body permeates all and the citizen is expected to give his all, even to the extent of worshiping the State that is not much different from the cultus of the ruler in imperial Rome.

There have been absolutist monarchies before, but this is not the same. It is not so much a *de facto* dictatorship as a doctrinaire view of humanity. The architects of modern totalitarianism were Machiavelli, who divorced public and private morality; Luther, who gave princes the right to pass judgment on bishops and popes; Comte, whose positivism favored social development and organization based on exact biological norms; Hegel, for whom history was the march of the Absolute Idea through the world, incarnated (in his day) in Prussia; and Marx, who merely changed Hegelian idealism into Communist materialism and adapted Hegel's "military class dictatorship" into "dictatorship of the proletariat." Thus positivist democracy on the lines of Comte led to the omnipotent bourgeois state; the Idealist nationalism of Hegel to the omnipotent state-nation; and Marx's Socialism to the omnipotent classstate. Totalitarianism is a combination or derivative of all three.

In order to realize the totalitarian state, there is first required complete administrative centralization, with the transfer of all authority to the government. The government becomes the blind executor of the will of a leader who is endowed (it does not matter how) with all moral, juridical, and political powers. For the dictatorial machine to gain momentum, it is necessary to suppress all civil and religious freedom, all the fundamental rights of persons and families, communities and churches.

The chief instrument of such powers is force. But since the ordinary force of the police is not enough, a secret police agency is created. This has assumed the well-known names of OGPU, originally Cheka, and later the NKVD (and MVD) in Russia; the OVRA in Italy; the Gestapo in Germany. Besides the official agencies, privately organized armed bands of surveillance and terror are also used.

The totalitarian State is secularist on principle. As long as the Church could be useful to bring about or maintain the dictatorship, its help is sought and even some degree of agreement reached. But once the Church as a whole, or any part of it, becomes an obstacle to complete control, it is first persecuted and, if it resists, put out of legal and (if possible) physical existence.

In Russia the Bolshevists tried to form a church of their own, then they suppressed it, proscribing its bishops and priests and closing its buildings. While they declared freedom of worship, they imposed so many restrictions on its exercise as to make it illusory. Hitler promised that the State would respect both Catholics and Protestants, and then tried to reform German Protestantism into an instrument of Nazism and make a concordat with the Catholic Church to suit his own plans. He ended up by setting in motion a complete dechristianization of the country. Mussolini settled the Roman Question with the Vatican and, for political reasons, accepted a concordat on Pius XI's terms. At first he tried to avoid open conflict with the Church but the Italians soon found that he respected no liberties that conflicted with his preconceived notion of the State.

CHRISTIAN CHURCH-STATES. At the other extreme to totalitarian secularism were the Church-States that existed in some cases for centuries but underwent radical changes since the turn of the present era.

The expression "Church-State" is ambiguous. It suggests a monolithic structure of the Tsarist type in Russia before the revolution of 1905, that actually paved the way (by reaction) for the Communist State of Marxism. Church-States in Europe were either Catholic or Protestant, as they had been in the colonies of North and South America before one country after another severed its dependence on the fatherland.

Among European countries that would qualify as Catholic, three had a national history which went back more than a millennium; one came into existence in 1949. In none of them was Catholicism, as a religion, the undisputed master of the State.

After confiscating the Papal States in 1870, Italy remained a kingdom until 1946, when a majority of the people voted for a republic. Meanwhile, the Lateran Treaty of 1929 established Vatican City as a sovereign State. On its side, the Holy See recognized the Italian State with Rome as capital. The Italian State recognized "the Catholic, Apostolic, and Roman Religion as the sole religion of the State," along with "the sovereign independence of the Holy See in the international field," and the Holy See's "sovereign jurisdiction in the Vatican City." Attached to the Treaty was a Concordat which provided for Catholic religious instruction in the schools, the civil recognition of marriages performed in accordance with canon law, the freedom of Catholic Action on condition of its being nonpolitically conducted, and the swearing of allegiance to the King by bishops before taking possession of their dioceses.[2]

Along with the recognition of Catholicism as the national religion, other religions were permitted, "provided it is clearly and loyally understood that the Catholic religion, and the Catholic religion alone, is the state religion with all the logical and juridical consequences, and provided that . . . the Catholic religion is not merely one of the many tolerated and permitted religions, but is what the letter and spirit of the Lateran Treaties and Concordat make it."[3]

After France's defeat in the Franco-Prussian War, it recovered quite rapidly. At first the government of the Third Republic was well disposed to the Church. But indifferentism and unbelief were widespread. This weakened the Church's influence before the government, especially when certain Catholic leaders (against the warnings of Leo XIII) urged the restoration of the monarchy. Under the guise of coercing the enemies of the Republic, anticlericals deprived Catholic schools of the right to grant academic degrees; clergy were made subject to military service; divorce was facilitated and religious instruction forbidden.

Republic Leftists were not satisfied. At the beginning of the century, a new storm was raised against religious orders and congregations. Until they were abolished, it was stated in Parliament, France could never gain its freedom from oppressive superstition. The law of July 1, 1901, regulating the formation of associations, was suddenly applied to religious orders not approved by the State. The main grievance was education. Within ten years, ten thousand Catholic schools directed by religious men and women were closed and their properties confiscated.

This was only the driving wedge for more. The real target was complete separation of Church and State, led by the Prime Minister, Emile Combes. In spite of the protests of the Pope, of French bishops and the laity still loyal to the Church, the bill was passed by the Chamber (341 to 233) and by the Senate (179 to 103), and became law on December 9, 1905. It nominally guaranteed full liberty of conscience and worship, but in practice made it next to impossible for the Church to carry out its extensive works in the apostolate. Other laws encouraged the formation of *associations culturelles* to take over the administration of church buildings and other property to be used under state supervision.

Pius X denounced the law in two encyclicals, *Vehementer Nos* and *Gravissimo Munere* (both in 1906), as contrary to justice and hostile to religion. The government reacted by taking an inventory of ecclesiastical holdings and confiscating everything. With minor variations, the Church's position remained precarious until after the Second World War. Yet, even the improved juridical status was constantly impeded by the strong Marxist element in France, where (in 1970) thirty per cent of the electorate voted Communist.

Mexico was the focus of antireligious persecution by a Marxist regime about the same time that the Russian Revolution broke in Europe. Communists capitalized on strong Mexican anticlerical and Masonic traditions, the unstable governments of the nineteenth century, and the sharp cleavage between the upper and lower strata of society. Venustiano Carranza seized the presidency in 1915 and held it until 1920, during which time the Church was oppressed in the extreme. When the new constitution was passed in 1917, bishops protested that this meant virtual slavery. Regarding the notorious Article 27, they asked, "By what power other than that of the tyrant can the state decree such spoilation?" The full text is still a classic instrument of subordination of Church to State.

> The religious institutions known as churches, irrespective of creed, shall in no case have legal capacity, hold or administer real property or loans made on such real property. All such real property or loans as may be at present held by the said religious institutions, either on

their own behalf or through third parties, shall vest in the nation, and anyone shall have the right to denounce property so held. Presumptive proof shall be sufficient to declare the denunciation well founded.

Places of public worship are the property of the nation, as represented by the Federal Government, which shall determine which of them may continue to be devoted to their present purposes. Episcopal residences, rectories, seminaries, orphan asylums, and collegiate establishments of religious associations, convents, or any other buildings built or designed for the administration, propaganda, or teaching of the tenets of any religious creed, shall forthwith vest as of full right directly in the nation, to be used exclusively for the public services of the Federation or of the State within their respective jurisdictions.

All places of public worship which shall later be erected shall be the property of the nation.[4]

Building on this legal foundation, the atheist President, Plutarco Calles (1924–28), spared no effort to implement what he said was the liberation of the people from ecclesiastical rule. Hundreds of priests, religious, and the laity died for the faith. Among the best known was the Jesuit priest Miguel Pro (1891–1927), who was arrested and shot to death by police in Mexico City.

Spain had a more violent Church-State history. After having been a monarchy for centuries, it became a dictatorship in 1923, under Primo de Rivera. King Alfonso XIII revoked the dictatorship in 1930 but was forced to leave the country in 1931. The new republic disestablished the Church, curtailed its privileges, and secularized education. A conservative reaction to these measures occurred in 1933, but was followed by a "Popular Front" (1936–39), composed of socialists, communists, republicans, and anarchists.

Army officers headed a revolt on July 18, 1936, led by Francisco Franco, with headquarters at Burgos. In the destructive war that followed, over a million people died. France, Mexico, and the Soviet Union were active on the side of the "Popular Front," until Madrid fell to Franco on March 28, 1939.

Franco re-established Catholicism as the State religion. Clergy were to be paid by the State. By the *Fuero de los Españoles* of 1945, specific provisions were enacted: "Profession and practice of the Catholic religion, which is that of the Spanish State, shall enjoy official protection. None shall be molested for their religious beliefs or their private practice. No other ceremonies or external demonstrations than those of the Catholic religion are permitted."[5]

While there was no persecution of Protestants in Spain (about two per cent of the population), strong representation from Protestant agencies in other countries and encouragement from Rome brought a mitigated policy in 1953.

In June of 1967 the Spanish Parliament passed a law, 391 to 9, granting full religious liberty to all denominations in Spain. It further guaranteed all Spaniards the right to worship in safety and peace, regardless of religious affiliation. The new law, passed overwhelmingly in a nationwide referendum, removed the previous restrictions on public worship and teaching of another religion than the Catholic. The opening preamble was almost a paraphrase of Vatican II's document on religious freedom: "The Spanish State recognizes the rights of religious liberty as founded on the dignity of the human person, and insures the necessary protection in providing immunity against any coercion in the legitimate exercise of this right."[6]

Unlike Spain, Portugal had taken a different approach already in 1933. At that time, it declared that "the relationship between the State and the Catholic Church shall be one of separation," while also stating that "the Catholic religion may be freely practiced, in public or private, as the religion of the Portuguese nation."[7]

The Mediterranean countries, therefore, made a remarkable change in their attitude toward religious minorities. The Irish Free State (1949), on the other hand, had no such change to make. Douglas Hyde, a Protestant, became the first President of Eire; Eamon De Valera, a Catholic, was Prime Minister.

The norms of Pope Leo XIII on the Christian concept of a State were closely followed in the drafting of the Irish Constitution. Unimpeachable from the viewpoint of Catholic theology, the Constitution is wide open to allow freedom of worship and belief to other religious bodies.

The preamble is an unqualified profession of the Christian faith: "In the Name of the Most Holy Trinity, from Whom is all authority and to Whom, as our final end, all actions both of men and State must be referred, We, the people of Eire, humbly acknowledging all our obligations to our Divine Lord Jesus Christ, Who sustained our fathers through centuries of trial, gratefully remembering their heroic and unremitting struggle to regain the rightful independence of our Nation . . . do hereby adopt, and give ourselves this Constitution."[8]

Also on the source of its authority, the Constitution declares that "all powers of government, legislative, executive and judicial, derive, under God, from the people, whose right it is to designate the rulers of the State."⁹

More specifically, as "the necessary basis of social order," the family is "indispensable to the welfare of the Nation and the State." Accordingly, "the State recognizes that by her life within the home, woman gives to the State a support without which the common good cannot be achieved." Then a forthright Catholic provision decrees that "no law shall be enacted for the grant of a dissolution of marriage, (and) no person whose marriage has been dissolved under the civil law of any other State but is a subsisting valid marriage . . . shall be capable of contracting a valid marriage . . . during the lifetime of the other party to the marriage so dissolved."¹⁰

But the most significant portion of the constitution deals with the status of the Catholic Church, along with other religious bodies within the juridical limits of the Irish Free State. First, in general terms, "the State also recognizes the Church of Ireland, the Presbyterian Church in Ireland, the Methodist Church in Ireland, the Religious Society of Friends in Ireland, as well as the Jewish Congregations and the other religious denominations existing in Ireland at the date of the coming into operation of this Constitution."¹¹

The term *special position* for the Catholic Church was derived from the Concordat between the Holy See and the French government under Napoleon, in 1801, when the papal representative accepted this status for the Church, in preference to "dominant religion," as a token gesture for certain concessions granted by the civil authorities.

Consistent with these norms, "Freedom of conscience, and the free profession and practice of religion are, subject to public order and morality, guaranteed to every citizen." Nevertheless, "the State guarantees not to endow any religion." Nor shall the State "impose any disabilities or make any discrimination on the ground of religious profession, belief or status."¹²

In order to implement the abstract theory of religious freedom, the law provides that "every religious denomination shall have the right to manage its own affairs, own, acquire, and administer property, movable and immovable, and maintain institutions for religious or charitable purposes." Moreover, "legislation providing State aid for schools shall not discriminate between schools under the management of religious denominations, nor be such as to affect prejudicially the rights of any child to attend a school receiving public money without attending religious instruction at that school."[13]

A small minority in Eire has campaigned for some years to revise the constitution on the ground that its religion clauses are a liberal compromise. But Catholic jurists generally accept the document as a fair interpretation of the Church's principles which may be adapted, without concession, to the needs created by religious pluralism in the modern State.

Much as the traditionally Catholic Mediterranean countries changed the course of their histories by giving juridical freedom to other religious bodies, so the Scandinavian nations did in favor of Catholicism.

In Sweden the offical religion was Lutheran. No Catholic could hold public office until 1870, and only in 1873 were dissenters allowed to open churches and acquire property without restriction. Even then minors were not permitted to leave the established religion before their majority, and all religious orders, except nursing sisters, were banned. The remains of the penal laws were removed on January 1, 1952.

Other countries in which Lutheranism was the established religion also gradually removed civil liabilities against Catholics. In 1929 Iceland had its first Catholic vicar apostolic since Reformation times. In 1942 diplomatic relations with Rome were established in Finland, and in 1953 both Norway and Denmark had the Catholic residential hierarchy formally restored.

Although England had established Anglicanism as the official religion in the sixteenth century, some measure of freedom was given to Catholics since 1778 in what have since come to be known as "Catholic Relief Acts." Most of the remaining liabilities were removed in 1926 under King George V, notably: prohibition of public religious celebrations, taking the title of the ancient episcopal sees, and the invalidity of marriage before a priest. Restrictions still remaining are a law which forbids either the King or Queen of England from being a Roman Catholic, with the same restraint applying to the Lord Chancellor and the Keeper of the Great Seal.

Parallel restrictions affect Roman Catholics in Northern Ireland. Brought into existence in 1920 by an act of the British Parliament, this segment of a divided country made world headlines in 1969 and 1970, when Catholic citizens of that State rebelled against what they considered discrimination because of their religion. Among other grievances, they pointed to the fact that for over forty years the dominant Unionist Party had not included a single Roman Catholic among its nominees for Parliament. Subsequent reaction indicated a gradual change of policy.

Among the remarkable creations of modern political history is the rise of non-Christian republics whose constitutions simultaneously recognize the preferred status of a non-Christian religion and grant full religious freedom to Christians within the country. Pakistan, founded in 1947, is a prime example.

After the preamble to the Constitution states that "Pakistan should be a democratic State based on Islamic principles of social justice," it goes on to provide, under *Freedom of Religion,* that "No law should prevent the members of a religious community or denomination from professing, practicing or propagating, or from providing instruction in their religion, or from conducting institutions in connection with their religion."[14] The one million Christians in Pakistan have found these provisions respected.

If Pakistan was not the exception, it was certainly not the rule among the newly founded Moslem states in Afro-Asia. In one after another, the status of Christians ranged from difficult to impossible, depending on how thoroughly the process of nationalization became the instrument of Islamization. The 1967–70 secession efforts of heavily Christian Biafra, seeking independence from chiefly Moslem Nigeria, are part of this tragic story.

One more type of political structure that came into being since 1900 is best known in North America. When the original Constitution of the United States was drafted, a first amendment was attached, declaring that, "Congress shall make no law respecting an establishment of religion, or prohibiting the free exercise thereof."[15] The intent of the American Constitution was to forbid the kind of state church that had prevailed in England and the colonies, and at the same time to insure the free exercise of whatever religion a person professed.

But in the next century and a half, America had greatly changed. The founding fathers of the nation were men of religious conviction who, in spite of personal differences, were steeped in the Judaeo-Christian tradition which they reflected for the country as a whole. What began in 1791 as the disestablishment of a national church (like Anglicanism in England or Lutheranism in Sweden) became by the mid-nineteen hundreds a gradual separation of religion from effective influence on civil society.

The key to understanding how this came about is the precise nature of the religious freedom originally guaranteed by the Constitution. Its focus was the personal liberty of the individual citizen. It was not the corporate freedom of any religious body. Every page in the writings of Madison, Jefferson, and Hamilton makes this clear. The last thing they wanted was established churches, whether one church (as obtained in England) or several churches, as some argued before the Constitutional Congress.

Through the nineteenth century and into the present one, groups of believers did have some of their religious practices approved by civil law and protected from encroachment either by rival church agencies or by the government. They might even have certain customs (or prohibitions) honored by special legislation—as the Quakers, who refused to bear arms, and the Methodists, who successfully promoted the Volstead Act. But such legislation was never based on the *a priori* grounds that the churches, as churches, had ecclesiastical status in the eyes of the law.

Their members could incorporate a church and enjoy legal personality for carrying out certain activities. But in this, they were essentially on a par with other, *secular* groups—industrial, commercial, or educational—enjoying the same privileges. It was not the Roman Catholics or the Lutherans being juridically treated as churches with claims to autonomy founded on Christian revelation.

By 1900 this position of the churches in America became more apparent, as Christian religious bodies grew in size and potential influence, through immigration and a rising birth rate. If the number of affiliated churchgoers increased, so did the number of the churchless who discovered that they could invoke the law on their side. A confrontation was inevitable and, as later events proved, the results were predictable.

Few men caught this insight better than John Dewey (1859–1952), dean of American philosophers. His analysis is basic to understanding contemporary Church and State relations not only in the United States but in other countries that follow the American prototype.

Writing in 1908 in the London *Hibbert Journal*, Dewey first gave the plausible reason:

If one inquires why the American tradition is so strong against any connection of state and church the immediate and superficial answer is not far to seek. The cause was not, mainly, religious indifference, much less hostility to Christianity, although the eighteenth century deism played an important role. The cause lay largely in the diversity and vitality of the various denominations, each fairly sure that, with a fair field and no favour, it could make its own way; and each animated by a jealous fear that, if any connection of state and church were permitted, some rival denomination would get an unfair advantage.[16]

But this is only a superficial explanation. The real reason lay deep in the development of the modern State:

> There was a deeper and by no means wholly unconscious influence at work. The United States became a nation late enough in the history of the world to profit by the growth of that modern (although Greek) thing—the state consciousness. This nation was born under conditions which enabled it to share in and to appropriate the idea that the state life, the vitality of the social whole, is of more importance than the flourishing of any segment or class.
>
> Our fathers naïvely dreamed of the continuation of pioneer conditions and the free opportunity of every individual, and took none of the precautions to maintain the supremacy of the state over that of the class, which newer commonwealths are taking. But the lesson of the two and a half centuries lying between the Protestant revolt and the formation of the nation was well learned as respected the necessity of maintaining the integrity of the state against all divisive ecclesiastical divisions. Doubtless many of our ancestors would have been somewhat shocked to realize the full logic of their own attitude with respect to the *subordination* of churches to the state (falsely termed the *separation* of church and state); but the state idea was inherently of such vitality and constructive force as to carry the practical result, with or without conscious perception of its philosophy.[17]

This is not one man's analysis of Church and State separation in one country. It is a fact of history, that as Church and State become consciously separated on the principle of statism, the result has been a gradual subordination of Church to State with the logic of this subordination following a certain pattern.

1. It begins with the avowed premise, more or less clearly assumed, that interests of State are paramount.

2. If the State is successfully to pursue its aims, it cannot permit

organized rivals (like churches), to its supremacy which threaten the interests of State.

3. The State feels increasingly threatened as its interests become more secular, i.e., this-worldly, while organized churches remain essentially sacred, i.e., beyond this-worldly.

4. In the defense of its secular interests, the State feels compelled to resist what it considers rival competitors, by ignoring their interests, by dulling their influence or, if necessary, by opposing the churches as a positive danger to the State.

5. The State may achieve this result either directly by executive mandate, by restrictive legislation or judicial decision; or indirectly by allowing and encouraging such domestic rivalry between the churches as to weaken their effective impact on the State.

In the United States, the civil government on federal, state, and local levels had been remarkably well disposed to the Christian churches all through the nineteenth century. The clergy and students for the ministry were exempt from military service, churches and religious agencies and institutions were exempt from taxation, army and navy chaplaincies were established by the government, protective legislation was passed in favor of conscientious objectors on religious grounds, people like the Quakers were not required to take oaths, and Congress passed strong anti-lottery laws urged by Baptists and others, Roman Catholics, Lutherans, and Adventists were allowed to build schools teaching religion as part of the regular curriculum, and the government supported such typically Christian practices as Sunday observance, Christmas, Thanksgiving, and (in most places) Good Friday.

In the realm of morals, the Mormon practice of polygamy was outlawed and the Supreme Court in 1878 decided against the followers of Brigham Young on remarkably Christian grounds: "As a law of the organization of society under the exclusive dominion of the United States, it is provided that plural marriages shall not be allowed."[18] Five years before, Congress enacted the Comstock Law against contraceptives (previously seen), and abortion was forbidden by the statutes of all the American states, beginning with the state of Connecticut in 1821. The Christian character of this legislation is indicated by the fact that neither the Jewish Talmud nor the Moslem Koran and Hadith forbid polygamy, contraception, or abortion.

While divorce was permitted, it was severely limited before 1900, on grounds that were often explicitly Christian in the wording of the law and in the statements of judicial permission to remarry.

By 1970 things had shifted immensely, to the point that some European commentators seriously asked how (in 1930) the highest court in America could still say, "We are a Christian people."[19]

Churchmen of the stature of John Courtney Murray echoed the Supreme Court's description as late as the fifties. If they were not ready to call America unqualifyingly Christian, at least they felt that American churches had untrammeled freedom to pursue their religious aims. Courtney Murray read the papal condemnations of nineteenth-century laicism in France and Italy and approved what men like Leo XIII wrote against the "juridical omnipotence and omnicompetence of the State." But America was different. "This thesis" of State above Church "was utterly rejected by the founders of the American Republic." Otherwise than the European approach, "the American thesis is that government is not juridically omnipotent. Its powers are limited, and one of the principles of limitation is the distinction between state and church." The State, on this premise, supposedly recognized its limitations: that it has no business meddling in church affairs, and so the churches are quietly left to attend to their own interests without interference from the government.

> It is obvious that the Church in America enjoys a stable condition in fact. That her status at law is not less stable ought to be hardly less obvious.
>
> The American Constitution does not presume to define the Church or in any way to supervise her exercise of authority in pursuit of her own distinct ends. The Church is entirely free to define herself and to exercise to the full of her spiritual jurisdiction. It is legally recognized that there is an area which lies outside the competence of government. This area coincides with the area of the divine mission of the Church, and within this area the Church is fully independent, immune from interference by political authority.[20]

Ten years are normally a short time. But in this case they were long enough to make people wonder if, perhaps, it was still true in 1970 that the Christian churches are "fully independent" in the pursuit of their "divine mission," and "immune from interference by political authority."

Christians who believed that direct abortion is murder were being told that this was an exercise of civic freedom; that the government was merely allowing some people to legally terminate pregnancies at will. Christian families were given no share in their own tax money for church-related schools because they were "sectarian," i.e., not "neutral" on matters pertaining to God.

Communist Domination

No single fact of the present century looms larger in Church-State relations than the rise of Communism. And no aspect of this relationship is more critical for Christianity than the opposition between the ideology of Marxism and the religion of Jesus Christ.

We have already seen what this opposition means, on principle, and how logically it follows that a government which subscribes to dialectical materialism will also oppose Christianity. What we now wish to see is how the contradiction in ideas became a conflict between peoples: of those dedicated to Marxism against those trying to live by the Gospels.

The key figure in reducing Marxism to practice and the one most responsible for Communist methodology against Christianity was Lenin. Without touching the essence of Marxism, he brought to it three effective ways of implementing what might otherwise have remained a nineteenth-century political theory. Lenin advocated: (1) the imposition of a centralized bureaucratic administration on the revolutionary movement, in order to integrate it, (2) complete separation of Church and State, with the State giving no juridical support for religion, and (3) massive indoctrination from childhood in submissive loyalty to the Party.

As we read the annals of Christian history since 1918, in Europe and Asia, and lately America—where Communism has taken control of the government—it was because Lenin's program was faithfully followed.

THE VARYING PATTERN. In its first fifty years of political existence, Communism had taken over in fourteen separate countries, excluding nations and peoples that, in the process, lost their national identity.

There are two versions of the actual state of affairs in Communist countries: the highly publicized version of the standard news agencies, and the witness of Christians who have actually lived in Red-controlled territories. It would be pointless to elaborate on the studied persecution of the Church in Russia, Hungary, Czechoslovakia, Poland, Yugoslavia, ever and his hope for the future was feverishly alive as a dynamic force for present action. Accepting Bloch as typical of human experience in today's unbelieving but hopeful world, they set themselves the task of wrestling with the Marxist's underlying metaphysics, including his "ontology of not-yet-being," in which the categories of possibility, of the new, and of futurity were given meanings that were foreign to historic Christianity.

Given his nontheistic view of the universe, Bloch postulated that the world was not freely created by an infinite Being at the beginning of time, but that the world itself was somehow in the process of reaching the fullness of being. Without having a beginning, therefore, the world did have a "destiny." It was "open to fulfillment" and constantly "reaching for perfection." But all of this excluded the hypothesis of a God who existed from eternity; who did not need the world to develop his own existence; and who stood absolutely independent of creation as a means of achieving his own beatitude.

Moltmann and Pannenberg accepted Bloch with these presuppositions. Instead of first clearing his eschatology of its metaphysics, they sought to adjust the principles of Christian hope to what they considered the necessary categories of modern man. It is not surprising that their efforts received so much attention, or the theology of hope acquired connotations that were unknown even at mid-century. They spoke of Bloch with unmitigated praise:

> As scarcely any other philosophy, *Das Prinzip Hoffnung* is suited to help in activating and elaborating the Christian doctrine of hope . . . *Das Prinzip Hoffnung* can, in the present situation of Christian theology, give us courage to try a new interpretation of the original Christian hope.[18]

> Perhaps Christian theology will have Ernst Bloch's philosophy of hope to thank if it regains the courage to return to its original category, the full concept of the eschatological. What remains decisive in this is the outlook on the future which is to be temporally understood. Bloch has taught us to understand anew the overwhelming power of the still open future and of hope which anticipates that future, for the life and thought of man as well as for the ontological quality of all reality.[19]

When they came to re-examine the meaning of hope on these premises, the adjustments were considerable. Moltmann began his *Theologie der Hoffnung* with a critical estimate of the Greek ontology which, he felt, had intruded itself into the Christian doctrine of eschatology. This ontology presupposes that language can grasp the truth about reality that is always there and already there. It assumes that reality is not open-ended; it has no real future. In Christian terms as formerly understood, this meant that the only future available to man was of reaching a God who had "always been there" and "already there." Man in no sense could be said to be shaping the God who constituted man's future, and much less be motivated to exert himself for the achievement of something which, except for man's effort, would never come to pass. So Christians became passive spectators of a religion whose inner essence is to effect perennial drastic change. Looking to eternity they lost their sense of time.

Although couched in language that may seem ambivalent in one or another passage, the dominant theme through several hundred pages of Moltmann's writings is clear enough:

> The more Christianity became an organization for discipleship under the auspices of the Roman state religion and persistently upheld the claims of that religion, the more eschatology and its mobilizing, revolutionizing, and critical effects upon history as it has now to be lived were left to fanatical sects and revolutionary groups . . . whereas the biblical testimonies which [Christianity] handed on are yet full to the brim with future hope of a messianic kind for the world.

> There is therefore only one real problem in Christian theology, which its own object forces upon it and which it in turn forces on mankind and on human thought: the problem of the future . . . The thing we cannot already think out and picture for ourselves on the basis of the given world and of the experiences we already have of that world, is one that confronts us with a promise of something new and with the hope of a future given by God. The God spoken of here is no intra-worldly or extra-worldly God, but the God of hope, a God with "future as his essential nature," as Ernest Bloch puts it.[20]

Pannenberg, who tends to be more philosophical, contraposes what this new theology of hope means, as against the archaic form still professed by most Christians:

> Although it is clear that faith in God and expectation of the future are indissoluble in the Old and New Testaments, Christian theology pays far too little attention to the future as a divine mode of being. The exegetical discoveries of the eschatological nature of the original message, as seen by the early Christians, have not received enough weight; they have been outbalanced by the pressures of theological tradition and the social position of Christianity.[21]

As Pannenberg read the Christian past, it was enslaved by its belief in a God who was completely transcendent with respect to man. This "concept of God as *summum ens* or as *ens perfectissimum* is hardly reconcilable with the notion of the future as a divine mode of being." Pannenberg correctly asked, "Is the future of God's lordship, of his Kingdom, something unessential to his divinity, only something that is supplementary to it?" On this basis, what has man to do with "making his future" and not merely reaching it. But change the concept of God and man enters into an exciting prospect of achievement. "As the power of the future, God is no thing, no objective reality." From this viewpoint, "he appears neither as a being among others, nor as the quiet background of all beings." This reflection, says Pannenberg, "on the power of the future over the present leads therefore to a new concept of creation, which is oriented not to a primeval event in the past, but to the eschatological future." The traditional doctrine of creation, he regrets, has been enveloped by an *Urzeit-Mythologie* (Mythology of Origin), without ever being converted to the true message of the Gospels.[22]

Does God still remain eternal under these conditions? Yes, but the meaning of eternal is transformed. For God is to be thought of as the future of every past, the future of every present, as ontologically prior in his futurity to every event at the remotest distance from us. "But there is a difference," according to Pannenberg, "whether eternity is thought of as timelessness and an endless continuation of something in existence from primeval times, or in terms of the power of the future over every present."[23] Eternity is thus not an attribute of an absolutely immutable being, but the future for which man as man hopes and toward which he is ever striving.

It is difficult to trace the precise line of influence from one theologian of hope to another. Moltmann's and Pannenberg's dependence on Bloch is certain. And the dependence of more recent writers on Moltmann and Pannenberg is admitted. Less certain is Bloch's overall impact on the whole thrust of this form of theology which remakes the essence of God, from absolute perfection to perfectibility contingent on man's action, and from the "static, unchangeable Lord" of Judaeo-Christianity to the "power of the future" whose fullness of being is yet to be reached by progressive realization.

Writing about the same time as Bloch was Teilhard de Chardin, whose ideas on total evolution are credited by some with similar

influence in redirecting the course of theology. Contributors to *The
Teilhard Review*, published by the Teilhard Association of Great
Britain and Ireland, commonly associate the two men as pioneers in
the same venture. So also Harvey Cox, who redefines eschatology with
Bloch as "the study of the not-yet" and leans heavily on the German
Marxist, regards Chardin (and not Bloch) as the turning point in the
history of theology. To Cox's mind, Chardin is normative for Bloch,
and not the other way around:

> In Bloch's view, not only man but the cosmos itself is an existence
> moving toward a still unfulfilled essence. Indeed he insists on this point
> so avidly that one cannot help being reminded of St. Paul's famous
> assertion in the eighth chapter of Romans that not only man but the
> creation itself groans and travails waiting for its redemption. But here
> Bloch adamantly stops short of any agreement with St. Paul. It is not
> God who is the source of this discontent or the ground of this hope.
> Drawing on the "left-wing Aristotelianism" that nourished Marx, Bloch
> contends that this restlessness of matter, it's longing for form, is
> an inner characteristic of matter itself. Here he seems closer to
> the vision of Teilhard de Chardin than he does to those theologians
> who posit a God who beckons to the cosmos from a radically other
> future.[24]

Cox finds in Chardin justification for his claim that, "The only
future which theology has is to become a theology of the future . . .
If theology can leave behind it the God who *is* and begin its work
with the God who *will be* (in biblical phraseology, 'he who cometh'),
then perhaps we stand at the beginning of a new and agitated epoch
in theology." Or again, "man at the helm of the world is the only point
of departure which we possess for a viable doctrine of God." On which
a Chardin specialist comments, "This is exactly Teilhard's thought in
Cox's phraseology." It was also an interpretation that Julian Huxley
gave to Chardin's idea of Omega, the end point toward which universal
evolution is tending. "He seems," according to Huxley, "to equate this
future hyperpersonal psychosocial organization with an emergent Divinity."[25]

Other Catholic writers, like the German Johannes Metz, likewise
favor a revision of the traditional concept of an absolute, transcendent
God, who always is. Speaking of the classic passage in Exodus, commonly rendered, "I am who am," he recalls how "a modern exegete has
taught us to translate, 'I will be who I will be.'" Unlike Bloch, how-

ever, he wants to retain, if he can, belief in God as a "God before us," whose "transcendence (in Bloch's language) is revealed as the power of our future." This should be understood as "a future which is grounded in itself and belongs to itself—as a future which does not come into being out of the possibilities of our human freedom, but which calls our freedom to its historical possibilities."[26]

Commentators generally distinguish three types of "theologians of hope" who often use the same language, but may be poles apart in their principles: Protestant writers (Braaten, Cox, Moltmann, Pannenberg) and professed Roman Catholics (Baum, Dewart, Lawler) who are not uncomfortable with a finite god that is reaching perfection through the exercise of man's freedom; and still others in the Catholic tradition (Metz, Rahner, Schillebeeckx), who are intrigued by the theories of Bloch and the universal evolutionists but shrink from admitting their full implication. Schillebeeckx declares, "all that we Christians can say, in the light of our faith in God as our future, is that faith is not based on what is empirically and objectively verifiable, but comes under the category of human existential possibility."[27] Such a statement is severely orthodox against the backdrop of traditional scholastic theology, but reveals deep tension when expressed (as Schillebeeckx does) with obvious dependence on Ernst Bloch and Jürgen Moltmann.

Protestant theologians closer to the classic Reformation ideas of man's spiritual depravity since the fall, and those who felt that Western society has for too long been victim of a denial of human freedom in working out its destiny have been especially well disposed to a Blochian, or at least Moltmann-Pannenberg, kind of theology of hope. But Catholics, too, under the impact of Teilhardism, have urged a radical change in the Church's eschatology. Some openly redefine God in finite terms; others would settle for less, but, while leaving God as the unchangeable Absolute, are ready to allow for drastic, even revolutionary changes in everything else. Only on these premises, they feel, does the future hold out the promise of human fulfillment.

Freedom of Expression and Communication

The last quality of contemporary theology, with growing intensity since 1900, is the freedom sought by theologians to teach what they consider useful in their science and the liberty to share these ideas with others. We have already seen what this meant at the turn of the century when Modernism arose in England and France, and how quickly it was condemned by Pius X. Something of the same tendency appeared in 1950, when existentialism seemed to threaten established Catholic doctrines and Pius XII warned the Catholic faithful in the encyclical *Humani Generis.*

The relative absence of comparable official pronouncements among the Protestants does not mean that similar challenges did not arise among the Churches of the Reformation. The organization of Protestant religious bodies did not allow for such authoritative action. But the equivalent took place through a series of schisms within denominations, or departures from the parent body, when ideas considered hostile to certain basic truths of Christian revelation were taught by scholars within the respective churches and then sanctioned (or at least not rejected) by denominational leaders.

Eastern Orthodoxy, for a variety of reasons, has not revealed a similar tension between theology and church authority, certainly not on the scale seen in Catholicism or Protestantism. One explanation is that since 1920 most of world Orthodoxy has been struggling for survival of the faith. In large parts of Europe it scarcely had the privilege to exercise its worship, let alone have the leisure (or desire) to indulge in religious speculation and therefore face the question of theological freedom.

From a practical standpoint, it seems more useful to confine this part of our analysis to the Catholic scene. For one thing, Catholicism is unique in its ecclesiastical structure to cope with problems of faith or discipline raised by questions of theology; moreover, what happens in the Roman Church, as Protestants explain, is a paradigm of similar phenomena elsewhere. In fact, some say that every shaking of the foundations of the Church by theologians of Rome has reverberations in the whole of Christendom.

NEW PROBLEMS OF THEOLOGICAL DIRECTION. Every facet of modern culture has contributed to the need felt for theological, and not merely practical or pastoral, direction in the Catholic Church. Increased educational opportunities have produced a laity in most countries that want to be informed about the faith, but also sense the need for a deeper understanding of why they believe, and how the mysteries of revelation are to be related to psychology and the social sciences. Just as they look for guidance in other fields to specialists, so in the sacred sciences they expect theologians to offer them leadership and help integrate their faith with the expanding knowledge of man and the world of space and time.

Church and State relations, as we have seen, in recent decades have produced conflicts of interest touching immediately on moral matters, e.g., the race question, peace and war, sexual morality, and the use of drugs. Laws passed by civil authority may be in conflict with the known precepts of the Gospel. But underlying the legal issues and the moral problems, are the deeper questions to which theologians have a right to address themselves. A single term like *civil disobedience* has dimensions that were scarcely considered a century ago, but that demand attention from those apparently qualified to offer direction to Christian believers caught in the dilemma between two loyalties.

The ecumenical movement also brought to the surface matters of doctrine that were long thought purely academic, like justification by faith or good works, merit and satisfaction, the efficacy of the sacraments, the nature of the Church and priesthood. As the movement took shape, many people began to re-examine these doctrines, compare theirs with the teaching in other Christian bodies, and look for assistance among men and women specially trained to handle such unfamiliar questions.

Rival ideologies, from dialectic materialism that denied every principle of historic Christianity to more urbane forms of naturalism that merely wondered about the relevance of Sunday Mass or sacramental Confession, posed problems for otherwise intelligent Catholics which they were frankly unable to deal with. They, too, wanted someone to help them at least sift the essentials from accidentals to know, as they said, what the Church still believes and "how I should react to the strange ideas that are circulating these days."

When the Second Vatican Council canonized the status of collegiality among bishops it created a new-felt need for theological counsel. The episcopate had always been regarded as the Church's divinely authorized teaching office, but now they were called upon in dramatic fashion to live up to their dignity. Karl Rahner made their obligation plain:

In this situation the bishops themselves have a duty. They can no longer, as has usually been the case up to now, simply wait for doctrinal decisions or political measures in doctrinal matters from Rome—happy that the heavy burden of being a teacher in the Church has been taken from them today by the Doctrinal Congregation. This points to a strange coincidence between the Second Vatican Council's theoretical teaching on the bishops' teaching office, namely, that it is by divine right and so must be taken seriously by them, and the concrete situation which requires just such a teaching office. The bishops cannot simply pass this responsibility on to the Roman Congregations nor to the theologians. What the Council's Dogmatic Constitution on the Church said about the teaching office of the bishops cannot remain a pious piece of paper.[28]

What this meant in practice was that bishops were either to become versed in theology themselves, or have easily available advisers who were at once thoroughly skilled in their discipline and committed to the inner principles on which the Catholic Church was founded. Many rose to the need with zeal and ability; some, in their laudable effort to instruct the people, began to exercise this function without sufficient acumen and with corresponding confusion among the faithful. A typical case was the multiplication of textbooks for the teaching of religion in the United States. Responding to widespread charges that the books taught a watered-down version of the faith, the bishops appointed a special theological commission to examine the texts. But given the post-factum situation and the emotion stirred by the prospect of a "doctrinal investigation," the prelates made only general recommendations and abstained from positive judgment on the disputed instructional material.

LIBERTY, AUTONOMY, AND PLURALISM. Inevitably the role of theologians entered a new phase in Roman Catholic circles. From their customary place on seminary faculties or schools of theology, they entered the mainstream of the Church's life and became, almost overnight, the recognized leaders for renewing the Church in the new age. The publicity they received as experts at the Vatican Council, and later as interpreters of the Council's documents, gave them status and a measure of authority they had never enjoyed before. Coupled with this was their work as consultants on national and diocesan commissions, all indicative of a sensed need for their services and the reliance on their judgment to help the clergy and laity adjust to the rapidly changing times.

But their new status also created new problems. If they were to be of genuine service, many of them said, they must have their position clarified. This meant they ought to identify their precise function in the Church and be given sufficient liberty to work with maximum efficiency.

One form of liberty they could easily assume: the freedom that over the centuries had given rise to theological pluralism, typified in the famous controversy on grace and free will and still represented in different schools of thought, e.g., Banezianism and Molinism, or on a broader scale between Thomism, Scotism, and Augustinianism.

The liberty they now sought was different and rooted in the changed meaning of theology in today's world. A dozen volumes and scores of articles in European and American journals wrestled with the question. All of them stressed the need for people-centeredness and avoidance of abstruse theorization. When the International Congress on the Theology of the Second Vatican Council met in Rome of 1966, Pope Paul VI underscored these features and added others that, he thought, should be brought to light.

> The council asks theologians to develop a theology which is no less pastoral than scientific; a theology that remains in close contact with patristic, liturgical and particularly with Biblical sources; a theology which always holds the teaching authority of the Church and especially that of the vicar of Christ in highest esteem; a theology which concerns humanity as seen in history and in concrete reality; a theology which is frankly ecumenical and sincerely Catholic.[29]

He had already told them to keep their "minds open to all the voices, all the needs and all the authentic values of our fast-evolving era," with emphasis on the term *authentic* to highlight the importance of openness, indeed, but also of discernment. Without the one, theology would be sterile or, at best, intellectual inbreeding; without the other, it ran the risk of promiscuity.

The problem was how to recognize "authentic values" and separate them from spurious ones. As later events were to prove, not all theologians saw eye to eye with the Pope on the norms of discernment. Those who were most ready to hold the teaching authority of the Church in the highest esteem were generally the least publicized; their confreres who believed they had charisms that ran parallel (or contrary) to the magisterium became more prominent. One of the unwritten volumes on the Catholic Church in the twentieth century would describe the uneven contest between these two classes of scholars.

At heart were deeper issues than obedience to the Church, although the moral aspects played their part. When in 1966 the pro-prefect of the

Doctrinal Congregation sent a letter to the bishops of the world, to inquire about "certain tendencies and dangers in Catholic theology today," some leaders in the theological sciences rose to the defense.

There was no denying that the tendencies and dangers indicated in the letter exist, and Rome was technically correct to issue a general warning. But theology in the second half of the twentieth century is not its namesake in the time of Pius IX. What good is it, they asked, to defend what the Church honestly believes is the truth unless what is taught also comes home to the people? Unless the faithful accept the Church's position, all the anathemas of Trent and the Syllabus of Errors will be wasted on deaf ears.

Karl Rahner isolated what he considered two possible approaches to the situation. He called one the "Pian monolith," named after Pius IX who authored the Syllabus of Errors, and the other "academic indifference" to contradictory interpretations of the Christian faith. The second was clearly impossible if the Church wished to remain true to its mandate from Christ to teach all nations—for all times— what the Master had revealed to the Apostles. But the first was also impracticable. Unlike the situation a century before, when Pius IX could leave the impression that "everything was clear, or in any case everything important could easily, unambiguously and, above all, quickly be decided," today's world (and Church) are different. Things are too complicated, and the general confusion in Western society too profound to expect Rome to have the talent for seeing its way through the maze and simply telling the faithful, "This is the truth," or "That is not true." Even if it had the extraordinary gift of supernatural insight which this predicated, it lacked the power of making its teachings easily believable.

Granting there must be some middle ground between these two extremes, Rahner would "not even try to give practical rules for following this *via media*." The best thing to do was wait.[30]

Not all scholars, however, felt that things were so bleak, nor that suddenly theologians held a sort of balance of power; until they cleared their own house, the hierarchy could not realistically face the confusion to restore some semblance of peaceful certitude. The Canadian Bernard Lonergan thought it was high time to distinguish between theology and religion, otherwise there was danger of confusing discord in one area with positive doubt in another:

Religion is one thing, and theology is another. Most saints were not theologians, and most theologians were not saints. Theology stands to religion as economics stands to business, as biology does to health, as chemistry to Du Pont industries.

Theology pertains to the cultural superstructure, while religion pertains to its day-to-day substance. Because of this difference, Cardinal Newman was quite right in saying that ten thousand difficulties do not make a doubt; the ten thousand difficulties are in the superstructure but doubt is in one's personal life.

By this, of course, I do not mean that theology and religion are totally independent of each other. Each does depend on the other, but before this dependence can function, they must be acknowledged as distinct, as each possessing its own proper features and modes of operation. To say that ten thousand difficulties in theology do not make one doubt in religion is like saying that ten thousand difficulties in economic theory are no reason for business firms declaring bankruptcy.[31]

Lonergan did not deny the existence of confusion among specialists as well as the rank and file of believers. He was also ready to admit there were both difficulties in theology and doubts in some people's religion. But the one was not the other, nor should the ventilation of theoretical problems be allowed to induce uncertainty and doubt in religious commitment. Failure to see this would lead to proposing the solution of theological questions as a remedy for the loss of faith. Some were making this equation, and making appropriate recommendations. "It is said that the Church had become a ghetto, that it had gone to excess in defensiveness and in rigidity, that it has to break away from its Byzantine and medieval trappings, that it has to learn to speak to the people of today, and so forth."[32]

On these grounds, theologians who thought that Rome had become excessively defensive, or rigid, or unable to speak to the people of today, would look with a jaundiced eye at any attempt to curb speculation which (in the Church's opinion) was a threat to the people's faith and endangered their religious commitment.

This was certainly the attitude of those who attended the World Congress on the Future of the Church in Brussels, in 1970, under the aegis of Cardinal Suenens and the chairmanship of Eduard Schillebeeckx.

They voted in resolutions that spoke of men "who have a charism for theology," but who often lack "the freedom to debate and pursue theogical issues." When they came to spell out the kind of freedom they wanted, and where "ecclesiastical authorities" were inhibitive, it was plain what they meant:

> The New Testament presents diverse types and even several principles of organization of the Christian communities, according to the different authors, places and times. On this basis, there have developed, in the course of history, multiple forms of Church order, each with its own advantages and disadvantages: papal, patriarchal, conciliar among others. In the light of history we ought today to respect and pursue diversity and complementarity in Church structures.[33]

Taking this resolution literally, it equated Roman Catholicism and Eastern Orthodoxy, Anglicanism and the various types of Protestantism as "multiple forms of Church order." They are objectively on a par and differ only because they have differently developed in the course of history.

As might be expected, opposite versions of the Brussels Congress emerged. One viewed the meeting, extensively covered by the press and television, as an *imprimatur* for Dutch and German theologians under Roman scrutiny. Another saw it as a public testimony to the collective strength of the theological community searching for its own identity. Still another believed that "the triumphalism of the Church had been replaced by the triumphalism of theologians."[34] The published reports from the men who led the Congress, notably Hans Küng, confirmed one more judgment: that contributors to the theological journal *Concilium* (which organized the meeting) wanted such autonomy as would permit Christians to remain Roman Catholic while redefining Catholicism, as the Congress title implied, less in terms of its history than of its still uncharted future. Above all, they wanted the freedom to pursue their investigations apart from the authority of Rome.

IX

MORALITY

It may seem unnecessary to look specifically at morality in the present century after seeing so many aspects of the Christian moral order in the past seventy years. After all, every event in a religious context has moral aspects that are inseparable from the religion and, with emphasis, from the one whose founder required his followers to prove their love in good works and "do all the things that I have commanded you."

But dealing with issues that reflect moral principles is not the same as examining the principles themselves or tracing their ebb and flow in the current of Christian history. These principles have been shaped, or at least affected, by the times; and the times are being influenced by the norms that Christians have decided are livable today. On both levels, it will pay to synthesize what future generations may refer to as *The Age of the Responsible Self* or, from another viewpoint, as *The Dialectic Between Love and the Law.*

Out of a welter of conflicting questions and at the risk of oversimplifying, certain features stand out in the way that secular culture has molded the Christian understanding and practice of morals in our day. If these features seem more characteristic of the present than, say, of the early decades of the century, they were years in the making and therefore may be considered representative of the age, either in its process of development or in actual realization.

The global unification of humanity, through physical transportation and psychological communication, has produced a sense of solidarity—quite unknown until modern times. This in turn has created an extraordinary need for social morality.

Externalism in its myriad forms, which for many people made etiquette a substitute for ethics, was bound to have a reaction. Hence the desire for authenticity and a positive horror of anything suggesting pretense. Sincerity and honesty have become sacred words in today's moral vocabulary.

Pressures from the most organized cultures in the history of Western man, including the tyranny of ideologies that assumed the dignity of law—Fascism and Nazism, Marxism and Secularism—clamored for release. Freedom has become a watchword in moral matters, and personal choice is near the center of contemporary Christian ethics.

Some would say ironically, but in any case certainly, the very drive inward to which a super-organized culture was directing modern man brought him to a deeper awareness of the Self and, within the Self, of his own inadequacy. Morality thus became a quest for contact with "the Ground of one's being" or "the Totally Other," which Christianity would say was a desire for union with God. This meant a reassessment of ethics as not only good behavior but, though often couched in obscure language, as sanctity.

Finally progress was too much in the air, and there were too many signs of human achievement not to leave their impress on the spirit. A "good Christian" did something; he put faith into action and was productive. Correspondingly a drive to the future entered the Christian mentality, with plans and projects and a desire for change that grew partly from disappointment with the present order but also from a sort of instinct that evolution in the natural sciences should have its counterpart in morals, that progress in the physical order should be matched with improvement in human conduct. The very existence of "behavioral sciences" symbolizes this trend and the practical redefinition of morals as mores—progressing from primitive to advanced—indicates the same tendency.

Christianizing Society

Among the living religions of man, Christianity stands unique in its stress on the practice of social virtues. St. Paul's apostrophe on charity in his letter to the Corinthians has been echoed in every century, from the first when Clement I wrote to the same Corinthians that "Love makes no schism; love does not quarrel; love unites us to God," to the twentieth when Paul VI told the Germans assembled at Trier for their annual *Katholikentag* that "Love is not only the constructive force in the Christian community, it is also its driving force, uniting it to overcome all difficulties in earthly life."[1]

Yet, until recent times, there was not the same awareness of Christian morality as social twice over: once because no virtue is ever practiced in total isolation, but once again because modern problems have made people more conscious of their obligations to society itself and not only to the individuals who entered their private lives.

The rise of Communism as a principle of government, and not only a paper theory of values, was brought on partly by the neglect among Christians of this second dimension of the Gospels interpreted for the present communitarian age. To love one's neighbor today means to love society and exert oneself in the interests of humanity, and not only of scattered human beings who happen to cross a Christian's path.

In a draft program for Soviet Communists, *The Worker* published in 1961 a series of obligations incumbent on every believing Marxist:

> Conscientious labor for the good of society—he who does not work, neither shall he eat.
>
> A high sense of public duty; intolerance of actions harmful to the public interest.
>
> Collectivism and comradely mutual assistance; one for all and all for one.
>
> An uncompromising attitude to injustice, parasitism, dishonesty and careerism.
>
> Friendship and brotherhood among all peoples of the USSR, intolerance of national and racial hated.
>
> An uncompromising attitude to the enemies of communism, peace and the freedom of nations.
>
> Fraternal solidarity with the working people of all countries, and with all peoples.[2]

Not all Christian ethicians were similarly aroused by the specter of atheist socialism as a burden on the *Conscience of the West*.[3] Many were satisfied with pointing out the defects of Communism and its inherent opposition to religion as an opiate of the people, who are drugged by the lessons of patience and humility if they are sufferers and by pious exhortations to charity if they are the exploiters. Others refused to admit any basic inconsistency between professing Communism and practicing Christianity. After the Lambeth Conference in 1947 declared that "in many lands there are Communists who are practising Christians," an Anglican committee on Moral Problems drew the logical conclusion: "It does not appear to accord with the wide tolerance of the English Church, that such a one (professed Marxist), if he is faithfully carrying out his spiritual duties, should be prosecuted for his opinions." This was in reply to the question of "Why does the Church, while condemning Communism, allow the Dean of Canterbury and other ministers to hold offices?"[4]

Gradually, however, the concept of moral responsibility as not only social but societal gained acceptance, until by 1970 it was rare to find a manual of Christian ethics which did not assume the distinction in its analysis of virtue.

Before the distinction became viable, a great deal of exegesis of the New Testament and some careful reading of patristic literature had to be covered. This became all the more important when some used the Gospels or the Fathers to expose, as they thought, the archaic nature of the Christian ethic when faced with the global needs of modern society.

It was first admitted that there is very little explicit in the way of a social (in the sense of societal) morality in the New Testament. One reason may have been that the tiny persecuted Christian minority had apparently no hope of influencing a hostile or indifferent society. Once Christianity became at least a permitted religion, we find some Christian writers, e.g., St. Athanasius, who urged the cleansing of society as paganism declined and Christian standards were more commonly accepted.

Most analysts pointed to the industrial revolution, the concentration of people in urban areas, and the abolition of distance which made all human life more and more dominated by large-scale social structures and thereby evoked latent potentialities in the Gospel ethic. Confronted with the spectacle, Christians slowly learned that even if the New Testament was written in terms of rural and familial patterns of life, its truths could be reinterpreted and applied to the contemporary situation:

> This means also a reawakening of Christians to the meaning of the gospel. Perhaps they have too often been content to pursue personal integrity, and have been too little aware of social evils. There are in our cities many fine churches gifted by pious nineteenth-century manufacturers, who sweated the money for them out of their workers, and these

churches may be regarded as ironic reminders of how Christians may be given to all kinds of good works and yet remain blind to social evils.[5]

But this awakening has not been uniform, and still less universal. No doubt industrialism kept growing in large countries like England, Germany, and the United States. Was there any correlation between such features of industrialism as its capitalist economy and a particular religious interpretation of society? Among other scholars credited with making the correlation, the best known was Max Weber (1865–1920), German economist and sociologist. His three volumes on the sociology of religion, published in 1920, were a milestone in the field. They are mainly an analysis of the relationship of religion to economic phenomena based upon an immense amount of factual material. He studied the economic ethics of Confucianism, Taoism, Judaism, and Christianity in the life of the people who profess these religions. But he centered on the connection between Western capitalism and Protestantism. A Protestant himself, he concluded that modern capitalistic organization is made possible by a definite psychology, conduct, and corresponding social conditions. He maintained that Western capitalism was originated by the Protestant religion and its economic ethics. The spirit of capitalism, therefore, is that of Protestantism, of its rules of conduct and practical morality.

One of his corollaries was that the individualism inherent in the capitalist system against which Marxists ranged their heaviest arsenal called for a complete re-evaluation, at the risk of becoming an unequal competitor for the ideological mastery of Western society.

But so-called Catholic cultures also needed updating. Weber made invidious comparisons between the prosperity of England and America and the poverty of Italy and Spain. But the main point of Weber's commentators was that he drew attention to the grave need for social consciousness in all Western nations. If the Protestant ethic made for secular development—thanks to rugged individualism—the Catholic ethic had to be developed to meet the rising industrialization and urbanization in the world world and not only in Anglo-Saxon countries.

This was also the message, from a different perspective, of Berdyaev to his Orthodox co-religionists. Their problem, he pleaded, was unlike that of the Protestants who could not find in the Bible such norms for social morality as the present age demanded; and unlike Roman

Catholics who had the norms but failed to apply them. Orthodox political leaders were urged to heed the lesson of religious history and see that just as there are two natures in Christ, the divine and human, so there are two components in a well-ordered Christian society, the spiritual and secular. Unless the crying social needs on the secular level were met, alien powers would rise to fill the vacuum with tragic consequences to Orthodox Christianity.

The encyclical *Pacem in Terris* (1963) of John XXIII was a comprehensive study of the same basic theme, elaborated as no comparable papal document had ever done. Its avowed purpose was to stimulate "all men of good will" and not only Catholics to read the times in which they live and not delay to put into practice the social mandate of Christ. Seeing the astounding "progress of science and the inventions of technology," there was no choice. Christians above all should labor strenuously for "the establishment of such a world community of peoples as is urgently demanded by the requirements of the common good."[6]

Part of the price of their new-found responsibility was the danger that Christians ran of misunderstanding their religion as merely another program for social improvement. Social-gospeling was as much a temptation in the twentieth as in previous centuries. There was also the risk, verified more than once in practice, that Christians would rush in with pronouncements on complex technical matters which they did not comprehend.

One way to obviate these difficulties was to have Christian laymen assume more responsibility in the social arena, where they could be expected to be more competent than the average churchman. This was the main thrust of the Life and Work branch of what later developed into a commission of the World Council of Churches. As early as 1925, in its meeting at Stockholm, it recommended that the laity "promote Christian influences on political, social, and economic life in the modern world."

Forty years later, the Second Vatican Council was even more explicit: "Secular duties and activities belong properly although not exclusively to laymen." Then, with a clear reference to their role in Christianizing society, compared with that of the clergy, "Laymen should also know that it is generally the function of their well-formed Christian conscience to see that the divine law is inscribed in the life of the earthly city; from priests they may look for spiritual light and nourishment."[7]

By implication, let priests concentrate on their contribution to the social order and allow the laity to exercise theirs.

Search for Authenticity

Expressions like "I want to be myself" or "I wish to be genuine" suggest the presence of a new spirit in moral thinking that is looking for the truth, even when the search is halting and angular, and sometimes tragic. When people use this language, they imply that so much of what they see about them is sham, even when the victims are unaware of the pretense, and they want to be authentic.

Volumes have been written on the elements in today's society that conspired to inhibit a man's "being himself," and that evoked the counterresponse in the direction of authenticity. Most of these elements have consequences in other ways, too, and will be seen in a later context. But two especially are pertinent to the creation of a "masked civilization" that bears on the immediate question of why people should now feel so strongly about honesty in the practice of morals. Anonymity and mobility are so characteristic of the large population centers of Europe and America as almost to define them. Both have been instrumental in producing the kind of mentality that wants nothing more than to be delivered from the burden of conforming to a make-believe code that urbanization and automation have imposed on millions who still believe (however vaguely) in Christianity.

Writers like Bultmann and Riesman spoke about the "standards of this world," which demand recognition and impose heavy sanctions on those who disobey. There are expectations in dress and place of residence, in eating and drinking customs, in reading habits and forms of recreation, in what to say in what words on what occasion, in where to stand or sit or posture to assume, in how to act "correctly" and not react "improperly" in a medley of social circumstances. They are accepted by millions whose conformity to external modes of behavior tends to atrophy their responsiveness to the inner norms of morality. There seems to be no escape from the dilemma. Familiarity is born of living in a familial (originally family) situation; but there is no intimacy in a crowd and nothing is more anonymous than a social security number.

Under these conditions, it is next to impossible really to know others, and they do not expect to be known beyond the occasional exposure of a chance remark or a sudden outburst of feeling.

So, too, the penchant for movement that has entered the bloodstreams of Western life. Harvey Cox stigmatized it in one paragraph:

> Every tendency in modern society points to accelerated mobility. Technology closes the saddlemaker's shop and opens electronic labs. Industrialization not only lures people off the farms and into the cities; it also invades the farms, transforming them into food factories and steadily diminishing the number of hands required to do the work. The modern city is a mass movement. It has been described by one writer as a kind of staging area where people pause in their complex movements from one place to another. Not only do we migrate between cities in search of improvement, but we migrate within cities to find more convenient or congenial surroundings. Commutation represents a small daily migration. We commute not only to work but also to play, to shop, to socialize. Everybody is going places, but what is happening to us as a people along the way?[8]

What happened is that anonymity was intensified. Another barricade was erected between human beings whose most intense desire is to exchange spirit with spirit in friendly, confidential intercourse.

The effect on many people was to make them rebel against these barriers to self-disclosure. They would insist on "saying what they think" and of "acting as they feel," with no let or hindrance from a society that for too long had stifled their desire to "be themselves."

Other factors have entered the picture, but this outlook was a contributing element in producing what certain ethicians call "moral authenticity." It denotes a style of conduct in which "the existent has become genuinely himself." The German equivalent is *Eigentlichkeit* (from *eigen*=own), implying that to be authentic is to be one's own self.

Strictly speaking this is not a moral concept, since authenticity as such has nothing to do with obedience to laws or fulfilling the universal principles of humanity. But existentialists have adopted the idea of authenticity to describe a person who does not take refuge in the accepted rules of society, but simply accepts himself for what he is—with all his foibles and tendencies—and seeks to realize the potentialities that are factually part of his own individuality.

Those who believe in objective norms of human conduct attribute the extraordinary popularity of situation ethics (to be examined later) partly to this reaction against the externalism of a congested culture. Its depersonalization has been just that, a deindividualization brought on by the massive accumulation of people, always in motion, who are now asserting their uniqueness as persons and their distinctiveness as individuals each with an autonomous human will.

Legalism and Law

Closely related to the search for authenticity is the quest for freedom which also typifies the mood of contemporary moral thinking. Where externalism, introduced by physical and psychological crowding, sparked the desire for "being oneself," as shown in the urge to reflect one's own real interior being, so legalism, developed to a fine art in societies where the civil government almost replaced organized religion as *custos morum,* has done its share to bring the meaning of law and its very existence under scrutiny. Law, by its nature, implies the imposition of limits on the freedom of members in a society for the sake of the common good. But this common good must be recognized, either by experience or on faith, for people to be willing to submit to laws which demand surrender of their personal liberty for the welfare of the community to which they belong. As the evidence of this welfare is obscured in practice or, worse still, when a society is positively harmed by what authorities prescribe, first the wisdom, then the value, and finally the need for law—any law—is called into question or even denied.

As usually defined, legalism is the type of ethic which seeks to prescribe rules for every conceivable occasion. It tends to induce the mentality in people which follows what is supposed to be the rule in every situation.

ORIGINS OF SITUATION ETHICS. Some ethicians who use the term in this sense contrapose to legalism what they call situationism; but they seldom trace the genesis of a legalistic mentality to its real source in modern times. The *bête noir* of legalism in today's culture, and especially in the present century, has been the modern state. We have already seen something of its demands on the human spirit and the heavy toll it has exacted, for example, in militarism in still nominally free countries, quite apart from its suppression of the most cherished liberties under Fascism, Nazism, and Marxism.

But how is the widespread legalism in many countries related to the emergence of situationism as a theory of Christian morality?

At least in Anglo-Saxon countries, Joseph Fletcher has become the unofficial spokesman for situation ethics, though he would be the first to give credit to many theoreticians who preceded him. Emil Brunner (1889–1966) in Switzerland, Dietrich Bonhoeffer (1906–1945) in Germany, William Temple (1881–1944) in England, H. Richard Niebuhr (1894–1962) in the United States are only a few prominent names among scores that looked at the current legal scene and turned away in horror at the inhuman demands which modern society—notably civil society—has been making on human liberty. Their reaction, and that of their followers, has taken on myriad forms. Situationism is no ethical monolith. But beneath it was the effort to release contemporary Christian man from the shackles to which he had been bound.

Behind Fletcher, as he admitted, was the shadow of Bonhoeffer, whose short life is too much part of the issue we are examining to be omitted. It gives the clue to situationism as an attitude, as distinct from situationism as an ideology. The attitude came first; only later was the ideology introduced.

As a young professor of twenty-seven, Bonhoeffer delivered a lecture broadcast over the Berlin radio in which he flayed the German public for its hankering after a "leader" who would inevitably become a "misleader" so long as he did not clearly refuse to become the idol of the led. The broadcast was cut short before he had finished. When it became apparent that Hitler, the idol, had succeeded, Bonhoeffer accepted a call to be pastor of two German congregations in London, for he refused to have any part in the "German-Christian" compromise with the Nazi government.

But Bonhoeffer was so involved in the dictator-dominated country from which he escaped that he could not feel comfortable "in flight from responsibility." He therefore returned to Germany, a marked man, whose days were numbered. During this time he devoted his spare moments to writing his *Ethics*, which he regarded as the special contribution he could make as a theologian. Moving about the country, preaching and talking to clandestine groups, or remaining in hiding in Berlin, he wrote whole chapters of his *Ethics* in the Benedictine abbey at Ettal and other temporary refuges.

The blow fell in early April 1943. He was arrested and put into prison at Tegel, where he remained until October of the next year. All the while he kept writing, and most of his prison letters are preserved. Then on Sunday, April 8, 1945, Pastor Bonhoeffer conducted a little service of worship for the inmates, at which he spoke on the text, "With his stripes are we healed." The next day he was hanged at Flossenburg.

Confronted with the tyranny that had enslaved his people, and that events proved would bring on the holocaust of whole nations, Bonhoeffer wrote in language that was born of anguish over the perversion of law. Christian citizens were being misled into "obedience" to a legal system that built the ovens of Dachau and that sought systematically to destroy the faith of believing Christians and Jews. Bonhoeffer's contemporary, Pope Pius XI, smuggled the encyclical *Mit Brennender Sorge* (With Deep Anxiety) into Germany in 1937, in which he warned that "Every attempt to dislodge moral teaching and moral codes from the rock of faith, and to build them on the unstable sands of human norms, sooner or later leads the individual and the community to moral destruction."[9]

Bonhoeffer shared these sentiments, and protested against the imposition of laws built on unstable sands—the Nazi myth of a superior race—with all the vehemence of his ardent nature. He said things and wrote things that must be read in the historical context in which they were given; and in that context they are intelligible.

Thus, according to Bonhoeffer, "The question of the good is posed and is decided in the midst of each definite, yet unconcluded, unique and transient situation of our lives, in the midst of our living relationships with men, things, institutions and powers, in other words, in the midst of our historical existence."[10] The "institutions and powers" to which he referred were painfully part of his historical existence. They were incredibly new and raised questions that were impossible to fit under neat moral categories. As a result, not only Bonhoeffer but thousands with him felt they had to decide then and there on what was good in the unique situation in which they found themselves.

Similar crises continue to face Christians in Soviet and satellite countries in Europe and their co-religionists in China and Mexico; they confront believers in nations that legalize the murder of unborn children or unwanted adults. They demand recognition in every society where the mores of a culture have become the law of the land, and where as a consequence to "break the law" is to be guilty before the law, although before God the lawbreaker may consider himself a witness to a faith that tells him, in that case or situation, it is better to obey God than man.

On a lower scale of intensity, but equally critical to explain the rise of situationism as an attitude, was the evidence of civil laws prohibiting actions which a man's religious convictions told him were permissible. The American Volstead Act (1917), better known as "Prohibition," put into the solemn instrument of the Constitution a law which absolutely forbade "the manufacture, sale or transportation of intoxicating liquors within, the transportation thereof into, or the exportation thereof from the United States and all territories subject to the jurisdiction thereof for beverage purposes."[11] For many Americans the Prohibition Amendment was a perfect symbol of legalism, which universally proscribed by federal mandate the legitimate consumption of a beverage which some people abused. It was also a classic example of distrusting the moral judgment of a nation because some citizens misjudged their capacity for drinking "intoxicating liquors."

IDEOLOGICAL SITUATIONISM. Against this background of several generations of legalism under civil law, reaching peaks of tragedy in countries that denied the most sacred liberties, it is not surprising that an attitude of situationism developed. It is equally understandable that writers like Barth, Bonhoeffer, and Tillich (apart from other reasons) should have favored a situationist ethic. All were victims of a legalistic behemoth against which they fought and, in Bonhoeffer's case, at the cost of their lives. It was Barth, too, who helped draft the *Barmen Declaration* which, in the teeth of Hitler's totalitarianism, declared that the Church's only *führer* was God.

What is less easily explained is why situationism grew into an ideology in countries where no such crisis existed as in Nazi Germany. England and America (or Canada and the Scandinavian countries) are not Nazi Germany or, for that matter, Cuba or Soviet Russia. How, then, explain not merely the attitude but a positive ideology of situationism promoted by ethicians in countries which did not seem to pressure their Christian citizens into a "here and now I must decide for myself" type of morality?

The key to an answer lay in the fact that the cultural pressure to conformity can be as effective as the legal pressure to obedience. We have seen the extent to which the mores of some nations have become decreasingly Christian, even when accepted customs have not yet been legally prescribed by the civil code.

It is enough that the civil law permits or encourages certain forms of conduct, or fails to restrain certain behavior, for those who wish to live up to the high demands of a Christian ethic to feel they are being forced into going along. Only when viewed in this light does the logic of systematic situationists appear in its full clarity. Without exception, they rest their case on the *de facto* conditions in which Christians are expected to live in today's world. Conditions are such that it is unthinkable for the Church to have laid down absolute precepts or, more often, absolute prohibitions in moral behavior.

Always the appeal is to a "new" morality, to the need for "Christians in each generation to help fashion and frame the moral net which will best preserve the body and soul of *their society*," to the fact that just as the first-century Christians tried to "relate the command of *agape* to their bewildering new environments," so today's Christian must "learn what the Spirit may be saying to the churches of the twentieth century."[12]

Consequently, behavioral practices accepted in contemporary society are first identified by situationist morality as relevant and then appraised on their relationship to the only precept known to Christianity, the commandment to love.

Essential to this logic, besides the sequence of priorities—first relevance and then relationship to love—is the fact that *relevance* for the situationists is not mainly the circumstance in which a particular individual finds himself at a given moment. It is above all the environment or milieu (situation) in which Christianity exists and Christians are expected to live at a given time and place in history. Once a behavioral pattern is established as characteristic, it is assumed that Christians will adjust the Gospel injunction of love to their environment. *How* this love will be expressed depends on the age or locality, i.e., its typical outlook; but there is nothing in the Christian religion that ever prescribes the expression.

Statements abound in the new ethicians to make it plain that the first norm of morality is relevance:

> The new morality, situation ethics, declares that anything and everything is right or wrong according to the situation.[13]
> This is the end from which the "new morality" begins . . . I believe that an ethic will have authority for most of our generation only as it is

empirical and starts firmly from the data of actual personal relationships as they now are.[14]

There is no such thing as a Christian ethic. The raw material of an ethic is provided by the ethos of a society or a century or a group. Times change and even Christians change with them.

As long as we allow for this relativistic factor in all ethical judgments and are not unduly afraid to face it as Christians, then we shall not be unduly disturbed by our divergent moralities.[15]

Since the first norm of conduct is its relevance to "the ethos of a society or a century or a group," whatever this ethos approves becomes normative for the Christian ethic. Applications of this principle are easy enough in theory, although in practice many Christians are still slow to avail themselves of the new morality. Take "our attitude to homosexuality. The notion, until recently almost universal, is now surely dying, that . . . homosexuals cannot inherit the Kingdom of God." The notion is becoming irrelevant "due to pressures from the empirical side. We have come to a much greater appreciation of the facts, particularly about the causes of homosexuality . . . and for the denial to a sizable minority of our population of any deep, free or secure personal relationships."[16]

The same with sterilization. "The situationist . . . is data-conscious because the alternative is to be sub-Christian and subhuman. He faces the information explosion of this scientific era unafraid. One recalls with joy the candor of a Church Assembly (Anglican) in 1962 which reported that the traditional legalistic prohibition of sterilization for nontherapeutic reasons should be acknowledged to be 'wrong,' after all, because of new data."[17]

Situationism, unlike traditional morality, is profoundly subjective. It does not presume to say that certain actions are objectively right or wrong. This is "the basic mistake of legalists. No law or principle or value is good as such—not life or truth or chastity or property or marriage or anything but love." But "love" cannot be defined in terms of law or principle or value. That would make it objective. It cannot be denied sexual expression between unmarried persons, or with someone else's spouse. The only norm for extramarital relations is the personal, undefinable sentiment of love. People are finally learning that "baby-making can be (and often ought to be) separated from love-making."[18] Love cannot even be denied homicidal intentions, since it is quite possible to favor abortion "simply on the ground that no unwanted and unintended baby should ever be born."[19]

PRACTICAL CONSEQUENCES. Once situationism took hold in modern ethical thought, it was only a matter of time before it was reduced to practice, far beyond the relatively small number of Christians who acted this way before the ideology became popular.

Its first and widest impact was among Protestants, but more especially among those whom Fletcher calls "non-fundamentalists." In North America and England, this would mean the majority of Protestant writers. Even when they sometimes took issue with the relativism of the situationist method, they admitted having no quarrel with it substantively. "Compared to the right-wing Evangelicals and their antisituational posture, employing such epithets as 'moral nihilism' and 'sneaky minimalism,' there is an imposing array of American Protestant moralists in the situational camp."[20] Written in 1966, this statement could be re-emphasized with the passage of every year, and applied with equal certainty to Protestant ethicians in most of Europe and the Americas.

Catholics were at first slow to adopt situationist ideas, and the repeated statements of the Vatican warning moralists against situation ethics were generally heeded until the end of Vatican II. An allocution of Pius XII in 1952 and a document of the Holy Office in 1956 were typical Vatican reactions to the "new morality," as Rome labeled it.[21]

As late as the mid-sixties, fully committed situationists could point to only a handful among Catholic moralists veering in the same direction. Among others, Bernard Häring was said to be making "an impressive effort to ease the law ethic by pleading the primacy of love over law, but at bottom he still identifies law with love, and when he stresses the spirit rather than the letter of the law, he is still distinguishing them, not *separating* them as a situationist would."[22] That was in 1961 and 1963 when Häring's two volumes on *The Law of Christ* were first published.[23] In less than ten years, Häring (with others whom Fletcher identified as kindred spirits) was applying the full weight of situation ethics to the moral laws of historic Catholicism. Under the subtitle of "Different Personal Situations," he examined typical cases in which a Christian couple are validly married in the eyes of the Church; they cannot obtain a declaration of nullity; but at least one of the partners is subjectively convinced that his first marriage was somehow improper. Häring advises such a person (and his new partner) to be admitted to the sacraments without receiving the Church's judgment on the previous marriage:

> It sometimes happens that those living a canonically invalid marriage are, for good reasons, convinced that their first marriage was not a proper one, but they are unable to prove this conclusively in terms that will satisfy modern legal requirements . . . Insofar as the subsequent marriage is a happy one, and the children well cared for, the couple will be firmly convinced that God blessed their marriage. In these cases there should be no hesitation in giving sacramental absolution.[24]

Situationists regularly use "legal" or "canonical" to describe what may be, as in this case, sacramental and therefore (by Catholic principles) divine law. Moreover, the situationist ethic applies equally to any law, whether civil or ecclesiastical. Accordingly, those who personally think that a contract was not properly made in the first place or "for good reasons" is no longer binding, are morally justified in terminating the contract without recourse to the public authority which claims jurisdiction over the matter to which they had ostensibly bound themselves. Even as socially important an institution as marriage thus becomes a private affair, whose conditions of entry or exit are uniquely determined by the fiat of the individual parties.

In Roman Catholicism, theoreticians who are presumably responsive to the Church's teaching set the direction for moral theology in books and in reviews such as *Theological Studies, Irish Ecclesiastical Record,* or *Stimmen der Zeit*. They in turn are echoed in scores of more popular magazines, read especially by clergy and teachers in schools and catechetical programs. The moral tone of these leaders of Catholic opinion then shapes the outlook of the rest of the faithful. At the opening of the 1970s, the tone was strongly situationist.

SACRAMENTAL CONFESSION. Unlike its impact in other Christian traditions, the effect of situationism in the Catholic Church was immediately felt in the one area where morality touches on the ritual life of the people, i.e., the practice of sacramental confession. Since the sacrament requires that the penitent tell his sins to a priest, everything depends on how "sin" is understood. Unless a person considers himself guilty of definite moral faults, he will have nothing to confess. Moreover, since the strict obligation to confess applies only to certainly committed grave sins, unless known moral failings are recognized as grave or "mortal," the obligation becomes a mere recommendation. In both cases, the results were predictable once either the notion of sin or of gravity was radically changed. Situationist morality introduced such a change.

Concretely the effects were anticipated by Pope Pius XII in a series of documents urging priests not to tamper with the laudable practice of frequent confession among children and adults. In 1943 he defended the custom and spoke of purveyors of "false doctrines" which are "not directed to the spiritual advancement of the faithful but turned to their deplorable ruin."[25]

A number of writers, mainly in Europe, supported the Pope with articles and even books. The best known was Dom Baur's *Die Haufige Beicht,* which went through nine editions in German by 1960, besides translations in other languages.

In 1947 the Pope returned to the same theme, using stronger words against those who discouraged the frequent use of the sacrament of penance. He recalled "with sorrow" the consequences of such an attitude, which is "most dangerous to the spiritual life."[26]

The drop in confessions across whole nations, notably in Belgium, Holland, and the United States, became a recognized fact. It was paralleled by a growing literature favoring delayed confessions for children—closer to adolescence, communal penitential exercises—without explicit confession of sins to a priest, and infrequent reception of the sacrament—unlike the monthly or weekly custom prevalent at mid-century.

A careful examination of this literature, European and American, showed that besides other arguments, drawn from psychology (confession tends to induce a guilt complex) or sociology (confession obscures the social aspect of sin), the main issue was the nature of sin in general and of grave sin in particular.

The notion of sin was re-examined in the light of the new morality, with a studied analysis of the Catholic Church's too long preoccupation with a legalistic concept of morals:

> In the past, training in morality had its basic orientation in the *law*—the Ten Commandments and the six precepts of the Church. If there was a moral question, the thing to ask was, "What does the law say?"
>
> Previously Catholics pictured the Church as having the answers to all questions—a bulwark of security in a changing world. But the Catholic Church today acknowledges that it doesn't have all the answers. Unfortunately, many Catholics, unknowingly perhaps, might prefer to pattern

their actions on the example of the nineteenth-century English intellectual who, it was said, liked to read at breakfast each morning a new papal decree. He had his marching orders for the day.[27]

Given this state of affairs in the past, the character of religious education was no different. "The image of the teacher of that era would have been that of the schoolmaster with a textbook in one hand and a ruler in the other."

Formerly, Catholics thought the Church had stable principles of morality and certain unchangeable provisions of the divine law. But the climate is no longer the same.

> It is important to realize that although the Church has definitely spoken out on moral matters, it has never done so in an . . . irrevocable way.
>
> The Church in its practice seems to realize, in spite of the denials of traditional theologians, that it does not enjoy an infallibly guaranteed competence to apply the moral vision of the Gospel to complex natural law questions.
>
> To date no exception has been admitted in many moral cases, such as abortion and birth control . . . Today Catholics are pressing for answers in many sensitive areas of the Christian moral life. They will not be satisfied with absolutism or evasion.[28]

The only way out, Catholics were told, was to rely on their conscience. Their own judgment of each situation as it comes up is their only true norm of morality. No doubt the Church still has a role to play; but it can only advise; it should never prescribe.

> This can only mean that the moral teaching of the Church in the future will give general directives.
>
> There are different opinions among people of good will. An absolutely authoritative statement is not possible. The facts and circumstances are not totally known. But the Church can give its evolving thoughts as a strong guide.[29]

Against this backdrop of situationism, Catholics were further told that the idea of mortal sin was being completely revised. For example, the Church's catechetical practice had been to teach that a person commits a mortal sin when the action he performs involves serious matter, about which he has sufficiently deliberated in his mind, and to which he gave complete assent with the will. In this definition, the operative term was the first of the triad, *serious matter*. Such sins as

adultery and murder, blasphemy and fornication were considered serious, and anyone who deliberately and with full consent did these
things was said to have sinned grievously and (as a Catholic) expected
to confess what he did.

But the new view was different. Instead of grave *matter,* the language
to be used is total *commitment;* and instead of saying that a person
sinned by performing a grave mis-*deed,* he should be called guilty of a
mis-*intention.* What therefore constitutes a sin is not *what* a person
does but *why* he does it. If he sinned grievously, it was not because
he broke a serious *law* of God but because he failed in *love.* The
essence of sin, on these premises, shifted from the objective to the
subjective; from having done a wrong action to acting from an unworthy motive. So that a sin becomes grave not because the act committed was a serious deviation from the divine law, but because the
sinner had seriously derogated from his love of God.

Accordingly, nothing less than total rejection of God's love constitutes mortal sin. To explain this, Catholic situationists drew on the
ideas of writers in the psychology of the will and coined such terms
as *fundamental option, capacity for totality, posture toward the ultimate
good,* all of which strived to explain what happens when a person
makes a total commitment of himself to another person, to a state of
life, or a basic course of action. As such, the concept was nothing new.
The Gospels, especially that of John, and the letters of St. Paul make
it clear that Christ wanted his followers to give themselves to God
with dedicated love; that charity is the epitome of the entire law, the
root of all the virtues, and the bond of perfection. Nor was it new
to conclude that those who refused to give this love and failed in
fundamental charity toward God would not be saved.

What was new, and introduced revolutionary ideas into Catholic
moral teaching and practice (including confession), was the exclusion
or at least minimizing of the content of the moral law in favor of
the intention in moral conduct. Many writers in the field carefully
distinguished between the new emphasis on intention, on why a person
did something, on the failure in basic love toward God hidden in
every sin—and what a sinner does when, in Augustine's terms, he
chooses himself even to the contempt of God. But while stressing this,
they did not minimize the objective fact that certain actions are closely
related to the self-disposition of human choice; that "as a general rule
only in grave matter will the sinner grasp in the depth of his person

that his relation to God is at stake"; that "in such matter will he be able to penetrate his act from the self-disposing center of his being."[30]

Not all moralists thought this way, and those with a situationist bent took the occasion to redefine grave sin as uniquely present in a complete rejection of God's love, done deliberately and explicitly as an act of defiance of infinite Goodness. "Theologians," they observed, "are clarifying the distinction between mortal sin and venial sin by speaking of mortal sin in terms of a fundamental choice against God."[31] They explained what this meant:

> Mortal sin is like that; it is a vocational decision—a fundamental choice—an act which involves the fullest dimension of one's personality; one's very life.
> The late Bishop Bekkers of Holland tried to clarify this question. He asked: Is it possible that a person could be in the state of grace at twelve noon some day, commit a mortal sin at five past twelve and then be in the state of grace at ten past twelve? Such a person would have certainty that he had not committed mortal sin. When the concrete act is followed by sorrow and real contrition, the necessary conditions for mortal sin cannot be considered present.[32]

The logic behind this conclusion was that, as the new morality defines sin, its essence is only in the intention. It is not, as historic Catholicism always taught, equally in the action (what is done), the circumstances (how it is done), and in the intention (why it is done).

Consistent with their position, those who so redefined sin also favored contraception, abortion, and the dissolubility of Christian marriage. Most people, they reasoned, who practice contraception, abort or divorce and remarry could honestly say their motives were good, and certainly their intention was not to defy God or simply reject his generous love. At the same time, they could excuse themselves, on Bekkers' terms, not only soon after an abortion or adultery, but in the very act itself. In traditional language, what they were doing is considered a grave sin, but the reason for doing it could be very noble— like protecting the reputation of an unwed mother or giving consolation to an estranged wife.

Aware of the personal problems which the new ethic has raised for priest confessors, they are being advised to look into their own conscience more closely than they ever did before situation morality had entered so deeply into Western thought.

In and out of the confessional, priests are considered representatives of the Catholic Church. One evidence of this is the fact that the Church trusts their maturity and competence, and on this basis gives them what are called "faculties" to hear confessions and confer absolution. Comparable permission, though less exacting, is commonly required for priests to act in an official capacity as teachers, lecturers, and counsellors in a diocese. Under pressure from a situationist morality, a priest may come to disagree with the known official teaching of the Church in moral matters. What should he do?

If his interpretation of the law itself should dissent from the positions generally admitted in the Church, he has no right to follow that personal opinion as norm for his conduct in the confessional. He must give his penitent the answer which the latter expects from him, the answer of the Church.

Outside of confession, the priest is entitled to his own opinion and is allowed to defend it, with the necessary discretion. He should however, be aware that even people who consult him outside of confession want not so much to hear his own opinion as to know what the Church thinks of the question at hand.

A fortiori it is unacceptable that a priest, in or outside of confession, in his capacity as a religious guide, should assume a negative attitude with respect to objective divine or ecclesiastical laws with which he can no longer agree. If he is convinced in good faith that honesty of conscience no longer allows him to accept certain laws, the same honesty will force him to function no longer as the representative of a Church of which he rejects some essential positions.[33]

This counsel by the Dutch author of *Vernieuwd Geweten* is only a sample of similar advice given in other countries. It shows how critical the issue had become in Catholic Christianity which entrusts so much of the moral direction of its members to ordained priests.

Ethics and Grace

Since the earliest days of Christianity there was a tension between two concepts of morality. They would approximately answer to the question of what makes a person good. Is it what he does by his own free choice, or what he does in virtue of God's grace?

St. Paul developed this theme in many of his letters, insisting not only on internal sincerity and humility of spirit, but pointing out that these, too, were fruits of the Spirit; that justification was more than correct behavior, more even than adherence to the divine will. It was above all the presence of God in the one justified. Speaking of himself, he said, "I live now, not I, but Christ lives within me."[34]

A similar concept has been surfaced by the modern search for authenticity, interiority, and true freedom in the moral order. What might be called "moral supernaturalism" is not a new idea, and at first may not seem to deserve special treatment in a history of contemporary Christianity. But the form it has taken and its significance for the future of the Church are unique, to a degree that some believe it offers the best hope for acculturating Christian morals without adjusting the ethical teachings of Christ to suit the mores of the times.

Until recently, Protestant ethicians who sought to ground moral teaching on the principles of their heritage based them on some variant of the Reformation idea of faith and good works. Many still subscribe to the classic position expounded by the early Reformers, and they are critical of others who appear to compromise. Thus according to the Scottish Presbyterian T. F. Torrance, "this is something that very badly needs to be reiterated today within the Churches of the Reformation." He feared a momentous change.

> Justification by Christ alone means the rejection of all self-justification, and all forms of justification by anything or out of any source other than Jesus Christ.
>
> At the Reformation justification by the Grace of Christ alone was seen to set aside all natural goodness, and all works-righteousness; but this applies to all goodness, Christian goodness as well, that is, to "sanctification" as it came to be called.[35]

According to this understanding, justification is so exclusively the expression of God's mercy that man contributes nothing of his own (natural goodness) to the virtues he performs. They are simply the unfolding of divine grace, once and for all received. They are not simultaneously (though mysteriously) the result of man's effort and of God's assistance, who gives man the power to collaborate in the practice of good works, and thus merit his salvation.

A dramatic shift from the traditional position is commonly traced to Kierkegaard, though more accurately it was due to his later, twentieth-century disciples. Gogarten and Tillich, Barth and Bonhoeffer, Reinhold and H. Richard Niebuhr tried to show, through an analysis of man's moral existence as reflected in the tragedies of our times, that more is needed to save human society than ethical principles and activity. Unless God enters history, here and now, to enable man to cope with the demonic forces unleashed in the present generation, they are sure to prevail and it is quite correct to predict an early "Post-Christian Age."

The term coined to express the new approach was *grace as empowerment to live the moral life*. It assumed that "man can recognize an obligation without being able to fulfill it, and that the actual moral experience is that of discovering a power beyond the self which enables man to make a right response. Grace is sometimes described as having a co-operating function once the initial restoration to right relationship is achieved by God's action."[36]

Others believed this was "the redemptive power of the divine working in history," and directly challenged the widespread notion of autonomous man who has no need of constant grace.

As might have been expected, such a view of grace as power and not merely mercy reopened in Protestant circles the thorny question of grace and free will. Some writers relied on Immanuel Kant's idea that the structure of moral obligation implies man's power to fulfill the moral requirement, because otherwise duty is meaningless. Moral action, they said, must be self-wrought to be truly moral, "even though there are environmental pressures and solicitations which render the will's action to an indefinite extent easier or more difficult."[37] Moreover, it seemed to them "a condition of the very being of a moral personality that a man's willing, in its goodness and in its badness, should be absolutely his own, into which in neither case does God's action enter constitutively."[38]

In spite of theoretical questions, however, the more common trend in Protestant pastoral theology has affirmed the need of God's assisting grace for moral living and the churches have been teaching accordingly. One of the clearest formulations of this belief was placed into the Methodist Social Creed, first drafted in 1908 and completely revised before the merger with the Evangelical United Brethren in 1967 to form The United Methodist Church. It faced the grave moral needs of the day, and declared the ongoing conferral of divine assistance to meet these needs.

The Methodist Church must view the perplexing times and problems which we face today in the light of the life and teachings of Jesus. We believe that "the earth is the Lord's and the fulness thereof." Our own capacities and all we possess are gifts of the Creator, and should be held and used in stewardship to him.

We believe that God in Christ is seeking to redeem all men and also society. This redemption is a continuing necessity.

We believe that the grace of God in Christ is available for redemption from individual and social sin as we seek in penitence and obedience to do his holy will.[39]

Such movements of Protestant origin as Alcoholics Anonymous, started in 1935, reflect the practical consequences of admitting one's own inability to solve a grave moral problem and relying on God's assistance to do the "humanly impossible."

But not only Protestantism was affected by this focus on grace as a superhuman means of overcoming bad habits or cultivating good ones. If it was in the nature of a discovery among Protestants, against the background of their theological tradition, it was a rediscovery among Catholics and Orthodox who had neglected this article of their faith. Many of them made the rediscovery through the experience and research of modern psychologists, notably of Carl Jung (1875–1961), whose years of clinical practice convinced him that an "integrated personality," a person with moral character, depended on belief in some form of available divine energy to secure and maintain his integration. Jung was a Christian who said, "I know so much of Protestantism that I could never abandon it."[40] As such, he frankly avowed his faith in Christ's indwelling in the human spirit:

Christ is in us, and we are in him! Why should the activity of God and the presence of the Son of Man within us not be real and observable? Every day am I thankful to God that I have been allowed to experience the reality of the Divine Image within me. Had this not been granted me, I should indeed have been a bitter enemy of Christianity, and of the Church especially. But thanks to this act of grace, my life has meaning.[41]

It was also Jung who claimed in 1932 that during thirty years of clinical practice, "among my patients in the second half of life—that is to say, over thirty-five—there has not been one whose problem in the last resort was not that of finding a religious outlook on life."[42] This outlook, he repeatedly said, included the belief that life was livable because it was not being lived alone. The man of faith had access to a Power above his own, yet within him, to meet life's problems and even profit from its inevitable conflicts.

Scientific and Moral Progress

The notion of progress has been so imbedded in modern thought that inevitably this would have its impact on morality. Words like *development* and *evolution, progress* and *improvement* have come to be used almost indiscriminately of physical organisms and of human behavior. The terminology reflects a variety of concepts that practically defy analysis and yet call for some clarification to understand the direction that Christian ethics has been taking in the post-Darwinian era.

The idea that cultural development should be seen as an extension of biological evolution was popularized by Herbert Spencer (1820–1903), the English philosopher who both anticipated Darwin and echoed his idea of evolution from simple homogeneity to complex heterogeneity. As stated by Spencer and refined by those who followed him, human society reflects definite stages of progress from simple primitive forms to the complex rational forms of Western civilization.

It was Spencer who gave the first impetus to a theory that was soon to have momentous consequences. He used the formula "survival of the fittest" to describe the essential principle of Darwinism, in which the superlative took on meanings that Darwin never intended. Professional geneticists try to explain what happened.

> This expression caught the imagination of biologists and non-biologists alike. There is something thrilling as well as forbidding in the image of "nature red in tooth and claw" commanding all its creatures to wage everlasting war of everybody else according to the motto "eat or be eaten." And this bloody mess was supposed to result not in universal debacle, but, miraculously, in progress itself. As one modern author puts it, "it was a cheerful thought that no good thing was ever lost and no lost thing was any longer any good."[43]

Applications of this reconstructed Darwinism to human problems were bound to come. They came in two ways: one was a literal interpretation of Spencer's "survival of the fittest," and the other was the use of statistics in inheritance studies.

A number of social theorists reasoned that if strife and bloodshed engender improvements in nature they would do the same in human society. This seemed to be nothing else than applying to man the inexorable "laws of nature." So the Superman created by Nietzsche was promptly identified with the surviving fittest. The late nineteenth and early twentieth centuries witnessed the rise of powerful nations building colonial empires. It was, therefore, satisfying to think that when savages with bow and arrow were killed by gunfire this was merely the unfolding of nature's laws, a biologically inferior stock was being replaced by a superior one.

It took men like Hitler to expand the theory into a racial myth, and engulf half the world in war as a corollary. Millions of Jews were put to death because their blood was inferior to that of the Aryan race. Racism for Hitler meant that a certain human stock, e.g., the Germanic, was naturally superior to others, e.g., the Semitic. The latter should be phased out to leave more room for the former.

But where Hitler's racism was militant and immediately devastating other forms were more urbane and subtle. They built not only on the survival theories of Spencer, but incorporated the ideas of what came to be known as eugenics, founded by Francis Galton (1822–1911), who first used statistics in the investigation of inheritance.

Cousin of Charles Darwin and his great admirer, Galton set about studying the heredity of men of exceptional ability in Britain. He found that many of them were related and that they also belonged to relatively few families. Preoccupied with biology, he prescinded from the fact that the ruling class in Britain during his time was a small minority, very much intermarried. He further did not take into account that the chances of success, even intellectual success, normally favor the children from cultured and well-placed families.

Galton's work marked the first crude use of statistics in inheritance studies. It led to the foundation of the sociobiological science of eugenics. Since Galton's time, eugenics has concerned itself with proving, on genetic grounds, the superior value of upper-class stocks and stressing the need to protect them against the careless breeding of the inferior, uneducated poor.

Historical scientists believe that this biological interpretation of mankind, with its emphasis on race and breeding, affected to a greater or lesser degree most "progressive" thinkers and planners in the social and political sciences. It was publicized by novelists like H. G. Wells (1866–1946) and George Orwell (1903–1950) who, in turn, stimulated research (mainly in England, America, and Germany) to improve the human race physically and mentally through control of mating and heredity by society.

As a science, eugenics is directed toward discouraging propagation by unfit and encouraging it in the fit. Part of its thesis is the postulate of an uneven development among different races, and the assumption that the peoples of Asia and Africa are at a lower stage of human development than the races of Europe and Euro-America.

The double transposition of social images into biology and back again was to have serious consequences when applied in political practice in the twentieth century. It struck at the roots of the older belief, established by Judaeo-Christianity, that man belonged to society and that his very individuality could find adequate expression only through society.

This biological view of humanity, as a race rather than a community affected otherwise Christian people in a way that could not even be said of the slave traders in the sixteenth through eighteenth centuries. Racism had become an ideology. It was the myth of a natural superiority of certain cultures in the West over other cultures, mainly in Africa and the Orient. Their inherent differences were considered inherent inequalities, which terms like *undeveloped* and *deprived* served to illustrate.

Organizations like the International Planned Parenthood Federation, consistently follow the racial dialectic in their global efforts to reduce the world's population by contraception, sterilization, and abortion. Started in 1952, the I.P.P.F. had ninety member nations by 1970. Supported financially and/or legally by most of the respective governments, the federation's program is explicitly conscious of the imbalance between population growth in countries of Northern Europe and America compared with those which are designated as underdeveloped. In the vocabulary of a kindred agency, the Center for International Economic Growth, backward peoples are "all countries and territories in Asia, Latin America, Africa and Oceania, excepting Japan, the Union of South Africa, Australia and New Zealand."[44]

The Center for International Economic Growth defined a backward people as those who had one or more of the following traits:

Low industrial output in relation to population.
A very high proportion of the labor force engaged in agriculture.
High illiteracy, low educational level.
High birth rates. In practically all the underdeveloped countries the birth rate ranges from 40 to 50 per thousand of population per year, as compared with 25 in the United States and 16 in some countries of Europe.[45]

The implicit premise of these and similar agencies, cooperating with the government, is the studied comparison between competitive cultures. The population pressure of backward races threatens the welfare of the world's more advanced societies.

Likewise implicit is the belief that some people are racially inferior to others, even when they settle in countries like America. Consequently, their fertility should be restrained.

Victims of social Darwinism are sensitive to its philosophy and some of their defenders are blunt in identifying it. At the first national Congress on Optimum Population and Environment, an American delegate told the assembly that "the whites" are afraid of "the blacks getting control. Otherwise, all their population control programs would not be directed at the ghettos." Another delegate, representing the American Psychiatric Association, saw "a parallel in white anxiety over growing black numbers and concern in Nazi Germany over Jewish population growth."[46]

Aware of this and similar ideologies, the Uppsala conference of the World Council of Churches denounced "contemporary racism" as a "blatant denial of the Christian faith" on three counts: (1) it denies the effectiveness of the reconciling work of Jesus Christ, through whose love all human diversities lose their divisive significance, (2) it denies our common humanity in creation and our belief that all men are made in God's image, and (3) it falsely asserts that we find our significance in terms of racial identity rather than in Jesus Christ.[47]

Three years earlier, the Second Vatican had specified what, in theological terms, is racial discrimination. It is the denial of fundamental rights to which everyone has a claim since "all men have a rational soul and are created in God's likeness, since they have the same nature and origin, have been redeemed by Christ and enjoy the same divine calling and destiny."[48] These reasons are accumulatively so Christian that no other religion adequately professes them, and, within Christianity, only those who stand in the fullness of the historic Christian faith.

Evolutionary Ethics

The most central feature of evolutionism in today's society is the rise of *evolutionary ethics*. Since the term has a variety of meanings, it will be useful to exclude those which are not the immediate focus of attention and isolate the one that calls for special analysis.

Evolutionary ethics is not merely the application of permanent moral principles to changing situations and times. It is not merely the growth in opportunities for man's moral progress created by his increased knowledge of the universe and of means for controlling the forces of nature. It is not merely the theory that *de facto* the rate or at least the pattern of man's moral behavior in the world is improving.

It is the affirmation that what Christianity calls basic moral principles are not immutable, that they are in a constant process of change either by some inexorable law of mutation or by virtue of man's conscious adjustment to keep pace with his progress in other areas of human existence.

Compared with other challenges to Christian morality, already seen, evolutionary ethics touches on the heart of the Christian religion and, as some of its proponents claim, shows promise of replacing the ethical system of Christianity with an evolutionary humanism better suited to man's condition in the new age.

Two main forms of evolutionary ethics have entered the stream of Western thought and, more than is commonly realized, affected large segments of still nominally Christian moral theory and practice. The secularist variety is an extension of the wider theory which unilaterally identifies man's existence with this world; the process variety is commonplace in Oriental philosophies of behavior, and has recently made headway in cultures that derive from Judaeo-Christian ancestry.

SECULARISM AND MORAL PROGRESS. Contrary to some of his critics, the secularist is not necessarily given to the pursuit of the grosser pleasures of food, drink, and sex. He may be a highly cultured person, absorbed in the pursuit of philosophy, art, or science, or in the promotion of the welfare of men and women less fortunately placed than himself. What makes him a secularist is his conviction, really a belief, that there is no other life than "this life," and no other world than "this world." If there is, and he is ready to grant the possibility, it is so uncertain and improbable that the hypothesis has no practical meaning in determining one's behavior. Thus "the essential characteristic of secularism is independent of the nature which secularism gives to what it regards as ultimately real; it is still secularist when that reality is mental or spiritual, and not only when it is material or biological."[49] All the secularisms of today have this in common, that they hold the meaning of the world to lie within itself.

No less than his theistic counterpart, the secularist recognizes the need for a moral order. Like the Christian believer, he also defines morality in terms of man's destiny. A Christian will say that human acts are morally good when they are conducive to the end or goal of human existence, which is the vision of God in eternity. In so far as a deliberate act deviates or detracts a man from his final reaching of God, it is morally evil. So that Christianity judges a person's goodness by the extent to which he is living in this life as he should, i.e., as God expects him to if he is to reach celestial glory.

Following the same ethical logic, the secularist defines morality as means to an end. Those human actions are praiseworthy which further a man's goal in life, or humanity's destiny; and conduct is blameworthy when it fails to advance these ends or, worse still, when they are consciously frustrated. The difference lies in how the secularist conceives the goal or destiny. Since he believes that there is no other life beyond the present one, and no other purpose than the ultimate of happiness—in duration, extension, and intensity—here and now, his norms of morality are determined accordingly.

He is willing to admit that before the scientific age religions as noble as Christianity had thought of man's destiny in postworldly terms. Consistent with this outlook, Christianity held that God had set the conditions of men's salvation and these conditions were, in essence, unchangeable. Their immutability lay in the objective fact that God was God and man was man; that God could not, without denying his nature, alter the essential relationship of creatures to their Creator; nor could he alter the essential relationships of man to man (or within man of one part of his nature to another) without denying man's humanity.

Few writers have improved on Julian Huxley's understanding of how the secularist views man's destiny, and therefore his moral outlook, from the evolutionary perspective:

> Twentieth-century man, it is clear, needs a new organ for dealing with destiny, a new system of religious beliefs and attitudes adapted to the new situation in which his societies now have to exist, including the new knowledge which they have discovered and amassed. The radically new feature of the present situation may perhaps be stated thus: Earlier religions and belief systems were largely adaptations to cope with man's

ignorance and fears, with the result that they came to concern themselves primarily with stability of attitude. But the need of today is for a belief-system adapted to cope with his knowledge and his creative possibilities; and this implies the capacity to meet and to inspire change.

In other words, the primary function of earlier systems was of necessity to maintain social and spiritual morale in face of the unknown; and this they accomplished with a considerable measure of success. But the primary function of any system today must be to utilize all available knowledge in giving guidance and encouragement for the continuing adventure of human development.[50]

All writers in the humanist tradition, and not only Huxley, agree that religions like Christianity have concerned themselves "primarily with stability of attitude." But today, in the light of such evident progress in man's capacity for earthly experience and on the basis of an evolutionary philosophy, the watchword is not stability but "creative possibility." Secularism, no less than Christianity, is a belief system; it does not claim to prove its presuppositions. Within this system, it postulates a destiny which is humanistic in the multiple sense of ending with man, for the unique fulfillment of man, to be achieved among men, and not through the help of some divine agency but only through other men.

A humanistic destiny implies a humanistic ethic, which was always changeable, depending on what terrestrial goals men would set themselves according to their different personalities in different circumstances at different periods of human history. What makes the humanistic ethic more variable than ever today is the discovery of astounding new potentialities of earthly fulfillment and the prospect of untapped resources for still further satisfaction in the years to come.

As recently as 1952, when Huxley began to publish his provocative essays on secularist morality, they were dismissed as "the rantings of an atheist." In less than twenty years, his fellow countryman, the ecclesiastic John Robinson, was saying almost the same thing and hailed as a liberator from an archaic morality. "My plea," he urged in *Christian Morals Today*, "is that Christians must not fear flux or be alarmed at the relativity of all ethics to the ethos of their day."[51] This ethos clearly includes what used to be called adultery, homosexuality, and a host of "sins" that Paul condemned in the first century. Paul's mistake was to identify morality with the unchangeable mind of God, once-for-all incarnate in the person of Christ. He not only came, but is repeatedly "coming in the flesh . . . and this means that the Christ of today is not simply the Christ of yesterday." For it is not in one man, Jesus of Nazareth, or in one age that God assumed human form. He "wills to become incarnate in, the contemporary of, every generation."[52] The ethos of each generation thus becomes the ethic of the Christ who is incarnated in the humanity of that age.

Moreover, the ethos of any one generation is *a priori* believed to be higher and more perfect than the ethical culture of generations which preceded, on the general assumption that what is later is necessarily better. This value judgment has been challenged by moralists who are willing to admit progress in the variety of ethical options and increased possibilities of action; but they are not ready to equate this with moral judgment.

> The belief that ethical conduct is conduct in accordance with the direction of evolutionary change, and that "good" means "more evolved," rests on a valuationally loaded view of evolution, by which it is seen as change in a line of direction, so that what follows is held to be more "advanced" and not only subsequent to what went before.
>
> There is some empirical support for this without an assumption of universal progress, insofar as more complex stages make possible the achievement of a greater range of possible types and activity and of relationships, and these more complex stages have generally been preceded by simpler and less differentiated stages. But the ethical question can still be raised whether, in human activities, the achievement of all "possibilities" is desirable.[53]

Underlying the issue is a confrontation between two world views of what constitutes morality, whether a moral act is essentially better because it involves greater freedom, e.g., in responding to a larger range of human choices, or whether it is ultimately better because it more truly responds to the order of reality, itself reflecting the mind and will of God.

The secularist ethician who believes in universal evolution assumes that subsequent cultures are necessarily superior to preceding ones. But he also assumes what is more significant here, that while there are no moral principles in the objective sense of unchangeable truths affecting man's behavior, there is such a thing as development in the moral order. How so? In virtue of growth in man's knowledge of the universe, including his own psychological being, in the spectrum of new choices which this greater knowledge opens up to human freedom, in wider motives for choice which increased possibilities of action offer a person, in the expansion of prospects for human satisfaction made increasingly possible by the discoveries of science and the creation of previously unheard of ways of self-fulfillment.

Christian morality would not deny the very real contribution to one side of human behavior which these developments imply. But, unlike the secularist ethic, it does not simply equate moral progress with increased variety of options or increased intensity of freedom because a person has more reasons to act in a certain way. The same man who decides to love his wife more intensely can also choose to love another woman more than his wife and act on his choice, which by Judaeo-Christian standards is adultery.

An unexpected revulsion against inevitable progress was being voiced by 1970 and may signal the dawn of a new era of secularist philosophy applied to human behavior on a massive scale.

Those who were accustomed to estimate human development uniquely by terrestrial standards became visibly worried as they saw the exercise of liberty "running rampant" in the pursuit of personal goals, without regard for the welfare of mankind. In less than ten years, ecology changed from a prosaic study of the reciprocal relations between man and his environment to an explosive subject that challenges the foundations of Christian morality.

As certain ecologists view the scene, the much-vaunted theory of cultural evolution calls for drastic reappraisal. Human beings have multiplied so fast and are consuming so much of the earth's available resources that what appeared to be progress threatens to become a world catastrophe. "Man's only hope for the survival of his species and his culture is to realize that he must curtail his breeding and his proclivities toward consumption and environmental destruction to keep within the tolerable limits of the ecosystem." Education and voluntary methods of curtailment should be supplemented by "intervention from the government."[54]

PROCESS THEOLOGY AND DEVELOPING MORALITY. Less well known but more deeply philosophical than secularist ethics is process ideology applied to morality. The name commonly associated with its origins is Alfred North Whitehead (1861–1947), English-American scientist turned religious philosopher. More subtle than the most speculative forms of secularism, it has also exercised a more pervasive influence on the Christian moral order.

Whitehead conceived a finite God, who is quite unlike the Yahweh of biblical revelation. In his vocabulary, "The limitation of God is his goodness. He gains his depth of actuality by his harmony of valuation," i.e., he becomes more actually perfect by synthesizing events into the most meaningful whole.[55] But just what events shall occur as material for this synthesis depends mainly on the inherent freedom or self-determination which is the essence of every event-unit of reality. Everything, not excluding God, is in process. In less technical terms, God is "perfect" only as the wise synthesizer of the universe; he is in the process of becoming more perfect as he directs the native liberty of being outside himself toward an ever more harmonious world of reality. Critical to Whitehead's moral thought is the idea of a universe (including God) which is growing in perfection through the exercise of myriad free wills throughout cosmic history.

Whitehead considered himself a Christian, regularly quoting the Gospels. But he leveled at all forms of Christianity "the charge of idolatry," which "rests with equal truth on all the main churches, Protestant and Catholic. Idolatry is the necessary product of static dogma."[56] Christian dogmas were static, for Whitehead, because they were founded on the notion of an infinite God who had no share in the world's sufferings and joys, who could watch the universe undergoing constant change and himself remain imperturbably unchanged.

It was not surprising that Whitehead also strongly criticized the traditional Christian conscience, or that modern situationists quote him in support of their aims. According to Whitehead, "The simple-minded use of the notions of 'right or wrong' is one of the chief obstacles to the progress of understanding."[57] He said this because consistent with a process theology of reality went a process theory of morals. Right and wrong in the process ethic is the greater or lesser (also accelerated or retarded) of the ongoing perfection of the universe, God and man included. It has nothing to do with man's fulfillment of God's antecedent will and with tending toward or away from the attainment of an already infinite, all-perfect God.

Under these suppositions, it would be naïve to still speak of unvarying moral principles, or of once-for-all ethical norms which derived their permanency from the immutable nature of God.

Process morality has been incorporated into existentialist ethics, whose principal affirmation is that "openness to the future has primacy over conformity to the past." In the language of Sartre, the past is not so much annihilated as merely "nihilated," which is to say, suspended in order to let the demands of the future emerge. The past tells a man what he ought to do. The future is a more reliable guide simply because it does not tell him what to do; it appeals to him to "invent" or "create" in the light of the emerging situation in which he finds himself at any moment of moral decision.

Among certain moralists, existentialist ethics is more or less closely tied in with process theology, depending on the writer's acceptance of an already-perfect Deity. Arguing from St. Paul as reducing Christ's whole ethical teaching to one word, "love," Tillich held that Christian behavior was rooted in "the trans-moral conscience," Ramsey wrote of "an ethic without laws," and H. Richard Niebuhr synthesized the existentialist approach in "responsivity."

They spoke of "the transcendence of laws," while insisting that this does not mean the abrogation of norms. For existential ethics, freedom, by which one transcends laws in the direction of creative action, is itself the norm for freedom. "Man is freedom. Freedom is the source of man's possibility of acting ethically, because freedom is nothing— a lack to be filled, a power of resoluteness which lets situations reveal their needs. And what is the norm by which to discern in any situation what is needful? One must so act as to let others be free while oneself remaining free."[58] Freedom here means the uninhibited capacity for acting or not acting, acting this or another way—in creative response and without hindrance from any law, human or supposedly divine, except the one "law" that I do not interfere with other people's liberty. If law is still defined as "limitation of freedom," the limitation is only in terms of other human beings, who have their own liberties to exercise; it bears no relation to an objective transcendent Being whose essence is the eternal norm of human morality, whose will has a right to claim obedience and whose love can elicit man's generosity.

X

ECUMENICAL MOVEMENT

The ecumenical movement is a dramatic symbol of modern Christianity. It was inevitable that, as human society everywhere was affected by the communications revolution, the Churches of Christendom would also feel the impact and be challenged to repair their broken unity.

Many aspects of the ecumenical movement have already been seen, and some in great detail. But ecumenism itself has not been examined from the single perspective of historical development and guiding principles—each within the Protestant, Orthodox, and Roman Catholic traditions. The merits of this approach are that the main stands of a complex religious phenomenon can be traced from its origins up to the present day and its direction almost predicted into the final decades of the current century.

World Protestantism

It is quite correct to say that the movement to restore Christian unity in modern times was started under Protestant auspices. Until recent years, most of the prominent leaders of ecumenism were Protestants. This was not surprising since the Protestant Churches were most affected by the separatist tendency that reached a high-water mark of sectionalism in the nineteenth century. In the sixteenth century, there were originally only four principal divisions among the Churches of the Reformation, Lutheran and Reformed, Anglican and Free Church or Congregational. By 1900 a single religious family, the Lutherans, had eighty-one distinct denominations in the United States.

Other affiliations had comparable divisions. By 1970 there were only three principal bodies of Lutherans in America, and even these were closing ranks with the prospect of still further mergers in the next generation.

DOMINANT PERSONALITIES. If Protestant origins were dominated by such figures as Luther, Calvin, Zwingli, and Cranmer, so, too, the growth of Protestant ecumenism. And as we can distinguish the spiritual ancestors of the Reformation from those who later organized and stabilized the various denominations, it is possible to isolate the charismatic persons who gave the primary impulse to Christian unity from their later followers who put the original ideas into concrete, organized practice.

Four names tower above the others as fathers of Protestant ecumenism: the American, John R. Mott; the Canadian, Charles H. Brent; the Swedish, Nathan Söderblom; and the Dutch, Willem A. Visser 't Hooft. Their biographies are part of the essential history of Christian reunification, and not only within Protestantism.

Born in New York in 1865, John Mott became student secretary of the International Committee of the Young Men's Christian Association at the age of twenty-three. Seeing the need for coordinating that segment of the Church which he felt offered the greatest potential for Christian unity, he founded at Vadstena in Sweden the World's Student Christian Federation to bring together the existing student organizations in America, Great Britain, the Scandinavian countries, and Germany. Chosen as its general secretary, Mott remained in that position for twenty-five years. The purpose which he formulated is still the guiding character of the World Federation:

> To unite student Christian movements or organizations throughout the world.
>
> To collect information regarding religious conditions of the students of all lands.
>
> To promote the following lines of activity: to lead students to become disciples of Jesus Christ as only Savior and as God; to deepen the spiritual life of students; to enlist in the work of extending the kingdom of Christ throughout the whole world.[1]

In 1910, at the historic Edinburgh World Missionary Conference, Mott headed the first of its preparatory commissions and became chairman of the Continuation Committee which he promoted and whose original charter he drafted. Mott served as the first chairman of the

International Missionary Council from its inception in 1921 until 1941, meanwhile continuing as president of the World's Committee of the Y.M.C.A. As with the Student Federation, so here, his main interest was to create "movements toward unity and cooperation in the mission field," on the premise that "Missionary Societies throughout the world must be in as close communication as possible with one another."[2]

All the while he was heading the international Y.M.C.A., Mott was prodigiously active in fostering the future World Council of Churches. Preparatory to the first Conference on Faith and Order, at Oxford, he directed the Advisory Council which coordinated the agenda. At the Conference in 1937, he presided as chairman and a year later, at Utrecht, he became vice-chairman of the Provisional Committee for the projected World Council. At its first assembly in Amsterdam, he served as one of the council's presidents.

Mott combined to an unusual degree a deep religious faith, evangelistic zeal, power over public assemblies and compelling, convincing speech. Most of his dozen published books deal with Christian unity, and his six volumes of addresses and papers read like a commentary on his favorite quotation, "that they all may be one." Even the 1958 merger of the World Council of Churches and the International Missionary Council only put into effect the idea conceived at the turn of the century by the first chairman of the I.M.C.

Charles Brent (1862–1929) was an Anglican missionary from Ontario, who became Episcopalian missionary to the Philippine Islands in 1910. Unlike Mott, who had a passionate zeal for unity based on the love of Christ, Brent was more conscious of the grave differences that separated the Churches. He also saw Anglicanism as the bridge that might span these differences. When the 1910 Missionary Conference at Edinburgh voted to explore ways of overcoming the conflicts among mission-sending societies, Brent carried the recommendation to his Anglican confreres at their triennial convention in Chicago. On his urging, the convention appointed a committee to invite "all Churches which accept Jesus Christ as God and Saviour to join in conferences following the general method of the World's Missionary Conference, for the consideration of all questions pertaining to Faith and Order of the Church of Christ."[3] Due to the approaching World War and its sequel, it was not until 1927 that the first World Conference on Faith and Order was held at Lausanne in Switzerland, where one hundred and fifty representatives from sixty-nine Churches met in August and passed a series of resolutions that laid the foundations for the future World Council, with headquarters in Geneva.

Brent was convinced that cooperation among Christian bodies was possible only if a certain degree of unanimity of faith had been reached. Faith and Order thus became synonymous with belief and worship, and was rooted in the doctrinal principles that he inherited from the Oxford Movement in England and America. He believed that disunity was essentially creedal and consequently ritual. Until these differences were resolved, there could be no question of authentic church unity.

Nathan Söderblom (1866–1931), Lutheran Archbishop of Uppsala in Sweden, was the founder and chief promoter of the ecumenical counterpart to Faith and Order, the Life and Work Movement. When he became archbishop in 1914, it was against the opposition of the more conservative elements in the Swedish Church which looked with suspicion at his apparent indifference to doctrinal issues that divided the Christian bodies.

Söderblom was certain that revelation was a continuous process, not limited to the apostolic age; that it reached varying degrees among both Christian and non-Christian religions; and that the future basis of church unity would not be doctrine but history. Each group would respect in the other what all had received, and thus share with the other their doctrinally diverse but ultimately one revelation to the human race. On these terms, revelation is the gradual unfolding of the sacred through the successive ages of man's history.

The archbishop was the mastermind behind the First Conference on Life and Work, held at Stockholm in August 1925, where five hundred delegates from thirty-nine countries and ninety-one Churches decided that the problems of social morality were too great to be solved by individual effort. The community must accept responsibility, "and must exercise such social control over individual actions as in each instance may be necessary for the common good."[4]

Among other elements of the historic faith which Söderblom criticized was faith in the two natures of Christ, which he said was unacceptable to modern man. He also formulated one of the leading ideas of ecumenical theology among certain Protestants: that holiness rather than the conception of God lies at the basis of religion. Religion is what a man is or what he does, irrespective of what he believes.

Willem Adolph Visser 't Hooft practically followed in the footsteps of John Mott. At twenty-four he became secretary of the World's Committee of the Y.M.C.A. and then served in the same capacity with the World's Student Christian Federation, while actively cooperating with the unity efforts set in motion by his predecessor. He made himself indispensable at the Life and Work meeting in Oxford (1927) by co-authoring a volume on *The Church and Its Function in Society* for use by the delegates; and the same year he played so prominent a role at the Edinburgh Conference of Faith and Order that no one was surprised at his appointment in Utrecht (1938) as General Secretary of the provisional committee for the later World Council of Churches.

More than any Protestant of his time, Visser 't Hooft determined the meaning of "ecumenical," which lay at the heart of the unity movement. He admitted that verbally the term "catholic" would have been just as accurate, since both mean "universal." But "catholic" had undesirable connotations. Unlike Roman Catholicism with its accent on universality as a historical fact, "ecumenical is interpreted in a substantial and spiritual rather than a formal and spatial manner," where "the point of reference is not the secular *Oikoumene* (already existing), but the Church Universal (still to be established)." No doubt, in the middle of the nineteenth century, "the time was not ripe for a general acceptance of this conception." But after one hundred years of growth in practical fellowship through such agencies as the Young Men's Christian Association, the "old etymological sense" of ecumenical (associated with general councils) has given way to a new meaning, "to embrace at one and the same time the truths that the Church of Jesus Christ is world-wide, supra-national, supra-racial; that it is essentially one, and that this oneness contains a variety of gifts," capable of uniting otherwise disparate churches into one *Ecclesia Christi*.[5]

As the first General Secretary of the World Council of Churches, Visser 't Hooft set the pace for the Protestant side of ecumenical theology, which is mainly of Calvinist lineage and strongly committed to the Reformed tradition. The international headquarters at Geneva are intended to symbolize this ancestry and confessional emphasis.

IDEOLOGICAL POSITION. There is no easy way to isolate the principles of Protestant ecumenism. From its origins in 1948, the World Council also included members from the Orthodox and Old Catholic communions. Moreover, among Protestants there is a wide range of ideas on the nature of the Church, of disunity, and consequently of reunification.

The best single exposition of the Protestant understanding of ecumenism is the Evanston Declaration, issued by the Second Assembly of the World Council in 1954. It came after the council was several years in existence and had a chance to reflect on its own (predominantly Protestant) identity. It also came seven years before the New Delhi conference, when the Orthodox Church of Russia was admitted to full membership to become the main voting body in the council and to radically change its ecumenical direction.

The declaration began with examining the nature and extent of the "oneness in Christ" which the members of the World Council of Churches presumably enjoy. "This oneness," they said, "is no mere unity of sentiment. We become aware of it because it is given to us by God as the Holy Spirit reveals to us what Christ has done for us."[6]

Searching for a viable basis of unity among the Churches, the assembly stated that "the New Testament conceives of the unity of the church, not as sociological, but as having its essential reality in Christ himself and in his indissoluble unity with his people."[7] Instead of defining unity in terms both of its divine Founder and its human members, who profess and practice a common faith, unity belongs only to Christ himself who, obviously, is the one Mediator between God and man. In answer, therefore, to the question: does the New Testament teach that the Church of Christ is one? the answer is affirmative, but in a qualified sense. It is one because Christ is one, because he is the one source of man's redemption and reconciliation with the Father, because through him alone men receive the Holy Spirit and hope for the glory of heaven.

But is this all? Essentially and substantially this is sufficient. Yet, there is a second kind of unity which Christ also desired his Church to have, which consists in the union of its members with one another, and which may be called "the oneness of the church in its earthly pilgrimage." Properly speaking, this is only a tendency toward unity that "will not be totally achieved until God sums up all things in Christ," that is, after the last day.[8]

An analogy was offered to help illustrate these two types of unity, the one given and existing, the other to become manifest and still in the making:

> In each Christian there is both the "new man" who has been created and yet must be put on daily, and also the "old man" who has been crucified with Christ and yet must be daily mortified. So the church is

already one in Christ, by virtue of his identification of himself with it, and must become one in Christ, so as to manifest its true unity in the mortification of its divisions.[9]

The Lord has given to his Church abundant means for the gradual, though never total, manifestation of unity among the members of his Mystical Body:

> Christ of his love and grace has given his church such gifts as it needs for its growth from unity to unity . . . Christ has given his Spirit, which is the bond of peace and love, and the guide to all truth . . . He has given apostles, prophets, evangelists, pastors and teachers, that the unity of the body may be continually built up . . . He has given the church the gift and power of prayer, by which the church can plead both for its own unity and for the reconciliation of men to God and to one another.[10]

Before entering into a diagnosis of the discord in Christianity, the assembly wished to give some evidence of existing unity among the Churches. "It would be ungrateful to a merciful God if we did not speak now of those gifts which assure us that the undivided Christ is present among us . . . in spite of our divisions."[11] The list of these gifts, it seems, is impressive. As regards faith, "We wait upon one Father, through the one Holy Spirit, praying that we may be ready to hear and obey when he takes the things of Christ and shows them to us."[12] As regards the Scriptures, all the Churches read them, "and proclaim the gospel from them in the faith that the Word speaking through them draws us to himself and into the apostolic faith."[13] Relative to the sacraments, "we all receive his gift of baptism whereby, in faith, we are engrafted in him even while we have not yet allowed it fully to unite us with each other." Moreover, "we all hear his command to 'do this' and his word 'This is my body . . . this is my blood' in the sacrament of the eucharist, even while our celebration of the Lord's Supper is not yet at one table."[14] In like manner, "we all receive a ministry of the Word and sacraments, even while our ministries are not yet recognized by all and not understood in the same sense."[15]

Here a careful distinction was made between the terms "common" and "uniform" as applied to the Churches. The gifts of Sacred Scripture, baptism, the Eucharist, and the ministry are not indeed being used in a uniform manner but, at least, "the fact of our *common*, though *diverse*, use of these gifts is a powerful evidence of our unity in Christ."[16] It is a "present reality," which affords some consolation as justice "compels us now to examine seriously how it is that our disunity as churches contradicts our unity in Christ."[17]

Disunity among the churches is not to be condemned out of hand. Understood as diversity, it is "not sinful because it reflects both the diversities of creation by one Creator." But diversity becomes sinful when it "disrupts the manifest unity of the body." The reason is because "it obscures from men the sufficiency of Christ's atonement, inasmuch as the gospel of reconciliation is denied in the very lives of those who proclaim it."[18]

But the real question still remains: how are the great divisions in Christian history to be estimated? Were they sinful or not? The answer must be ambiguous. Objectively the alienation of one Christian body from another is always sinful, but subjectively all the great divisions in Christianity have been sincerely instituted.

Thus during the first millennium, "some believed that others were departing from the God-given structure and faith of the church by unwarrantable claims and unfounded doctrines. So came the schism between East and West" completed by the year 1054 and, except for temporary and partial reunions with Rome, still extant in the Orthodox churches which number upwards of one hundred fifty million communicants.[19]

Others again "believed that God had called them to such reformation of the faith and order of the church as would restore it to its primitive purity. They found their work could not be completed within the framework of Roman Catholicism; thus came the separate churches of the Reformation."[20] These represent the parent churches of Luther, Calvin, and Zwingli, which have since divided into scores of denominations.

"Some believed that the faith must indeed be reformed but within the framework of ancient and historic episcopacy. So the Anglican and Old Catholic communities became separated both from Rome and from many of the Reformed churches."[21] Generically they may be called "episcopalian," as distinct from the Roman Church which is papal, and the Orthodox which claims to be conciliar.

Finally "some believed that the established churches of their day would not give free course to the Word of salvation. So the older free churches and the Methodist connection felt themselves forced to adopt independent church orders."[22] In this group belong the majority of

Protestant Churches affiliated with the World Council, which are founded on the principle of "self-determination" in matters of doctrine and discipline.

Disunity among the churches is only another proof of man's utter depravity. "We shall never, in this life, escape from our sinfulness."[23] Then on an opposite, hopeful note, "we can repent of sin when it is revealed to us," as in the present situation.[24] However, before proposing a number of remedies as a means of repentance, it is recommended that the Churches in the World Council make an ecumenical examination of conscience, asking themselves a series of searching questions:

> We ask each other whether we do not sin when we deny the sole lordship of Christ over the church by claiming the vineyard for our own, by possessing "our church" for ourselves, by regarding our theology, order, history, nationality, etc., as our own "valued treasures," thus involving ourselves more and more in the separation of sin. The point at which we are unable to renounce the things which divide us, because we believe that obedience to God himself compels us to stand fast—this is the point at which we come together to ask for mercy and light.[25]

The remedy for disunity, therefore, is blind self-surrender, "even unto death." Churches which have cherished doctrines and traditions for centuries "have to be prepared to offer up some of their accustomed, inherited forms of life in uniting with other churches, without complete certainty as to all that will emerge from the step of faith."[26] Several practical means were suggested to give tangible expression to this self-surrender which lies at the spiritual basis of the ecumenical movement.

First and of paramount importance for healing the disunity in Christendom is humble repentance. "Not the repentance we may expect of others, but that which *we* undertake ourselves—cost what it may—even when others are not willing to follow." This means a sincere "acknowledgment before God that we have sinned so as to be caught in the net of inexplicable evil and rendered unable to heal our divisions by ourselves."[27]

After repentance should come thankfulness to God "for the actual oneness he has given us in the World Council of Churches." Concretely this means that the present members of the council resolve "to stay together [and] beyond that, as the Holy Spirit may guide us, we intend to unite."[28]

The guidance of the Holy Spirit must come through "our Lord

speaking to us through Holy Scripture." This is a hard thing to do because "we still struggle to comprehend the meaning and authority of Holy Scripture." Hence an earnest study of the Word of God is recommended, but, above all, a firm resolution "to be obedient to what we are told" by the inspired text. Then "we are on our way toward realizing the oneness of the church in Christ in the actual state of our dividedness on earth."[29]

Special and studious attention should be paid to the importance of baptism and the Eucharist as instruments of unity. "For some, but not for all, it follows that the churches can only be conformed to the dying and rising again in Christ, which both sacraments set forth, if they renounce their eucharistic separateness."[30]

And lastly, "the measure of our concern for unity is the degree to which we pray for it. We cannot expect God to give us unity unless we prepare ourselves to receive his gift by costly and purifying prayer." Especially valuable is communal prayer, for "to pray *together* is to be drawn together." Therefore "we urge, wherever possible, the observance of the Week of Prayer for Christian Unity, January 18–25 (or some other period suited to local conditions) as a public testimony to prayer as the road to unity."[31]

ISSUES AND DEVELOPMENT. Since Evanston, the theological premises of world Protestantism on the ecumenical movement have not greatly changed, even though the World Council of Churches and its national affiliates have altered considerably. Besides the entrance of Russian Orthodoxy into the council, other forces have also been operative —to the point that by the Uppsala Assembly in 1968 other issues than doctrine or worship preoccupied the council's delegation and practically created a new entity in the twenty years of existence since Amsterdam.

The heavy inroads of secularism in the Churches evoked a lively response at Uppsala; also concern for social questions like racism, war and peace, poverty and unemployment, alcoholism and drug addiction, and the women's liberation movement have become so integral to the councils of Churches in various countries that the specific aim of fostering reunion among the dismembered church bodies has been left increasingly to other agencies and institutions.

These agencies have been remarkably successful in the promotion of church unity among the divided families of Protestantism. In the United States, where denominationalism had been most pronounced, some thirty large-scale mergers of Churches were effected from 1900 to 1970, including such major creations as The United Methodists and United Presbyterians. In some cases, they were reunions of church bodies that had split over such issues as the race question in the nineteenth century (Methodists), or of denominations that originally stemmed from the same ancestry (Baptists), or of groups in the same tradition that had emigrated to America from different countries (Lutherans).

Outside the United States, the most significant merger was the Church of South India, formed in 1947 through the union of three religious bodies: the Anglican Church of India, Burma and Ceylon; the South India Province of the Methodist Church; and the South India United Church, itself the result of a movement which brought Presbyterian, Congregational, and Dutch Reformed bodies into organic union in 1908 and was joined in 1919 by the Malabar District of the Basel Mission, which drew its workers from Continental Lutheran and Reformed Churches.

The significance of the Church of South India lay in the fact that it meant the formal recognition by the Episcopalians, through the Lambeth Conference, of the ministry of non-episcopal Protestant denominations. Anglo-Catholics viewed the merger as an implicit denial of the historic episcopate; but the majority of world Anglicans hailed it as a milestone in ecumenical progress.

Actual mergers have stimulated further possibilities of reunion among the Protestants in Europe, Afro-Asia, and the Americas. The most ambitious of such explorations was the Consultation on Church Union (COCU), which drafted its principles in 1966 for the eventual formation in America of one ecclesiastical body out of some ten major denominations, including The Methodist Church, the Protestant Episcopal Church, and the Christian Churches or Disciples of Christ. First spearheaded by James Pike, Episcopal Bishop of California, and Carson Blake who later became General Secretary of the World Council of Churches, the Consultation is undergirded by three general ecclesiological positions: congregationalism, presbyterianism, and episcopalianism. Yet, the new Church is to be in the episcopal tradition, claiming "visible historic continuity with the Church of all ages, before and after the Reformation," with the understanding that "the bishops together personify the continuity of the Church's trusteeship of tradition and pastoral oversight."[32] Strongest opposition to the union has been from the evangelical Protestants who see the proposed merger as a compromise with Reformation principles, notably of local church autonomy and the universal priesthood of the faithful. Symbolic of its evolutionary character, the Consultation changed its name to the Church of Christ Uniting. The new title implied an open-ended organization that allows a constant addition of affiliating members without the corresponding need for constitutional adjustment.

As important as the realized and projected church unions have been within Protestantism, this is only a third of the Protestant ecumenical movement; the other two thirds concern its relationship with Eastern Orthodox and Roman Catholic Churches. On both levels the effects have been mutual and so far-reaching that no phase of Christianity has been left untouched and in some cases more deeply affected than by any comparable development in Orthodoxy since the thirteenth and in Roman Catholicism since the sixteenth century.

Eastern Orthodoxy

Though less well known, the ecumenical movement among the Orthodox also began with the domestic task of reuniting Churches which had originally been together. While no single term covers the precise differences that divided them, two sets of expressions are commonly used: Ephesian or Nestorian, and Chalcedonian or Monophysite.

Nestorianism, named after its founder, Nestorius, was the theory that there were two distinct persons in the incarnate Christ, one human and the other divine. It was condemned by the Council of Ephesus in 431. The Monophysites, from the Greek *monos* (one) and *phusis* (nature), went to the other extreme, claiming that Christ had only a divine nature, and not also a human one. The Council of Chalcedon (451) declared this was heresy.

Many Nestorians remained organized as ecclesiastical bodies, notably those who belonged to the Persian Empire of the fifth and sixth centuries, which once extended to East China and South India and now survives as the Church of the East. The Monophysites represented a split within the Byzantine Empire, essentially between the Hellenic and Latin peoples on the one hand and Christians of Syria and Egypt on the other. Both groups were united in their rejection of Chalcedon, the fourth ecumenical council of the undivided Church.

DIALOGUE WITH THE NON-CHALCEDONIANS. There the matter stood until the present century. After years of study and private dialogue, a formal consultation was held at the University of Aarhus, Denmark, in 1964, at which theologians from the Eastern Orthodox (Chalcedonian) and Oriental Orthodox (Non-Chalcedonian) reached an historic decision. They concluded that the Council of Chalcedon substantially represents the official teaching of both traditions. Their joint statement was the first of its kind in fifteen hundred years:

> Ever since the second decade of our century, representatives of our Orthodox Churches, some accepting seven ecumenical Councils and others accepting three, have often met in ecumenical gatherings. The desire to know each other and to restore our unity in the one Church of Christ has been growing all these years.
>
> We have spoken to each other in the openness of charity and with the conviction of truth. All of us learned from each other. Our inherited misunderstandings have begun to clear up. Fifteen centuries of alienation have not led us astray from the faith of our Fathers.
>
> In common study of the Council of Chalcedon, the well-known phrase used by our common Father in Christ, St. Cyril of Alexandria (the one *Phusis* or *hypostasis* of God's Word Incarnate) with its implications, was at the centre of our conversations. On the essence of the Christological dogma we found ourselves in full agreement. Through the different terminologies used by each side, we saw the same truth expressed.[33]

Along with the theological statement at Aarhus, decisions were also reached by the Churches themselves. The Conference of Heads of Oriental Orthodox Churches, which met at Addis Ababa (Ethiopia) in January 1965, decided to "institute a fresh study of the Christological doctrine in its historical setting," in order that the "controversy which caused the division" might be resolved in the interests of "the reunion of Christendom."[34] A comparable statement was issued on the side of the Eastern Orthodox Churches, at their Synod of the Ecumenical Patriarchate of Constantinople, in June of the same year. The synodical decision outlined the steps in restudying the position of their respective bodies, and then "a joint meeting shall be convened of the heads of the Churches, on both sides, for finally ratifying and proclaiming before the world their union and to give liturgical expression to the great event."[35]

These decisions were later reaffirmed in a patriarchal memorandum, but the appointment of the commissions was proceeding at the usual Orthodox pace. Among others, the major Churches of Russia, Romania, and Greece took prompt action; others have been moving more slowly. But eventual organic union appears certain.

More familiar ecumenical involvement of the Eastern Orthodox Churches concerned their relationship with Protestants and Roman Catholics and, between the two, with the Anglican Communion.

RELATIONS WITH ANGLICANS AND PROTESTANTS. Theological colloquia with the Anglicans began as early as 1874 with the Bonn Conferences, sponsored by the Old Catholics (who broke with Rome over Jansenism and papal infallibility) and attended by Orthodox and Anglican representatives. But it was not until the sixth Lambeth Conference in 1920 that delegates from the Orthodox Churches were invited to attend as observers and to take part in unofficial discussions during its session.

It would be misleading, however, to suppose that the Anglicans were more reluctant than the Orthodox in advancing mutual relations. The Anglicans had sought for years to obtain recognition of their priestly and episcopal ordinations by the Orthodox, especially after Leo XIII in 1896 declared that Anglican orders were invalid. Study and dialogue finally reached a point of decision in 1922, when the Patriarch of Constantinople, Meletius, supported by his synod, officially declared Anglican ordinations, "possessing the same validity as those of the Roman, Old Catholic and Armenian Churches possess, inasmuch as all essentials are found in them which are held to be indispensable from the Orthodox point of view for the recognition of the charisms of the priesthood derived from Apostolic succession."[36]

In the following year, the Patriarch of Jerusalem supported this decision, along with the Church of Cyprus. The same was approved by the Church of Alexandria in 1930, and the Romanian Orthodox in 1936. But in 1948 a startling reversal took place, when a consultation of the autocephalous Church held in Moscow decided that Anglican orders cannot be recognized until the Anglicans themselves further clarified their doctrinal attitude toward their own orders, because they seemed to be uncertain whether ordination is one of the seven sacraments. The present Orthodox position, therefore, is one of suspended judgment on the validity of the Anglican priesthood.

Ecumenical relations with Protestants have been varied and yet predictable. Two schools of thought exist among the Orthodox on the subject, and both have been crystallized in their respective attitudes toward the Faith and Order movement and the World Council of Churches. One party holds that Orthodox should take no part in either, or at most send observers to the meetings but not full delegates. They claim that full participation in the ecumenical movement would compromise the principle that the Orthodox Church is the one true Church of Christ, and would imply that all Churches are alike. A typical statement to that effect was made in 1938 by the Synod of the Russian Church in Exile:

> Orthodox Christians must regard the Holy Orthodox Catholic Church as the true Church of Christ, one and unique. For this reason, the Russian Orthodox Church in Exile has forbidden its children to take part in the ecumenical movement, which rests on the principle of the equality of all religions and Christian confessions.[37]

That was ten years before the charter assembly of the World Council. When the council met at Amsterdam, the Orthodox Churches of Constantinople, Greece, and the Romanian Church in America were officially represented. Since then, most of world Orthodoxy has actively participated in formal ecumenical relations with Protestant Churches on the national and international level.

Yet, while actively cooperating, the Orthodox have always been careful to distinguish their part in the venture from that of the Protestants. This was dramatically illustrated in 1954, at the Evanston meeting of the World Council, when Orthodox delegate Georges Florovsky took issue with the council's commentary on the main theme, "Christ, the Hope of the World." What the Orthodox found missing was the awareness of the saints' and especially of Mary's place in the Church, and of the work of the Holy Spirit.

> It is misleading to describe the Church simply as "the pilgrim people of God" and to forget that the Church Triumphant and Church Militant are but One Body. It is precisely in this unity that the Christian Hope is grounded. The Church is the great Communion of Saints. We upon earth live and strive in communion with the glorious "cloud of witnesses" revealed through the ages and are strengthened by the intercession of the Theotokos and the Saints with whom we join in adoration of Christ our Redeemer.
>
> It would be in vain to preach Christ as the Hope of the World without mentioning Divine action and acknowledging the reality of Grace which is the sole source of this hope. The tragedy of the fallen world consists

precisely in its inability to hope in Christ without the help of Grace. Moreover, this hope is meaningful and fruitful only inasmuch as it leads man into the real life in Christ which pre-supposes the continuous action of the Holy Spirit within us.[38]

The entrance into the World Council of the massive Orthodox delegation from Moscow did not greatly change the essential position. Always at strategic points of ecumenical deliberation, the Orthodox as a group or individual synods as voting delegates made it abundantly clear that their stance in Christian reunion was unique, and unequivocally opposed to any suspicion of compromising with the idea that the fullness of Christianity resided in Orthodoxy. But the focus changed considerably.

Orthodox delegates generally took the view that whatever might eventually come of the ecumenical movement, it was a mistake to promote unity in structure or administration, and still less in juridical forms, in the face of an already given spiritual unity found among believing Christians. Speaking for the Protestant membership at Uppsala, a British theologian confessed that some of the "sharpest criticism" came from the Orthodox on the meaning of "Catholicity" toward which the World Council was striving. They repeatedly expressed the fear of "a false dichotomy or confusion between some secular, 'horizontal' notion of catholicity and the unity given by and in Christ; between catholicity as an essential attribute of the Church and catholicity as something to be sought (as if it were not already there). There was a danger of presenting catholicity as 'quantitative' rather than 'qualitative,' or as 'visible' versus 'interior,' instead of 'total.' "[39]

This was consistent with the known attitude of the Moscow delegation that a too visible concept of the Church, in terms of authority or canonical discipline, ill-accorded with the essentially "interior" role of Christianity in serving man's spirit. Needless conflict with the civil government was inevitable when the Church made claims to jurisdiction in externals of conduct or, worse still, in conformity to ecclesiastical standards.

As a rule, the Russian Orthodox Church stressed the need for advancing the cause of peace, and of cooperation in social welfare among the members of the World Council of Churches. Conversely, the Byzantine Church, notably through its Patriarch of Constantinople, placed a heavy accent on the actual restoration of unity among the dismembered Churches.

Significantly, the important Secretariat for Religious Liberty which had been active until 1967, was phased out by the Uppsala Assembly the following year. After stating that the "Structure Committee" fully "recognized that a contribution of outstanding quality and permanent value was made by the Secretariat for Religious Liberty during the period of its existence," Uppsala reported that the same Structure Committee "would not recommend the continuation of the Secretariat."[40] Not stated was the fact that discontinuance was part of the known mind of Orthodox Churches behind the Iron Curtain. Their participation in the World Council was conditioned on avoiding any semblance of criticism of the political policy of their respective governments.

TOWARD REUNION WITH ROME. The breach between Rome and Eastern Orthodoxy goes back to a series of disagreements over policy, which started in the ninth century when Pope Nicholas I excommunicated Photius, the Patriarch of Constantinople, for ousting Ignatius, whom the Pope supported. Photius proceeded to excommunicate the Pope on five charges, all but one of which arose from legitimate differences between Greek and Latin discipline. He accused the Latins of heresy for: fasting on Saturdays in Lent, beginning Lent on Ash Wednesday instead of Monday, disapproval of a married clergy, objection to confirmation by a priest, and insertion of the *Filioque* (and from the Son) in the Creed. The last objection made theological history and marked the beginning of Eastern accusations of heresy against the See of Rome.

In the eleventh century another Patriarch of Constantinople, Michael Caerularius, charged Pope Leo IX with three other heresies, besides inserting the *Filioque*. The Western Christians, he said, established clerical celibacy, fast on Saturdays as well as Fridays, and use unleavened bread for the Eucharist. When the Pope's delegates in Constantinople solemnly excommunicated Caerularius in 1054, the schism was complete. The charge of cruelty and oppression by the Crusaders aggravated the division, climaxed by the sack of Constantinople in 1204.

Sporadic and unsuccessful attempts to heal the breach occurred many times, and on a major scale the Council of Florence in the fifteenth century made the last major effort to reunite Eastern and Western Christianity.

Since the turn of the present century, more progress has been made and with more promising results than at any time since that fateful day, July 16, 1054, when the Roman legates laid Pope Leo's excommunication on the main altar of St. Sophia's.

The one historical fact most certainly responsible for the changed relationship was the rise of Communism. Persecution of the clergy and laity, suppression of monasteries and the mass closing of religious edifices rocked the Orthodox Church to its foundations. At every stage in the process, the Catholic Church identified itself with the persecuted, defended their rights, and its people suffered along with the Orthodox as victims of a concerted effort to root out Christianity, first in Russia and its satellites and then in mainland China.

The papal relief mission to Russia (1920–1921) when ten million died of starvation and other millions were saved only by reason of such "foreign intervention," strong documents like Pius XI's *Divini Redemptoris* against "Atheistic Communism" (1937), daily prayers "For Russia" at the Eucharistic liturgy throughout the Catholic world, the training and commissioning of Catholic priests for pastoral work among the Orthodox in Marxist countries, and the constant preoccupation in Catholic circles with the suffering Church in occupied lands—all contributed to a sense of kinship that prepared the way for ecumenical developments between Rome and the "Separated Churches of the East."

Outside the Iron Curtain, the main discernible factor that operated in the same direction was the years of diplomatic service by the Vatican prelate Angelo Roncalli, who later became Pope John XXIII. After four years (1921–1925) with the office of the Propagation of the Faith, Roncalli went to the largely Orthodox Bulgaria as Apostolic Visitor. He became successively Apostolic Delegate to Bulgaria, to Turkey and Greece, and Apostolic Vicar in Constantinople. In each country the majority of Christians were Orthodox, and everywhere his kindness and exquisite tact endeared him to the people and gave him an extraordinary knowledge of their faith and Christian piety. One of his first public acts as Pope was to declare how eagerly he sought the restoration of organic union between Rome and his "beloved Orthodox."

The climax was reached on January 5, 1964, when the Ecumenical Patriarch of Constantinople, Athenagoras, and Pope Paul VI, met in Jerusalem to symbolize the dawn of a new period in the Church's history. A commentary on the meeting issued by the Greek Orthodox Archbishop of North and South America made no secret of how momentous it was:

> This was no mere meeting of two ecclesiastical heads, or two personalities, but of two Churches torn asunder into East and West. It was moreover the fulfillment of David's prophecy, "Mercy and truth are met together; righteousness and peace have kissed each other."
> In reality the Jerusalem encounter was a meeting of three: of Athenagoras and Paul, and of the "Pioneer and Perfecter of our faith," Jesus Christ, who on this very mountain (of Olives) had shown the way for His disciples, but also for those who would, through them, believe in Him.
> The 1964 meeting was not just a stage of progress, but a wholly new beginning of a toilsome journey, but with the end, unity in Christ, clearly in view.[41]

Two years later, December 7, 1965, was published the mutual lifting of anathemas, which the Orthodox called "those obstacles that had barred the road toward dialogue on equal terms." The initiative for removing the excommunications was due to the personal efforts of the Ecumenical Patriarch, responding to a letter from Cardinal Augustin Bea, head of the Vatican Secretariat for Christian Unity.

The common declaration began with a brief rehearsal of the "painful incidents" which in 1054 resulted in Rome's sentence of condemnation of the Patriarch of Constantinople, and the reciprocal anathema against Rome. By comparison with the emotion of those days, the situation can be judged today "more fairly and serenely." Patriarch and Pope wished to "express the common desire for justice and the unanimous sentiment of charity which moves the faithful." Accordingly they formulated, in three statements, a solemn renunciation of the past:

> They regret the offensive words, the reproaches without foundation, and the reprehensible gestures which, on both sides, have marked or accompanied the sad events of this period.
> They likewise regret and remove, both from memory and from the midst of the Church, the sentences of excommunication which followed these events, the memory of which has influenced actions up to our day and has hindered closer relations in charity; and they commit these excommunication to oblivion.
> Finally, they deplore the preceding and later vexing events which,

under the influences of various factors—among which, lack of under-standing and mutual trust—eventually led to the effective rupture of ecclesiastical communion.[42]

As consequential as this declaration was, it should be noted that the Patriarch did not hold the same position in his Church as the Pope had with respect to Catholicism. Orthodoxy is a family of self-governing Churches. It is held together, not by a centralized organiza-tion or a single prelate, but only by the "double bond of unity in the faith and communion in the sacraments." There is not, in Orthodoxy, anyone equivalent to the Pope. Nevertheless, the Patriarch of Con-stantinople is known as the "Ecumenical" (universal) Patriarch, and since the schism between the East and West he has enjoyed a position of special honor among all the Orthodox communities; but he does not have the right to "interfere in the internal affairs" of other Churches. His place resembles that of the Archbishop of Canterbury in the world-wide Anglican Communion.

Moreover, to avoid any misunderstanding of what lifting of the anathemas really meant, the same Patriarch wrote to the heads of scattered Orthodox bodies throughout the world on how they should deal with the delicate subject of intercommunion. "The impression prevailed," noted Athenagoras, "that our Orthodox could Confess and take Communion from Roman Catholic priests." In this they were mistaken. Only "where no Greek Orthodox Church exists," may this be allowed. Indiscriminate approach of the sacraments in any non-Orthodox Church, including the Catholic, is forbidden, "since no decision of this kind was ever taken and since intercommunion between the Orthodox and other Churches does not yet exist."[43]

Similar provisions were made with regard to marriage. Barring ex-ceptional cases for which permission must be sought, a marriage which involves an Orthodox person must be performed before his own priest in order to receive the sacrament and contract a valid union.

Roman Catholicism

The Catholic side of the ecumenical movement may seem to have started almost reluctantly. From 1910, when the World Council of Churches was first conceived, to 1968, when Catholic observers at the council presented their formal statement on ecumenism, appears like a long time. And as lately as 1969, Pope Paul VI cautioned against the false irenicism which does more harm than good to the ecumenical movement. Those who think they can "re-establish unity at the expense of doctrinal truth" are following a mirage.[44]

Actually Roman Catholic interest in restoring Christian unity was never more keen, and the development of an ecumenical outlook in every phase of the Church's life and practice is one of the most prominent features of Catholicism in modern times.

When the inaugural Missionary Conference was held at Edinburgh in 1910, no Catholic representative was present. But a detailed letter was sent to the conference by the Catholic Bishop of Cremona, in Italy. Monsignor Bonomelli's message was highly encouraging:

> The elements of faith in which you all agree are numerous and are common to the various Christian denominations, and they can serve as a point of departure for your discussion. It is, therefore, legitimate to aspire to a unity of faith and of religious practice, and to work for its realization by the consecration of all energies of mind and heart. This is a work in which we in our day may well cooperate.[45]

During the pontificate of St. Pius X, a lively correspondence began between Robert Gardiner, one of the organizers of Faith and Order and the papal secretary of state, Cardinal Gasparri. Gasparri said Rome's hope was that "the one and only Church which Jesus Christ has decreed and sanctified by His divine blood be always carefully guarded and kept entire, unsullied, and ever overflowing with love." Speaking in the Pope's name, Gasparri expressed the wish that the Mystical Body of Christ "will cease to be scattered," and that finally "unity of faith will triumph" through cooperative effort among those who bear the name of Christian.[46]

Benedict XV was invited to send representatives to the preliminary meetings of the Faith and Order Conference. The Pope courteously declined. When, in 1919, a deputation called at the Vatican to repeat the invitation, the answer they received was inevitable, given the status of Protestant ecumenism at the time. They were told that "the teaching and practice of the Roman Catholic Church regarding the unity of the visible Church of Christ are well known to everybody, and therefore it would not be possible for the Catholic Church to take part in a congress such as the one proposed." Nevertheless, "His Holiness by no means wishes to disapprove of the congress in question for those who are not in union with the chair of Peter."[47]

MALINES CONVERSATIONS TO UNA SANCTA. In 1921 at Malines,

Belgium, began the first intensive involvement of the Catholic Church in the ecumenical movement. A series of meetings was held between Anglican theologians, led by Lord Halifax (1839–1934), and Roman Catholic scholars, headed by Cardinal Mercier (1851–1926). Initiative for the conversations came from Halifax, an Anglo-Catholic, who was impatient with the slow progress of the Oxford Movement to come to grips with the "Roman Question." Halifax was joined by Abbé Portal to request Mercier for the dialogue. On the Anglican side, besides Halifax, were the patristic writer J. A. Robinson (1858–1933); Walter Frere (1863–1938), Bishop of Truro; Charles Gore (1853–1932), Bishop of Oxford; and B. J. Kidd (1864–1948), warden of Keble College. Along with Mercier and Portal, the Catholic contingent had the Church historian Pierre Batiffol (1861–1929) and Abbé Hippolyte Hemmer (1864–1945), and Cardinal Joseph van Roey (1874–1961), who replaced Mercier.

Five sessions took place, under the episcopal sponsorship of Malines and supported by Rome and Canterbury. At the first meeting, December 6 to 8, 1921, the Anglicans declared that the Thirty-Nine Articles no longer had sufficient authority to stand as an obstacle to approaching the Roman Church. They showed themselves rather conciliatory on the Council of Trent, but reticent on papal infallibility and the Vatican Council. The second session occurred in March of 1923 along more practical lines, but recognizing the need for doctrinal agreement before ritual and moral issues could be resolved. In November of the same year, Gore and Kidd entered the conversations for the Anglicans, with Batiffol and Hemmer joining the Catholic ranks. At the third meeting, the principal Anglican difficulty, the authority of the Pope, was raised. Robinson analyzed the position of Peter in the primitive Church and gave the traditional Anglican explanation that the promises made by Christ to Peter were later extended to all the Apostles, and that St. Paul in particular exercised superiority over Peter in all independence. But he reached an unexpected conclusion:

> Do we insomuch affirm that in what has been said above we have exhausted the significance of the promises addressed to St. Peter by Our Lord? Personally, I cannot affirm it. In conformity with what I believe to be the principle of the *Ecclesia Anglicana*, I cannot accept as definitive an interpretation of Scripture which does not take into account that given by the first Fathers or of the providential conduct of the Church

such as it is revealed by history. The words, 'Thou art Peter and upon this rock I shall build my Church' have pervaded the spirit of Christianity, and have been, at least partially, the cause of the Church of Rome's eminent position throughout the centuries.[48]

At the fourth session, was discussed the critical question of how bishops were related to the papacy, centering on the basic issue of what kind of primacy was enjoyed by the Bishop of Rome. The Anglicans, represented by Gore, opted for a primacy short of the one defined by the Vatican Council, allowing for "Unity in Diversity," including diversity in matters of doctrine, for example, some Christians believing in a Eucharist with and others without transubstantiation. After the fifth meeting, which merely summarized the preceding, Halifax published the first report of the Malines Conversations in 1928, the same year that Pius XI issued *Mortalium Anomos*, the first papal encyclical on ecumenism.

It is possible to misread Pius XI's document, coming on the heels of Malines, as a conscious barrier to the cause of Christian unity. Certainly the Pope forbade Catholics to participate in the Faith and Order program, and he charged the men directing the movement with trying to establish a "Pan-Christianity" built on mutual love but without basic agreement in faith. Protestant historians, however, concede that the warning was timely and actually saved the cause of unity from lapsing into a vague sort of fellowship that ignored the grave issues which divide the Churches of Christendom. Authentic unity, according to the Pope, "can be born of but one single authority, one sole rule of faith, and one identical Christian belief."[49]

While the Malines program had been formalized and intended to advance the reunion of Anglicans with Rome, the *Una Sancta* movement was less ambitious. Its founder, Max Joseph Metzger (1887–1944), was a Catholic priest who saw how closely Catholics and Protestants had worked and suffered together during the war. He first organized a religious community, the League of the White Cross, later renamed the Society of Christ the King. Transferred from Austria to Germany, it became the forerunner of *Una Sancta*, whose purpose Metzger clearly identified:

The members undertake to pray, using the Lord's Prayer common to all Christians, and also the high-priestly prayer of Christ, for the coming of the kingdom of Christ on earth, and for its unity in faith and love, and to urge such prayer on their fellow Christians. They will endeavor to build bridges, intellectual and spiritual, between the separated Christian Confessions, emphasizing that which unites rather than that which divides; clearing away misunderstandings; honoring the truth in all, deepening brotherly love, and seeking to promote brotherly intercourse and common service in tasks of Christian helpfulness.[50]

Metzger wrote a letter to Pius XII in 1939, in which he asked the Pope to convoke a general council in the cause of Christian unity. His main contention was that Christians are less divided in matters of doctrine than in "the spiritual attitude on both sides." His argument was that dogmatic differences, though real, are more easily soluble than prejudice born of ignorance. Moreover, the greatest need among Christians is the spirit of prayer and fidelity to grace. Where these are present, divergences in doctrine can be resolved; but in the absence of "deep humility" and responsiveness to "the guidance of the Holy Spirit," true reunification is impossible. Metzger spoke of promoting "an inward drawing nearer of the religious Communions" as precondition for the visible reunion of Churches. After several temporary arrests by the Nazis, he was executed "for treason" in 1944.

PIUS XII AND JOHN XXIII. The former Cardinal Pacelli, who became Pius XII, followed the growth of unity with keen interest. His encyclical on the Mystical Body (1943) set the groundwork for a theology of adherence to the Church for Christians who are not professed members of the Roman Catholic Church. His public addresses to scores of groups that were not Catholic reflected a sure understanding of a kinship of spirit in spite of doctrinal differences. And the evidence he had of spiritual brotherhood among Catholics, Protestants, and Orthodox suffering persecution in Germany, Russia, and Central Europe further confirmed his conviction that the Catholic Church should be officially involved in a movement so clearly manifesting "the work of the Holy Spirit."

He cautiously refrained from authorizing Catholic observers to attend the first assembly of the World Council of Churches in 1948. But in the following year he published an instruction, *Ecclesia Catholica*, that was later used by the Second Vatican Council as the foundation for Roman Catholic ecumenism. His concern was to further the process while insuring that the principles of faith were not jeopardized:

The work of "reunion" belongs above all to the office and charge of the Church. Hence it behooves bishops, whom "the Holy Spirit has placed to rule the Church of God," to bestow on it their special attention. They should therefore not only carefully and efficaciously keep this movement under vigilant observation, but also prudently foster and guide it to the twofold end of assisting those who are in search of the truth and the true Church, and of shielding the faithful from the perils which readily follow in the tread of the movement.[51]

Pius XII encouraged the foundation in Rome of the Unitas Association to study of ways of promoting Christian unity. The quarterly review of the association, *Unitas,* did pioneer service in arousing and sustaining interest among Catholic scholars. Under the editorship of Charles Boyer, Jesuit ecclesiologist, and the direction of the Graymoor Friars of the Atonement, *Unitas* became the forerunner of dozens of similar Catholic publications that gradually came into existence in all the major languages of Euro-America. In its first number, the quarterly quoted the Pope's address to the German people assembled at Mainz, when he told them, "We know how urgent among many of your people, Catholics as well as non-Catholics, is the aspiration toward unity in the Faith. And who could feel more intensely this desire than the Vicar of Christ himself?" At the same time, he pointed out the Church must remain "inflexible before all that could have even the appearance of a compromise, or of an adjustment of the Catholic Faith with other confessions." The reason was that the Catholic Church "knows that there has always been and always will be one sole infallible and sure rock of the whole truth and of the fulness of grace come to her from Christ; and that this rock, according to the explicit will of her divine Founder, is herself and simply herself."[52]

With the accession of John XXIII to the papacy, the road was clear for a full-scale entrance of Roman Catholicism into the ecumenical movement. His familiarity with the Churches of the East prepared him for convoking the Second Vatican Council to heal the breach in ecclesiastical unity. "The Council," he wrote in 1959, "will certainly present an admirable spectacle of truth, unity, and charity. We have confidence that such a manifestation will be for Christians separated from Rome a gentle invitation to seek and find that unity for which Christ offered to His Father such an ardent prayer."[53]

There was paradox in Pope John's desire for Christian unity and his concept of this unity as the result of heeding the "gentle invitation" of Rome where, he believed, the only true source of oneness could be found. Identical statements by his predecessors were ascribed to "Roman triumphalism," as though Christianity could not be united except on Roman terms. But John XXIII was listened to and his ideas, though as intransigent as those of Pius XI and Pius XII, were received sympathetically by the Protestant and Orthodox world. One observation, out of hundreds that have since been publicized, reveals what this meant:

> At no other time, perhaps, during the past centuries, has the Church of England, as a whole, nurtured such warm regards for the Vatican, as today. There are many reasons for this, but the truly decisive one is to be found in the personality of John XXIII himself. Because it is not only by his ecumenical intentions and declarations, but by his personality, so full of charity and compassion, that he overcomes all barriers of nationality and religion and gains access even to the conscience of millions of Europeans who grew up in a post-Christian age.[54]

Pope John did not stop with convoking the Council and suggesting that one of its aims would be to foster Christian solidarity. He implemented this aim in every possible way.

In 1960 he directed that one of the preparatory commissions for the Council should deal with "Promoting Christian Unity." Under the direction of the biblical scholar, Augustin Bea (1881–1968), the commission became a full-fledged secretariat with extraordinary freedom to guide the fortunes of Catholic ecumenical efforts and promote relations with non-Catholic Christian bodies since the close of the Council.

The next year, when the World Council of Churches met at New Delhi, the Pope gave permission for five Catholic observers to attend the meeting. Having established this precedent, it was logical for non-Catholic observers to be invited to attend the deliberations of the Vatican Council. While the observers had neither voice nor vote at the meetings, the Protestant and Orthodox churchmen made their presence felt. As explained by one of them, "observers were asked to comment frankly on the documents under discussion, and—particularly when the documents dealt with ecumenical matters—the opinions of the observers were taken with real seriousness by the leaders of the Council. Frequent changes in the wording or the tone of the final documents can be traced to these briefing sessions."[55]

As the Council moved into its assemblies and published one after another of its documents, a note of interest in the whole Christian world, and not only Roman Catholicism, pervaded every major issue debated by the delegates. Part of the original agenda was to have a separate decree on ecumenism. This was issued a year after Pope John died, but its principal contents and basic approach had been outlined by the Secretariat for Christian Unity.

SECOND VATICAN COUNCIL. While other documents of the Vatican conclave also dealt with Christian unity, notably the Constitution on the Church and the statement on the Eastern Catholic Churches, the Decree on Ecumenism was intended to synthesize the Catholic position in principle and practice. And in the few years since it was published (1964), it has become the focal point of ecumenical progress also outside the ambit of Roman Catholicism. Its inherent logic has made the decree unexceptional to those who are not Catholic but who recognize Rome's historic stance of maintaining its own identity while remaining open to the presence of revealed truth in every religious tradition.

The document *De Oecumenismo* begins with the overarching premise that God became man to reveal his love to mankind by giving men a new divine life as individuals and a new supernatural life as social beings. The latter was to be achieved by incorporation into that Mystical Body of which Christ is the invisible head, and those who believe in him are its members.

To establish and insure visible unity in this Body, which is the Church, Christ entrusted to the twelve Apostles and their successors the task of teaching, ruling and sanctifying the people of God whose docility, obedience and sanctification in the Church would unite them until the end of time.

Among the Apostles, Christ chose Peter (and his successors) to be the visible head of the new society, with bishops as shepherds of the flock.

While there had been rifts in Christian unity from the beginning, they became more serious with the passage of time. As a result, many persons are now separated from visible unity with the successors of the Apostles under Peter. But these people cannot now be charged with sin which brought on the separation. Indeed, they are embraced by the Catholic Church as brothers, and are regarded by the Church with respect and affection.

Such persons are Christians, as long as they believe in Christ and have been truly baptized. They are, consequently, "in communion with the Catholic Church, even though this communion is imperfect." Moreover, "they are incorporated into Christ," and they possess "some and even very many of the significant elements and endowments which together go to build up and give life to the Church itself." Thus they have: "the written word of God, the life of grace, faith, hope and charity, with the other interior gifts of the Holy Spirit, and visible elements too."[56]

Nor is this all. They also use various liturgical actions which are channels of grace and means of salvation for themselves and those to whom they minister. In a word, their "Churches and Communities," though deficient by Catholic standards, pertain to the mystery of salvation. "For the Spirit of Christ has not refrained from using them as means of salvation which derive their efficacy from the very fulness of grace and truth entrusted to the Church."[57]

Having affirmed so much, the Vatican Council then added one inevitable limitation. These Christians are not blessed with the unity which Christ wants his followers to possess. They also lack the fullness of God's "blessings of the New Covenant" that Christ entrusted "to the apostolic college alone, of which Peter is the head."[58]

By implication, therefore, the objective plenitude of revealed truth and of the divinely instituted means of salvation and sanctification are to be found only in the Roman Catholic Church. Or, taken subjectively, as the Constitution on the Church declared, "They are fully incorporated in the society of the Church who, possessing the Spirit of Christ, accept her entire system and all the means of salvation given to her, and are united with her as part of her visible bodily structure and through her with Christ, who rules her through the Supreme Pontiff and the bishops."[59] To have said less would have been to deny the essence of Catholic Christianity.

At this point, the function of ecumenism becomes lucidly clear. It is a movement, inspired by God, which comprehends all "the initiatives and activities, planned and undertaken to promote Christian unity, according to the Church's various needs and as opportunities offer."[60]

In practice, this means that Catholics must avoid any words, judgments, or actions which do not correspond to what other Christians believe or do. Positively they should enter into dialogue with their separated brethren, in discussion, cooperative action, and corporate prayer. All of thus further demands study and the desire to learn how Protestants, Anglicans, and the Orthodox worship, what they believe and what their religion means to them.

Yet towering above all unitive efforts is the need for "spiritual ecumenism." Since the main reason historically for Christian disunity was the failure of their forebears to live up to the demands of the faith, Catholics today cannot do better to promote the ecumenical movement than to be as loyal as possible to Christ and responsive to his grace. If reunification has been so long delayed, this can be set down in large measure to the failure among Catholic Christians to become what their religious profession tells the world they should be. In plain language, "there can be no ecumenism worthy of the name without a change of heart."[61] Conversion to Christ in the practice of virtue, especially of charity, will assure divine blessings on human enterprise and inspire sacrifice, without which no progress in the moral order has ever been achieved.

Crucial to an understanding of the Catholic attitude toward unity is the distinction which the Council made among different classes of persons with whom ecumenical relations were encouraged. Many of the problems in ecumenism since the Council arose through failure to recognize these distinctions. At least five different groups of people were envisaged by the Vatican documents as worthy objects of ecumenical effort on the part of Catholics, where the term "ecumenical" is taken in its broadest possible connotation. Among Christians there are the Orthodox, Anglicans, and Protestants; and outside Christianity are believers like Moslems, Hindus, Buddhists, and the Jews; and finally others who may be called atheists, agnostics, or simply unbelievers.

The highest priority was given by the Council to prospective reunion with the Eastern Orthodox bodies which, "though separated from us, yet possess true sacraments and, above all, by apostolic succession, the priesthood and the Eucharist, whereby they are linked with us in closest intimacy (*arctissima necessitudine adhuc nobiscum coniunguntur*)."[62] Next in nearness to Roman Catholics are the Anglicans, which the Council carefully distinguished from other descendants of the Reformation. Thus, while "many Communions, national or confessional, were separated from the Holy See" as a result of the upheaval in the sixteenth century, "among those in which Catholic traditions and institutions in part continue to exist, the

Anglican Communion occupies a special place (*locum specialem tenet Communio anglicana*)."[63]

After the Orthodox and Anglicans comes the spectrum of Protestant denominations which "differ greatly from one another not only by reason of their origin, place and time, but especially in the nature and seriousness of questions bearing on faith and the structure of the Church."[64] Reunion between them and the Roman Catholic Church is correspondingly more remote and difficult, and almost postulates prior unification among the denominations themselves.

Properly speaking, ecumenism ends here, and other ventures that have since become known as ecumenical are really extensions of the term. Reunion presupposes that there had once been unity that later was shattered, which can be applied only to existing Christian Churches and ecclesiastical bodies. Two other documents than *De Oecumenismo* dealt with this "wider ecumenism," the declaration on the relation of the Church to Non-Christian Religions (*Nostra Aetate*) and the pastoral constitution on the Church in the Modern World (*Gaudium et Spes*), both issued in 1966. They pertain to interfaith relations that belong to the larger context in which the Church finds itself today, confronted with a development of non-Christian religions that challenges the zeal of Christians in every tradition; and faced with the spread of ideologies that deny, on principle, the very existence of a personal God and of man's responsibility to a higher power than the creation of his own individual or collective will.

Since the Council. Nothing more accurately describes Roman Catholicism since the Council closed in 1965 than to say it has become ecumenical. Every aspect of the Church's life and practice, and every aspect of its outreach to other religious institutions has been affected by the desire to heal the divisions of the past and, as far as possible, present to the non-Christian world the vision of a single Christ with a single, unambiguous message to the human race.

Among the developments that have taken place, the revision of theological studies for seminarians and priests-in-training will perhaps be the most influential for the Church's future. In a comprehensive directory published by the Vatican in April 1970 the whole of higher education, including studies for the priesthood, was reassessed and guidelines issued for making this education truly ecumenical.

In stating the primary purpose of ecumenizing higher studies, the focus was on inward renewal and a better grasp of the Catholic faith already professed:

> The purpose of programs of this type is to increase among students a deeper knowledge of the faith, the spirituality and the entire life and doctrine of the Catholic Church, so that they may wisely and fruitfully take part in ecumenical dialogue, each according to his capabilities.
> Its aim, moreover, is to direct their attention both to that inward renewal of the Catholic Church itself, which will help so much to promote unity among Christians, and to those things in their own lives or in the life of the Church which hinder or slow down progress towards unity.[65]

Throughout the instruction ran a bifocal theme: to further the progress of ecumenism by every means consonant with active charity, and to make certain that basic principles of Catholic belief and polity were deepened and clarified. It was assumed that knowledge can only be liberating, and that increased familiarity with one's own and other traditions would bring greater loyalty to the Catholic Church and a heightened dedication to Christian unity.

Some would say that the first decade since the Council witnessed such preoccupation with ecumenicity that the fidelity of many Catholics to their Church was gravely impaired. They pointed to such statistics as a constant decline of adult converts to Catholicism since Vatican II, a drop of ten thousand less each year in the United States, with comparable figures in other countries. They urged the notorious fall in attendance at Catholic schools as partly brought on by an amorphous religious education that was embarrassed to be "too Catholic" in an ecumenical age. They argued that Catholic church leaders have compromised by their silence on such ecumenically unpopular subjects as divorce and contraception. And they quoted some sobering data on the gradual elimination of Catholic publishing houses in strongly pluralistic societies like America, and the practical impossibility (in some places) of finding books and periodicals that still reflected the fullness of the Catholic approach to modern life without apologizing for papal infallibility or Marian piety or devotion to the reserved sacrament of the altar.

Pope Paul VI gave voice to these concerns each time, in three successive years, that he spoke on ecumenism during the Church Unity Octave. Each year he seemed to grow more anxious that a great movement might be harmed through coldness born of ignorance or through intemperate zeal.

We intend to make conciliar ecumenism a new, original and magnanimous exercise of charity. This is easy to say. But in reality this exercise demands overcoming inner attitudes which have become a habit and considered normal. It demands great humility and generosity, fighting one's selfishness and renouncing one's prestige. It demands great love.[66]

Those who see everything perfect in the camp of the separated brothers, and everything heavy and blameworthy in the Catholic camp, are no longer able to promote the cause of union effectively and usefully. As one of the best contemporary ecumenists, a Protestant, pointed out with sad irony, "the greatest danger for ecumenism is that the Catholics should become enthusiastic about everything that we have recognized as harmful, and abandon everything which we have rediscovered as important."[67]

Ecumenism seems to be wearing itself out in an illusory effort! . . . Some say, could not Peter drop his numerous demands? Could not Catholics and dissidents celebrate together the highest and most definitive act of the Christian religion, the Eucharist? Could they not then proclaim that the yearned for unity had at last been attained? Unfortunately, no. Unity cannot be achieved by a *fait accompli,* by intercommunion, as they say. How could there be unity without the same faith, without the same valid priesthood?[68]

Yet, for all his anxiety about indifference in some and intemperance in others, the Pope who approved the teachings of the Second Vatican Council never doubted that God would bless the Church's sincere quest for unity. But from the Catholic side, "there cannot be a watered down, approximate and camouflaged Catholicism," by a failure to present the faith in its historic integrity. Nor can the people expect divine grace on their unitive efforts with Orthodox and Protestants, unless they are first united among themselves. "All divisions, quarrels, separations, all egoism within our Catholic communion, harm the cause of ecumenism," since "they belie the Church whose members are marked by mutual love, as the Lord taught."[69] A divided Catholicism cannot help to unite a divided Christianity.

The supreme test of ecumenism came within five years of the close of the Council, when forty men and women were canonized as martyrs of the Reformation, for having defended the primacy of the Holy See. For months before the final consistory at which the canonization was decided, the religious and secular press of England and Wales, America and continental Europe was scrutinized to assess the possible reaction which the canonization might evoke. All the while, news agencies in these countries were supplied with up-to-date information of proceedings and invited to give their frankest appraisal. As reported by the specialists in charge, eighty-five percent of the reaction was not only well disposed but highly favorable; and the rest who seemed negative based their attitude on insufficient knowledge of the real issues at stake.

When the time for canonization approached, the Anglican hierarchy expressed their satisfaction with the event in terms that showed more than anything else the distance that separated the tragic era of division in the sixteenth century and the present age of unification. The Anglican Archbishops of Canterbury, York, and Wales wrote a joint letter of commendation to the Pope, speaking for their constituency:

> In these days of ecumenical progress, we Christians should not look back too much to the conflicts of the sixteenth century. When we do look back, we should have penitence for much that was done and should reverence all on either side who died for the sake of conscience. We can also link them in our thoughts and prayers with those who in these days and in many parts of Christendom are still resisting tyranny or oppression, or who are still being persecuted because of their Christian faith.[70]

A capstone was placed on these sentiments by the Anglican Bishop of London in whose territorial jurisdiction most of the martyrdoms took place. "To read the lives of the Forty Martyrs," he wrote, "is to be transported into a world in which people were prepared to put the claim of God first, to suffer for conscience' sake and for the glory of God. That is why I rejoice in their canonization and believe that it should bind Christians together more closely."[71]

It was to advance this togetherness, the Pope told the audience at the ceremony, that these "heralds of the faith" were raised to the honors of the altar.[72]

XI

THE NON-CHRISTIAN WORLD:
MISSION AND DIALOGUE

The history of Christianity cannot be separated from the non-Christian world into which it came in the first century. In the intervening years Christians have always been conscious of their responsibility to the Gentiles, to bring them, as they felt, the saving message of Jesus Christ and to deliver them from "the powers of darkness."

After the Edict of Constantine in A.D. 313, three periods of the Christian missions can be distinguished, up to (but excluding) the present day. There was the massive conversion of the people of Northern and Central Europe, featuring such giants of zeal as Patrick and Boniface, Cyril and Methodius, Augustine and Ansgar; then a period of relative immobility, through the Dark Ages and the Renaissance, with sporadic efforts to reach the "pagans" of the Orient. With the discovery of America and the opening of routes to the Far East, evangelization became the typical expression of Christian fervor. Thousands embraced the faith in North and South America, China and India, and the farthest reaches of Africa.

Surprisingly the new churches of the Reformation made only feeble efforts to evangelize until the end of the eighteenth century. One reason was that Protestant churches in England, Germany, and Scandinavia had domestic work to do that occupied most of their attention. Only with the rise of Anglo-Saxon colonialism, comparable to the Spanish, French, and Portuguese colonial efforts in the sixteenth and seventeenth centuries, did the churches seriously undertake to preach the Gospel outside of continental Europe.

The nineteenth century witnessed such widespread missionary enterprise among non-Christian nations that some writers seriously expected the whole world to become Christian in the foreseeable future. Tribes and villages and what seemed like whole races were attracted to the Gospel and willing to exchange their customs for a simple faith in the God of the Christians.

But many thought that all was not as well as it seemed. Converts to Catholicism were generally among the unlettered and least influential members of society. They were often ostracized from their tribe or people for having turned their backs on the religion of their ancestors. Isolation, persecution, and, in many cases, martyrdom were the only reward that fidelity to Christ brought the neophytes. Protestant missionaries found that, in spite of numerical conversions, there was lack of organization, competition, and sometimes positive hostility between representatives of different denominations or mission-sending societies.

With the rise of the present century Christian missionaries inherited a host of problems from the past. Some were soluble, others were so complex that solution was humanly impossible, and still others were only implicit in the external difficulties that a widespread evangelization created.

At this point, it is impossible to deal with the churches' outreach to the non-Christian world without distinguishing between Protestantism and Catholicism in their respective efforts to bring the message of Christ to an "unbelieving world." For one thing, the missionary posture of Catholic and Protestant evangelism was different, arising as it did from different interpretations of the faith. Moreover, before the dawn of the Modern ecumenical movement missionaries were generally unaware of how much they either shared in common as Christians, or in how much they could cooperate for the welfare of the non-Christian nations without compromise to their own creedal and theological principles.

Catholic Missionary Enterprise

It is remarkable that for all the far-flung mission work of the Roman Catholic Church, it was not until well into the twentieth century that stock was taken of two great obstacles which stood in the way of effective evangelization: the practical identification of the Church with the culture of the missionaries, and the corresponding absence of an indigenous clergy and ritual with which the people of Afro-Asia could identify themselves. Pope Benedict XV in 1919 published what is justly regarded as the magna charta of contemporary Catholic missiology. He said it was "a tragedy" that some missioners spent themselves "in attempts to increase and exalt the prestige of the native land" that had sent them to preach the Gospel. The chief aim of missionary labor, he said, was to make the missionary from foreign lands superfluous by promoting such development among the natives as would give them their own clergy, religious, and lay leaders to establish and cultivate the Church where the Gospel had been implanted. No country, he said, has ever been converted except by the leaders of its own native land.

The problem of adjusting the Church's worship to the cultural practices of the people had plagued Catholicism for centuries. Not until 1936 did Pope Pius XI publish a decree permitting ceremonial usages in Imperial Shinto along with certain marriage and funereal customs which had previously been forbidden to Christians. Then in 1939 Pope Pius XII concretized the new policy by his decree on Chinese rites. For anyone familiar with the sad experience in the eighteenth century, this decree marked the end of an era in the Catholic approach to the non-Christian cultures of the East.

The preamble made the observation that certain ceremonies, formerly linked to heathen rites, now have only a civic sense of piety toward the ancestors or of love for the fatherland or of courteous relations with the neighbor. Four statutes followed, giving pastoral direction on how Catholics should react to the centuries-old Confucian practices:

1. It is lawful for Catholics to give public honor to Confucius before his portrait or honorific scroll in Confucian edifices or schools. In order to give substance to this innovation, Rome invoked the repeated denial of the Chinese government that any religious cultus was intended by these "rites." Their only purpose is to foster and express recognition of an illustrious person, which itself was part of the universal veneration for ancestors among the Chinese.

2. Not only might Catholics venerate the image or name tablet of Confucius, but such emblems can be placed in Catholic schools, especially if the public authorities require it and salutation to the emblem

is made by a head bow. Whenever there is danger of scandal, a Catholic should indicate what his real intention is.

3. If Catholic civil officials or students are obliged to attend public functions of a religious nature, they may participate provided they maintain a passive attitude and do only such things as can be interpreted as purely civil. In case of doubt, they should make known their real sentiment in order to avoid giving the impression that they are compromising their faith.

4. The veneration of the dead, which is the nerve center of Chinese Universism, is now open to Catholics. Thus the Chinese faithful may bow their head before the deceased person or even before a tablet inscribed simply with his name. Similar gestures are designated as not only morally permissible (*licitae*), but even commendable (*honestae*).

Five years later the Vatican added three more provisions on the subject, which to this day are normative. They paved the way for the teaching of the Second Vatican Council on the need for acculturation in the Church's work of evangelism. The original directive was intended for China. It was first stressed that there are too many variations in place, time, and circumstances to assemble a catalogue of permitted and forbidden ceremonies. Rather the bishops of each province should give rules and define general standards, but not descend to details. And even priests and good Christian laymen may be left to direct themselves according to their own lights in particular cases.

Historians of the Catholic missions consider these changes a sign of how pliable Catholicism can be to the changing times, while preserving the integrity of faith.

When the Second Vatican Council came to treat of the missions it built on the past, including the recent developments typified by the Chinese rites, but it also opened the door to a vastly different and wider concept of the Church's approach to the non-Christian world than had ever been dealt with by an ecumenical Council. Each of the sixteen documents of Vatican II somehow touched upon the relationship of Christianity to those who were religious, indeed, but not Christian. Several documents explicitly analyzed this relationship, each from a different perspective, and each probing a new issue that clamored for attention in the communications age.

THE PURPOSE OF THE MISSIONS. Building on generations of scholarly reflection and research by missiologists, the Council faced the critical question of why there should be missions at all. It was obvious that the present age is not the sixteenth century when Xavier pleaded with his fellow Europeans to help him save the people of India and China from damnation. Nor, for that matter, is it the first century when St. Paul urged the necessity of preaching the Gospel so that men might hear, and hearing might believe, and believing might be saved. For one thing, Christianity had already been evangelizing for almost two millennia; for another, the natives of the Orient and of Africa today are not the Romans and Greeks of apostolic times. So much was clear. Less clear was what difference this should make, not in missionary methods but in the very concept of the missions.

It was in this context that the Council defined missionary activity in terms of the evident changes in human history and in what Catholicism believes is the unchanging truth of God's communication to man:

> Missionary activity derives its reason from the will of God, "who wishes all men to be saved and to come to the knowledge of the truth. For there is one God, and one mediator between God and men, himself a man, Jesus Christ, who gave himself as a ransom for all," "neither is there salvation in any other." Therefore, all must be converted to him, made known by the Church's preaching, and all must be incorporated into him by baptism, and into the Church which is his body. For Christ himself, by stressing in express language the necessity of faith and baptism, at the same time confirmed the necessity of the Church, into which men enter by baptism, as by a door.
>
> Therefore those men cannot be saved, who though aware that God, through Jesus Christ, founded the Church as something necessary, still do not wish to enter into it, or to persevere in it. Consequently, although God in ways known to himself can lead those inculpably ignorant of the Gospel to find that faith without which it is impossible to please him, yet a necessity lies upon the Church, and at the same time a sacred duty, to preach the Gospel. And hence missionary activity today as always retains its power and necessity.[1]

In the light of this statement, it was plain that the Church felt evangelization of the non-Christian world was no less necessary today than in the time of Xavier or Paul. In explaining this necessity two principles of historic Christianity were clarified. One has to do with the relationship of baptism to the Church, and the other with the need of the Church for salvation.

Catholic theology always taught that baptism was the door of the Church, and that actual membership in the Mystical Body was obtained only by those who were baptized in water and the Holy Spirit. More obscure, in missionary terms, was the notion that faith in the necessity of baptism prompts those who believe to baptize others or receive the sacrament themselves. Who else but a person instructed in the need of baptism would believe in its necessity?

The second clarification was connected with the first. If no one will be baptized who has not had the Gospel preached to him, it is equally true that no one will actually be incorporated in the Church unless he has been sacramentally baptized. Accordingly, Christ's condition for salvation was not only faith but also incorporation in his Church. The non-Christian world, therefore, has a right to hear the message of Christ and be offered the option of believing in him and receiving his baptism.

No doubt, Divine Providence has ways of conferring grace on people who have not been actually baptized. There is such a thing as baptism of desire and virtual membership in the Church, if a person believes in God and is faithful to the graces conferred on him. This is a simple restatement of God's universal salvific will. Saying this, however, is only to affirm that God is not limited by human means to achieve his own predetermined ends. The correlative is equally true: that God lays down certain conditions which he expects men to use in order to achieve the destiny to which he calls them. It is no comfort to take refuge in calling this a paradox. The fact is he wants those who have received the faith to share its fullness with others, including the need for baptism and through baptism, the Church, as divinely instituted means of reaching heaven. To neglect using these means on the excuse that God has other ways may be clever theological reasoning, but it puts an awful responsibility on those who evade their duty in order to lay the responsibility on God.

Less than a year after the decree on the missions was published, the head of the Vatican Secretariat for the Missions took strong issue with those who indulged in just that kind of reasoning. He excoriated the idea that God's will through Christ could be neglected because some shrewd theologian found a way out:

> To refuse to offer the Gospel message to those who do not yet know it, or who know it only imperfectly, would not only be contrary to the express and solemn command of Christ, to the economy of salvation willed by him, which obliges those who have received the faith to spread it in their turn. It would also be a deliberate abandonment of a human person to the slavery of ignorance concerning his destiny and to deny him the human freedom to make that sublime personal com-

mitment to which he has a right by reason of the universality of the Redemption. That is, in effect, to shut off from mankind access to "regeneration unto a lively hope."[2]

Part of the problem to which Cardinal Agagianian reacted was the idea that modern man (including the non-Christian) should not have his liberty imposed upon by an aggressive evangelization. Some were saying the Council's *Declaration on Religious Freedom* forbade, or at least discouraged, evangelization as an outmoded form of proselytism. Agagianian explained that there is a world of difference between respecting the liberty of others and ignoring their religious needs. Certainly indiscreet pressure should not be brought to bear on anyone, nor was this rule of prudence first discovered in our times. So far from being intolerant by preaching the Gospel to non-Christians, missionaries would fail in due respect to the true freedom of their neighbor if they did not offer him the option of accepting the message of Christ. It all depends on how we define freedom; whether we identify it with physical liberty to do anything, or whether we see it as the liberty which God has given all men to hear and freely respond to his revelation.

ACCULTURATION. Another major issue to which the Vatican conclave addressed itself was the delicate subject of adjusting the Christian religion to the culture of people who had for generations lived in a non-Christian society. This had more than one level of practical implication. It meant a predisposition on the part of the missionary to shed his own background in favor of the new ethos into which he hoped to bring the Gospel. It meant a reassessment of the modes of expression, linguistic forms, and social customs—in a word, a total re-examination of how the Christian faith and ethic could be presented to non-Christians and not repel them by its strangeness and discord with the prevailing outlook and practices of the people. It further meant such sympathy for those whom the missionary converted that they could, in many ways, remain what they were in the externals of daily life and yet become truly Christian and professed believers in Jesus Christ.

The Council realized that too little of this had been done in the past. One reason may have been that missionaries were often unfamiliar with the real meaning of the social and religious customs of those to whom they were preaching. In the laudable effort to avoid one extreme—not to compromise the true faith—they had perhaps gone to the other extreme—not retaining or incorporating cultural practices that the converts could follow as Christians.

A new generation of missionaries had to be trained to adjust to the new approach. They were now being told to "acknowledge themselves to be members of the group of men among whom they live," to "share in cultural and social life by the various exchanges and enterprises of human living," to become "familiar with their national and religious traditions, gladly and reverently laying bare the seeds of the Word which lie hidden in them."[3]

The reference to "laying bare the seeds of the Word" touched on what may prove to be a break-through in Catholic missionary thinking. It states at once that, in mysterious ways known to God alone, the Word—who is Christ—somehow has been present and active in all mankind, not excluding those who may not have explicitly heard the teachings of the Gospel.

But the problem remains, as only those who are working on the missions fully recognize. They see so much good in the culture of the people among whom they labor, even though this society is not Christian. At the same time, they know that Catholic Christianity must be uncompromising on the essentials of faith, worship, and moral conduct. How far can they go in adapting what is nominally unchristian to a religion that is faithful to the spirit of Christ?

While acculturation is a universal problem, it poses special challenges and offers unique opportunities in countries where recent events have produced a strong national consciousness. Such are some of the new nations in Africa. But the best contemporary example on a large scale is India.

A number of factors have conspired to make India the testing ground for the Church's missionary labors since the Vatican Council. India became a republic in 1950. Its Constitution is surprisingly broad in recognizing all religions as equal. The founders of the Indian Republic fully allowed for belief in God and the acceptance of the higher laws of the universe which govern the physical world of space and time. But there is no constitutional privilege in favor of Hinduism, and conversely, other religions are given parity before the law. "Subject to public order, morality, and health," the provision reads, "all persons are equally entitled to freedom of conscience and the right freely to profess, practice and propagate religion."[4]

At the same time, Hinduism is recognized as having a special status in the country. Nothing, it is said, in the Constitution should be construed as preventing the State from "providing for social welfare and reform or throwing open of Hindu religious institutions of a public character to all classes and factions of Hindus."[5]

It would seem, therefore, that, on the one hand, India opens the door wide to the Christian religion. It allows either missionaries from other lands or natives to practice and promote their faith without let or hindrance from the government. On this basis, acculturation becomes only a matter of effort on the part of Christians to adjust themselves to the ethnic and social customs of the country. On the other hand, since the Constitution recognizes Hinduism as somehow identified with the national culture, acculturation is not as simple as it may seem. It involves more than good will on the part of Christians or the willingness of missionaries to shed their European or American ways. At issue is the deeper question of what Indian culture includes and consequently what Indianization, as the term goes, really means.

It can mean the acceptance and integration into the Christian way of life of such practices as have traditionally been part of India, which covers every phase of Indian culture: social and political, religious and moral, juridical and institutional. Taken in this sense, Indianization among Christians implies a certain degree of Hinduization. Missionaries are now asking themselves how far they can go since Christianity is not Hindusim and the external profession of one religion is not the expression of the other.

Indianization can also mean that Christians are willing and eager to adopt such practices of the Indian people as are clearly not religious, nor rooted in Hinduism as a divergent religious ideology and therefore may be assimilated into Christian society at no risk to the essentials of Christian worship and conduct.

Three areas of recent development illustrate the complexity of the problems which this raises and the direction which Catholic missionaries in India are taking: in the field of education; community life among missionaries, particularly religious women; and the liturgy.

For generations the English medium schools have been operated by Catholic and Protestant missionaries in the urban areas of India. Historically they were organized to care for the children of the English colonists or the products of English colonization, the Anglo-Indians. Until recently the English language had been stressed in these schools with only small attention paid to the vernacular languages.

Since the founding of the Republic, educators in increasing numbers began to change this policy. Among other institutions, the "Cambridge Schools" were slowly Indianized. Where formerly the final examinations were issued by Cambridge University, the tests were now being set and corrected in India. The curriculum was revised to include more Indian history and literature. Where formerly, in some cases, English history was taught almost exclusively to Indian children, now their native country and its past became primary. Indian dancing, music and art came to be included in the curriculum.

A similar situation obtained in the community life of the religious women from England, Ireland, the Netherlands, France, and America, working among the natives of India. Communities were known not to accept Indian girls into their novitiates. When they entered, they were often accepted only as lay sisters, had to undergo formation in the mother country of the community, and were rarely placed in decision-making positions. Speaking for an American community which reversed this policy, a missionary (who must remain anonymous) writes that: "Our Indian candidates were immediately taken into the community—not only *physically* but *psychically* accepted. Ten years from the profession of our first novices, one of the Indian sisters was appointed Directress of Novices, and another Directress of our young professed. The administration in India has kept in the foreground of community thinking and planning the development of a strong, responsible, trained and intellectually formed native community. And at the moment, just twenty years after our first sisters went to India, many of us strongly feel that we could place all the administrative reins into the hands of our native sisters."

Others are following suit. They are gradually entrusting the government of their institutes to native members and seriously wish to make amends for the past. In more than one novitiate the program of training is, if anything, thoroughly Indian. The religious eat, study, pray, sleep on the floor. They have the choice of being vegetarians and they are regularly given lectures on the value of cultivating a religious life in keeping with the culture of the land.

The process of Indianization has deeply affected the liturgy. When the Council approved the vernacular, the response among the people received almost unanimous acceptance. That was only the beginning. Details of ritual practice that may seem trivial to Western eyes, take on momentous importance in a country where nothing is trivial in worship and where the least gesture may have centuries of symbolic meaning.

Catholics may remove their shoes and sit on the floor for liturgical functions; the priest need not kiss the altar but may touch it and his forehead, and the same for the Bible; he can be met at the door of the church or the sanctuary in the traditional Hindu manner with the *arti* for incensing; oil lamps are used instead of candles at the Offertory; the people may bow instead of genuflecting; and reverent Indian dance steps are used during the celebration of the Eucharist.

As might be expected, not everyone was pleased with the innovations, or satisfied with the kind of external changes just mentioned. Some complained that even the Hindu Scriptures were used, on occasion, in the Mass—along with the Bible. No doubt the practice (though limited) grew out of the broader permission which the bishops gave for using the *Upanishads* and *Bhagavad-Gita* in nonliturgical functions.

All of this reflects the ferment in a nation that prides itself on having a religion that reaches back to the time of Abraham. Some see in the desire to accommodate the Gospel to Indian life a belated attempt to correct the mistakes of former days. They consider even these adjustments only passing concessions that do not touch on the heart of the matter.

While India is a unique example of the needs and opportunities that lie ahead, other countries put the same questions to missionaries intent on Christianizing the non-Christian world. Most of them are not professional missiologists and only mildly interested in such theoretical issues as "the ultimate finality of the Church's apotolate" in Afro-Asia. Most of them are practical men and women interested in bringing the message of Christ to those who never knew him. They are asking themselves: What are we here for? Is it to convert these people to the Faith or to help them live more human lives whether they ever become Catholic Christians or not? They are so immediately pressed by the social problems of starvation, poverty, overpopulation, sickness, and malnutrition that some are wondering if traditional missionary activity should not at least be postponed to another day. Veterans who have spent years in the direct apostolate of preaching and catechizing are told to re-examine all that had been done. The value of their work is unquestionable and the benefits in the order of grace are certain—for those who believe that man's greatest need on earth is in the realm of the spirit. What many fear, however, is that Christianity needs a suitable climate even to survive and certainly to flourish. Should they not devote their efforts to making this environment more favorable to the Christian religion, and only then seek to make converts?

Fortunately others than active missionaries are also assessing the situation and planning the future. Social scientists who are not missionaries and, in most cases, have never lived outside Europe or America are not so sure that a real dilemma faces the foreign missions: either evangelization or social amelioration.

In 1970 Pope Paul gave aggressive support to the missionary apostolate in preference to social improvement. He recognized the conflict of interest but insisted on respect for a hierarchy of values. "There should be no dilemma," he said. "Before, during, and after evangelization (which always retains its essential priority), development, with its use of pastoral means, may be given pastoral priority." Two kinds of primacy are involved: of objective importance and of practical concern. The two are not the same.

> In the rethinking of the Church's missionary vocation, there is one question that stands out in particular, opposing two different concepts of what the general direction of missionary activity should be. These concepts may be summed up in the two words, evangelization and development.
>
> The confrontation between these two concepts is a serious one and entails two dangers: that we may consider them as mutually exclusive, and that we may fail to establish a correct relationship between them.
>
> For us believers it would be unthinkable that missionary activity should make of earthly reality its only or principal end and lose sight of its essential goal, to bring all men to the light of faith.
>
> At the same time it would be inadmissible for the Church's missionary activity to neglect the needs and aspirations of developing peoples and for its religious aims to ignore the fundamental duties of human charity.[6]

There is no easy way of resolving the conflict, which is not surprising in any human activity and certainly in the mission work of the Church. But there is a threat, which the Pope made sure no one missed, of excluding evangelization in favor of social improvement. That would be an inversion of Christ's purpose in sending the apostles (Latin= *missionarii*) to preach the Gospel (Latin=*evangelium*) to the whole world.

In one sense, countries like Pakistan and India, Kenya and the Congo are "undeveloped" by the norms of Western technology. But by the standards of intelligence and native insight and such things as family stability or respect for human life (born and unborn) it is not clear that these nations are as backward as some Western commentators suggest.

Instead of seeing a dichotomy between preaching and material improvement, those on the missions were urged to work on both fronts but to concentrate where the emphasis belongs: on the Gospel of salvation.

ANONYMOUS CHRISTIANS. Another problem, and the most serious, is the fear in some Catholic circles that the whole missionary enterprise of the Church is misplaced. The misplacement, some claimed, came from ignorance of the non-Christian world. With increased knowledge of the higher religions outside of Christianity—Hinduism, Buddhism, and Islam—the West is coming to appreciate their depth of spiritual insight and capacity for moral virtue. Would it not be more accurate, they argued, to change the focus of what used to be called evangelism?

Instead of trying to convert these people, would it not be better to help them become more loyal Hindus, Buddhists, or Moslems? All of this is premised on the assumption that the so-called non-Christian religions are really Christianity in embryonic form that needs development rather than a radical change from one faith commitment to another.

There seems to be good reason for this attitude, if men like Gandhi were to be taken at their word. The Mahatma had little patience with the efforts of Christian missionaries evangelizing the Hindus, with a view to bringing them the message of salvation. One of his statements has since become famous: "If I had power and could legislate, I should stop all proselytizing."[7]

This was consistent with his concept of Christianity as only a partial, even inferior, insight into religious truth. He was so opposed to the whole idea of conversion that he said people should not "even secretly pray that one should be converted, but our inmost prayer should be that a Hindu should be a better Hindu, a Muslim a better Muslim, and a Christian a better Christian." As far as he was concerned, "Hinduism with its message of *ahimsa* (nonviolence) is to me the most glorious religion in the world, as my wife to me is the most beautiful woman in the world." Religion was such a personal matter, he wrote, that "I believe there is no such thing as conversion from one faith to another" in the accepted Christian sense of the term.[8]

In the light of all this, it would have been surprising if some Western Christians had not become impatient with a policy which, in their eyes, failed to see that Hindus and Buddhists were actually anonymous Christians. In the future, the focus of the Church's apostolate should not be to preach the Gospel but to perform works of social charity. Instruction in Christian doctrine should be replaced by humanitarian welfare. This witness by Christians is all that "the pagans" need to actuate the grace of Christ already present in their hearts. It is immaterial if they will ever be baptized or come to profess the Christian faith.

A typical expression of this new view came from an Oriental national who was also an educational leader among the Catholics in his country. He spoke of the revolution through which Christians are going in "a newborn appreciation of the spiritual riches and treasures of non-Christian religions and cultures, chiefly the great ones like Hinduism, Islam, Buddhism, which have sustained the life and spirit of millions of people for thousands of years." Inasmuch as "the 'Christian' West itself seems to have abandoned its faith in its own religion [and] to have lost its inner moorings and to be suffering from spiritual starvation," the last thing that Western missionaries should do is try to evangelize the Orientals.[9]

In that case, why the missions at all? What possible good can they serve to those who already have a deeper faith if not a superior culture? The answer erases one millennium of the Church's apostolic zeal to the nations:

> What is the purpose of the missions if people can be, nay are being saved through their own religions, and if the living God and the living Christ act on them through the channel of their own religious traditions? The Church's mission is not primarily to bring salvation to individual souls but to be the sacrament and sign of the living God, of Christ and his saving action on behalf of the whole world. It is, therefore, the task of the Church to make Christ present in every age and culture and race.[10]

Reactions among missionaries and missiologists were immediate. If ever this attitude prevailed, they urged, the propagation of the faith as the Catholic Church understands it, would come to an end. Unquestionably, it has always been important to have the Church make

Christ present in every age and culture and race. But how is this to be done? To substitute the end for the means and, in fact, discard the means in favor of the end is either to indulge in vain rhetoric or to have lost the vision of St. Paul.

Christian syncretism is a new term to describe what actually has a long history. It was raised more than once over the centuries and found its classic expression back in the days of Ambrose of Milan. His dialogue with the pagan senator Symmachus stands for all time as a confrontation between two opposing views of man's relationship to God. Symmachus opposed the removal from the Senate house of an image of the Roman goddess Victoria. Ambrose insisted that the image should be removed as a sign of the triumph of Christianity in the Roman Empire. The senator argued that "It is impossible for a mystery so great [as religion] to be accessible by one road alone." Christian syncretists in the fourth century and the twentieth reprove Christianity for never answering Symmachus. They side with the senator against Ambrose and state their position in unambiguous terms. "We cannot harden our hearts against Symmachus," they say, "without hardening them against Christ."[11]

It all depends on how Christ is understood and what his religion is believed to be. If he is a historic Person whose life, death, and resurrection are God's revelation to the world, and if his teaching is God's wisdom in history on which the salvation of the world depends, it becomes less than plausible to speak of Christianity hidden under a layer of Hindu ritual or of Christ's truth in the pages of the *Upanishads.*

Somewhat parallel was the notion that instead of a mission apostolate there should be only witness, that evangelization be replaced by dialogue, and kerygma by pre-catechesis. Christians should testify only by the simple radiation in their milieu of good example.

Those who saw a danger in such theologizing said it would be a tragedy if, under the pretext of bearing witness, Christians remained on the threshold of encounter and if, under the pretext of dialogue, they were satisfied to talk with others without transmitting to them the Christian message. Such attitudes would result in a crisis of the direct apostolate, of vigorous evangelization as understood by all the great apostles of Christ. Cardinal Suenens, who has more than once appeared in these pages, saw here nothing less than the demon of silence trying to paralyze the missionary endeavors of the Church:

There is a certain uneasiness in the air. Has the time come to put the very witness of the mission itself in the background? Is this the hour of silent witnesses? Or, is there still a place for witnesses who speak out, who are channels of the witness of God's living word to the modern world? We must throw off this cloak of silence . . . exorcise this dumb diabolic spirit.[12]

Observers of what is going on in Catholic missiology suggest that this is more than method or a new way of reaching the 2000 millions who never heard of Christ. They believe the basic question centers on what kind of Christianity should be communicated to a world which is nominally not Christian. Should it be a religion of the spirit, built on the Gospels and living in the sphere of the divine; or a secular philosophy clothed in the language and externals of faith? Jean Daniélou, a ranking scholar in modern Catholicism on the religious cultures of the East, posed the choice that lies ahead:

The danger for Christianity at present is that it should become secularized, worldly, reduced to a kind of socialist humanism. This is not what the world needs; and, if Christians were reduced to offering the world only this humanism, they would soon be set aside and rightly so, since there have always been socialists, teachers of morality and organizers of society: they have rendered service, but they have never saved anyone.
The world today does not need greater social organization but a Savior: man today needs someone who will answer the fundamental problems of his existence, which no social structure has ever been able to answer. And it would be sheer madness if once again, fifty years behind their times, Christians were to teach a Christianity that was nothing but social humanism, just when the men of today are beginning to discover its deficiencies and once more feel the need of God. It would be a distressing sight to see men ask for God from a Church no longer able to offer Him.[13]

The issue at stake, as Daniélou saw it, is neither semantic nor pragmatic. It rests on one's understanding of who is Christ and why he came into the world: whether to improve man's social existence on earth or prepare him for a divine participation in heaven. If the two purposes are related, they are also distinct.

Protestant Evangelization

The modern phase of the Protestant "evangelism to the Gentiles" began in 1910 when missionaries from all the major countries met at

Edinburgh in Scotland and agreed to form what later became the International Missionary Council. Organized at London in 1921, it divided its work with a coordinate office in New York from 1924 and has since provided for an agency in the Far East. It soon became the chief organ of liaison for the Protestant missions and a major factor in the whole ecumenical movement.

The Council derived from its constitutive bodies the mandate to promote consultation, investigation, publication, and cooperation in "the work of presenting the Gospel to non-Christian peoples." Variety of belief was recognized as a fact, but subordinated in practice to "fellowship in the total task of the missions."[14]

At the time of its proposed merger with the World Council of Churches (1958) it accounted for sixty per cent of Protestant missionary activity throughout the world. It was more than a financial detail that the Ghana assembly, which voted the merger, also reported that a four million dollar theological education fund was made available to members of the I.M.C. "to render a new and more far-reaching service to the training of the ministry and the Christian world mission." Typical of the American support of the Council, half of this sum was the gift of John D. Rockefeller, Jr. The other half came from nine major United States boards of missions. As a result of this heavy financial backing from the United States, delegates to the Ghana conference publicly stated that "Americans are resented because they provide the dollars" which practically keep the International Missionary Council in existence. There is no doubt that Americans in the I.M.C. fairly controlled its policy as illustrated in the move to unite with the World Council of Churches. All the proponents of the merger were Americans, including such eminent liberals as Drs. MacKay and Van Dusen, while a substantial block in the I.M.C. was conservative and suspicious of the ecumenical theology in the Council of Churches.

Although in literature on the subject the International Missionary Council may have appeared to hold a monopoly on Protestant evangelism, it was actually in competition, by a ratio of three to two, with other societies who preferred to sacrifice material advantage in favor of a more evangelical and frankly biblical form of apostolate. "Faith Missions" they are still called by others than themselves, because of their continued insistence on faith to provide the necessary means. More accurately their express function is to preach the word of God and not primarily, as with less dogmatic groups, to promote the temporal welfare of their clients. The best known of these groups, the International Foreign Mission Association, affiliates more than thirty lesser bodies. It strongly expresses a biblical perspective:

> In the face of the disposition today in some missionary circles to disparage and discard evangelism in favor of a more popular program of social studies, higher education, and other things, we boldly assert that the substitution of any other policy or program of work has signally failed in achieving anything like equal returns for the energy and money expended.
>
> We are strongly convinced that the truest criterion of a missionary's success, judged by the test of time, is the degree in which his efforts are the means of producing truly regenerated men and women who, united together in indigenous churches, will propagate their faith, win others to Christ, and exert a vital and ever-increasing spiritual and moral influence in the community and the nation.[15]

A balanced estimate of the Protestant missions since 1961, when the I.M.C. merged at New Delhi with the World Council, must look at both forms of the Churches' outreach: the social and the evangelistic. By 1970, however, the differences had polarized not only between the World Council and the Faith Missions but within the Council of Churches itself.

GROWTH AND VARIETY. Due in large measure to the generous support from America, Protestant missions grew in number and influence to a degree unparalleled since the Reformation. In estimating the size of these missions, a number of distinctions should be made.

First we note the difference between indigenous Protestant population in a given territory and what are reported as recent converts. The former may go back several generations, the latter are often too recent and fluctuating to give anything but a vague approximation. Thus in 1930, before the recent Protestant influx into Latin America got under way, the Protestant figure for Brazil was reportedly 1.3 per cent of the total population. In 1950 it rose to 3.3—which does not distinguish beween old-time conservative bodies like the Igreja Evangelica Lutherana and evanescent American imports like the Assemblies of God.

Still, no matter how severely qualified, Protestant missionary zeal has been successful, to the point where it poses a serious challenge to the Catholic Church.

For sheer numerical increase, Latin America offers the most sobering example. On the eve of World War II there were half a million Protestants in Hispanic America, or less than one-sixth the present calculation. Figures now range as high as ten million Protestant adherents below the Rio Grande. This represents a growth of more than one hundred per cent in less than ten years. Heaviest concentration was in Brazil, with two million, and Mexico with a million. In 1970 Asia reported fifteen, Africa thirteen, and Australia eleven million adherents respectively. Preferred Churches in Latin America are fundamentalist bodies like the Baptists, and post-Reformation groups from the United States, especially the Spiritualists, Pentecostals, and Seventh-Day Adventists.

Some idea of the variety of Churches on the missions may be gained from the situation in India. About two hundred juridically distinct and autonomous Protestant bodies were active in the country at the beginning of 1971. They fall into six classes or types: national organizations like the Church of South India; national societies with no denominational affiliation and small membership; Australian and British groups, of which the largest is the Church Missionary Society of England; a handful of Church affiliates from the continent; and about forty denominations from the United States and Canada, among which the American Baptists have the largest membership. Many Protestant converts on the missions do not belong to any denomination, like the Methodist or Lutheran. They are simply joined to whatever society gave them baptism and instruction in the Bible. This shows the flexible character of Protestant faith and worship; people become Christians without belonging to any Church, except the society of those who accept Jesus Christ as their Lord and Savior.

METHODS AND TECHNIQUES. The method of evangelism is determined by two factors in particular: whether the mission agency stresses the social aspect of Christianity or direct and personal indoctrination. In practice the two functions are closely related; but as one or the other predominates it affects the orientation of missionary effort down to the smallest details.

Easily the best example of an organization mainly concerned with the social Gospel is the Young Men's Christian Association. The Y.M.C.A. has fully established national alliances in forty-five countries, including India and Japan, besides local foundations in twenty-seven other territories like Madagascar and Thailand. Its program is to advance the kingdom of Christ under Protestant auspices, as appears from the whole structure and history of the Association. For twenty years (1926–1947) the international president of the Y.M.C.A. was

John R. Mott, one of the pioneers in the Protestant ecumenical movement and vice-president of the World Council of Churches until his death in 1955. His administrative genius and dozen volumes on the Christian apostolate under such titles as *Cooperation and the World Mission* and *The Larger Evangelism* played a major role in setting the tone of Protestant missionary work among the member churches of the World Council.

As far back as the last century, delegates to successive world conferences have been told to "look on the Young Men's Christian Association as an important and practical auxiliary to the Foreign Missions' effort." Over the years, this policy has not changed except to be intensified. Leaders in the Protestant mission field had long sensed the injury done to their cause by sectarian divisions in their ranks. Something had to be done to neutralize the bad effect and the Y.M.C.A. furnished the answer.

At the turn of the century, when the offer was first made to Association representatives at Stockholm, they were told that, "when the devotees of other religions are asked to embrace the religion of Jesus, it does appear to them a stumbling block of no small moment to find that the followers of Jesus, instead of presenting a united front and walking side by side with each other in loving harmony, are often so rent asunder by ecclesiastical strife that all traces of Christian unity disappear." No section of Asia or Africa is more aware of this sectarianism and therefore prejudiced against missionaries than intelligent young men, the future leaders of their people. The moral was clear.

> If, side by side with the missionary efforts of the Churches on the foreign field, there were placed an effective Young Men's Christian Association holding forth its all-embracing arms to everyone who loves the name of Jesus and cooperating in loving harmony with every earnest effort of every faithful section of the Christian Church, much of the evil resulting from sectarian division would be dissipated, and the essential unity of the followers of Jesus placed upon a platform that all might see. This is a kind of testimony no argument can refute, and the relation of the Young Men's Christian Association to Foreign Missions would be felt to be no uninfluential one, if in all our Foreign Missions' centres it thus let its light shine.[16]

In the years since this proposal was made and adopted, the Y.M.C.A. has done yeoman service in every major country of the world, to a degree that some rank the Association among the leading instruments of Protestant evangelism; others would say it is the most influential. Its concentration in urban areas and access to American revenue, both secular and ecclesiastical, make it a potent arm of the Christian apostolate in the Afro-Asian (and Latin American) world.

On a broader scale the building and maintenance of welfare institutions are the main vehicle for the Protestant message in the Foreign Missions. When the question arose whether they are merely instrumental or positively integral to the Christian Gospel, the answer was unequivocal. "Christian institutions," the World Council of Churches was told, "are the exhibitions in collective and social life of the new power in Jesus Christ and therefore part and parcel of the declaration of the Gospel." The impressive network of Christian hospitals, dispensaries, and other organizations of service, which stretches from one end of a mission country to the other, has grown out of the impulse to express the power of the Gospel, however dimly conceived, in the presence of immediate need.

Hence the problem is only one of balance and proportion, and perhaps of deciding how far a hospital, for instance, should go in proselytizing among its patients. Some institutions, notably those connected with the ecumenical movement, consider the proclamation of the Gospel beyond the scope of their immediate purpose. But this is rare and frequently criticized, within and outside the Council of Churches, as a "half-hearted" attempt to prepare for Christ without openly declaring his message.

An Asiatic conference on *Hospital Evangelism* showed that a great deal of proclamation of the Gospel takes place in medical institutions. When hospitals in the Far East were criticized for being used to evangelize, the spokesman for a medical college replied that "We rarely find a non-Christian patient who does not ask for Christian services." And again, "We decided it was not right to have prayers in the wards with non-Christian patients. So we stopped. After twenty-four hours we had to resume as the protest from the patients was so strong."[17] A recent model for combining Protestant evangelism with high-minded social welfare was the late Albert Schweitzer, whose volumes in liberal theology pale in comparison with his care of the sick in French Equatorial Africa.

As a promotional medium, educational institutions are the most permanently effective. They differ according to the needs and, incidentally, according to the weight of evangelism that a local situation will bear. In Latin America schools enjoy the highest priority for long-range Protestant mission enterprise. There are more than a thousand such institutions, from elementary grade to university.

Early in 1957 the American ambassador from Bolivia was invited to speak on cooperation with Latin America. Victor Andrade used the occasion for a personal testimony to the influence that a Protestant high school—Instituto Americana, of La Paz—had exerted on his life. During the plastic years of his adolescence, he said, "we learned there the great teachings which are not written in books. We learned there the spiritual values of evangelical love which translated itself into the good life as to morals and into the democratic style of government as to politics. And now in retrospect I realize that these values are nothing but the Protestant style of life."[18]

Not only the ambassador, but most of the government officials at the time, including the Bolivian President, were reportedly graduates of that Methodist institution.

Given the broad spectrum of doctrinal positions in Protestantism, there is no easy way of telling what creedal message is communicated in any one sector of the Protestant missionary world.

At one extreme are religious bodies commonly associated with less privileged churches of Protestantism. The Gospel Mission of South America, active in Chile and Ecuador, requires of all its members (including office workers and staff) unquestioned faith in the divine inspiration of the Bible, the Trinity, the fall of man, his need of regeneration, salvation through Christ, heaven for the saved and eternal punishment for the lost, and, typically, Christ's premillennial return before the last day.

More common are the numerous sending societies sponsored by the World Council of Churches. Their members or constituent Churches may be quite conservative, but they generally permit a wide latitude in Christian belief, ritual, and practice.

Part of the history of contemporary Christianity is the dialectic that has emerged in Hispanic America. Centuries of State domination of the Church, social inequity between the very wealthy and the very poor, and a strong nationalism that resented native Spanish and Portuguese clergy had reduced Catholicism to a shadow of its former self. Within weeks of his accession to the papacy, John XXIII assembled the Latin American hierarchy to take immediate emergency action to meet what he considered a crisis.

Protestant Christians saw in these countries an opportunity (and duty) to bring Christian ideas and institutions to the people. The result was inevitable. Roman Catholics began to see themselves "face to face with Anglo-American Protestantism, which means to repeat with its neighbors to the south what its ancestors did in Europe in the sixteenth century. We face a true invasion, systematic and perfectly synchronized and perfectly planned."[19]

In 1936 one out of fourteen Protestant missionaries in the world came to Latin America; by 1970 the ratio was one out of three. In Argentina the number of denominations had increased from 20 to 150 in twenty years. By mid-century about five thousand Protestant missionaries, mostly from the United States, were entering South America every year. The uniform impression on Protestants was highly favorable. "In few parts of the world," according to an official observer, "is there more continuous and more fruitful day-to-day evangelism than in Latin America. Visitors are impressed by the immense vigor of the work and the determination to grasp to the full the almost fantastic opportunity which confronts the Church."[20] This in turn stimulated a missionary zeal in North American Protestantism that has no parallel in modern history. It is the Reformation come to life again.

A number of factors explain the shift in emphasis. They were thoroughly discussed at the Madras missionary convention in 1938, where the basic strategy of the new approach was formulated. Delegates at Madras sensed the rise of a spirit of nationalism in Asia and Africa that would inhibit the preaching of Christianity as a foreign commodity. Since then China fell into the hands of the Communists, and India placed restrictions on visas to prospective missionaries. Spanish America offered a likely substitute for the Oriental apostolate. Actually, Latin America, was more than a substitute; it was a deliberate choice. A singular unity of language and culture, material conveniences and protection from the politically interested States made the diversion from the Orient highly prudential. Only one difficulty arose, which for years had checked the Protestant advance—Latin America is nominally Catholic and possesses what the Protestants offer except for allegiance to Rome.

Great poverty, undeveloped natural resources, sickness and a scaling death rate, widespread illiteracy and the need for social reform are sample motivations to inspire many Protestants, often at great sacrifice, to enter South America. When doctrinal differences are considered unimportant, this attitude has more than a degree of logic on its side.

Protestant commentators object when this is called a foreign invasion. They explain that the spirit of the movement is actually native. At least in Brazil, Chile, Cuba, Argentina, Mexico, and Guatemala the growth should be called indigenous and a product of the soil. The "invasion" occurred generations ago; it was the sowing of the seed. It was Paul crossing the Hellespont into Macedonia and the West. "At present the problem for our Roman Catholic brethren would be rather to spot the tropical growth of the Evangelical forest." Millions of Protestants in Hispanic America now speak of their faith as "the religion of our fathers and of our grandfathers." As these sentiments become more frequent, they raise some grave questions for a dominant but complacent Catholicism.

WELFARE OR CONVERSION. Not unlike the dilemma facing the Roman Catholic Church, world Protestantism has reached a critical point of decision on its missionary purpose. After the International Missionary Council fused with the World Council of Churches, the latter took a missionary turn which had not been characteristic before. In ten years after the merger at New Delhi, this had become more social than evangelistic, with consequent polarization in its own ranks. By 1968 it became clear where the World Council stood on the purpose of the missions. Its officially approved report at Uppsala spelled out this purpose in seven premises, of which the last three are radically new:

> The growth of the church . . . both inward and outward, is of urgent importance. Yet our ultimate hope is not set upon this progress, but on the mystery of the final event which remains in the hand of God.
>
> The meeting with men of other faiths or of no faith must lead to dialogue . . . Dialogue and proclamation are not the same. The one complements the other in a total witness. But sometimes Christians are not able to engage either in open dialogue or proclamation. Witness is then a silent one of living the Christian life and suffering for Christ.
>
> We must see achievements of greater justice, freedom, and dignity as a part of the restoration of true manhood in Christ. This calls for a more open and humble partnership with all who work for these goals even when they do not share the same assumptions as ourselves.[21]

Although Christian in spirit and responsive to the Christian principles of charity, the foregoing statement of policy was not acceptable to those churches which saw here "the humanistic turn that Protestant missions have taken." By 1970 they had drafted a counter statement, which came to be known as The Frankfurt Declaration. Missiologists in Germany took the lead in raising the question: *"Humanization—the Only Hope of the World?"* What added gravity to the question was that most missionary societies in Germany belong to the World Council. Those who honestly felt that the Council was abandoning the true goals of evangelization asked the Council to reverse its stand. They took each of the elements of the Uppsala manifesto and rewrote it in dialectic form: one part expressing the role of the missions in positive terms and the second taking issue with the world assembly of Protestants and Orthodox. Again one passage from the last three of these "Indispensable Basic Elements of Mission" identifies their point of contrast:

> The primary visible task of mission is to call out the messianic, saved community from among all people. *We therefore oppose* the view that the Church, as the fellowship of Jesus, is simply a part of the world.
>
> The offer of salvation in Christ is directed without exception to all men who are not yet bound to him in conscious faith. *We therefore reject* the false teaching that the non-Christian religions and world views are also ways of salvation similar to belief in Christ.
>
> The Christian world mission is the decisive, continuous saving activity of God among men between the time of the resurrection and second coming of Jesus Christ. We refute the identification of messianic salvation with progress, development, and social change. *We do, however, affirm* the determined advocacy of justice and peace by all churches, and we affirm that "assistance in development" is a timely realization of the divine demand for mercy and justice as well as of the command of Jesus: "Love thy neighbor."[22]

Only the future can tell what direction Protestant missions will take. Some feel that things have moved too far to coordinate these opposites. They admit that a practical solution is to tell each side to sit down and quietly listen to its counterpart. Social-minded humanitarians would profit from the apostolic zeal of the evangelicals who, in turn, could integrate the social awareness of humanitarians with their own proclamation of the Gospel. This will be done in many countries with benefit to both sides.

But there seems to be no resolution of the deeper fact of history which this confrontation reveals. It is the gradual manifestation of two different, even divergent, positions which call themselves Christian. One represents involvement in the world of human affairs and sees in this involvement the unique fulfillment of Christ's message to love others as he had loved men. Doctrine and ritual, creed and moral precepts are secondary and frankly unnecessary in the pursuit of the real goal.

The other approach is really another missiology. Men as individuals and mankind as society are sinful. They need a Savior, who is Christ the Lord, without whom no one can have lasting peace on earth or the prospect of joy in eternity. Earthly issues are unimportant and social concerns are not ignored but minimized. All the effort is placed on restoring friendship with God and such things as preaching and prayer, the Bible and the Lord's Supper are dominant—with stress on the life of God which is not the same as preoccupation with the affairs of man.

Needless to say, the same dichotomy appears in the missionary development of the Roman Catholic Church and, to a limited extent, in Eastern Orthodoxy. All of Christendom is being challenged with the growth of modern science and the expansion of human knowledge, with its prospects of political freedom, social improvement, and cultural acquisition that were scarcely conceivable in the past. The question is partly one of balance between fidelity to the difficult ethic of Christianity and acceptance of this-worldly gains. More deeply it touches on a choice which Christ had said allows of no compromise.

The Coming Dialogue

Less than a century ago it would have been strange to talk about a dialogue between Christianity and the non-Christian religions of the world. A dialogue presumes a conversation, where two people or two cultures meet and discuss in a common effort to understand the other's viewpoint and profit from their exchange of ideas. But until the present century, about the only contact between Christians and others was on the missionary level in Africa and the Orient, and in the secular fields of commerce and politics, where religion (to say the least) is not the real concern.

A new situation has arisen that knowledgeable Christians in every tradition recognize needs attention. Both sides of the prospective encounter sense the need. The people of the East admire the West for its achievements in science, education, and social welfare. They sense that somehow the Christian value system of Western nations has contributed to these achievements. Even the most caustic critics of Euro-America concede that Western peoples have more than business and industry to export, and that the East could profit from the inner spirit of Western society. Shortly before his death, Jawaharlal Nehru paid an unexpected tribute to this hope:

It is a commonplace that in the modern industrial West outward development has far outstripped the inner, but it does not follow, as many people in the East appear to imagine, that because we are industrially backward and our external development has been slow, therefore our inner evolution has been greater. That is one of the delusions with which we try to comfort ourselves and try to overcome our feeling of inferiority.[23]

If the Christians of the West seldom saw their external achievements related to the inner spirit, they are learning that others, who are not Christian, see the relationship and feel they could profit from contact with both demands.

From the side of Christianity, this tribute has been more than reciprocated in a discovery of the religious wisdom of the East. A stream of books and monographs, journals and popular writings is being published in Europe and America on every aspect of Hinduism and Buddhism, Chinese Universism and Islam. Programs in Eastern studies at institutions of higher learning and whole departments concerned with the culture of the non-Christian world have no parallel in educational history. Protestant scholars like Kraemer and von der Leeuw, the Orthodox Eliade and the Roman Catholics de Lubac and Daniélou illustrate the quality of research that Christians have been doing in the living religions of the Orient.

One reason for this resurgence is that the sacred writings and religious commentaries of the Eastern religions have only recently become available on a large scale in accurate translations and critical editions for people in the West. It was in 1953 that the first English translation of the Koran was published by a Moslem Englishman.

These developments have not remained religiously sterile. Christians see them as signs of a special providence for the future of the human family. The experience in Roman Catholicism typifies what is happening in the rest of Christendom. Its Vatican Council had originally planned only a short statement on the relations of the Church with the Jewish people. Yet in three years, 1962 to 1965, the momentum at the Council had built up to such proportions that a separate and elaborate declaration on the non-Christian religions of mankind was finally produced. The present age called for nothing less:

> In our times in which the human race benefits by being drawn more closely together day by day and interdependence grows between peoples, the Church considers with closer attention the nature of her relations with non-Christian religions. In her task of promoting unity and charity between men and also among peoples, she examines here first of all what men have in common and which leads them then to live out their common destiny together.[24]

Some would interpret this as only the nostalgia for unity which torments today's world. But the roots in Christianity lay deeper. As physical distance between nations was diminishing so, too, believing Christians thought, should the distance in spirit be diminished between members of the human family. They have a single origin, for God is the Father of all. They have the same end, God, whose providence, goodness, and design "extend to all men until the day when the elect will be united in the Holy City, ablaze with the glory of God, where the nations will walk in his light."[25]

These words expressed a new mandate to Christians to exercise the charity of Christ toward all men. Evangelization was presumed and the Church's apostolate was not being impugned. But this was different. It meant the recognition that God's grace is active in all souls of every religious persuasion. It also meant that this grace should be encouraged by all the means at a Christian's disposal. It finally meant that, in God's own way, humanity would be enriched by untold numbers in every country, who would show good will toward the millions professing other faiths than their own. Their corporate effort would produce a new world, bound together by ties of love, even as the genius of science was uniting them across the reaches of what used to be the obstacles of space and time.

REFERENCES AND ACKNOWLEDGMENTS

QUOTED REFERENCES

References follow the numerical sequence in the book, with complete bibliographical information on published writings. The author is deeply grateful for the use of hitherto unpublished documentary material. In each case, the writer is identified.

The author is personally responsible for translations from other languages, although he generally relied on existing versions as the basis for quotations given in this volume.

Special thanks are due to Mrs. Warren Joyce, whose secretarial assistance through more than two years of research was indispensable in finally bringing the manuscript to completion.

THE TWENTIETH CENTURY: DAWN OF A NEW ERA

1. C. De Vaucouleurs, *Discovery of the Universe* (London, 1956).
2. L. S. Silk, *The Research Revolution* (New York, 1960).
3. V. Bush, *Science, the Endless Frontier* (Washington, 1945).
4. The two world wars (1914–1918 and 1939–1945) were the main immediate occasion for the development in medical science affecting the treatment of injuries and numerous diseases.
5. Carl Jung, *Modern Man in Search of a Soul* (New York: Harcourt, Brace and World, 1933), p. 174
6. Sigmund Freud, *The Future of an Illusion* (Garden City, N.Y.: Doubleday, 1953), p. 54.
7. Paul Tillich, *Systematic Theology* (Chicago: University of Chicago Press, 1957), vol. II, p. 7.
8. Socrates, quoted by Plato, *Phaedrus*, 275, A-B.
9. William Shakespeare, *King John*, II, i.

10. Thomas Carlyle, "Heroes and Hero-Worship," *Thomas Carlyle's Works* (New York: Publishers Plate Renting), p. 383.

11. Charles R. Wright, *Mass Communication* (New York: Random House, 1965), p. 91.

I. FAITH AND UNBELIEF

1. St. Augustine, "Enarrationes in Psalmos," 54:22, *Corpus Christianorum*, Turnholdt, 1953, vol. 39, pp. 672–73.

2. Immanuel Kant, *Groundwork of the Metaphysic of Morals* (London: Hutchinson's University Library, 1947), pp. 99–100.

3. Romans 8:28.

4. Friedrich W. Nietzsche, *The Antichrist*, I, 15 (Walter Kaufmann, *The Portable Nietzsche*, New York: Viking, 1954, pp. 581–82).

5. St. Pius X, "Pascendi," *Enchiridion Symbolorum*, 3475.

6. Rudolf Otto, *The Idea of the Holy* (London: Oxford University Press, 1931), p. 108.

7. George Tyrrell, *Autobiography* (London, 1912), vol. II, pp. 26–27.

8. S. Paul Schilling, *God in an Age of Atheism* (New York: Abingdon, 1969), lists over three hundred titles of books and monographs on atheism published in English between 1960 and 1969.

9. *The Observer*, London, March 24, 1963.

10. John A. T. Robinson, *Honest to God* (London: S.C.M. Press, 1963), p. 14.

11. *Ibid.*, p. 47.

12. Rudolf Bultmann, *Kerygma and Mythos* (Tübingen: Mohr, 1948), vol. V, p. 18.

13. Dietrich Bonhoeffer, *Sanctorum Communio: Eine Dogmatische Untesuchung zur Soziologie der Kirche* (*Theologische Bucherai*), (Munich: Kaiser, 1954), pp. 88, 166, 177–78.

14. Paul Tillich, *Systematic Theology* (Chicago: University of Chicago Press, 1963), vol. I., p. 15; idem, in *Ultimate Concern: Tillich in Dialogue*, ed. by D. MacKenzie Brown (New York: Harper and Row, 1965), p. 12; idem, *The Protestant Era* (Chicago: University of Chicago Press, 1962), p. 82.

15. Robinson, *op. cit.*, p. 78.

16. *Ibid.*, p. 8.

17. *Der Christliche Sonntag: Katholisches Wochenblatt* (New York: Herder, April 12, 1964).

18. Basilea Schlink, *Und Keiner Wollte Es Glauben* (Darmstadt: Verlag Evangelische Marienschwesterschaft, 1965), pp. 50–52.

19. II Vatican Council, *Gaudium et Spes*, I, 19.

20. II Vatican Council, *Dei Verbum*, I, 5.

21. Pedro Arrupe, *Council Daybook*, Session IV (Washington: National Catholic Welfare Conference, 1966), p. 61.

22. Julian Huxley, *Religion Without Revelation* (New York: New American Library, 1957), p. 13.

23. Yu. A. Levada, "Church and State in Soviet Society," *Religions and the*

Promise of the Twentieth Century, UNESCO (New York: New American Library, 1965), p. 103.

24. Robert S. McNamara, *Population Bulletin* (Washington: Population Reference Bureau, November 1968), p. 75.

25. Juan Jose Espinosa, *ibid.,* p. 59.

26. Lenin, *Selected Works* (New York: International, 1943), vol. X, p. 94; idem, *op. cit.,* vol. XI, p. 661.

27. Paul Tillich, *The Protestant Era* (Chicago: University of Chicago Press, 1951), pp. 166, 259–60.

28. United Nations, "Universal Declaration of Human Rights," *Human Rights* (London: Allan Wingate, 1949), p. 277.

29. *U.S. News & World Report,* November 1969, p. 10.

30. H. J. Skornia, *Television and Society* (New York: McGraw-Hill, 1965), p. 197.

31. *Ibid.*

32. *Holy Trinity Church v. United States,* 143 U.S. 457, 470–71.

33. Bertrand Russell, *Marriage and Morals* (New York: Bantam, 1959), p. 38.

34. Lepp, *The Christian Failure* (Westminster, Md.: The Newman Press, 1962); Alasdair C. MacIntyre, *Difficulties in Christian Belief* (London: S.C.M. Press, 1961); Michael de la Bedoyère, *Objections to Roman Catholicism* (New York: Lippincott, 1965); H. C. Rümke, *The Psychology of Unbelief* (New York: Sheed and Ward, 1962).

35. Rudolf Heiler, *Prayer: A Study in the History and Psychology of Religion* (New York: Oxford University Press, 1958), p. iv.

36. II Vatican Council, *Sacrosanctum Concilium,* IV, 86.

37. *The Uppsala 68 Report,* Norman Goodall, ed. (Geneva: World Council of Churches, 1968), pp. 79–81.

38. Albert Camus, *The Rebel* (New York: Vintage, 1965), pp. 303–4.

39. Pope Paul VI, "Present Sufferings of the Church," *L'Osservatore Romano,* March 4, 1968.

40. John Dewey, *A Common Faith* (New Haven, Conn.: Yale University Press, 1934), p. 46.

41. II Vatican Council, *Gaudium et Spes,* II, 25.

42. Pope Paul VI, "The Credo of the People of God," *op. cit.,* June 30, 1968.

43. Piet Schoonenberg, *Man and Sin: A Theological View* (Notre Dame, Ind.: University of Notre Dame Press, 1965), p. 113.

44. *Documents of Christian Unity,* G. K. A. Bell, ed., "Evanston Assembly," (London: Oxford University Press, 1958), p. 240.

45. II Vatican Council, *Lumen Gentium,* November 21, 1964, Introduction.

46. *Acta Apostolicae Sedis,* vol. LIV (1962), p. 526.

47. H. Richard Niebuhr, *Christ and Culture* (New York: Harper and Row, 1956), pp. 195–96.

II. THE BIBLE AND TRADITION

1. *Augsburg Confession,* Article 4.

2. *Westminster Confession,* Chapter I, no. 1, 6.

3. Frederick C. Grant, "Form Criticism and the Christian Faith," *Journal of Bible and Religion* (February 1939), pp. 11–12.

4. Martin Dibelius, *The Sermon on the Mount* (New York: Scribner's, 1940), p. 97.

5. Analyzed by L. G. McGinley, "The Principles of Form-Criticism," *Theological Studies*, 1941, pp. 451–80.

6. Oscar Cullmann, *Peter: Disciple, Apostle, Martyr* (New York: Meridian, 1961), p. 207.

7. Luke 3:5–6.

8. Adolph Harnack, *What Is Christianity?* (New York: Harper and Row, 1957), pp. 24–25.

9. *Ibid.*, p. 26.

10. Rudolf Bultmann, "New Testament and Mythology," *Kerygma and Myth* (London: S.P.C.K., 1953), vol. I, p. 1.

11. *Ibid.*, p. 3.

12. *Ibid.*, p. 5.

13. Henry T. Buckle, *History of Civilization* (London, n.d.), p. 738.

14. John 6:60.

15. Matthew 8:27.

16. Quoted in G. F. Abbott, *Thucydides: A Study in Historical Reality* (London: Routledge, 1925), p. 11.

17. R. G. Collingwood, *Human Nature and Human History* (London: British Academy, 1936), pp. 12 sqq.

18. Fritz Buri, "Albert Schweitzer," *A Handbook of Christian Theologians*, Marty and Peerman, eds. (New York: World, 1965), p. 123.

19. II Vatican Council, *Dei Verbum*, V, 19.

20. I Corinthians 3:17.

21. Titus 1:1; I Peter 1:1.

22. *Zadokite Document*, 5; Mark 10:4–6.

23. *Manual of Discipline for the Future Congregation of Israel*, ad finem.

24. John Calvin, *Institutes of the Christian Religion*, Book I, Chapter 7, no. 2.

25. Robert M. Grant, *The Interpretation of the Bible* (New York: Macmillan, 1963), pp. 13–14.

26. Wilhelm Niesel, *Bekenntnisschriften und Kirchenordnungen* (Zürich: Zollikon, 1948), pp. 328, 336.

27. Wilhelm Niesel, *The Gospel and the Churches: A Comparison of Catholicism, Orthodoxy and Protestantism* (Philadelphia: Westminster, 1962), pp. 230–31.

28. John H. Leith, *Creeds of the Churches* (Chicago: Aldine, 1963), p. 524.

29. II Vatican Council, *Dei Verbum*, II, 9.

30. *Ibid.*, II, 10.

31. *Acta Apostolicae Sedis*, vol. XL (1948), pp. 45 sqq.

32. New York *Times* (Robert C. Doty), May 14, 1964, p. 37; *The New York Herald Tribune* (Sanche de Gramont), May 14, 1964, p. 7.

33. Pope Benedict XV, "Spiritius Paraclitus," Commemorating the fifteenth

centennial of the birth of St. Jerome, *Acta Apostolicae Sedis*, vol. XII (1920), pp. 385–422.

34. Pope Pius XII, "Divino Afflante Spiritu," *Acta Apostolicae Sedis*, vol. XXXV (1943), p. 319.

35. Hans Küng, *The Church* (New York: Sheed and Ward, 1967), pp. 355–58.

36. Gregory Baum, "Does God Punish?" *Guide*, March 1967, p. 7.

37. Romans 1:17.

38. Timothy McDermott, "The Devil and His Angels," *New Blackfriars*, October 1966, pp. 16–25.

39. Avery Dulles, "Dogma and Ecumenism," *Theological Studies*, September 1968, pp. 397–98.

40. *Ibid.*, pp. 401–2.

41. *Ibid.*, p. 405.

42. *Ibid.*, p. 408.

43. J. P. Mackey, *Tradition and Traditions* (Dublin: Cahill, 1968), pp. xxi–xxii.

44. *Ibid.*, pp. xxii–xxiii.

45. *Ibid.*, p. 96.

46. *Ibid.*

47. Ruud J. Bunnik, *Priests for Tomorrow* (New York: Holt, Rinehart and Winston, 1969), p. 49.

48. *Ibid.*, pp. 33–34.

49. St. Ignatius of Antioch, *Letter to the Smyrneans*, 8.

50. Bunnik, *op. cit.*, p. 58.

51. Olivier A. Rabut, *Faith and Doubt* (New York: Sheed and Ward, 1967), p. 98.

52. *Ibid.*, p. 107.

53. *Ibid.*

54. Pope Paul VI, Addresses of July 2, 1969; January 22, 1969; and November 16, 1967.

55. *Time*, November 1, 1968, p. 86.

56. Justus George Lawler, "Due Season," *New Book Review* (October 1969), p. 11.

57. James P. Shannon, "The Church and Change," *The Priest* (June 1969), pp. 338–47.

58. *Sala Stampa Della Santa Sede*, "Sinodo Straordinario die Vescovi," (Vatican City, October 13–24, 1969).

59. "Divino Afflante Spiritu," p. 319.

60. Instruction of the Biblical Commission, "De Historica Evangeliorum Veritate," *Acta Apostolicae Sedis*, vol. LVI (1964), p. 716.

III. WORSHIP AND MINISTRY

1. *Decree of the Holy Office*, December 7, 1690.

2. *Leonis XIII Acta*, vol. XIII (Bruges), 1894, p. 134.

3. Decree, "Sacra Tridentina Synodus," December 16, 1905, *Pii X Acta*, vol. II, p. 251.

4. Alphonsus Liguori, *Homo Apostolicus* (Mechlin: 1849), p. 148.

5. Decree "Quam Singulari," August 8, 1910, *Acta Apostolicae Sedis*, vol. II, p. 580.

6. *Ibid.*, p. 582.

7. *Pii X Acta*, p. 253.

8. Pius X, "Tra Le Sollecitudini," November 20, 1903, *Acta Apostolicae Sedis*, vol. XXXVI, pp. 332–33.

9. Odo Casel, *Das Christliche Kultmysterium* (Regensburg: Pustet, 1932), p. 37.

10. Decree of Congregation of Rites on Dialogue Mass, August 4, 1922; Apostolic Constitution *Divini Cultus*, December 20, 1928.

11. Joseph Stedman, "The Liturgy in Military Life," *Proceedings of the National Liturgical Week*, Liturgical Conference, 1944, pp. 107–8.

12. *Acta Apostolicae Sedis*, vol. XLV, p. 15.

13. Pope John XXIII, "Mater Ecclesia," *Acta Apostolicae Sedis*. vol. LII (1960), pp. 355–56.

14. II Vatican Council, *Sacrosanctum Concilium*, I, 5–11.

15. *Ibid.*, I, 6.

16. Ibid., 16.

17. *Ibid.*, Introduction, 2.

18. II Vatican Council, *Lumen Gentium*, II, 11.

19. II Vatican Council, *Sacrosanctum Concilium*, I, 22.

20. *Ibid.*, 23.

21. *Ibid.*, 24.

22. *Ibid.*, 27.

23. *Ibid.*, 28.

24. *Ibid.*, 33.

25. *Ibid.*, 36.

26. *Ibid.*, 37.

27. *Ibid.*, 38.

28. A. Bugnini, *L'Osservatore Romano*, December 11, 1969.

29. Justin Martyr, *Apology*, I, 66.

30. *Didache* (The Teaching of the Twelve Apostles), 10, 3.

31. *A New Catechism* (New York: Herder and Herder, 1967), pp. 363–64.

32. *National Opinion Research Center Questionnaire* (Chicago: December 1969), Introduction.

33. *Ibid.*, pp. 5–6.

34. *A Critical Study of the New Order of the Mass* (London: Lumen Gentium Foundation, 1969), p. 3.

35. *The Ministry of the Priest*, European Assembly of Priests (Italian Group), Draft Text, A VI:1.

36. Constitution of the Sacred Liturgy, *Sacrosanctum Concilium*, I, 13.

37. Louis Bouyer, *Liturgical Piety* (Notre Dame, Ind.: University of Notre Dame Press, 1966), p. 7.

38. Second Vatican Council, *De Presbyterorum Ministerio et Vita*, II, 4.

39. Theodore Andrews, *The Polish National Catholic Church in America and Poland* (London: S.P.C.K., 1953), p. 35.

40. "Private Letter of the Sacred Congregation of the Sacraments," December 27, 1955, *Canon Law Digest* (Milwaukee: Bruce, 1958), vol. IV pp. 307–13.

41. Monsignor Loris Capovilla (Archbishop of Chieti), *L'Osservatore Romano*, February 19, 1970.

42. *Presbyterorum Ordinis*, III, 16.

43. *L'Osservatore Romano*, February 5, 1970.

44. *Ibid.*

45. *Ibid.*, April 30, 1970.

46. The New York *Times*, May 12, 1970.

47. Charles Davis, Editorial, *The Clergy Review*, July 1966.

48. Pastoral of the American Hierarchy, *The Church in Our Day* (Washington: United States Catholic Conference, 1968), p. 45.

49. *Third World Conference on Faith and Order*, Oliver S. Tomkins, ed. (London: S.C.M., 1953), p. 47.

50. *Ibid.*, p. 281.

51. *Ibid.*

52. *Ibid.*, p. 282.

53. Arthur C. Piepkorn, *Worship and the Sacraments* (St. Louis: Concordia, 1952), p. 17.

54. *Ibid.*, p. 18.

55. *Ibid.*, p. 26.

56. *Confirmation* (Helsinki: Lutheran World Federation, 1963), Preface.

57. *Ibid.*, p. 58.

58. *Ibid.*

59. *Ibid.*

60. *Ibid.*

61. Ernest B. Koenker, *The Liturgical Renascence in the Roman Catholic Church* (Chicago: University of Chicago Press, 1954), p. 187.

62. Hebrews 10:12–14, 26; 13:15.

63. *Ways of Worship* (Report of Theological Commission of Faith and Order) (London: S.C.M., 1951), p. 34.

64. "Confession of Dositheus," *Creeds of the Churches*, John H. Leith, ed. (Chicago: Aldine, 1963), p. 504.

65. *Ways of Worship* (Arthur Graf, Reformed Church of Switzerland), p. 239.

66. Collection *Eglise et Liturgie*, no. 1.

67. "Act of Uniformity," (Elizabeth I) 1559, *Documents of the Christian Church* (New York: Oxford University Press, 1961), p. 326.

68. *The Peoples' Anglican Missal in the American Edition* (New York: Frank Gavin Liturgical Foundation, 1962), p. 250.

69. *The Book of Common Prayer According to the Use of the Anglican Church of Canada* (Toronto: Anglican Book Center, 1959), p. 92.

70. *Basis of Union of the United Church of Canada* (June 10, 1925), Article XVI, paragraph 2.

71. *Lambeth Conference, 1930* (London: Society for Promoting of Christian Knowledge), p. 62.

72. *The Lambeth Conference, 1968* (London: Society for Promoting of Christian Knowledge), p. 127.

73. *Ibid.*

74. *Ibid.*, p. 123.

75. *The Living Church*, July 14, 1968.

76. Cf. *The Art of Building Worship Services*, Thomas B. McDormand (Nashville: Broadman, 1946).

77. S. F. Winward, *The Reformation of Our Worship* (London: Carey Kingsgate, 1964), p. 7.

78. Horton Davies, *Worship and Theology in England* (London: Princeton University Press), p. 236.

79. Thomas B. McDormand, *The Art of Building Worship Services* (Nashville: Broadman, 1946), p. 101.

80. Vladimir Solovyev, *Russia and the Universal Church* (London: Centenary, 1948), p. 207.

81. *Ibid.*, p. 208.

82. *Ibid.*

83. John of Cronstadt, "Rites and Customs of the Church," *A Treasury of Russian Spirituality*, G. P. Fedetov, ed. (New York: Sheed and Ward, 1948), p. 373.

84. *Ibid.*, pp. 374–75.

85. Alexander Schmemann, "Problems of Orthodoxy in America." *St. Vladimir's Seminary Quarterly*, 1964, vol. 8, no. 3, p. 164.

86. *Ibid.*, p. 165.

IV. AUTHORITY AND FREEDOM

1. J. J. Servan-Schreiber, *The American Challenge* (New York: Avon, 1969), p. xxii.

2. Clement I, *Epistle to the Corinthians*, 59.

3. Pope Leo XIII, "Testem Benevolentiae," *Leonis XIII Acta* (Rome, 1899), pp. 6 sqq.

4. *Ibid.*

5. George Tyrrell, *Medievalism* (London: Longmans, 1908), p. 38.

6. *Ibid.*, pp. 38–39.

7. *Ibid.*

8. *Acta Apostolicae Sedis*, vol. X (1918), p. 282.

9. *Ibid.*, vol. XII (1920), p. 395.

10. *Casti Connubii*, II, 45.

11. *Ibid.*, I, 39.

12. *Ibid.*, I, 32.

13. *Ibid.*, II, 54.

14. *Ibid.*, II, 64, 67, 73; III, 112.

15. "Vegliare con Sollecitudine" (October 29, 1951), *Acta Apostolicae Sedis*, vol. XLIII, pp. 835–54.

16. "Munificentissimus Deus" (November 1, 1950), *Acta Apostolicae Sedis*, vol. XLII, p. 770.

17. "Humani Generis" (August 12, 1950), *Acta Apostolicae Sedis*, vol. XLII, pp. 567–69.

18. *Ibid.*

19. John B. Janssens, *De Executione "Humani Generis"* (Rome, 1951), p. 1.

20. Pope John XXIII, *Journal of a Soul* (New York: McGraw-Hill, 1965), p. 317.

21. Pope John XXIII, *Acta Apostolicae Sedis*, vol. LIII (1961), pp. 785–803.

22. Pope John XXIII, *"Veterum Sapientia,"* February 22, 1962, *Acta Apostolicae Sedis*, vol. LIV, p. 134.

23. *L'Osservatore Romano*, November 15, 1961.

24. *Ibid.*

25. *L'Osservatore Romano*, September 11, 1969.

26. Romans 10:15.

27. Matthew 28:19; 18:18; Luke 22:19.

28. I Vatican Council, *De Ecclesia*, "Prologus," Chapter I.

29. II Vatican Council, *Lumen Gentium*, "Nota Explicativa Praevia," num. 2.

30. *Ibid.*

31. II Vatican Council, *Lumen Gentium*, III, 21.

32. *Ibid.*, 22.

33. *De Ecclesia*, Chapter III.

34. St. Ignatius, *Spiritual Exercises*, "Rules for Thinking with the Church," num. 1.

35. John L. McKenzie, *Authority in the Church* (New York: Sheed and Ward, 1966), pp. 84–85.

36. Matthew 16:19; 18:18; II Corinthians, 10:5–6.

37. Acts of the Apostles 14:23; 20:17–35.

38. Hans Küng, *The Church* (New York: Sheed and Ward, 1967), p. 405.

39. M. A. Kopp, *Collegial Christians* (Chicago: Argus, 1968), p. 44.

40. *Ibid.*, pp. 36–37.

41. Francis Simons, *Infallibility and the Evidence* (Springfield, Ill.: Templegate, 1968), pp. 105–20.

42. *A New Catechism: Catholic Faith for Adults* (New York: Herder and Herder, 1967), p. v.

43. *De Volksrant*, December 29, 1967.

44. *L'Osservatore Romano*, December 12, 1968.

45. *L'Osservatore Romano*, January 22, 1970.

46. *L'Osservatore Romano*, February 5, 1970.

47. *Letter of the Sacred Congregation of Religious* (N. 493/65), February 21, 1968.

48. *Time*, February 23, 1970, p. 55.

49. James P. Shannon, "The Church and Change," *The Priest* (June 1969), p. 339.

50. II Vatican Council, *Christus Dominus*, I, 5.

51. Motu Proprio, "Apostolica Solicitudo," *Acta Apostolicae Sedis*, vol. LVII (September 15, 1965), pp. 776 sqq.

52. Allocution of Paul VI to the First Synod of Bishops, September 30, 1967, *Acta Apostolicae Sedis*, vol. LIX, p. 971.

53. Leo J. Suenens, *Un Problème Crucial: Amour et Maîtresse de Soi* (Bruges: Desclée, 1956). Citation from English translation, *Love and Control* (Westminster, Md.: Newman, 1961), pp. 94–95.

54. Suenens, *La Coresponsabilité dans L'Église d'Aujourd'hui* (Paris: Desclée, 1968); *Coresponsibility in the Church* (New York: Herder and Herder, 1968).

55. *The Tablet*, May 17, 1969, p. 489.

56. *Ibid.*, p. 486.

57. *Sala Stampa della Santa Sede*, October 11, 1969.

58. *Ibid.*, October 16, 1969.

59. *Ibid.*, October 15, 1969.

60. *Ibid.*

61. *Ibid.*

62. *Ibid.*

63. *Ibid.*, October 14, 1969.

64. *Ibid.*, October 16, 1969.

65. *Ibid.*

66. *Ibid.*, October 13, 1969.

67. *Ibid.*, October 14, 1969.

68. *Ibid.*

69. *Ibid.*, October 15, 1969.

70. *Ibid.*

71. *Ibid.*

72. *Ibid.*, October 13, 1969.

73. *Ibid.*, October 16, 1969.

74. Martin Luther, *Werke* (Weimar edition), vol. XI, pp. 405–15.

75. Harry E. Fosdick, *The Man from Nazareth* (New York: Harper, 1949), p. 80.

76. Ernst Troeltsch, *Zur Religiösen Lage: Religionsphilosophie and Ethik* (Tübingen: 1913), p. 522.

77. Otto W. Heick, *A History of Christian Thought* (Philadelphia: Fortress, 1966), vol. II, p. 254.

78. *Formula of Concord*, I, Article 1.

79. Heick, *op. cit.*, p. 271.

80. Karl Barth, *Church Dogmatics* (Edinburgh: Clarke, 1958), vol. III, Part 4, pp. 506–8.

81. *The Basic Theology of Evangelism*, World Congress on Evangelism (Washington, 1966), num. 1–3, 5.

82. *Southern Baptist Abstract of Principles*, Article 1.

83. G. B. A. Gerdener, *Recent Developments in the South African Mission Field* (London, 1961), p. 188.

84. L. D'Epinay in *The Ecumenical Review*, January 1968, p. 16.

85. *Statement of Fundamental Truths*, General Council of the Assemblies of God, "Constitution," 1961, pp. 7–8.

86. *The Uppsala 68 Report* (Geneva: World Council of Churches, 1968), pp. 340–41.

87. *Ibid.*, p. 342.

88. *Confession of Dositheus* (in *The Acts and Decrees of the Synod of Jerusalem,* J. Robertson, tr., London: Baker, 1899), Decree X.

89. E. I. Petrovsky, "Atheistic Education in the School," *Sovietska Pedagogika* (Moscow: Soviet Academy of Pedagogical Service, 1955), num. 5, pp. 8–9.

90. Friedrich Engels, "Socialism: Utopian and Scientific," *The New Left* (New York: Barnes and Noble, 1962), p. 106.

91. V. I. Lenin, Address to the Third All-Russian Congress of the Russian Communist League, October 2, 1920, *Collected Works* (Russian Edition), Moscow, vol. XXV, pp. 403–4.

92. *Ibid.*

93. "Program of the All-Russian Communist Party, adopted at the Eighth Congress," March 18–23, 1919 (Moscow: Communist Library, 1920), num. 6.

94. Message of Patriarch Tikhon, *Kratkii Obzor Istorii Ruskoi Tserkvi ot Revolutsii do Nashikh Dnei* (Jordanville, N.Y.: Holy Trinity Monastery, 1952), pp. 21–22.

95. *Rabochaia Moskva* (Moscow), June 27, 1923.

96. *Izvestia,* June 17, 1923.

97. Philaretus Gumilevsky, *Pravoslavnoe Dogmateskoe Bogoslovie* (Petersburg, 1882), II, p. 221.

98. Yu. A. Levada, "Church and State in Soviet Society," *Religions and the Promise of the Twentieth Century* (New York: New American Library, 1965), p. 106.

99. Nicholas Berdyaev, *The End of Our Time* (New York: Sheed and Ward, 1933), p. 195.

100. *Ibid.*, pp. 163–64.

101. Serge Verkhovskoy, "The Highest Authority in the Church," *St. Vladimir's Seminary Quarterly,* 1960, vol. 4, num. 2–3, p. 83.

102. *Ibid.*

103. Constantine Dyabouniotes, *Ta Musteria* (Athens, 1912), pp. 153–54.

104. Eutaxia, *Tou Kanonikou Dikaiou tes Orthodoxou Anatolikes Ekklesias ta peri Hieratikes Exousias* (Athens, 1872), p. 161.

105. Nicholas Zernov, *Orthodox Encounter* (London: Clarke, 1961), pp. 84–85.

V. CHRISTIAN MARRIAGE

1. John Calvin, *Institutes of the Christian Religion,* Book IV, Chapter 19, num. 34.

2. *Lutheran Agenda* (St. Louis: Concordia, n.d.), p. 53.

3. *Smalcald Article,* "Of the Power and Jurisdiction of Bishops," *Book of Concord,* pp. 155–56.

4. *Westminster Confession,* XXIV, 6.

5. "Westminster Confession," XXIV, 2, *The Book of Confessions* (Philadelphia: The United Presbyterian Church, 1967), item 6, 124.

6. *The Shorter Catechism* (Notes by J. L. M. Haire and John Thompson) (Belfast: Nicholson and Bass, n.d.), p. 61.

7. *The Lambeth Conference of 1968*, Resolution 23 (London: Seabury), p. 37.

8. *Southern Baptist Abstract of Principles* (1961), Article 18.

9. *The Confession of Dositheus* (Text published by Robertson, London, 1899), Decree XV.

10. *Nomologia tou Oikoumenikou Patriarcheiou* (Constantinople, 1897, pp. 256–60; *Collectio Decretorum et Statutorum Synodi Ecclesiae Russicae Orthodoxae* (Moscow, 1918), fasciculus 3, 4.

11. Demetrios J. Constantelos, *The Greek Orthodox Church* (New York: Seabury, 1967), pp. 86–87.

12. Nicolas Zernov, *Eastern Christendom* (London: Weidenfel and Nicholson, 1961), p. 255.

13. Council of Florence, "Exsultate Deo," (November 22, 1439), *Enchiridion Symbolorum* (Barcelona: Herder, 1963), pp. 336–37

14. Pope Pius XI, "Casti Connubii," *Acta Apostolicae Sedis*, vol. XXII (1930), p. 552.

15. *Council Daybook* (Washington: National Catholic Welfare Conference, 1966), vol. III, p. 69.

16. *Ibid.*, p. 91.

17. *A New Catechism* (New York: Herder and Herder, 1969), pp. 396–97, 570–71.

18. Norman E. Himes, *Medical History of Contraception* (New York: Gamut, 1963), p. xxxv.

19. *Soranos' Gynecology* (Owsei Temkin, tr.) (Baltimore: Johns Hopkins, 1956), p. 63.

20. "Adversus Haereses Panarium," *Patrologia Graeca* (Migne), 41, 339.

21. "Casti Connubii," p. 561.

22. Johannes Mansi, *Sacrorum Conciliorum Nova et Amplissima Collectio*, vol. II, c. 668.

23. Demetrios J. Constantelos, *The Greek Orthodox Church* (New York, 1967), p. 88.

24. *The Lambeth Conference of 1920*, Resolution 68, London.

25. *The Lambeth Conference of 1958*, Resolution 115, London.

26. Alfred M. Rehwinkel, *Planned Parenthood and Birth Control in the Light of Christian Ethics* (St. Louis: Concordia, 1959), p. 41.

27. *The Uppsala 68 Report* (Geneva, 1968), p. 92.

28. Pope Paul VI, *Humanae Vitae*, II, 14.

29. Karl Rahner, *Stimmen der Zeit* (September 1968), pp. 193–210.

30. Bernard Häring, "The Encyclical Crisis," in *The Catholic Case for Contraception* (Daniel Callahan, ed.) (London: Collier-Macmillan, 1969), pp. 80–81.

31. *Protest Statement of 87 Theologians* (Washington: July 30, 1968).

32. II Vatican Council, *Lumen Gentium*, III, 25.

33. Joseph F. Costanzo, "Papal Magisterium and *Humanae Vitae*," *Thought*, Autumn 1969, vol. XLIV, num. 174, pp. 377–412.

34. Alan F. Gutmacher, *Birth Control and Love* (London: Collier-Macmillan, 1969), pp. 158–59.

35. "Statement of the French Hierarchy" (Lourdes, November 1968), *Catholic Mind*, January 1969, p. 52.

36. "Pastoral Letter of the Joint Philippine Hierarchy" (October 1968), *Catholic Mind*, p. 58.

37. Discourse of Cardinal Wyszynski (June 29, 1969), *L'Osservatore Romano*, November 27, 1969.

38. *Washington Protest Statement*, signed (among others) by Leo Bakker (Netherlands); J. P. Mackey (Ireland); Bernard Häring (Germany); Walter Burghardt, Charles Curran, Justus Lawler, Roland Murphy, Hugh McElwain, Kevin Ranaghan, Gabriel Moran, Peter Riga, Godfrey Diekmann (U.S.A.).

39. *Stockholm Statement of the Scandinavian Hierarchy* (N.C. News Service), November 1, 1968.

40. *Human Life in Our Day* (New York: Paulist Press, 1969), pp. 30–32.

41. *Humanae Vitae*, II, 9.

42. Dietrich von Hildebrand, *Die Enzyklika "Humanae Vitae"—Ein Zeichen des Wiederspruchs* (Regensburg: Habbel, 1968); English Translation: *Humanae Vitae—A Sign of Contradiction* (Chicago: Franciscan Herald, 1969), pp. 12–13.

43. *Ibid.*, p. 13.

44. *Humanae Vitae*, II, 9–10.

45. *Christian Marriage* (Pastoral of the Irish Hierarchy: William Conway, Cardinal of Armagh; Archbishops John McQuaid of Dublin, Joseph Walsh of Tuam, and Thomas Morris of Cashel) (Chicago: Scepter, 1969), p. 28.

46. Alexander Schmemann, *Sacraments and Orthodoxy* (New York: Herder and Herder, 1965), pp. 111–12.

47. *Ibid.*, p. 116.

48. Carnegie S. Calian, "Social Consciousness in Eastern Orthodoxy," *The Christian Century* (October 20, 1965), p. 1285; Vitaly Borovoy, "Theology and Social Revolution," *Concern*, vol. VIII, 16 (September 15, 1966), p. 21.

49. André S. Bustanoby, "Love, Honor and Obey," *Christianity Today* (June 6, 1969), p. 804.

50. *Ibid.*

51. *Ibid.*

52. *The Uppsala Report 68*, "Towards New Styles of Living," no. 18, (Geneva, 1968), p. 92.

53. *Ibid.*, p. 93.

54. Leland Foster Wood and Robert Latou Dickinson, *Harmony in Marriage* (New York: Round Table, pp. 99–100.

55. *Ibid.*, p. 101.

56. *If I Marry a Roman Catholic* (New York: National Council of Churches, 1962), pp. 10–11.

57. *Lambeth Conference of 1968*, "Relations with the Roman Catholic Church," p. 136. Also *Declaration on Religious Freedom*, num. 5.

58. *Responsible Parenthood* (New York: National Council of Churches of Christ in the U.S.A., 1961), p. 5.

59. *If I Marry a Roman Catholic*, p. 14.

60. George H. Demetrakopoulos, *Dictionary of Orthodox Theology* (New York: Philosophical Library, 1964), pp. 129–30.

61. *Guidelines for the Orthodox in Ecumenical Relations* (Leonidas Contos), Standing Conference of Canonical Orthodox Bishops in America, 1966, p. 27.

62. *Ephemerides Iuris Canonici*, vol. IV (1948), p. 158.

63. II Vatican Council, *Lumen Gentium*, II, 11; *Gaudium et Spes*, II, 1, 48.

64. Latin text of the petition and dispensation in *American Ecclesiastical Review*, vol. LXII, p. 188.

65. II Vatican Council, *Orientalium Ecclesiarum*, no. 18.

66. Decree "Crescens Matrimoniorum," *Acta Apostolicae Sedis*, vol. LIX (1967), pp. 165–66.

67. Instruction, "Matrimonii Sacramentum," *Acta Apostolicae Sedis*, vol. LVIII (1966), pp. 235–39.

68. *Rite of Marriage*, Revised by the Sacred Congregation of Rites (March 19, 1969), no. 8.

69. Pope Paul VI, "Apostolic Letter on Mixed Marriages," (March 31, 1970), *L'Osservatore Romano*, May 14, 1970.

70. *Ibid.*

71. Pope John XXIII, "Ad Petri Cathedram," *Acta Apostolicae Sedis*, vol. LI (1959), p. 509.

VI. RELIGIOUS LIFE

1. Matthew 19:21.

2. *Augsburg Confession*, XXVII, "Monastic Vows" (1531).

3. *Thirty-Nine Articles of the Church of England*, XXXII, "Of the Marriage of Priests" (1563).

4. *John Wesley's Articles of Religion*, XI, "Of Works of Supererogation" (1784).

5. *Canones et Decreta Concilii Tridentini* (Mechlin: Velsen, 1860), p. 251 (Canons on Marriage, 9–10).

6. *La Diaconesse* (April–June 1957), pp. 12–18.

7. Francois Biot, *The Rise of Protestant Monasticism* (Dublin: Helicon, 1963), p. 99.

8. *Ibid.*, p. 97.

9. *The Rule of Taizé*, Les Presse de Taizé, 1965, "Preamble" and Rules on "Prayer . . . The Council . . . Interior Silence . . . Mercy."

10. *Ibid.*, Preamble.

11. Roger Schutz, *Unanimity in Pluralism* (Chicago: Franciscan Herald, 1966), pp. 14–15.

12. *Ibid.*, p. 22.

13. *Ibid.*, p. 30.

14. *Ibid.*, p. 34.

15. *Ibid.*, pp. 39–40.

16. *Ibid.*, pp. 44–45.

17. *Ibid.*, pp. 50–51.

18. *Ibid.*, p. 61.

19. *Ibid.*, p. 62.

20. *Ibid.*, p. 63.

21. *Ibid.*, pp. 63–64.

22. *Ibid.*, p. 64.

23. *Ibid.*, p. 10.

24. Karl Barth, *Kirchliche Dogmatik*, IV, 2 (*Church Dogmatics*, Edinburgh: Clark, 1958), p. 18.

25. *Ibid.*

26. *Ibid.*, pp. 18–19.

27. John Calvin, *Institutes of the Christian Religion*, IV, 4, 2.

28. Barth, *op. cit.*, p. 17.

29. *Directory of the Religious Life* (New York: Macmillan, 1957), pp. 28–29.

30. *Constitution and Canons for the Goverment of the Protestant Epsicopal Church in the United States of America*, 1964, pp. 129–30.

31. St. *Gregory's Priory*, 1964, p. 3.

32. *Ibid.*, p. 1.

33. *The Lambeth Conference* (London: S.P.C.K., 1968), p. 30 (Resolution 5).

34. Karl Marx and Friedrich Engels, *Works*, vol. XIV, p. 322.

35. Savelii Tuberozov, "Monasteries and Theological Schools in the U.S.S.R.," *Eastern Churches Review*, Spring 1966, p. 60.

36. Kallistos Timothy Ware, "Monks and Monasteries in the Near East" (Book Review), *Eastern Churches Review*, p. 93.

37. Paul Verghese, "The Role of Monasticism and a New Askesis for Our Time," *The Ecumenical Review* (April 1963), p. 317.

38. *Ibid.*, pp. 317–18.

39. Konstantin Bonis, "The Orthodox Conception of the Spirituality of the Church in Relation to Daily Life," *Ibid.*, p. 305.

40. T. Lincoln Bouscaren and Adam C. Ellis, *Canon Law* (Milwaukee: Bruce, 1948), p. 4.

41. Canon 487.

42. Canons 499–502.

43. Canon 522.

44. II Vatican Council, *Perfectae Caritatis*, 2.

45. *Ibid.*, 15.

46. *Ibid.*

47. *Ibid.*, 13.

48. *Ibid.*

49. *Ibid.*

50. *Ibid.*, 12.

51. *Ibid.*, 14.

52. *Ibid.*

53. *Ibid.*, 2.

54. *Ibid.*

55. *Ibid.*, 17.

56. Pope Paul VI, Address to International Union of Superiors General of Religious Congregations of Women, March 7, 1967.

57. *Perfectae Caritatis*, 11.

58. "Appropriate Renewal," Father Arrupe's Letter to the Jesuits, *The Tablet*, December 6, 1969.

59. *Ibid.*

60. Leo Josef Cardinal Suenens, *The Nun in the World* (Westminster, Md.: Newman, 1963), pp. 10–14.

61. Gerard Huyghe (Bishop of Arras), "Renewal of the Religious Life," *Religious Orders in the Modern World* (London: Chapman, 1965), pp. 123–24.

62. Statement to the C.M.S.W. Membership, from the St. Louis (Missouri) Conference of Men and Women Superiors, September 3–5, 1970, p. 2.

63. Gabriel Moran, "Religious Community: A Call to be Born," *National Catholic Reporter*, December 18, 1970, p. 9.

64. Gabriel Moran, *The New Community* (New York: Herder and Herder, 1970), pp. 73, 14, 74, 129.

65. *National Catholic Reporter*, p. 10.

66. Position Statement on the Religious Life from the Watertown (New York) Conference of Major Superiors of Religious Women, October 13, 1970.

VII. CHURCH AND STATE

1. Luigi Sturzo, *Nationalism and Internationalism* (New York: Roy, 1946), p. 40.

2. *Acta Apostolicae Sedis*, vol. XXI (1920), pp. 209–71 (Lateran Treaty), pp. 274–94 (Concordat).

3. Cardinal Gasparri, in *The Vatican: Yesterday, Today, and Tomorrow* (George Seldes) (New York: Harper, 1934), pp. 383–87.

4. *Constitution of Mexico*, Article 27, Section II.

5. English text in Newman C. Eberhardt, *A Summary of Catholic History* (St. Louis: Herder, 1962), vol. II, p. 741.

6. The New York *Times*, June 26, 1967.

7. *Political Constitution of the Portuguese Republic* (Lisbon: National Incorporation of Publicity, 1957), Article 45.

8. *The Constitution of Eire* (Adopted December 29, 1937) (Dublin: Government Publication Office, 1945).

9. *Ibid.*, Article 6.

10. *Ibid.*, Article 41, Section 2, num. 1; Section 3, num. 2–3.

11. *Ibid.*, Article 44, Section 1, num. 2–3.

12. *Ibid.*, Section 2, num. 1–3.

13. *Ibid.*, num. 4–5.

14. *The Constitution of the Republic of Pakistan*, Section 6, num. 7a.

15. *First Amendment*, adopted September 15, 1791.

16. John Dewey, "Religion and Our Schools," *The Hibbert Journal*, VI (July 1908), p. 800.

17. *Ibid.*, p. 801.

18. *Reynolds v. United States*, 98 U.S. 145–67.

19. *Holy Trinity Church v. United States*, 143 U.S. 457, 470–71.

20. John Courtney Murray, *We Hold These Truths* (New York: Sheed and Ward, 1960), pp. 76–78.

21. *American Churchmen Visit the Soviet Union*, Signed by Paul B. Anderson (Y.M.C.A.), Boswell P. Barnes (National Council of Churches), Eugene C. Blake (Presbyterian), Franklin Fry (Lutheran), Herbert Gezork (Baptist), Bishop D. Ward Nichols (Methodist Episcopal), Charles C. Parlin (Methodist), Bishop Henry K. Sherrill (Episcopal), Walter W. Van Kirk (National Council of Churches) (New York: National Council of Churches, 1956), pp. 14–15.

22. *Ibid.*, p. 15.

23. *Hearing Before the Committee on Un-American Activities, House of Representatives* (August 10, 1967) (Washington: United States Government Printing Office, 1967), pp. 543–44.

24. Document in *The Church of Silence in Slovakia* (Theodore J. Zubek) (Whiting, Ind.: John J. Lach, 1956), p. 70.

25. *Ibid.*, p. 192.

26. *Jednota*, May 20, 1970.

27. *The Catholic Church and Cuba* (Peking: Foreign Language Press, 1959) (Translation published by the Committee on the Judiciary, United States Senate) (Washington: United States Government Printing Office, 1967), p. 2.

28. *Ministry of Education Revised Regulations for Private Schools*, Article 6, May 7, 1946.

29. Pius XII, "Ad Apostolorum Principis," *Acta Apostolicae Sedis*, vol. L (1958), pp. 606–7.

30. Dries van Coillie, *Brainwashed in Peking* (Nederlands: Boekdruk Industries, 1969), pp. 35–36.

31. *Ibid.*, pp. 217–18.

32. *Mao Tse-tung: An Anthology of His Writings* (edited by Anne Fremantle) (New York: New American Library, 1962), p. 260.

33. *United Nations Charter*, I, 1,1.

34. Pitirim A. Sorokin, *The Crisis of Our Age* (New York: Dutton, 1941), p. 225.

35. Albert Camus, *The Rebel* (New York: Random, 1956), pp. 3–4.

36. Romans 13:1.

37. *An Act Relating to the Right to Die with Dignity; Providing an Effective Date*, House Bill 318, Legislature of the State of Florida (1970).

38. *Catholic Hospital* (Official Organ of the Catholic Hospital Association of Canada), September 1969, p. 2.

39. Thorstein Velben, *Absentee Ownership* (New York: Huebach, 1923).

40. "Article 231, Treaty of Versailles," *Treaty of Peace with Germany* (Washington: Senate Document, No. 49, 1919).

41. *Giovinezza*, verses by M. Manni, music by G. Blanc. Copyright 1923 by Mauro V. Cardilli.

42. Statement of President Harry S. Truman (August 6, 1945), *The Great Documents of Western Civilization* (Milton Viorst) (New York: Grosset and Dunlap, 1967), Document 102, p. 364.

43. *Pope Paul VI in New York* (Washington: National Catholic Welfare Conference, 1965), p. 8.

44. *Ibid.*, p. 11.

45. *Ibid.*, p. 10.

46. "Decree of the Soviet Commissars Concerning Separation of Church and State, and of School and Church," *Compilation of Decrees* (Moscow, January 23, 1918), p. 263.

47. George Seldes, *The Vatican: Yesterday, Today, and Tomorrow* (New York: Harper, 1934), p. 721.

48. *Communist-Christian Encounter in East Europe* (Meador) (Indianapolis: School of Religion Press, 1956), pp. 481–82.

49. *Ibid.*, p. 464.

50. Pope Pius XI, "Divini Illius Magistri," (Encyclical on Christian Education), *Acta Apostolicae Sedis*, vol. XXII (1930), p. 62.

51. II Vatican Council, *Gravissimum Educationis*, 6.

52. John Cardinal Carberry, "The Need for Orthodox Catholic Teaching," (Cleveland, 1969), p. 1.

53. *Ibid.*, p. 4.

VIII. THEOLOGY

1. Leslie Dewart, *The Future of Belief: Theism in a World Come of Age* (New York: Herder and Herder, 1966), pp. 92, 111.

2. Arman Maurer, *The Ecumenist*, V (January–February 1967), p. 25.

3. Joseph Heller, *Catch-22* (New York: Modern Library, 1961), pp. 183–85. Cited by William Hamilton, "A Note on Radical Theology," *Concilium*, IX, November 1967, p. 40.

4. E. L. Mascall, *Theology and the Future* (New York: Morehouse-Barlow, 1968), p. 63.

5. Philippians 2:6–8.

6. T. J. J. Altizer, "Creative Negation in Theology," *Frontline Theology*, Dean Peerman, ed. (Richmond: John Knox, 1967), p. 82.

7. Harvey Cox, *The Secular City*, pp. 22 f.

8. Mascall, *op. cit.*, pp. 163–64.

9. *Uppsala Report* (Geneva: World Council of Churches, 1968), p. 45.

10. *Ibid.*, p. 48.

11. II Vatican Council, *De Ecclesia in Mundo Huius Temporis*, III, 34.

12. *Ibid.*, 37.

13. *Ibid.*, 39.

14. John Bright, *The Kingdom of God in Bible and Church* (London: Lutterworth, 1955).

15. Emil Brunner, *Das Ewige als Zunkunft und Gegenwart* (Zürich: Zwingli Verlag, 1955).

16. Jean Daniélou, *Le Mystère de L'Avent* (Paris: Editions du Seuil, 1948).

17. Oscar Cullmann, *Immortality of the Soul; or Resurrection of the Dead?* (New York: Macmillan, 1958), passim.

18. Jürgen Moltmann, in *Ernst Bloch zu ehren* (Frankfurt: Suhrkamp, 1965), pp. 243–244.

19. Wolfhart Pannenberg, *ibid.*, p. 213.

20. Jürgen Moltmann, *Theology of Hope* (New York: Harper and Row, 1967), pp. 15–16.

21. Pannenberg, *op. cit.*, p. 39.

22. Carl E. Braaten, "Toward a Theology of Hope," *Theology Today*, (July 1967), pp. 208–26; Pannenberg, *op. cit.*, p. 217; *ibid.*, p. 218.

23. *Ibid.*, p. 219.

24. Harvey Cox, Foreword to Ernst Bloch's *Man on His Own* (New York: Herder and Herder, 1970), pp. 12–14.

25. Harvey Cox, "Afterward," in *The Secular City Debate* (New York: Macmillan, 1966) pp. 197–98; S. M. Daecke, "Teilhard de Chardin and Protestant Theology," *The Teilhard Review* (Summer 1969), p. 12; Julian Huxley, Introduction to *The Phenomenon of Man* (New York: Harper and Row, 1961), p. 19.

26. Johannes B. Metz, "Creative Hope," *New Theology No. 5*, edited by Marty and Peerman (Toronto: Macmillan, 1969), p. 134.

27. *Ibid.*

28. Karl Rahner, "Kirchliches Lehramt und Theologie nach dem Konzil," *Schriften zur Theologie*, VIII, Einsiedeln: Benziger, 1967, pp. 120–21.

29. Paul VI, Letter to the International Congress on the Theology of the Second Vatican Council (September 21, 1966), *Acta Apostolicae Sedis*, vol. LVIII, p. 879.

30. Rahner, *op. cit.*

31. Bernard Lonergan, "Belief Today," *Catholic Mind* (May 1970), p. 18.

32. *Ibid.*

33. *Documentary Service, U. S. Catholic Conference*, Washington, October 1, 1970, p. 3.

34. Jan J. Van Capelleveen, "Brussels Conference: While Theologians Talked," *Christianity Today*, October 9, 1970, p. 50.

IX. MORALITY

1. St. Clement, *Letter to the Corinthians*, 49, 2; Paul VI, Letter to the 83rd Katholikentag, *L'Osservatore Romano*, September 24, 1970.

2. *The Worker*, August 6, 1961, p. 3.

3. Fulton J. Sheen, *Communism and the Conscience of the West* (Indianapolis: Bobbs-Merrill, 1948).

4. *Moral Problems: Questions on Christianity with Answers by Prominent Churchmen* (London: Mowbray, 1957), pp. 61–63.

5. John Macquarrie, "Social Ethics," *Dictionary of Christian Ethics* (Philadelphia: Westminster, 1967), p. 325.

6. John XXIII, *Pacem in Terris*, Introduction, 3, 7.

7. Second Vatican Council, *De Ecclesia in Mundo Huius Temporis*, IV, 43.

8. Harvey Cox, *The Secular City* (London: SCM Press, 1965), pp. 49–50.

9. Pius XI, "Mit Brennender Sorge," *Acta Apostolicae Sedis*, vol. XXIX (1937), p. 180.

10. Dietrich Bonhoeffer, *Ethics* (New York: Macmillan, 1955), p. 185.

11. *Eighteenth Amendment to the American Constitution*, Ratified January 16, 1919–Repealed December 5, 1933.

12. John A. T. Robinson, *Christian Morals Today* (Philadelphia: Westminster, 1964), p. 31.

13. Joseph Fletcher, *Situation Ethics* (Philadelphia: Westminster, 1966), p. 124.

14. Robinson, *Christian Morals Today*, p. 37.

15. *Ibid.*, p. 14.

16. *Ibid.*, pp. 40–41.

17. Fletcher, *op. cit.*, pp. 84–85.

18. *Ibid.*, pp. 68, 140.

19. *Ibid.*, p. 39.

20. John C. Bennett, "Ethical Principles and the Context," unpublished presidential address, American Society of Christian Ethics, 1961; Daniel Williams, *What Present-Day Theologians Are Thinking* (New York: Harper and Row, 1959), pp. 114 f; Fletcher, *op. cit.*, p. 147.

21. *Acta Apostolicae Sedis*, vol. LIV (1952), pp. 413–19; vol. 48 (1956), pp. 144–46.

22. Fletcher, *op. cit.*, p. 70.

23. Bernard Häring, *The Law of Christ*, 2 vols. (Westminster, Md.: Newman, 1961, 1963).

24. Häring, "Pastoral Work among the Divorced and Invalidly Married," *The Future of Marriage as Institution*, Franz Bockle, ed. (New York: Herder and Herder, 1970), *Concilium* vol. 55, pp. 127–28.

25. Pius XII, *Mystici Corporis Christi*, 88.

26. Pius XII, *Mediator Dei*, 177.

27. John E. Corrigan, *Growing Up Christian* (Dayton, Ohio: Pflaum, 1968), pp. 18, 20.

28. *Ibid.*, pp. 22–23.

29. *Ibid.*, pp. 30–31.

30. Richard McCormick, "The Moral Theology of Vatican II," *The Future of Ethics and Moral Theology* (Chicago: Argus, 1968), p. 15.

31. Corrigan, *op. cit.*, pp. 78–79.

32. *Ibid.*

33. Louis Monden, *Sin, Liberty and Law* (New York: Sheed and Ward, 1965), pp. 142–43.

34. Galatians 2:20.

35. T. F. Torrance, "Justification: Its Radical Nature and Place in Reformed Doctrine and Life," *Scottish Journal of Theology*, 13 (1960), pp. 225–46.

36. Daniel Williams, "Grace," *Dictionary of Christian Ethics*, p. 140.

37. W. G. Maclagan, *The Theological Frontier of Ethics*, (London: Allen and Unwin, 1961), p. 131.

38. *Ibid.*, p. 118.

39. *Methodist Social Creed*, Section II (Lovick Pierce and Donald A. Theuer, publishers, 1967), pp. 38–39.

40. Carl Jung, Letter dated September 22, 1944, in *God and the Unconscious* by Victor White (London: Collins Clear, 1952), pp. 270–71.

41. Jung, Letter dated January 13, 1948, *Ibid.*, pp. 272–73.

42. Jung, *Modern Man in Search of a Soul* (London: Paul, Trench, Trubner, 1933), p. 264 f.

43. L. C. Dunn and Theodosius Dobzhansky, *Heredity, Race and Society* (New York: New American Library, 1960), pp. 65–66.

44. *Does Overpopulation Mean Poverty?* (Joseph M. Jones) (Washington: Center of International Economic Growth, 1952), p. 25.

45. *Ibid.*, p. 25.

46. Chicago *Sun-Times*, June 9, 1970.

47. "Protection of Individuals and Groups in the Political World," Report adopted by the Assembly, *The Uppsala Report* (Geneva: World Council of Churches, 1968), p. 65.

48. II Vatican Council, *Gaudium et Spes* (December 7, 1965), Part I, I, 29.

49. V. A. Demant, *Religion and the Decline of Capitalism* (New York: Scribner's, 1952), p. 113.

50. Julian Huxley, *Knowledge, Morality and Destiny* (New York: New American Library, 1960), p. 260.

51. Robinson, *Christian Morals Today*, p. 18.

52. *Ibid.*, p. 19.

53. Dorothy Emmet, "Evolutionary Ethics," *Dictionary of Christian Ethics*, p. 123.

54. "Population Education—Evolution or Revolution," *Population Bulletin*, vol. XXVI, 3 (1970), p. 5.

55. Alfred North Whitehead, *Religion in the Making* (New York: World, 1961), p. 147.

56. *Ibid.*, p. 142.

57. Whitehead, *Modes of Thought* (New York: Macmillan, 1938), p. 15.

58. Carl Michalson, "Existentialist Ethics," *Dictionary of Christian Ethics*, p. 124.

X. ECUMENICAL MOVEMENT

1. John R. Mott, *The World's Student Christian Federation* (New York, 1920), p. 5.

2. *World Missionary Conference*, vol. VIII, (1910), p. 144.

3. William A. Brown, *Toward a United Church* (New York: Scribner's, 1946), p. 58.

4. *Ibid.*, p. 208.

5. W. A. Visser 't Hooft, *The Meaning of Ecumenical* (London: SCM Press, 1954), pp. 21, 27.

6. Report of Section I on Faith and Order, Adopted by the Evanston Assembly August 29, 1954, No. 101–AS, p. 1.

7. *Ibid.*, p. 2.

8. *Ibid.*, p. 8.

9. *Ibid.*, p. 3.

10. *Ibid.*, pp. 3–4.

11. *Ibid.*, p. 5.

12. *Ibid.*

13. *Ibid.*

14. *Ibid.*

15. *Ibid.*

16. *Ibid.*

17. *Ibid.*, p. 6.

18. *Ibid.*

19. *Ibid.*, p. 7.

20. *Ibid.*

21. *Ibid.*

22. *Ibid.*

23. *Report on Faith and Order*, p. 7.

24. *Ibid.*

25. *Ibid.*, pp. 7–8.

26. *Ibid.*, p. 8.

27. *Ibid.*, p. 9.

28. *Ibid.*, p. 10.

29. *Ibid.*

30. *Ibid.*, p. 11.

31. *Ibid.*

32. *Plan of Union*, Church of Christ Uniting, 1970, p. 49.

33. *Eastern Churches Quarterly*, Autumn 1966, pp. 137–38.

34. *Ibid.*, p. 139.

35. *Ibid.*, p. 140.

36. Letter of Patriarch Meletius to the Archbishop of Canterbury, July 28, 1922, *Orthodox Statements on Anglican Ordinations* (E. Hardy), New York, 1946, p. 2.

37. Timothy Ware, *The Orthodox Church* (Baltimore: Penguin, 1964), p. 330.

38. *Declaration of the Orthodox Delegates Concerning the Main Theme of the Assembly*, August 25, 1954, Document 97-A, p. 1.

39. *The Uppsala Report*, p. 19.

40. *Ibid.*, pp. 368–69.

41. *Be Reconciled to Your Brother*, 1967, pp. 8–9.

42. *Ibid.*, p. 13.

43. *Ibid.*, pp. 19–20.

44. Paul VI, *Genuine Ecumenism*, January 22, 1969 (Chicago: Scepter), no. 147, p. 3.

45. *World Missionary Conference*, 1910, vol. VIII, p. 221.

46. Max Pribila, *Um Kirchliche Einheit* (Freiburg, 1929), p. 315.

47. R. Rouse and S. C. Neill, editors, *A History of the Ecumenical Movement, 1517–1948* (Philadelphia: Westminster, 1948), p. 416.

48. Jacques de Bivort de la Saudée, *Documents sur le problème de union anglo-romaine* (1921–1927), Paris, 1949, p. 95.

49. Roger Aubert, *Le Saint-Siège et l'Union des Églises* (Brussels: Universitaires, 1947), p. 138.

50. Lillian Stephenson, *Max Josef Metzger* (London, 1952), passim.

51. *Documentation Catholique*, March 12, 1950, pp. 330–31.

52. *L'Osservatore Romano*, November 9, 1948.

53. *Unitas*, V. XIV, no. 2 (1952), p. 93.

54. *The Church Times*, September 1, 1961.

55. Robert McAfee Brown, *The Ecumenical Revolution* (Garden City, N.Y.: Doubleday, 1967), p. 66.

56. II Vatican Council, *De Oecumenismo*, I, 3.

57. *Ibid.*

58. *Ibid.*

59. *Lumen Gentium* II, 14.

60. *De Oecumenismo*, I, 4.

61. *Ibid.*, II, 7.

62. *Ibid.*, 15.

63. *Ibid.*, 13.

64. *Ibid.*

65. *L'Osservatore Romano*, May 28, 1970.

66. *Ibid.*, January 25, 1968.

67. *Ibid.*, January 30, 1969.

68. *Ibid.*, January 29, 1970.

69. *Ibid.*

70. *Ibid.*, October 29, 1970.

71. *Ibid.*

72. *Ibid.*, November 5, 1970.

XI. THE NON-CHRISTIAN WORLD: MISSION AND DIALOGUE

1. II Vatican Council, *Ad Gentes Divinitus*, I, 7.

2. *Vatican Council II and the Missions*, address given on August 10, 1966, by His Eminence, Gregory Cardinal Agagianian at the Spanish Missionary Congress.

3. II Vatican Council, *Ad Gentes Divinitus*, II, 11.

4. *Constitution of India*, Article 25, paragraph 1.

5. *Constitution of India*, Article 25, paragraph 2.

6. N. C. News Service, June 26, 1970.

7. *Harijan*, May 11, 1935.

8. *Harijan*, September 28, 1935.

9. T. A. Mathias, Address to the National Council of Churches Division of Overseas Ministries Assembly (November 20, 1968).

10. *Ibid.*

11. Arnold Toynbee, *Christianity Among the Religions of the World* (New York: Scribner's, 1957), pp. 111–12.

12. Leo Josef Cardinal Suenens, quoted by Cardinal Agagianian, *Vatican Council II and the Missions.*

13. Jean Cardinal Daniélou, *Christian Faith and Today's Man* (Huntington, Ind., 1970), pp. 9–10.

14. *International Missionary Council* (New York), pp. 1–2.

15. *What Is a Faith Mission?*, International Foreign Mission Association (New York), pp. 5–8.

16. Clarence P. Shedd, *History of the World's Alliance of Young Men's Christian Associations* (London: S.P.C.K., 1955), pp. 245–56.

17. *Journal of the Christian Medical Association of India, Pakistan, Burma and Ceylon* (September 1952), p. 271.

18. Alberto Rembao, "The Reformation Comes to Hispanic America," *Religion in Life,* (Winter 1957–58), p. 9.

19. Prudencio Damboriena, *Cuadernos Hispanoamericanos* (Madrid, August 1956).

20. "Evangelism Around the World," *Faith and Order Commission Papers,* num. 18 (New York, 1954), p. 37.

21. *The Uppsala 68 Report,* Norman Goodall, ed. (Geneva: World Council of Churches, 1968), pp. 28–29.

22. *Christianity Today* (June 19, 1970), pp. 5–6.

23. Jawaharlal Nehru, *Autobiography* (London, 1953), p. 379.

24. II Vatican Council, *Nostra Aetate,* 1.

25. *Ibid.*

INDEX

Relation of the Church to the War in the Light of the Christian Faith, The (Federal Council of Churches), 98

Religious life, 276–313; "Actual Poverty," 304; Anglican renewal, 287–91; Barth on, 285–87; Calvinist women, 279, 280; celibacy, 304–5, 312–13; under Code of Canon Law, 298–302; "Distinctive Spirit Inherited from the Founder," 306; "Ecclesial Obedience," 305–6; "Eucharistic Community Life," 304; historical antecedents, 276–78; "Lifelong Celibacy," 304–5; Lutheran, 279–80; in modern Protestantism, 278–91; Orthodox monasticism, 291–97; Orthodox (outside U.S.-S.R.), 294–97; post-conciliar crisis, 308–13; "Pursuit of Holiness in the Following of Christ," 303–4; Reformation and, 277–78; "Religious Habit," 306–8; Roman Catholic, 297–313; Taizé brethren, 280–85; in U.S.S.R., 291–94; Vatican II and, 302–8; vows, 301

Religious Society of Friends, 155, 211, 234, 321, 324, 326

Renaissance, 16, 121, 451

Renan, Ernest, 42, 78

Revelation: Bible as, 94–104; as communal experience, 95–99; scripture and, 99–104

Revolution of 1905, 224, 225, 337–38

Revue Biblique (quarterly), 101

Riesman, David, 389

Ritschl, Albrecht, 78

Ritualism: Anglican, 149–55; compared to word *creed*, 115; distinctive features of, 112–16; Eastern Orthodoxy, 158–65; Free Church tradition, 155–57; as index of religion, 112; Lutheranism, 142–46; Protestant churches, 141–57; Reformed churches, 146–49; Roman Catholic, 116–41

Rivera, Primo de, 319

Riverside Church, 200

Robinson, Bishop John A. T., 42–45, 46, 356, 413–14

Robinson, J. A., 439–40

Robinson, Wheeler, 59

Rockefeller, John D., Jr., 467

Roey, Joseph, Cardinal van, 439

Roman Breviary, revision of, 120, 129–30

Roman Catholic Church: anonymous Christians and, 463–66; apostolicity, 178–79; authority and freedom, 167–98; birth control issue, 137–38, 167, 174, 194, 245–57; Bishops' Pastoral Office, 190–94; breach between Eastern Orthodoxy and, 434–37; California nuns' case, 188–89; canonization of Reformation martyrs, 449–50; challenge to marital stability, 237–40; Chinese Universalism and, 453–54; Christian marriage, 237–40, 268–75; clergy crisis, 135–41; clerical celibacy controversy, 135–41, 167, 188; collegiality and, 179–98, 377–78; communist treatment of, 331–34; contemporary theology, 375–82; contraception and conscience, 245–57, 347; decline in devotional practices, 133–34; Dutch hierarchy and, 131, 138, 186–88, 239–40, 382; ecumenical movement, 437–50; first encyclical